Springer Proceedings in Business and Economics

Springer Proceedings in Business and Economics brings the most current research presented at conferences and workshops to a global readership. The series features volumes (in electronic and print formats) of selected contributions from conferences in all areas of economics, business, management, and finance. In addition to an overall evaluation by the publisher of the topical interest, scientific quality, and timeliness of each volume, each contribution is refereed to standards comparable to those of leading journals, resulting in authoritative contributions to the respective fields. Springer's production and distribution infrastructure ensures rapid publication and wide circulation of the latest developments in the most compelling and promising areas of research today.

The editorial development of volumes may be managed using Springer Nature's innovative EquinOCS, a proven online conference proceedings submission, management and review system. This system is designed to ensure an efficient timeline for your publication, making Springer Proceedings in Business and Economics the premier series to publish your workshop or conference volume.

This book series is indexed in SCOPUS.

Antonio J. Guevara Plaza ·
Alfonso Cerezo Medina · Enrique Navarro Jurado
Editors

Tourism and ICTs: Advances in Data Science, Artificial Intelligence and Sustainability

Proceedings of the TURITEC 2023 Conference, October 19–20, 2023, Málaga, Spain

 Springer

Editors
Antonio J. Guevara Plaza
Andalusian Institute for Research
and Innovation in Tourism
Campus University of Málaga
Málaga, Spain

Alfonso Cerezo Medina
Andalusian Institute for Research
and Innovation in Tourism
Campus University of Málaga
Málaga, Spain

Enrique Navarro Jurado
Andalusian Institute for Research
and Innovation in Tourism
Campus University of Málaga
Málaga, Spain

ISSN 2198-7246   ISSN 2198-7254 (electronic)
Springer Proceedings in Business and Economics
ISBN 978-3-031-52606-0   ISBN 978-3-031-52607-7 (eBook)
https://doi.org/10.1007/978-3-031-52607-7

Organization

Scientific Committee

Mohamed A. Nassar, Pharos University
Alexandre Augusto Biz, Universidade Federal de Santa Catarina
Manuel Alector Ribeiro, University of Surrey
Aurkene Alzua-Sorzabal, Universidad de Nebrija
Salvador Anton Clavé, Universitat Rovira i Virgili
Rodolfo Baggio, Università commerciale Luigi Bocconi
Enrique Bigné, Universitat de València
Dimitrios Buhalis, Bournemouth University
Jacques Bulchald, Universidad de Las Palmas de Gran Canaria
José Luis Caro Herrero, Universidad de Málaga
María Jesús Carrasco Santos, Universidad de Málaga
Alfonso Cerezo Medina, Universidad de Málaga
Esther Chavez Miranda, Universidad de Sevilla
Cihan Cobanoglu, University of South Florida Sarasota-Manatee
Andres Coca-Stefaniak, University of Greenwich
Eduard Cristòbal Fransi, Universitat de Lleida
Natalia Daries Ramón, Universitat de Lleida
Stefano De Cantis, Università degli Studi di Palermo
Pablo Díaz Luque, Universitat Oberta de Catalunya
Francisco Femenía Serra, Universidad de Nebrija
Antonio Fernández Morales, Universidad de Málaga
Berta Ferrer Rosell, Universitat de Lleida
Cristina Figueroa Domecq, Universidad Rey Juan Carlos
José Antonio Fraiz Brea, Universidad de Vigo
María García Hernández, Universidad Complutense de Madrid
Josefa García Mestanza, Universidad de Málaga
Ramón García Marín, Universidad de Murcia
Manuel Enciso García-Oliveros, Universidad de Málaga

Germán Gémar Castillo, Universidad de Málaga
David Giner, INVAT·TUR
Joan Miquel Gomis López, Universitat Oberta de Catalunya
Ulrike Gretzel, University of Queensland
Alfonso Infante Moro, Universidad de Huelva
Juan Carlos Infante Moro, Universidad de Huelva
Josep Ivars Baidal, Universidad de Alicante
Mª del Amor Jiménez Jiménez, Universidad de Huelva
Jose Luis Leiva, Universidad de Málaga
Carmelo León González, Universidad de Las Palmas de GC
José Antonio López, Universidad de Cádiz
Enric López C., CETT—Universidad de Barcelona
Estela Mariné Roig, Universitat de Lleida
Eva Martín Fuentes, Universitat de Lleida
Sebastián Molinillo Jiménez, Universidad de Málaga
Soledad Morales Pérez, Universitat Oberta de Catalunya
Eugenio Olmedo Peralta, Universidad de Málaga
Eduardo Parra López, Universidad de La Laguna
Noemí Rabassa Figueras, Universitat Rovira i Virgili
Ricardo Remond Noa, Universidad de La Habana
Miguel Ángel Ríos Martín, Universidad de Sevilla
Isabel Rodríguez, University of Surrey
Carlos Romero Dexeus, SEGITTUR
Carlos Rossi, Universidad de Málaga
José António Santos, University of Algarve
Marianna Sigala, University of South Australia
Pilar Talón Ballestero, Universidad Rey Juan Carlos
José Fernando Vera Rebollo, Universidad de Alicante
Maria José Viñals Blasco, Universidad Politécnica de Valencia
Mariemma I. Yagüe del Valle, Universidad de Málaga

Preface

The 14th International Conference on Tourism and Information and Communication Technology, TURITEC 2023, showcases the latest research and case studies on the use of Information and Communication Technologies (ICT) in the field of travel and tourism. The event is organized by the Faculty of Tourism of the University of Málaga and the Andalusian Institute for Research and Innovation in Tourism of the Universities of Granada, Málaga, and Seville (IATUR). The conference took place in Málaga on October 19 and 20, 2023, with the theme "Advances in Data Science, Artificial Intelligence, and Sustainability."

The research tracks of TURITEC 2023 received a total of 50 full paper submissions covering a diverse range of fields related to ICT and tourism. Each research paper went through a rigorous double-blind review process, resulting in the acceptance of 25 full papers for presentation at the conference. These accepted papers are included in the proceedings to facilitate the exchange and dissemination of tourism technology research on a global scale. We are grateful to the organizers and sponsors for publishing the proceedings in an open-access mode to support this goal.

The papers presented in these proceedings contribute to the current knowledge of the intersection of ICT and tourism. The scientific committee proposed three main tracks for the papers: digitalization, mobility, and tourism distribution; artificial intelligence; and sustainability, platform economies, and new realities. Since the last edition of TURITEC, in the midst of the pandemic, the trends that are transforming the tourism sector have accelerated towards an increase in local sustainability, adaptation to the climate crisis, and especially an advance in technology, with the digitalization of companies and destinations, the incipient use of artificial intelligence, etc. These changes are not assimilated in the same way depending on the size of companies and destinations, so technological solutions must be democratized in different future scenarios. In this edition, we are moving forward on familiar topics, but with multiple novelties with the increase in digitization applied to mobility, user-generated content, Big Data, business intelligence, and platform economies; and we incorporate other disruptive topics such as data platforms, artificial intelligence and its impact on tourism, circular economy or smart governance.

The first part of the book focuses on *Digitalization, Mobility and User-Generated Content (UGC)* in the context of tourism. It sheds light on various methodological processes such as the analysis of tourist flows using Wi-Fi sensor technology, best practices for using technology to promote music festivals, and optimizing tourist data extraction and analysis as an integral methodology. The book features numerous contributions to user-generated content, including hotel reviews on Booking, analysis of social media followers on Facebook, Instagram, and Twitter in World Heritage Cities, and user opinions on Tripadvisor. Furthermore, it explores the relationship between metaverse and tourism by studying lexical competences in these new digital environments and researching the tourist perception of "intelligence" in a destination.

The impact of Artificial Intelligence and Big Data on the tourism industry has been a widely discussed topic due to their vast potential and that is the scope of the second part of this book. These technologies are now viewed as opportunities to revive the sector. Big Data has long been used in the industry, but its significance has increased in recent times. It is now seen as an essential tool, be it for data platforms for tourism organizations, real-time management of tourism destinations, or Business Intelligence for cruises. In restaurant management, it can be used for unsupervised modelling of ticket data to forecast sales. Moreover, Machine Learning is used to analyze predictors of yacht charter success.

The last part of this book focuses on a growing trend—the application of information and communication technology (ICT) to promote greater sustainability, highlighting the sensitivity of researchers to the impacts of tourism. The topics covered in this section are quite varied, but can be grouped under the research from the social dimension, where the focus is on analyzing the connections between tourist destinations, the digital ecosystem, and the technological actors. The part also explores how to apply an intelligence system based on knowledge governance, or the creation of a framework to enhance the social impact of tourism. In the environmental dimension, research is carried out on how circular economy can benefit hotel and catering companies, or how measures to reduce carbon footprint can influence the choice of accommodation booking. We hope that these proceedings will serve as a valuable source of information for researchers and practitioners in the tourism industry worldwide, fostering better understanding and collaboration between universities and tourism professionals.

We hope that these proceedings will serve as a valuable source of information for researchers and practitioners in the tourism industry worldwide, fostering better understanding and collaboration between universities and tourism professionals.

We would like to express our sincere gratitude to all the members of the TURITEC 2023 Scientific Committee for their valuable time and effort in ensuring the high quality of the research papers. We also extend our thanks to the organizing board,

Mario Blanco, Natalia Hustova, Marta Lozano, and Irene Baquero, for their unwavering support in managing the conference. Finally, we would like to acknowledge the authors whose willingness to present their latest research at TURITEC 2023 made this conference possible. Without their contributions, this conference would not have been a success.

Málaga, Spain   Antonio J. Guevara Plaza
                                                                                            Alfonso Cerezo Medina
                                                                                            Enrique Navarro Jurado

About This Book

This open-access book showcases the latest research and case studies on the use of Information and Communication Technologies (ICT) in the field of travel and tourism. It presents the proceedings of The 14th International Conference on Tourism and Information and Communications Technology, TURITEC 2023. The papers presented in this book contribute to the current knowledge of the intersection of ICT and tourism in three main topics: *Digitalization, Mobility and User-Generated Content (UGC)*; *Artificial Intelligence and Tourism*; and *Sustainability, Platform Economies and New Realities.*

Contents

About the Editors

Antonio J. Guevara Plaza is the Dean of the Faculty of Tourism at the University of Málaga and Professor in the Computer Sciences Department. He began his relationship with tourism studies since its creation at the University of Málaga in 1995. He is currently president of the Spanish Conference of Deans of Tourism (CEDTUR), involving 45 Spanish universities with undergraduate, postgraduate, and Ph.D. studies in Tourism. His research interests focus on Information Technology and Communication (ICT) applied to tourism. He is the principal researcher of the SICUMA research group (Cooperative Information Systems, University of Malaga). He has directed several projects for R&D related to the implementation of ICT in tourism and published research works at relevant journal publications.

Alfonso Cerezo Medina has participated in over a dozen tourism projects as a researcher. His main research line has been the relationship between tourism and information technologies, which led him to write his doctoral thesis on IT training needs in tourism companies in Andalusia. He is a co-opted member at the International Federation for IT and Travel and Tourism (IFITT). He is developing new research areas such as wine tourism, food tourism, platform economies, and security in tourism. Alfonso serves as a reviewer for international academic tourism journals and has extensive experience as a member of the organizing board for the International Conference of Tourism and

Information Technology TURITEC. Over the last 4 years, he has also worked as an assistant professor in tourism and gastronomy.

Enrique Navarro Jurado holds a Ph.D. in Geography and is the Director of the Andalusian Institute for Tourism Research and Innovation (Málaga). His research focuses on tourism destinations, planning, and management, limits to growth and tourist carrying capacity, sustainability indicators, and technologies applied to sustainability, tourism, and climate change. Principal investigator of several R+D+i projects and has participated in more than 30 research projects (Brazil, the Dominican Republic, Cuba, Mexico, Argentina...) and in technology transfer contracts. He published more than 40 publications in journals of international impact. He is the member of several boards of trustees, scientific associations, and journal editorl; and Advisor to the Blue Plan (UNEP-UN) and various regional and local plans.

Digitalization, Mobility
and User-Generated Content (UGC)

Best Practices in Technology Usage for Promotion of Music Festivals in Spain

Diego R. Toubes⊕, Noelia Araújo-Vila⊕, and José Antonio Fraiz-Brea⊕

Abstract Technology plays a crucial role in the success of festivals and music events, contributing to the promotion of tourist destinations, optimization of dissemination processes, accessibility for attendees, and overall enhancement of their experience. This article presents a case study of best practices in the use of technology in festivals and music events in Spain, based on award-winning technological initiatives from the Talkfest Music Fest Summit, which promotes the Iberian Festival Awards. A cooperative benchmarking methodology is employed, and the challenges and directions in the face of the technological paradigm shift posed by artificial intelligence (AI) are assessed. The results provide updated insights into the best practices in technology usage in music events in Spain, as well as identifying challenges and trends in this field.

Keywords Event management · Cooperative benchmarking · Tourist promotion · Artificial intelligence · Cashless

1 Introduction

The festivals and music events industry has experienced significant growth in recent decades, both in Spain and globally. These events serve as a cultural expression that attracts millions of people each year, particularly the young and digitally savvy audience. Music festivals have a positive impact on the tourism development of hosting destinations, enhancing their image, generating socio-economic benefits, and enriching the cultural offerings. However, incorporating new technologies

D. R. Toubes (✉)
Business Administration and Tourism School, University Campus, 32004 Ourense, Spain
e-mail: drtoubes@uvigo.es

D. R. Toubes · N. Araújo-Vila · J. A. Fraiz-Brea
Universidade de Vigo, Vigo, Spain

© The Author(s) 2024
A. J. Guevara Plaza et al. (eds.), *Tourism and ICTs: Advances in Data Science, Artificial Intelligence and Sustainability*, Springer Proceedings in Business and Economics, https://doi.org/10.1007/978-3-031-52607-7_1

throughout the event lifecycle, from promotion and ticket sales to staging and audience interaction, is necessary for achieving success and attendee satisfaction. Technology can improve the quality, accessibility, and innovation of festivals and music events, enhancing the experience for the predominantly young and digitally native attendees.

According to the Cultural Statistics Yearbook (Ministerio de Educación, Cultura y Deporte, 2022), music events primarily attract a young audience aged between 25 and 34. However, the age range may vary depending on the type and theme of the festival, encompassing a broader market segment. Given that most attendees are digital natives, it is natural for new technologies to increasingly play a part in these events, from accessing information and purchasing tickets to on-site experiences and consumption within the venue, particularly during performances.

This article aims to identify best practices in the use of technology in festivals and music events to enhance tourist destination promotion, optimize dissemination processes, improve consumption and access for attendees, and amplify their overall experience. The study conducts a case study of best practices in technology usage in festivals and music events in Spain based on award-winning technological initiatives. It also evaluates the challenges and directions in the face of the technological paradigm shift posed by the advancement of artificial intelligence. Finally, recommendations are proposed for the festivals and music events sector on offering innovative, applicable, and accessible services using technology, adding value to the festivals and indirectly benefiting the tourist destinations where they are held.

2 Theoretical Review

2.1 Festivals, Musical Events and Tourism

Festivals and events have become integral parts of the tourism product in many destinations (Getz & Page, 2016), attracting visitors and tourists and contributing to the economic and social well-being of the destination. Therefore, they are increasingly included in tourism policies and strategies (Mair & Whitford, 2013). Destination Management Organizations (DMOs) have been investing in the creation and promotion of festivals and music events to enhance the appeal of destinations (Araújo & Domínguez, 2012). These products align with cultural tourism, offering characteristics that meet the current demands and desires of consumers, such as socialization, novelty, prestige, relaxation, intellectual enrichment, and experiential tourism.

Music festivals create a dynamic and fluid soundscape within a specific space, which is the tourist destination, and a short period of time, providing attendees with an opportunity to enjoy and interact not only with the music but also with other visitors (Anderson et al., 2005; Ballantyne et al., 2014). Modern music festivals offer diverse genres and styles, catering to different tastes and preferences, and often incorporate other elements such as art installations, food vendors, and immersive experiences. This multi-dimensional approach contributes to the overall appeal and attractiveness of the festival, attracting a wide range of attendees. In modern festivals, particularly music festivals, a line-up of singers and musical groups is organized to perform over several days, usually centered around a specific theme (Pan & Wang, 2019). Thus, attendees can enjoy a social, cultural, and leisure experience during these days (Gibson & Connell, 2003).

Music festivals and other music events have always been popular activities in Western countries (Ballantyne et al., 2014), and their numbers have also increased in recent decades in other countries, such as China, where they have become a rapidly growing industry since the beginning of the century (Han et al., 2017). Therefore, in recent decades, the number of festivals and other music events has increased, becoming a significant part of the tourism sector with great potential for the development, repositioning, and economic restructuring of a destination. According to Leenders (2010), branding, atmosphere, image, and emotions act as attractive factors for tourists, leading to their loyalty and increased spending. If the destination has a long-term vision, variables such as pricing, online sales, and the use of technologies must be addressed to achieve long-term success and consolidate the event (Cardoso et al., 2019).

Regarding the promotion of festivals through social media, various studies indicate that social media usage has a significant influence on festival engagement (Hudson et al. 2015). This influence evidently impacts the destination image, which is why for destination managers it is especially important to have a clear understanding of the desired theme and image of the destination they wish to project (see Song et al., 2021), and to learn how to work on each specific platform in order to oversee the different destination visions and their resources (Garay & Morales, 2017).

2.2 The Use of New Technologies in Music Festivals

Many music festivals fail because the experiences they offer do not ensure relevance and meaning for attendees. By experimenting with enhanced sensory feelings and utilizing the wide range of technologies available today, the broadcasting, accessing, and consumption of these events can be significantly optimized (Robertson et al., 2015).

Advancements in information and communication technologies (ICTs) have transformed communication worldwide, including the festival sector. ICTs have become a key element of the experience in these events. The Typology of Human Capability (TCH) introduces digital opportunities that enhance the festival experience and acknowledges that digital technology provides people with opportunities to connect. The theories describing technology acceptance by users offer a comprehensive understanding of the factors affecting the adoption of ICTs in festival settings, relevant to current and future technologies. Integrating emerging technologies into festivals allows for the provision of novel experiences and adds value for attendees when properly incorporated (Van Winkle et al., 2018).

The purchase process for attending a festival begins with recognizing the need (Kotler & Keller, 2006). In this case, it is the need to attend a particular festival. This need may be motivated or amplified through information disseminated by the festival itself, such as advertising, or through feedback from other users or friends familiar with the festival. Here, the use of new technologies can provide a competitive advantage by reaching a larger target audience or making the festival more appealing. Most festivals have their own websites where users can perform essential actions, such as purchasing tickets or accessing event information. Additionally, they utilize social media platforms like Instagram, Facebook, or Twitter, which provide information and serve as important sources of feedback (Oklobdžija, 2015). Streaming music platforms like YouTube or Spotify also enhance the festival experience (UOC, 2019).

Technological alternatives continue to increase within the festivals themselves. The development of festival-specific applications is becoming more common. Through these apps, attendees can check artist schedules, transportation options, festival areas or maps, some of which are interactive with points of interest (Monllor, 2023). Another technological advancement used during events is cashless payment, which is revolutionizing the festival experience and gaining acceptance from both attendees and event organizers. Also, internationally renowned festivals like Coachella in California, United States (http://www.coachella.com), or Tomorrowland in Belgium (http://www.tomorrowland.com), have embraced RFID (Radio Frequency Identification) technology, which is incorporated into the access wristband chips. Others use NFC (Near Field Communication) technology instead. Through these wristbands, attendees can participate in raffles, vote, share impressions on social media, engage in games, or download exclusive content. These wristbands not only offer utilities for users but also provide valuable information to event organizers and promoters for improving the event, known as big data analysis. For example, they can analyze the number of people entering at any given time, points of high flow, the number of attendees yet to arrive, the most consumed drinks and food, peak consumption times, etc. (BBVA, 2017).

Facial recognition technology, well-known for its common use in smartphones, has also been implemented in music events. For instance, Taylor Swift concerts have used it to detect potential harassers. It has also been utilized in a more positive sense to create artistic expressions reflecting real-time emotions. Blockchain technology has also made its way into the festival sector. Firstly, in music dissemination through streaming platforms like Musicoin or Bitsong, which offer payment security for royalties using blockchain (traceable and monitorable transfer blocks). Secondly, in the creation of new music festivals. An example of this is Our Music Festival in 2018 (https://www.facebook.com/OurMusicFest/), a festival supported by blockchain technology where tickets are purchased using a specific cryptocurrency, and investments are made in cryptocurrency (UOC, 2019).

3 Methodology

The objective of this study is to conduct a case study on best practices in the use of technology in festivals and music events in Spain. To achieve this, the awarded technological initiatives in the last two editions of the Talkfest Music Fest Summit have been taken as a reference. This summit promotes the Iberian Festival Awards (IFA), specifically the category of "Best use of Technology". Two representative cases from different areas of technology application have been selected: the interaction with an artificial intelligence image generation model at the Icónica Sevilla Fest, developed by Prodigioso Volcán, and the contactless payment systems at festivals held in Spain and Portugal, developed by Easygoband under the brand Gofun.

The case study is a qualitative research method that employs multiple sources of evidence and explores the object of study within its context. Its objective is to gain an in-depth understanding of a complex and unique phenomenon, including its causes, consequences, and implications (Yin, 2014). Within the case study, benchmarking analysis has been applied as a technique to identify and compare best practices in the field of technology in festivals and music events. Benchmarking offers several advantages, such as gaining knowledge of the state of the art, identifying improvement opportunities, establishing realistic and measurable objectives, and fostering innovation and quality (Kotler & Keller, 2006). Different types of benchmarking exist based on the field, objective, or source of comparison (Zairi, 1994). In this study, a cooperative benchmarking approach has been used, involving collaboration between participating organizations to share information and experiences. By selecting two awardees from the IFA, a cooperative benchmarking methodology is employed, investigating organizations recognized for their excellence in the use of technology in music events and their willingness to share experiences. This enables valuable insights to be gained from their best practices and adapted to other contexts (Ramabadron et al., 1997). The following steps have been followed to conduct cooperative benchmarking: defining the activity, identifying organizations implementing best practices, collecting and analyzing information about these practices, comparing them with other solutions, and evaluating the benefits obtained.

For each case study, a documentary analysis of available sources related to the project has been conducted, including websites, social media, press releases, videos, and reports. Special attention has been given to the objectives, characteristics, results, and benefits of the technology used. Finally, semi-structured interviews were conducted with the heads of the winning projects in the IFA 2022 and IFA 2023, aiming to delve deeper into the benefits derived from the use of technology in festivals and music events. They were contacted via the social network LinkedIn, and once they agreed to be interviewed, the interview was conducted in writing and the content of the questions was shared with the respondents. The interviews focused on evaluating four key benefits related to destination promotion, operational optimization, user experience, and added value. The answers of the interviewees were collected after two days.[1]

3.1 Identification of the Activity

Talkfest Music Fest Summit is the premier event in the Iberian Peninsula for all topics related to music festivals. It features a program that is entirely focused on the present state of music festivals. The first edition took place in 2012 and included conferences, showcases, and exhibitions. In 2022, Talkfest-Music Fest Summit offered an event supported by three clusters: Main Event, Night Event, and Iberian Festival Awards (IFA).

IFA recognizes the contributions and achievements of event organizers and other stakeholders in the festival industry. The awards consist of 26 categories, including the category of "Best use of Technology". Brands and organizations that present technological and innovative solutions in festivals in Spain and Portugal, which contribute to and add value to the festival experience and/or the attending audience, can participate in this category. The IFA 2022 was held in Barcelona, and the 2023 edition will take place in Maia, Portugal.

The IFA provides a platform for recognizing the exceptional contributions of event organizers and technology providers in the music festival industry. It plays a crucial role in fostering collaboration and establishing effective synergies between Spain and Portugal. The awards aim to acknowledge the efforts of various agents involved in festival organization and shed light on aspects that are often invisible to the public eye (IFA, 2023).

3.2 Best-Practice Organizations

The technologies awarded at the IFA serve as catalysts for innovation, promoting excellence and collaboration in the Iberian music festival industry. Below, we present the proposals of the winners from the last two editions.

The winner of the IFA 2022 was the brand Gofun, developed by Easygoband. Gofun is a pioneering platform that digitizes festival operations and payments. It integrates cashless payment systems, enabling users to make transactions seamlessly. With a hybrid device that supports NFC wristband/card payments and contactless bank card payments, Gofun offers festival-goers a wide range of payment options, thereby reducing queues and enhancing the overall user experience. A key feature of Gofun is its provision of comprehensive data analysis and sales reports. These reports

---

[1] The interview was conducted in Spanish; the authors of the article have translated the answers into English.

empower festival promoters with detailed insights into sales information, enabling them to optimize resources and improve profitability.

Gofun combines various payment methods seamlessly. Festival attendees can utilize NFC cashless payments, contactless payments, QR payments, and an on-demand web app for ordering and receiving goods or services. The all-in-one payment solution increases user convenience and streamlines transactions. The award for the best use of technology recognizes the platform's versatility, comprehensive data analysis, and focus on user experience (Easygoband, 2022).

The winner of the IFA 2023 was the company Prodigioso Volcán with their proposal "Icónica I-Art" at the Icónica Sevilla Fest, held in the Plaza de España in Seville from September 16th to October 15th, 2022. In this case, music and artificial intelligence were blended in the first collaborative exhibition of AI art and music at a festival. The attending audience contributed their ideas through social media, focusing on their music experience, and the company translated these combinations into artistic creations using image creation tools that employ generative AI algorithms (see Fig. 1).

The "translation" of the audience's ideas into images is the key process. Prompt engineering seeks ways to assist in training and adapting AI tools to make the most of new large language models (LLMs), which may yield results that are not always accurate or suitable. In text-to-image algorithms, the user writes a prompt or command containing instructions for the machine, and the AI model generates an image that matches the given description. The image creation tool used in this

Fig. 1 Deep purple in the recording studio, in the style of El Greco. *Source* Image created by Pablo Escobedo via Midjourney.

case was Midjourney. It is during the conception, writing, and refinement process that Icónica I-Art channels its creative intention. The resulting small artistic pieces from this co-creative experience represent a gallery showcasing the potential of AI applied to visual creation and communication (Prodigioso Volcán, 2022).

3.3 Evaluation of the Benefits Obtained

The selected case studies present two examples of how technology can enhance festivals and music events in different aspects. On one hand, Prodigioso Volcán demonstrates how AI can create a novel and creative interaction between the audience and the event, generating a unique and distinctive experience. On the other hand, Easygoband shows how NFC technology can facilitate payment processes, access control, and overall management at festivals, improving security, convenience, and efficiency. Table 1 provides a summary of the objectives, characteristics, results, and benefits obtained from the two case studies.

The systems used in payment platforms have revolutionized festival operations and the consumer experience. For example, the O Son do Camiño festival, held in Santiago de Compostela, was a finalist at the IFA 2023 for its use of Weezevent, an event management platform that offers technological solutions for festival organizers, such as ticket sales and access control. Weezevent and Enterticket provide a cashless payment system with NFC wristbands that can be recharged online or at the event venue. They also offer an online ticketing system with various formats (e-tickets, thermal tickets, passbooks). Imply offers Elevencash, a cashless payment platform for different segments that uses RFID technology in cards, wristbands, or printed tickets with QR codes.

Cashless payment systems offer several advantages to festivals, including reducing waiting times at bars and points of sale, ensuring the security of money flows by limiting the circulation of cash and preventing fraud, real-time monitoring and tracking of all operations with detailed sales reports, fostering audience loyalty through various promotions, and offering alternatives such as donations or ticket purchases for the next edition. Cashless systems also enhance sponsorship by featuring on the cashless wristband and improve promotions based on collected data (Weezevent, 2022). However, it is necessary to educate the public about the use of the cashless system, address their questions or complaints, and there is always the possibility of wristband failures or losses.

Results of the Interviews

The benefits of using technology in festivals are supported by the evaluations obtained in the expert interviews. The creative director at Prodigioso Volcán, argues that "the technological paradigm shift posed by the advancement of AI requires the sector to be attentive to technological changes, and we are entering an uncertain era where SEO and advertising space payments will not be enough". Regarding the added value and experiential aspect for attendees provided by the Icónica I-Art solution, this expert

Table 1 Summary of selected case studies

Case study	Objective	Characteristics	Results	Benefits
Prodigioso Volcán Icónica Sevilla Fest	Provide the music event attendees with the opportunity to interact with an image-generating AI model	A large screen displayed images generated by an artificial neural network based on the festival's ambient sound Attendees could send messages to the model through a web app and see how it responded with images The model constantly learned from audience feedback	Over 5,000 interactions recorded More than 1,000 images generated Significant media and social impact	Enhance creativity and audience participation Create a unique and innovative experience Differentiate the festival from other similar events
Easygoband Gofun	Gofun facilitate payment systems used in festivals held in Spain and Portugal	A smart bracelet that allows cashless and cardless payments at festivals Attendees can recharge the bracelet online or at physical points Organizers can monitor capacity, consumption, and access with the bracelet	Over 50 festivals implemented the solution More than 1 million users utilized the bracelet 30% increase in average attendee spending	Improve safety and convenience for attendees Reduce queues and fraud Obtain data and insights on audience behavior

notes that "the ability of this model to transform (the audience's) words into images, their experiences and memories into art, is what provided Icónica with innovative value and a new type of relationship with the audience. It hasn't been a year yet, and the technological possibilities available to us now would allow us to offer an even more astonishing experience". Easygoband's CEO also emphasises how technology enhances the attendee experience: "(attendees) leave the concert with an impressive live experience", and continues, "people are going to enjoy the event. Anything that facilitates that enhances the experience, and that's where technology has a lot to contribute".

Another aspect to highlight is the optimisation of access, consumption and sales processes. In the words of the head of Easygoband "it is about reducing friction in all cases, both in the purchase and payment, as well as in recharging, access, etc.". Many technological solutions are emerging, but they all need to demonstrate an economic return to the festival organizer, which is not always the case. In this sense, this expert points out that the technological solution presented by Gofun "increases sales, reduces collection times and avoids the hassle of queues for wristband recharging".

A new challenge arises, openly discussed as a paradigm shift in technological innovation, and as one expert notes, "the generative AI revolution, the great paradigm shift of our time, brings an explosion of creativity and the ability to create new experiences for the audience. The improvement brought by AI algorithms to live sound engineering, beyond visual experiences personalized both on and off stage, is one of the fields where significant evolution will be observed". He believes that large language models (LLMs) will bring greater efficiency in production management and improve the ability to provide personalized information to the audience through chatbots and assistants. The diffusion of innovation has its timelines, and not always do new technologies have the success they were predicted to have. It is important for companies and organizations to carefully study how innovative products or ideas are disseminated and perceived by consumers or users (Rogers, 2003). In this regard, one expert points out that "the challenge lies in knowing how to offer these services in an innovative way".

4 Conclusions

The cooperative benchmarking methodology employed in this work allows for a panoramic and up-to-date view of best practices in technology usage in festivals and music events in Spain, as well as identifying the challenges and trends to be pursued in this field. In summary, the case studies highlight two key benefits of technology usage in festivals—enhancing the audience experience through AI creativity, and optimizing operations via improved payment systems. The technological paradigm shift posed by the advancement of AI requires the sector to be attentive to technological changes. As one of the experts commented, the challenge lies in knowing how to offer these services in an innovative way, meaning that technology should be applicable, accessible, and reach most of the market.

The analysis conducted has both theoretical and practical implications for the study of festivals and music events. From a theoretical perspective, it contributes to expanding knowledge about the role of technology in these types of events, as well as the dimensions of destination promotion, operational optimization, and user experience. From a practical standpoint, it provides a guide for organizers and professionals in the industry on best practices in technology usage, as well as the challenges and trends to follow.

This study has some limitations and suggestions for future research. The generalizability of the results is affected by the specific context of the selected case studies, as they may not be representative of other music events with different characteristics, and only two interviews were conducted with company managers, so the results may not be representative of the entire sector. Additionally, the selection of case studies has been based on a subjective criterion that may not reflect the quality or relevance of other technological initiatives in festivals and music events. It is suggested that future research expands the number and diversity of analyzed case studies and compares or contrasts the obtained results with other contexts or scenarios.

Acknowledgements This work is part of the research project: "Retos para la transición digital en turismo: análisis de la inteligencia turística y propuestas normativas", MCIN/AEI/https://doi.org/10.13039/501100011033 y Unión Europea "NextGenerationEU"/PRTR". Reference: TED 2021-129763B-100.

References

Anderson, B., Morton, F., & Revill, G. (2005). Practices of music and sound. *Social & Cultural Geography, 6*(5), 639–644.

Araújo Vila, N., & Domínguez Vila, T. (2012). Los festivales de cine como elemento potenciador de destinos turísticos. El caso de San Sebastián. *Vivat Academia. Revista de Comunicación*, 31–49.

Ballantyne, J., Ballantyne, R., & Packer, J. (2014). Designing and managing music festival experiences to enhance attendees' psychological and social benefits. *Musicae Scientiae, 18*(1), 65–83.

BBVA. (2017). *Cómo la tecnología mejora los festivales, y no sólo la música.* https://www.bbva.com/es/tecnologia-mejora-festivales-solo-musica/. Retrieved 02 May 2023

Cardoso, L., Araújo Vila, N., Almeida, Â. D., & Fraiz Brea, J. A. (2019). *Los festivales de música como inductores de imagen de destino turístico.* El caso del Festival Vodafone Paredes de Coura.

Coachella. (2023). www.coachella.com

Easygoband. (2022). *The iberian music festival party awards technology.* Tecnología para eventos. October 24, 2022. https://gofun.easygoband.com/en/blog/the-iberian-music-festival-party-awards-technology/

Garay, L., & Morales Pérez, S. (2017). Understanding the creation of destination images through a festival's Twitter conversation. *International Journal of Event and Festival Management, 8*(1), 39–54.

Getz, D., & Page, S. J. (2016). Progress and prospects for event tourism research. *Tourism management, 52*, 593–631.

Gibson, C., & Connell, J. (2003). 'Bongo Fury': Tourism, music and cultural economy at Byron Bay, Australia. *Tijdschrift voor economische en sociale geografie, 94*(2), 164–187.

Han, J., Wang, W., Zheng, C., & Zhang, J. (2017). Host perceptions of music festival impacts: Time and space matter? *Asia Pacific Journal of Tourism Research, 22*(11), 1156–1168.

Hudson, S., Roth, M. S., Madden, T. J., & Hudson, R. (2015). The effects of social media on emotions, brand relationship quality, and word of mouth: An empirical study of music festival attendees. *Tourism Management, 47*, 68–76.

IFA. (2023). *Iberian festival awards.* https://www.talkfest.eu/ifa

Kotler, P., & Keller, K. L. (2006). *Dirección de marketing.* Pearson educación.

Leenders, M. A. (2010). The relative importance of the brand of music festivals: A customer equity perspective. *Journal of Strategic Marketing, 18*(4), 291–301.

Mair, J., & Whitford, M. (2013). An exploration of events research: Event topics, themes and emerging trends. *International Journal of Event and Festival Management.*

Ministerio de Educación, Cultura y Deporte. (2022). *Anuario de Estadísticas Culturales 2021.* https://www.culturaydeporte.gob.es/dam/jcr:f595ecde-9965-4204-a134-7c569931eb1e/anuario-de-estadisticas-culturales-2021.pdf

Monllor Alonso, L. (2023). Aplicación para la centralización de la gestión e información en festivales musicales. UOC.

Oklobdžija, S. (2015). The role and importance of social media in promoting music festivals. In *Synthesis 2015-international scientific conference of IT and business-related research* (pp. 583–587). Singidunum University.

Our music Festival. (2018). https://www.facebook.com/OurMusicFest/

Pan, J. Y., & Wang, J. L. (2019). *Music festival goes to the mass.*

Volcán, P. (2022). *Así sacamos de la chistera una expo de arte IA*. https://www.linkedin.com/pulse/as%C3%AD-sacamos-de-la-chistera-una-expo-arte-ia-prodigioso-volcan/?originalSubdomain=es

Robertson, M., Yeoman, I., Smith, K. A., & McMahon-Beattie, U. (2015). Technology, society, and visioning the future of music festivals. *Event Management, 19*(4), 567–587.

Rogers, E. M. (2003). *Diffusion of innovations* (5th ed.). Free Press.

Song, S., Park, S., & Park, K. (2021). Thematic analysis of destination images for social media engagement marketing. *Industrial Management & Data Systems, 121*(6), 1375–1397.

Tomorrowland. (2023). www.tomorrowland.com

UOC. (2019). *5 novedades tecnológicas de los festivales de música*. https://blogs.uoc.edu/gestioneventos/es/5-novedades-tecnologicas-de-los-festivales-de-musica-gestion-de-eventos/

Van Winkle, C. M., MacKay, K. J., & Halpenny, E. (2018). Information and communication technology and the festival experience. In *The Routledge handbook of festivals* (pp. 254–262). Routledge.

Ramabadron, R., Dean, J. W., Jr., & Evans, J. R. (1997). Benchmarking and project management: A review and organizational model. *Benchmarking for Quality Management & Technology, 4*(1), 47–58.

Weezevent. (2022). *Cashless para festivales para una gestión inteligente*. https://weezevent.com/es/cashless-festival/

Yin, R. K. (2014). *Case study research: Design and methods* (5th ed.). Sage.

Zairi, M. (1994). Benchmarking: The best tool for measuring competitiveness. *Benchmarking for Quality Management & Technology, 1*(1), 11–24.

Tracking Tourist Flows Through Wi-Fi Sensor Technology in Seville

Irene N. Franco, Concepción Foronda-Robles, Federico Rollán, and Pino Canales

Abstract The study of tourism flows consists of understanding the spatial-temporal relationship of tourists with the space they visit, which has become a key aspect for the management of destinations. The advance of communication and information technologies nowadays allows the extraction and storage of a large amount of data of different types and at different scales, which can be very useful for decision-making. In this context, this study aims to use WiFi sensor technology to track and record the movement patterns of tourists. The methodology used focuses on the measurement and analysis of this variable through the extraction of real-time data from WiFi points in the Barrio de Santa Cruz, Seville. The results obtained demonstrate the viability of this instrument for analysing tourist flows at the destination as opposed to the use of other instruments that involve higher costs and/or limitations. Likewise, in terms of its applicability, the results show the need for its use, in combination with other tools and techniques, for the planning and management of tourist destinations.

Keywords Tourist flows · ICT · WiFi sensors · Tracking · Seville

1 Introduction

The spatial structure of a destination is constantly shaped and reshaped by the movements of tourists. In this sense, spatio-temporal behavioural patterns in the destination are defined by the movements of visitors moving from one attraction to another (Vu et al., 2018).

I. N. Franco (✉) · C. Foronda-Robles
University of Seville, Seville, Spain
e-mail: infranco@us.es

Andalusian Institute for Research and Innovation in Tourism (IATUR), Granada, Spain

F. Rollán · P. Canales
Smart Tourist Office-Sevilla City Office of Seville City Council, Seville, Spain

© The Author(s) 2024
A. J. Guevara Plaza et al. (eds.), *Tourism and ICTs: Advances in Data Science, Artificial Intelligence and Sustainability*, Springer Proceedings in Business and Economics,
https://doi.org/10.1007/978-3-031-52607-7_2

In the last decade, there has been an increase in research on this issue, but studies are still limited and the methodologies employed are multiple and varied, lacking uniformity and complementarity (Zheng et al., 2022). Against this background, the need for a more developed and nuanced theoretical framework, as well as the application, clustering and improvement of research techniques in this field is evident. The present study aims to contribute in providing a theoretical-methodological framework to this field of study and proposes as its main objective to study the use of WiFi sensorics to track and record tourists' movement patterns.

The origins of research on the spatio-temporal behaviour of tourists at destination level date back to the 1980s. Hartmann (1988) pioneered the analysis of American and Canadian visitor flows in Munich in order to describe their behavioural patterns, using various methods such as direct observation and questionnaires. From this, a literature on the mobility and travel patterns of tourists visiting a destination began to take shape. In terms of purposes, most of them have focused on internal (tourist's own) or external (destination's) factors (Karagöz et al., 2022). The former encompass the study of those behaviours related to the capabilities and socio-demographic and psychological factors that influence the tourist's own decision-making. In this line, studies have been conducted to find differences in movement patterns according to the role of tourist or resident (Murphy, 1992), time of year (Keul & Küheberger, 1997) or nationality (Caldeira & Kastenholz, 2015), as well as in relation to psychological aspects (Fennell, 1996), establishing demand classifications (Galí & Donaire, 2006).

Other research focuses on factors external to the tourist and inherent to the destination itself, such as the distribution and characteristics of the tourist offer. Thus, trips from accommodation to attractions are considered first-order movements (Neutens et al., 2011), since tourist attractions are a source of motivation (Salazar et al., 2001), in addition to the distribution of supply, accessibility and transport infrastructure, or the demographic and economic environment itself (Lew & McKercher, 2006; Xiao-Ting & Bi-hu, 2012).

Similarly, when managing destinations and tourist demand, it is important to examine behaviour through their movement within a destination. In relation to this, there have been studies that have analysed the evolution of the tourist space (Lepan, 2013), as well as its spatial delimitation (Bauder, 2015) and the urban transformations that are related to these movements (Freytag & Bauder, 2018). Similarly, others have addressed tourist flows in the analysis and management of the destination, with a view to decentralising and decongesting overcrowded spaces (Cavaillès et al., 2016).

Tourism flows are analysed at different scales. Under the present research and for a better understanding of this variable, the following classification of tourist flows according to the scale of analysis is provided in a novel way (Fig. 1), being the meso level the one that corresponds to this study.

It should be added that most of the meso-scale research has been carried out in urban destinations. Regarding the tracking instruments used (Fig. 2), whatever the scale, these have been based on both quantitative and qualitative techniques, with mixed methodologies being very common. Likewise, both the instruments used to collect mobility data and those used to analyse them have evolved in line with technological advances.

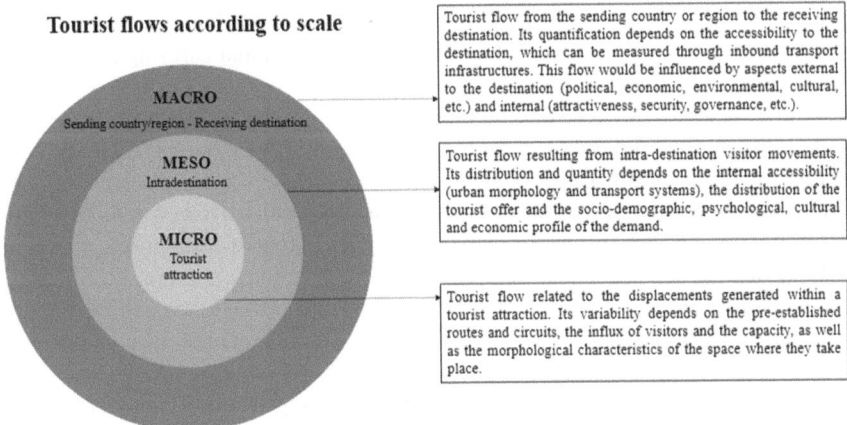

Fig. 1 Tourist flows according to scale. Own elaboration

Types	Instruments	References	Scale of analysis
Analogues	Direct observation	Hartmann, 1988	Meso: Munich, Germany
		Galí & Donaire, 2006	Meso: Girona, Spain
	Travel diaries	Haldrup, 2004	Meso: North Sea, Denmark
	Behavioural maps	Thornton et al., 1997	Meso: Newquay, United Kingdom
		Molz, 2010	Macro: global destinations
	Surveys and interviews	Stienmetz & Fesenmaier, 2019	Meso: Baltimore, USA
Digital	Statistical databases	Park et al., 2020	Meso: South Korea
		Zheng et al., 2022	Meso: Xiamen, China
	GPS tracking	Xiao-Ting & Bi-Hu, 2012	Micro: Summer Palace, Beijing, China
	Bluetooth tracking	Ahas et al., 2007	Meso: Estonia
		Versichele et al., 2014	Meso: Gant, Belgium, Brussels.
	Social Networking	Vu et al., 2018	Meso: Hong Kong, China.
	Wi-Fi sensors	Gao, Y. & Schmocker, 2021	Meso: Higashiyama Ward, Kyoto, Japan.

Fig. 2 Tracking tools for the analysis of tourism flows. Own elaboration

This paper employs Wi-Fi sensors to track tourists' movement patterns. With the rapid development and diffusion of smartphones, Wi-Fi packet sensors provide new possibilities for obtaining flow data (Advani et al., 2020; Martchouk et al., 2011). These sensors are designed to detect and record all Wi-Fi enabled electronic devices within an average radius of about 40 m. The detected devices are identified by the use of a Wi-Fi packet sensor. The detected devices are identified by an anonymous tag encrypted from the MAC address of the device. In addition to the encrypted MAC address, Wi-Fi packet sensors also record the timestamp, packet sensor ID, received signal strength indication (RSSI) and device vendor ID. Multiple detections and the above attributes allow observing the routes of any individual carrying a detectable device (Gao & Schmocker, 2021).

With regard to Wi-Fi sensors, although numerous studies have been carried out in the field of engineering, others have focused on military operations, environmental monitoring in the face of climate change and natural disasters, agriculture, energy efficiency, home automation, means of transport or smart cities. However, there is little research associated with the use of sensor technology in tourist destinations, although, with the incorporation of smart destinations, there is an integration of technological infrastructures and user devices to improve the tourist experience and destination management (Buonincontri & Micera, 2016). This sensor technology could be very useful for collecting real-time data (number of visitors, movement of people, hotel occupancy, vehicle traffic, energy consumption, among others) (Femenia-Serra & Ivars-Baidal, 2021).

2 Methodology

This research focuses on the movements of tourists at the meso level, which is called Tourist Flow Destination (TFD). According to Foronda et al. (2022, 3), the TFD is "the quantified flow of visitors who, during their stay at the destination, move from one geographical point to another to visit a tourism product, consume a service or satisfy a basic or tourist need, either on foot, in their own vehicle or through the means of transport and mobility systems (public and private) offered by the destination".

Likewise, with respect to the instruments for data extraction, Wi-Fi sensors will be used. It should be clarified that a Wireless Sensor Network (WSN) is a set of nodes composed of a microcontroller, various sensors, communication devices and, in some cases, actuators, which allow collecting and transmitting data from and influencing the physical environment in which they are applied. Each technology is exploited for its range and bandwidth characteristics. Wireless sensor networks (WSN) have different fields of application because they give the possibility to develop the nodes in a customised way for use in each specific area, as well as to adapt the network topology to the needs of the problem.

The case study where wifi tracking is applied is the Santa Cruz neighbourhood, one of the most emblematic places in Seville. Its ad hoc urban development, at the beginning of the twentieth century, was carried out to increase the attractiveness of the tourist offer, being "the first of the medieval historic quarters to undergo renovation for tourist purposes" (Moreno Garrido, 2005). Even today, it is the urban space with the highest intensity of tourist use in the city.

The study area of this neighbourhood is delimited with those points that have been considered most relevant from the point of view of congestion and traffic of people (residents and visitors), taking into account the access points (entrances and exits), as well as the main stops for visitors to the neighbourhood. Although 10 WiFi sensor points are planned, there are currently 4 of them, which provide real-time data on the capacity, affluence and flow of visitors in the area.

2.1 Phases of Analysis

2.1.1 Measurement and Observation Phase

The installation of the Wifi Location and Presence Analytics sensors is carried out by the company Galgus. This infrastructure connects the devices providing location analytics. Mobile devices use MAC (Media Access Control) address randomisation to be less traceable and protect personal information, but this interferes with traditional WiFi device counting methods. The company's patented device fingerprinting algorithm (Pérez-Hernández et al., 2023) overcomes MAC randomisation to accurately count WiFi devices without compromising the Intelligent Peripheral Interface (IPI). With these sensors, the study allows for location analytics (position estimation of nearby devices, heat maps, tracking, etc.) and presence (counting, segmentation, dwell times, gauging control, typical movements within the installation, recurrence estimation, etc.) using exclusively WiFi, through devices connected (associated) and not-connected (not associated) to the network. These WiFi frames of the "Probe Request" subtype are emitted by the devices when they are searching for nearby networks. They are frames sent by devices automatically and in bursts of several frames at a time, with the time interval and the number of frames per interval being configurable (Freudiger, 2015). Probe requests are interesting because they are the only frames sent by the device without being connected to an AP (Access Point) and they are the only frames sent by a device on all channels.

The Grafana OSS (Open-Source Software) operating system is a data analysis and visualisation software for processing time series data. A time series data set consists of several data points, each together with a time stamp. These data sets can be used to draw graphs and draw conclusions as the data changes over time (Salituro, 2020).

2.1.2 Prototyping Phase

All the information is processed and analysed from different areas. Contursa is the company responsible for the coordination to process and analyse the information, build and design the prototype solutions that will be incorporated in the implementation phase. In the future, the datasets extracted from the sensors will also be accessible from an open data portal so that users can work with them and offer possible solutions.

2.1.3   Implementation Phase

In advance, there are a multitude of actions, technological or otherwise, which may be recurrent in order to provide answers to questions such as:

- The identification of tourist routes established by tourist guides and free tours, where entry and exit points are recognised, as well as stops for explanations of the main tourist attractions (Foronda et al., 2022).
- The normative development of strategies related to the regulation of mobility in the destination, the regulation and control of the accommodation offer, the activation of peripheral points of attraction, the restriction of affluence in tourist resources and public spaces, among the most frequent (Mendoza et al., 2019).

3   Analysis and Results

In accordance with the methodology for accessing information, a series of analyses have been constructed, which are presented as preliminary results in the Santa Cruz neighbourhood of Seville.

Counting users by zones provides information on the flow of people, in a given area, by accesses, time slots, etc. and extracting ratios such as the number of people according to the distance from the WiFi. This information is used to obtain data on average occupancy, peak times, etc. This data is displayed in real time and recorded in the database to obtain historical reports.

Dwell time and Profiling. Emerging urban IoT infrastructures enable novel ways of detecting how urban spaces are used. However, the data produced by these systems are context-independent, making it difficult to discern what patterns and anomalies in such data mean. The profile of users has been classified according to time spent:

- Passers-by, who pass through the space for less than 1 h. In this sense, they walk on public roads, have no fixed abode and are visiting or passing through. The streets in this neighbourhood are narrow, without vehicles and there are no traffic lights.
- Visitors. The statistical concept of visitor is not used verbatim. In this case, the visitors counted are those who travel through the neighbourhood between 1 and 5 h, a duration that is used, for example, for cruise ship stopovers, short-haul flights or GPS tracking experiences (Dane, 2018).
- Long duration, users stay more than 5 h, either because they stay overnight in tourist accommodation or because they live in that neighbourhood.

Network segmentation is another variable within the architecture that divides the network into several sub-networks. This allows traffic flow to be controlled at short (over -60 dBm), intermediate (between -61 and -80 dBm) and far (less than -81 dBm) distances, which facilitates monitoring, increases throughput, identifies technical problems and, most importantly, improves security. As a future line, this segmentation can build micro-perimeters to set alarms for over-capacity.

Visitor tracking. Tracking provides information on the behaviour of visitors within the neighbourhood, identifying where they move. This technique identifies through continuous tracking where tourists spend the most time and at what times they are most likely to be visited, as well as tracking between nodes to establish the routes travelled.

In later phases, the aim is to carry out flow analysis with contextual intelligence, both with WiFi sensor technology and with other technological tools developed by intelligent systems. All this, providing relevant recommendations and suggestions to tourists, improving their experience and satisfaction during the trip, as well as providing destination managers with a greater understanding of the behaviour and needs of tourists, allowing them to make more informed decisions, personalise the tourist experience, optimise resource management and promote the destination more effectively in relation to the prediction of crowds and prescription of actions, alarms for exceeding capacity or warnings when someone enters or leaves a restricted area.

4 Conclusions

The study has demonstrated the use of WiFi sensors as a tool to track and record the spatio-temporal behaviour of tourists and, specifically, the TFD. Through this technology and the data obtained, it has been possible to count people in real time in the areas in range. It has also made it possible to identify the user profile according to the time spent, the most frequented routes and spaces and network segmentation. With such information, more valuable insights are provided for destination planning, service design and management (Lew & McKercher, 2006), as well as for decentralising and decongesting crowded spaces (Shoval, 2018). However, as a future line of research, it is intended to deepen the categorisation of users based on the movement patterns detected and taking into account not only the length of stay, but also other socio-demographic issues that allow us to distinguish more precisely the movements between tourists and residents.

Likewise, the study demonstrates the effectiveness of Wi-Fi sensors as a tool for data extraction compared to other digital instruments such as GPS, since both tracking accuracy and applicability on a larger scale are greater and at a lower cost, as has already been demonstrated in previous studies (Foronda et al., 2022; Gao & Schmocker, 2021). Although this research has relied on 4 WiFi sensor points, which is a limitation, the results demonstrate their usefulness in view of the possibility of installing a greater number of points in other tourist areas.

Thus, as future research, there is a need to continue to deepen the use of this tool in combination with other technological solutions, which should be integrated under a holistic perspective aligned with Location Intelligence. With this, it would be possible to build a theoretical-methodological framework that would allow the design, evaluation and improvement of tourist destinations, both analytically and empirically, especially in the case of cities, which carry a large amount of data generated in the context of "smart" evolution.

Acknowledgements This work was supported by the TED2021-131577B/AEI/https://doi.org/10.13039/501100011033/Union Europea NextGenerationEU/PRTR and TUR-RETOS2022-033, financed by the Ministry of Industry, Trade and Tourism and by the EU "NextGenerationEU/PRTR".

References

Advani, C., Thakka, S., Arkatkar, S., & Bhaskar, A. (2020). Performance evaluation of urban arterial network using Wi-Fi sensors under heterogeneous traffic conditions. *Transportation Research Procedia, 48*, 1022–1037.

Ahas, R., Aasa, A., Mark, L., Pae, T., & Kull, A. (2007). Seasonal tourism spaces in Estonia: Case study with mobile positioning data. *Tourism Management, 28*(3), 898–910.

Bauder, M. (2015). Using GPS supported speed analysis to determine spatial visitor behaviour. *International Journal of Tourism Research, 17*(4), 337–346.

Buonincontri, P., & Micera, R. (2016). The experience co-creation in smart tourism destinations: A multiple case analysis of European destinations. *Information Technology Tourism, 16*, 285–315.

Caldeira, A., & Kastenholz, E. (2015). Spatiotemporal behaviour of the urban multi-attraction tourist: Does distance travelled from country of origin make a difference? *Tourism Management Studies, 11*(1), 91–97.

Cavaillès, C., Laurent, M., Maurin, S., & Sánchez, J. (2016). Tourists in the historic centre of Salamanca: Transit, perception and (dis)knowledge. *Cuadernos de Turismo, 37*, 37–67.

Dane, G. Z. (2018). Experiences of event visitors in time and space: GPS tracking at Dutch design week. In *Proceedings of the AGILE.*

Femenia-Serra, F., & Ivars-Baidal, J. A. (2021). Do smart tourism destinations really work? The case of Benidorm. *Asia Pacific Journal of Tourism Research, 26*, 365–384.

Fennell, D. (1996). A tourist space-time budget in the Shetland Islands. *Annals of Tourism Research, 23*(4), 811–829.

Foronda Robles, C., García López, A. M., & Navarro Franco, I. (2022). The redistribution of Tourist Flow in Destination from the spatio-temporal concentration. Sevilla fluye. *Investigaciones Turísticas, 23*, 1–23.

Freudiger, J. (2015). How talkative is your mobile device? An experimental study of Wi-Fi probe requests. In *Proceedings of the 8th ACM conference on security & privacy in wireless and mobile networks* (pp. 1–6).

Freytag, T., & Bauder, M. (2018). Bottom-up touristification and urban transformations in Paris. *Tourism Geographies, 20*(3), 443–460.

Galí, N., & Donaire, A. (2006). Visitors' behavior in heritage cities: The case of Gerona. *Journal of Travel Research, 44*(4), 442–448.

Gao, Y., & Schmocker, J. (2021). Estimation of walking patterns in a touristic area with Wi-Fi packet sensors. *Transportation Research Part C, 128*(2021), 103219.

Haldrup, M. (2004). Laid-Back Mobilities: Second-home holidays in time and space. *Tourism Geographies, 6*(4), 434–454.

Hartmann, R. (1988). Combining field methods in tourism research. *Annals of Tourism Research, 15*(1), 88–105.

Jensen, M., Gutierrez, J., & Pedersen, J. (2014). Location intelligence application in digital data activity dimensioning in smart cities. *Procedia Computer Science, 36*, 418–424.

Karagöz, D. G., & S.A. & Mert Y.K. (2022). Spatial analysis of the relationship between tourist attractions and tourist flows in Turkey. *European Journal of Tourism Research., 31*, 3102.

Keul, A., & Küheberger, A. (1997). Tracking the Salzburg tourist. *Annals of Tourism Research, 24*(4), 1008–1012.

Lepan, L. (2013). L'espace touristique de la grande ville: Une approche par les pratiques et les mobilités touristiques Le cas de la destination Paris. *Mondes du Tourisme, 8*, 75–78.

Lew, A., & McKercher, B. (2006). Modeling tourist movements: A local destination analysis. *Annals of Tourism Research, 33*(2), 403–423.

Martchouk, M., Mannering, F., & Bullock, D. (2011). Analysis of freeway travel time variability using Bluetooth detection. *Journal of Transportation Engineering, 137*(10), 697–704.

Mendoza, S., García, M., & de la Calle, M. (2019). Tourist use regulation in overcrowded historical centres in Spain. In search of good practices. In *Proceedings of the 6th UNESCO UNITWIN conference 2019*.

Molz, J. (2010). Performing global geographies: Time, space, place and pace in narratives of round-the-World Travel. *Tourism Geographies, 12*(3), 329–348.

Moreno Garrido, A. (2005). Elite tourism and tourist administration of the time (1911–1936). *Estudios Turísticos, 163–164*, 31–54.

Murphy, P. (1992). Tourism and visitor behavior. *American Behavioral Scientist, 36*(2), 200–211.

Neutens, T., Schwanen, T., & Witlox, F. (2011). The prism of everyday life: Towards a new research agenda for time geography. *Transport Reviews, 31*, 25–47.

Park, S., Xu, Y., Jiang, L., Chen, Z., & Huang, S. (2020). Spatial structures of tourism destinations: A trajectory data mining approach leveraging mobile big data. *Annals of Tourism Research, 84*, 102973.

Pérez-Hernández, A., Barreras-Martín, M. N., Fernandez-Manzano, J., & Aguilera, P. (2023). On radio signatures to mitigate the MAC addresses randomization for Wi-Fi analytics in real-world scenarios. In *2023 IEEE radio and wireless symposium (RWS)* (pp. 11–13). IEEE.

Salazar, J. P., Chang, S., & Girard, T. C. (2001). Visitor sharing among country attractions and hotels. *Journal of Hospitality & Leisure Marketing, 8*(1/2), 33–43.

Salituro, E. (2020). *Learn Grafana 7.0: A beginner's guide to getting well versed in analytics, interactive dashboards, and monitoring.* Packt Publishing Ltd.

Shoval, N. (2018). Urban planning and tourism in European cities. *Tourism Geographies, 20*(3), 371–376.

Stienmetz, J. L., & Fesenmaier, D. R. (2019). Destination value systems: Modeling visitor flow structure and economic impact. *Journal of Travel Research, 58*(8), 1249–1261.

Thornton, P. R., Williams, A. M., & Shaw, G. (1997). Revisiting time-space diaries: An exploratory case study of tourist behaviour in Cornwall, England. *Environment and Planning, 29*, 1847–1846.

Versichele, M., Groote, L. D., Bouuaert, M. C., Neutens, T., Moerman, I., & Nico, V. (2014). Pattern mining in tourist attraction visits through association rule learning on bluetooth tracking data. *Tourism Management, 44*(13), 67–81.

Vu, H. Q., Li, G., Law, R., & Zhang, Y. (2018). Tourist activity analysis by leveraging mobile social media data. *Journal of Travel Research, 57*(7), 883–898.

Xiao-Ting, H., & Bi-Hu, W. (2012). Intra-attraction tourist spatial-temporal behaviour patterns. *Tourism Geographies, 14*(4), 625–645.

Zheng, W., Li, M., Linb, Z., & Zhang, Y. (2022). Leveraging tourist trajectory data for effective destination planning and management: A new heuristic approach. *Tourism Managment, 89*, 104437.

Lexical Competence in New Digital Environments: The Metaverse and Its Application to Tourism Science

Isabel Serra-Pfennig⊕

1 Introduction

This work is based, on the one hand, on the experience with the metaverse carried out in an exhibition that took place at the *Matadero Contemporary Creation Center* in Madrid (09.22.2022–January 29, 2023), titled *Metaverses, Realities in transition (see Nave O. Centro de creación contemporánea, Madrid 22 de septiembre del 2022 al 29 de enero de 2023)*. Exploring new digital territories through art, and, on the other hand, we have based ourselves on the report *The metaverse and the soul: Journey to the next challenge of tourism*. Both works have been fundamental to developing the glossary around the metaverse and its application to the science of tourism.

2 The Metaverse: Exploring Digital Territories

The term "metaverse" refers to a futuristic concept of a virtual world in which people interact and participate in various activities through virtual reality. It is an extension of the concept of virtual reality, but instead of being an isolated environment, the metaverse would be a persistent digital universe shared by multiple users. Of the many definitions of the metaverse, we have chosen the most plausible within the virtual universe network.

The metaverse is the closest to stepping into thinking a lucid dream in which everything is possible or is possible to the extent that its creator allows us to interact. It is an evolution to an Internet of experiences where users can live incredible adventures in fictional places or travel with their friends to impossible destinations, such as a

I. Serra-Pfennig (✉)
Universidad de las Islas Baleares, Palma, Spain
e-mail: isabel.serra@uib.es

A. J. Guevara Plaza et al. (eds.), *Tourism and ICTs: Advances in Data Science, Artificial Intelligence and Sustainability*, Springer Proceedings in Business and Economics, https://doi.org/10.1007/978-3-031-52607-7_3

25

planet millions of light years away. [...] Perhaps it is the most important step since the appearance of cinema as a catalyst for the human imagination, since here the viewer is teleported to another world, and that world is believable (Martín-Blas, 2022: 12–13).

It has been more than three decades since the term metaverse was first introduced in Neal Stephenson's science fiction novel *Snow Crash* (1992). Stephenson was seeking a word to describe and predict the cyberspace of the future. In this work, he not only predicted what cyberspace would be like today but also anticipated a "dystopian future" in which the American author foresaw a future marked by viruses and hyperinflation, leading to an irreversible loss of government power in favor of large corporations and global economic power. Stephenson, who has also published under the pseudonym Stephen Bury, is famous for his novels, short stories, and essays and is considered a pioneer of the post-cyberpunk genre. His goal is to apply his studies in physics and geography to his works and blend computer and nanotechnology concepts with other areas of historical, mythological, and political knowledge.

3   The Metaverse: Opportunities Versus Risks

A paradigm shift arrived in our society in the first decade of the twenty-first century, when significant technological changes at the social level began to affect our lives with the emergence of Generation Z, or digital natives, drastically altering our social habits. Social media became a priority in our lives. However, the Covid-19 pandemic brought about a second paradigm shift, as social restrictions and the need for remote work generated new technological needs whose impact is still unknown. The inability to travel due to the pandemic and the shift to remote work through video conferences raised concerns among technological strategists (as we experienced firsthand with virtual learning in our university environment). In this recent stage, the scientific community has paid special attention to the metaverse as a tool that a considerable portion of the population will use in the near future. However, experts point out, "[...] we should consider whether the arrival of the metaverse will pose a bigger problem for us or, on the contrary, will allow us to consider the world's inequalities as a point of connection for every human being, regardless of race, religion, borders... and whether our digital counterparts will have the same ideals or thoughts as ours" (Reyes & Alonso, in Turium et al., 2022: 10).

The expansion of metaverses is not without controversy within the scientific community and also gives rise to political and strategic debates. On one hand, it is a subject of discussion among computer scientists, physicists, philosophers, medical professionals, and anthropologists. On the other hand, it is a topic of concern for public institutions due to the inherent problems that arise within the virtual world, such as digital crimes. In an article in El Periódico Digital (May 5, 2023), Pratel, N. J., a psychotherapist and activist against sexual crimes in cyberspace, pointed out that "What is illegal and harmful in the physical world should also be in the virtual synthetic world." Additionally, in the same newspaper article, the State Secretariat for Digitalization and Artificial Intelligence (SEDIA) states that "The EU already has a strong regulatory framework to address potential impacts that the metaverse may have on areas such as competition, cybersecurity, artistic creation, and privacy." However, according to experts, these measures are not sufficient to address many metadigital grievances (Muñoz, in Turium et al., 2022).

From the perspective of neuroscience, scientists predict a decline in mental health that can result not only from human isolation but also from disconnection from the real world, a phenomenon known as the *Metacurse*. On the other hand, environmental and sustainability issues, often caused, among many other factors, by the excessive and consumerist use of digital products, including metaverses, are reported to worsen the climate emergency due to the increased energy demand for the proper functioning of the required servers. Conversely, in a positive light, in reference to the Sustainable Development Goals (SDGs), significant economic, social, and environmental challenges need to be met. In this regard, virtual spaces can also contribute to reducing CO_2 emissions and polluting waste from many human activities that do not require physical presence.

4 Network Space and Virtual Travel

Currently, in the university context, we are rapidly immersed in courses for learning about and understanding ChatGPT, a symbol and result of Artificial Intelligence (AI), among many other technological advancements. All of this has fully introduced us to the Network Society, a term coined by sociologist Manuel Castells, who pointed out that "The term network society refers to the social structure resulting from the interaction between social organization, social change, and the technological paradigm centered on digital information and communication technologies" (Castells, 2009: 21). Its goal allows us to interact with others through digital technology and create a new social structure. However, the major current debate concerns the limits and dangers posed by these innovations and their effects on ethics and society.

This social structure has changed rapidly in the last two decades, with new technologies becoming indispensable in our lives, both professionally and personally. However, facing new cutting-edge technological advancements requires not only learning to use them but also, since their social structure is multidimensional, understanding different logics and values in our society.

The advancement of technology has significantly changed the way we travel and has had a drastic impact on both users and the tourism industry. Platforms and various apps have transformed the way people choose travel destinations, offering many advantages to tourists and travelers. However, how can we classify the metaverse in the world of tourism? What sociological impact will it have on people? Will we adapt to experiencing the world, enjoying sounds, smells, colors, and the "essence of being" through AI? In short, the paradigm has shifted as human behavior has evolved, from exploring virtual social networks to exploring immersive technological spaces.

One of the experiments related to the metaverse can be observed in *Metaverse: Pioneers on a Journey Beyond Reality* by Martín-Blas (2022). In this work, the author recorded the first immersive F1 championship at the Mugello circuit in Italy in 360° as part of various experiments. "The goal was to experience it as if you were a co-pilot" (Martín-Blas, 2022: 71).

A group of experts came up with the *Virtual Voyagers, the Virtual Travelers* planning new areas of exploration in the metaverse sector whose slogan "the value of the team above all" provided them with the basis to investigate this virtual environment. One of the examples provided by this team was making a video game to attract tourists to Catalonia. The idea was:

> The concept was to take users to a real place in Catalan geography and decorate it with a layer of fantasy, such as the Sant Jordi dragon, Dalí's elephants, etc., so that, once the adventure had been experienced, the visitor would discover that much of what was seen in that experience really existed, it was not fantasy. These were places that could be visited. Finally, once all the phases of the game had been overcome, an immersive piece appeared that took a trip to the real Catalonia and visited those dream places, but without that fantastic layer, showing the tourist part (Martín–Blas, 2022: 96).

This combination of tradition, culture, and geospace can be experienced by millions of users who can feel, and perceive the essence of a place from very distant places, and at a global level, and at the same time-space instant can visit a tourist route, a concert, a theater or a theme park.

Both experts and visionaries anticipate that the metaverse is already a reality, in the same way that the Internet came into our lives many decades ago, a new universe of communication that will allow us to connect with unimaginable spaces, from visits to theme parks with dinosaurs to experiencing other planetary systems, and finding out the origins of a city and its first settlements and in turn changing the behavior of people and society, enriching the imagination with experiences shared with creators can be an improvement of human communication, a way to democratize the way of knowledge in our society, as long as the ethical codes and the bases of sustainability and respect and inclusion are respected, in short, that it is accessible to all people.

5   The Metaverse and the Soul: Journey to the Next Tourism Challenge

When reading the introduction of the report *The metaverse and the soul: Journey to the next tourism challenge* (2022), you realize the complexity of combining the concepts of the "metaverse" and "the soul" into a common denominator. In this regard, the report has used several scientists- including philosophers, neuroscientists, technologists, developers, publicists, marketing experts, and anthropologists- to analyze with the highest academic rigor this complexity. Despite many pioneering studies, this complexity remains at the center of media debates as the General

Director of Turium writes in the introduction of the report.[1] "One approach is the humanistic approach that aims to understand how this new technological development will affect us on a social and individual level. The other the sector: the tourism industry. The impact of the metaverse on the travel environment and its potential are exponential" (Jiménez, in Turium et al., 2022: 4). The State Society of the State Secretariat for Tourism (SEGITTUR), since its creation in 2002, has been betting on the use of new technologies, including the metaverse, anticipating not knowing the consequences of this, "[…] where people are the key and part of the travel experience" (Martínez, 2022: 5).

Although these statements are true to a greater extent, still, to what extent and in what way will these technological realities influence our lives at the behavioral level? As sociologist Zygmunt Bauman states, "Virtual proximity manages to deactivate the pressures that non-virtual proximity usually exerts. In turn, it sets the parameters of any other proximity. The merits and defects of all proximities are now measured in relation to the standards of virtual proximity" (Bauman, 2013: 88). Even personal relationships have been conditioned for decades to a greater extent by new technologies.

It is not surprising, then, that virtual proximity is the option of choice, practiced with greater zeal and abandon than any other kind of closeness. Solitude behind the closed door of a private room and with a cell phone at hand is a safer and less risky situation than sharing the common ground of the domestic sphere (Bauman, 2013: 90).

However, a new form of design of the world around us was already anticipated by the anthropologist Marvin Harris (1927–2001) in his work *Theories of Postmodern Culture* (2000), showing us how postmodern guidelines were anticipated in the years 40 of the last century, where they tried to replace science and reason with other mental activities of the human being such as "emotion, diversity of sensations, introspection, intuition, autonomy, creativity, imagination, fantasy, and contemplation" (Harris, 2000: 155) among many other characteristics of human potential. In this context, we refer to the heading referring to: "The questioning of reality and the suitability of language to describe reality" (Harris, 2000: 152), this explains that certain evolutionary processes have an impact on a progressive change in society and are essential for the evolution of the human being. Among other things, the anthropologist and philosopher of science Donna J. Haraway (1944–), takes as a reference the concept of *cyborg*, a cybernetic organism, a hybrid between machine and organism, a creature in social reality and in fiction. According to these premises, she developed the theories that have led us to this new reality reality and expressed in his work *Science, Cyborgs and Women. The reinvention of nature.* In this regard, Haraway anticipated that "the technologies of the body that produce the modern subject are becoming increasingly weaker and are gradually being replaced by technologies of a completely different order" (Haraway, 1991: 11).

---

[1] Report title: *El metaverso y el alma: Viaje al próximo desafío del turismo* (2022). Edited by Turium and SEGITTUR.

These gradual changes in our lives with the technological revolution of the twenty-first century have substantially changed our habits in pursuit of the digital world. They have also conditioned communication at a linguistic level, in relation to lexical competition around virtual realities.

6 The Metaverse for Tourism Purposes

As observed in the report "The Metaverse as a Tourist Destination" (Reyes & Alonso, in Turium et al., 2022: 6–12), a reflection is made starting from the world of video games to help understand the process of the metaverse in real contexts. Video games are indeed the authentic precursors of the transition from the real world to the virtual world. In addition, virtual games have largely driven technological development towards the metaverse, a concept that, despite abundant literature, remains somewhat abstract. Both researchers have used examples from games like *Pong* (2D representations) to hyper-realistic graphics like *Assassin's Creed*, where players could explore cities like Damascus or Jerusalem in the twelfth century or visit Florence during the Renaissance. Games like *Spider-Man* (2018), where the hero recreates New York City. Finally, they have taken *Cyberpunk 2077* (2020), as an example in order to show us a certain aspect of a city of dreams that could be Macau (Hong Kong) where reality can be confused with virtuality.

In all these recreations, the cities have been represented subjectively, however, within everyone's reach it is possible virtually, which is why it is an unprecedented advance in the transition from the real world to the virtual one and a challenge in the world of technological advances, both at the hardware and software level, as commented by the authors of the aforementioned report. Additionally, virtual travel will become accessible to everyone, democratizing it in the sense that individuals, regardless of economic, personal, mobility-related, or other limitations (including social and religious reasons), will have the opportunity to visit tourist destinations and interact with them from the comfort of their homes. Through virtual guides, users can explore museums, monuments, enjoy cultural experiences, and participate in various tourism-related activities specific to each destination. This transformation will be achieved through immersive and haptic technologies that allow users to observe real scenes, even perceiving scents, sounds, and more.

On the one hand, the devastating impact of the Covid-19 pandemic on the tourist industry, set the need for reinvention by a potentially vulnerable industry, with the possibility of creating interactive virtual worlds and interacting in them. On the other hand, awareness of climate change is another factor to take into account in the spacing of tourist destinations, which is why these emerging needs have developed new trends in technological innovation. The possibility of traveling to virtual spaces will undoubtedly modify the way we travel and see the world. However, are we willing to experience virtual travel through an alternative fictional recreation of human reality? Fernando Broncano, a professor of Logic and Philosophy of Science, writes in his article *"Metaverse: Between Reality and Fiction"* that "the metaverse has emerged in just a few months as a transhumanist promise to create a new virtual reality where the border between fiction and reality ends up being confusing" (Broncano, 2022: 14). Furthermore, referring to tourism, he believes that it has been one of the human activities that have undergone the greatest transformations in our society and in this regard, he considers to what extent travel through immersion in virtual reality will affect tourism with the dilemma that perhaps it creates a new competition between physical and cyberspace travel, among the many other observations made.

The metaverse has also been studied in Neuroscience, as researchers in this field point out: How does the brain interpret digital reality? David Bueno and Diego Redolar start from the hypothesis "[…] how the nervous system interprets digital spaces and can compare them with a real environment" (see Turium et al., 2022: 21). Furthermore, these researchers consolidate in their study the relationship between the digital and physical world and its implications in relation to the brain, and how this relation influences learning contexts both in the educational field, as well as in tourism, thus forming a common dichotomy, comparing it between different environments:

> In a sense, education should be a kind of "intellectual tourism". Thus, if tourism is defined as "the set of relationships and phenomena produced by the movement and stay of people outside their home, for reasons of leisure, sport or culture", education would be "the set of relationships and learning phenomena produced by displacement and permanence beyond knowledge and intellectual and cognitive limits. Education understood as intellectual tourism means that both concepts can be intertwined.

Finally, viewing the metaverse from an anthropological standpoint and its impact on individuals provides a new way of understanding human societies. Based on anthropological theories by Marvin Harris, which suggest that humans are in constant evolution, the anthropologist Pablo Mondragón (see Turium et al., 2022: 30) observes "that humans may prefer to live in parallel realities rather than in their own". He suggests that this is the most recurrent debate when imagining the possible social impacts of metaverse popularization.

7 Lexical Competition in the Field of Tourism

There are many didactic tools in the context of lexical competence around the teaching-learning of tourism lexicon and their purpose enriches the work of teachers, as well as students and tourism professionals who require very rigorous lexical competence regarding lexicon.

To achieve this, we have access to digital dictionaries that are equipped with corpora related to various tourism areas. These dictionaries can be monolingual, bilingual, and multilingual and are increasingly extensive in thematic areas, among which are: specialized monolingual dictionaries for tourism, bilingual dictionaries or multilingual tourism glossaries, and monolingual, bilingual, and multilingual repertoires, all of which favor the acquisition of vocabulary in various thematic areas, generally provided with multilingual textual reference corpora and which are increasingly extensive and complete in the digital field. Among them, we highlight here, the *Multilingual Tourism Dictionary* prepared by COMETVAL, in the three reference languages, Spanish, French, and English, whose information is connected by hyperlinks that offer additional information offering linguistic and regulatory clarifications, it is designed with new technologies and free online access and offers the user to make all kinds of queries in relation to the science of tourism. In various fields of science, glossaries with specialized corpora are available online to users. As an illustration, we can mention the SEAH (*Sharing European Architectural Heritage: Innovative Language Teaching Tools for Academic and Professional Mobility in Architecture and Construction*) glossary, developed by five European universities, composed of an academic corpus and designed for architecture and construction and carried out in five languages. In addition to the dictionaries collated on the internet, we have not found lexical varieties around the metaverse. To do this, and after comparing several texts on the matter, we have developed an example of a glossary that allows us to understand not only the word but also the definition in order to be able to apply it in specific contexts and situations adapted to this regard.

8   Lexical Competence Around the Metaverse

Concerning the lexicon of tourism related to the metaverse, there is not yet a specific language that we can use, as it is a concept still in development and has not been fully implemented. However, if we examine various bibliographies, we find that it is already possible to use generalized terms and concepts applied to tourism and adapt them to the virtual environment. The lexicon of tourism in these virtual spaces includes terms related to virtual travel booking, navigation of virtual destinations, descriptions of virtual tourist attractions, interaction with other users, and participation in virtual events and activities. Nevertheless, we will limit ourselves here to using basic definitions and glossary terms to be able to transfer them to the language of tourism in the very near future.

Below, we propose a selection of terms specific to this area of knowledge as a sample. For this purpose, a lexical search has been carried out based on the cited work by Edgar Martín-Blas (2022) *Metaverse: Pioneers on a Journey Beyond Reality*, together with other works and manuals (See Reference list for an overview). These can help not only in understanding the term itself but also in expanding its definition. According to this author, the pillars of the metaverse, even though they are virtual worlds, should be based on human principles, including *Identity, Exploration, Group Membership, Experimentation, and Ownership.*

8.1 Pillars of the Metaverse: Metaverse Principles

Glossary compiled from the previously cited work (Martín-Blas, 2022: 15–20).

Glossary	Definition
Identity	According to the RAE "Set of traits characteristic of an individual or a community that characterize them compared to others". Within this new world, each person will have an appearance, a role, and a personality that may be similar to reality or invented"
Exploration	We will enter a virtual world where we can visit each house, each city, each world, each universe, etc. There will always be a new horizon to aim for [...] Since there are no physical laws, the places we will find will surprise us and we will always want to travel to the next metaverse
Belonging to the group	In each metaverse, we will find ourselves in a world with a story that is happening in real-time, from an intergalactic war to a historical event. [...] Once trapped by this background, we will be another inhabitant of this place and we will belong to it
Experimentation	Here we can really live experiences that are very close to reality. Virtual devices already offer us interaction with hands, head, and body that allows us to drive cars, fly, dive, fight, or even walk in these virtual worlds of the metaverse
Ownership	This is the last fundamental pillar of the metaverse and the most widespread in the world in which we live, the one that moves markets, and the one that has even caused the rise and fall of empires. [...] Currently, these belongings are only available in each metaverse in isolation, but work is already underway so that we can take these properties from one to another as if they were real assets, thanks to *blockchain* technology

8.2 Immersion Within the Metaverse (Martín-Blas et al., 2022: 13–15)

However, according to Harris (2000), human language is unique in possessing semantic universality, or the ability to produce an unlimited number of new messages without loss of informative effectiveness. The objective of this communication is to update and define concepts in this regard, which are sometimes somewhat diffuse from the perspective of semantics. Therefore, we will limit ourselves to providing examples based on the literature consulted.

Glossary	Definition
Virtual reality (100% immersion)	(VR) A technology that allows users to immerse themselves in a computer-generated simulated environment, which can be a part of the metaverse. This is achieved by wearing a headset that completely blocks our view of the real world, replacing it with a digitally generated one
Mixed reality (50% immersion)	A combination of elements from both virtual reality and augmented reality in a single experience. It is a recent typology, still in the phase of early prototypes, but it will almost certainly be the massive way to enjoy the metaverse in future decades
Web3D (10% immersion)	It is based on displaying the metaverse on a classic PC, mobile, or tablet screen version using a 3D programming and visualization language called *Web Graphics Library* (WebGL). This is what we call *transition technology or protometaverses* and is intended for users who do not yet have virtual or mixed viewers
Augmented reality	(AR): Technology that combines real-world elements with computer-generated virtual elements. Augmented reality based on pattern recognition. Augmented reality based on image recognition. Augmented reality based on geolocation
User interface (UI)	How users interact with the metaverse, usually through devices such as virtual reality headsets, haptic gloves, motion controllers, or other peripheral devices
Immersive experience	Refers to an experience in which users are completely immersed in the metaverse, feeling present and actively participating in it
Content creation	Users can create and customize their own content within the metaverse, such as objects, virtual spaces, clothing for avatars, etc
Virtual socialization	Social interaction between users within the metaverse, which may include voice conversations, chat, virtual meetings, events, and more

It is important to keep in mind that the lexicon of the metaverse is constantly evolving, and according to experts the various classifications and typologies change depending on the new challenges of technology and new terms that constantly emerge as this technology develops and expands. Here we have limited ourselves to naming certain concepts and definitions that will be applied in the field of tourism in the very near future. A great challenge between the real world and the virtual world and new approaches is appearing at a dizzying pace, benefits will be expanded and functionalities will be extended. Furthermore, it is planned in the imminent future that we will already use concepts about specialized professions in the metaverse, such as *Metaverse Hardware Engineer, Metaverse Marketing Specialist, Metaverser Metahuman Doctor, Metaverse Tour Guide,* etc.

9 Conclusions

With this brief exposition of the glossary around the metaverse and its possible applications in the science of tourism, we show that it is important, to perceive the world around us, be critical of the alternative reality, and not to confuse it with the real world. With the virtual world, our task as teachers is to create teaching methods for all students and transmit knowledge in order to perfect their skills. The use and expansion of disruptive technologies such as AI and ChatGPT in the field of teaching–learning is currently a topic of debate in the scientific community in general and in the educational community in particular. Antonia Pades, Doctor in psychology and communication, in a recent article (*El economico* 1. 6. 2023) referring to the communicative abilities of *Sophia the humanoid robot*, asks herself "Where will the curiosity and desire for learning of students be left?".

Lastly, for those of us who believe that the writing process is a consequence of human intellect, stemming from ideas, study, knowledge, and extensive reading, we continue to ask ourselves: How can AI manage the mental and emotional capacities of human beings, given that we are biologically unique and irreplaceable? In conclusion, we wonder if one of the latest works created exclusively through AI, *Death of an Author*, published under the pseudonym of Aidan Marchine (2023), an analogy taken from Roland Barthes' concept of *the death of the author* (1915–1980), following the premise that "infinite ideas intersect in every text" Here, AI adapts to the text as it recreates or replicates an existing idea. However, the question remains: Will a work of such nature be considered part of the canon of Universal Literature? Therefore, we believe that AI represents the evolution of our technological society, a step beyond postmodernity, and the most immediate consequence is a progressive increase in the use of digital technologies in our educational context, potentially overcoming physical limitations in the learning process.

References

Bauman, Z. (2013). *Amor líquido. Acerca de la fragilidad de los vínculos humanos*. Fondo de Cultura Económica de España.

Broncano, F. (2009). *La melancolía del Ciborg*. Herder. https://keepcoding.io/blog/tipos-de-rea lidad-aumentada/#Tipos_de_realidad_aumentada. Retrieved 2 June 2023.

Castells, M. (Ed.). (2009). *La sociedad red: Una visión global*. Alianza.

Haraway, D. J. (1991): *Ciencia, ciborgs y mujeres. La reinvención de la naturaleza*. Cátedra.

Harris, M. (2000). *Teorías sobre la cultura en la era posmoderna*. Crítica.

Marchine, A. *Death of an author*. https://www.nytimes.com/2023/05/01/books/aidan-marchine-death-of-an-author.html. Retrieved 15 June 2023.

Martín-Blas, E. (2022). *Metaverso. Pioneros de un viaje más allá de la realidad*. Almuzara.

Nave O. Centro de creación contemporánea Matadero (Madrid 22 septiembre 2022 al 29 enero 2023): *Metaversos. Realidades en transición. Explorando nuevos territorios digitales*.

Pades, A. (2023): *Sophia, el robot humanoide* en El Económico (26 de mayo al 1 de junio de 2023).

SEAH (Sharing European Architectural Heritage: innovative language teaching tools for academic and professional mobility in Architecture and Construction). http://www.seahproject.eu/index.php. Retrieved 10 May 2023.

Turium, S., Jiménez, G., & Martínez, E. et al. (2022). El metaverso y el alma: Viaje al próximo desafío del turismo. https://www.turium.es/wp-content/uploads/sites/2/2022/07/METAVERSO-2.pdf. Retrieved 12 May 2023.

Optimizing Tourism Data Extraction and Analysis: A Comprehensive Methodology

José Javier Galán-Hernández⊙**, Ramón Alberto Carrasco-González**⊙**, and Gabriel Marín-Díaz**⊙

Abstract Objective: There are various sources that provide data related to tourism. However, at times, this data lacks structure or is found in sources that do not facilitate its easy, automatic, or unsupervised collection. In such situations, a methodology employing data science techniques offers a significant advantage to researchers. They can leverage the tools available through the proposed methodology to extract, process, and analyze information efficiently. While this methodology is applicable to various disciplines, this work presents a specific case focused on tourism in Spain. Methodology: Employing data science techniques like graph analysis and unsupervised machine learning, we collect and process data on tourists' origins and numbers in Spain, using Python, R, and VOSViewer. The analysis uncovers primary tourism sources and origin-country patterns. It delves deep into Andalusia due to its high tourist influx. Results: Our study reveals key Spanish tourism sources and visitor behavior patterns. Visual data illustrates tourist origins, visit numbers, and interactions. Additionally, Andalusia is thoroughly examined for visit counts and origin countries. Conclusions: Employing data science, our study yields insights into Spanish tourism, identifying core sources and understanding origin-country interactions. These findings inform strategic decisions and enhance Spain's tourism promotion and management.

Keywords Tourism · Data science · Vosviewer · Python · Methodology

J. J. Galán-Hernández (✉)
Departamento de Sistemas Informáticos y Computación, Facultad de Estudios Estadísticos, Universidad Complutense de Madrid, 28040 Madrid, Spain
e-mail: josejgal@ucm.es

R. A. Carrasco-González
Departamento de Marketing, Facultad de Estudios Estadísticos, Universidad Complutense de Madrid, 28040 Madrid, Spain

G. Marín-Díaz
Departamento de Sistemas Informáticos y Computación, Facultad de Estudios Estadísticos, Universidad Complutense de Madrid, 28040 Madrid, Spain

© The Author(s) 2024
A. J. Guevara Plaza et al. (eds.), *Tourism and ICTs: Advances in Data Science, Artificial Intelligence and Sustainability*, Springer Proceedings in Business and Economics, https://doi.org/10.1007/978-3-031-52607-7_4

1 Introduction

Tourism plays a fundamental role in Spain's economy (Gonzalez & Moral, 1996), making it one of the most visited countries in the world. Understanding the primary source of tourism and obtaining relevant visitor information is essential for driving the development and promotion of the sector. Fortunately, in the era of data science and advanced technologies, we have effective tools and methodologies to address this challenge (Medina-Munoz et al., 2013).

In this study, we employ a proprietary methodology applying data science techniques to analyze tourism in Spain. Using technologies like Python, R, and VOSViewer (Moral-Muñozet al., 2020), we gather, process, and visualize information about the origin and number of tourists visiting the country. This methodology allows us to draw significant conclusions about the main sources of tourism and understand patterns and interactions among the countries of origin of tourists.

In particular, this study focuses on the autonomous community of Andalusia, one of the most prominent regions in terms of tourist reception in Spain (Martínez & Nicolás, 2014). We examine in detail the number of visits received and the countries of origin of tourists in Andalusia. With this information, we aim to gain a better understanding of the flow of tourists in the region and make strategic decisions to boost its tourism development.

Data analysis and network visualization through graph theory play a key role in this study (Abbasi-Moud et al., 2021), allowing us to effectively represent and explore information about tourism in Spain. Through this data science methodology, we seek to obtain an evidence-based, in-depth view of tourism in Spain, with an emphasis on Andalusia, to contribute to sustainable development and informed decision-making in the tourism sector.

2 Methodology of Analysis

To achieve the introduced objectives, a proprietary methodology is carried out, see Fig. 1, based on an adaptation of the CRISP-DM methodology (Moine et al., 2011), widely used in the field of data mining (Burbano & Anderson, 2023). This methodology has been specifically adapted to address the study of tourists visiting Spain and has been enriched with advanced network visualization techniques using graph theory.

Each stage of the methodology is analyzed in the following sections.

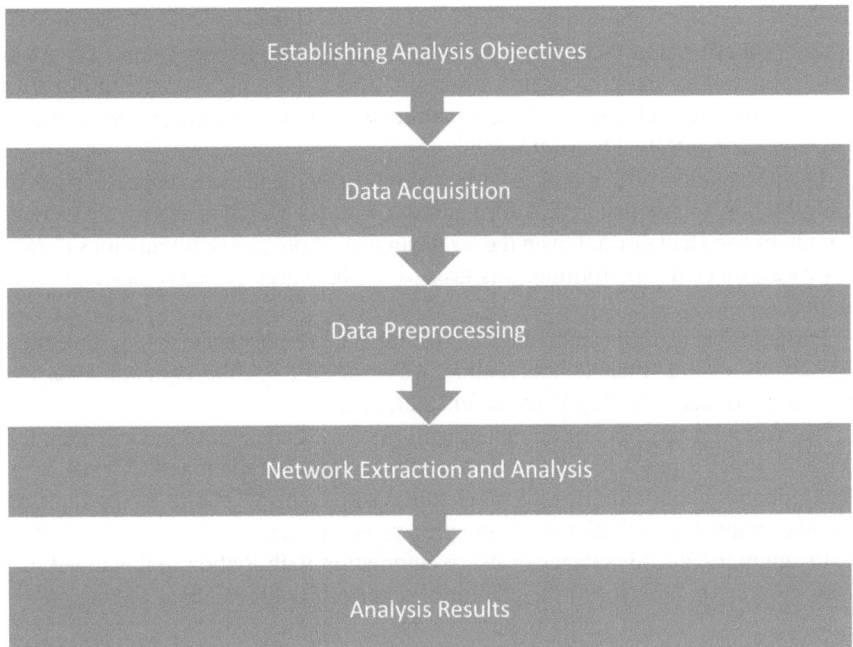

Fig. 1 Methodology used

2.1 Setting Analysis Objectives

Following the methodology outlined in Chap. 2, the objective is established, which is to collect data related to tourist visits to each of the autonomous communities of Spain by international tourists during the year 2022. This data is available on the official website https://www.dataestur.es/ (Diezma, 2021). Since the manual collection process would be extremely time-consuming, we have automated the data download and processing. Once the processed data is collected, we intend to create a network graph that allows us to perform a visual analysis of the flow of tourists to Spain, as well as a more specific analysis focused on the autonomous community of Andalusia.

2.2 Data Acquisition

As previously mentioned, the first objective is to obtain data from the official website https://www.dataestur.es/, which offers the option to consume its web service to obtain the desired information. However, this process involves numerous steps, as it is necessary to select each country for each autonomous community. With a total of 15 countries and 19 autonomous communities, there are a total of 285 possible combinations. Performing this task manually would consume a significant amount of time and effort. For this reason, we have decided to use Python (Stančin & Jović, 2019) to automate the process and efficiently download a file with the information corresponding to each combination. Thanks to this automation, we can complete the task in approximately 2 h, unattended.

The automation of this process offers several significant advantages. Firstly, by using Python to automate the information download, we can save a considerable amount of time and effort. Given the large number of possible combinations (285 in this case), manually performing this task would be extremely laborious and error-prone.

Furthermore, using an automated approach ensures higher accuracy in data collection. By eliminating manual intervention, we reduce the possibility of human errors, providing greater reliability in the results obtained.

Another advantage is that automation allows us to carry out the task unattended. Once the process has been programmed in Python, we can run it and let it run in the background without requiring constant supervision. This allows us to use our time for other important activities while the process is ongoing.

In summary, the advantages of using automation with Python to download data from different combinations include time and effort savings, increased accuracy in data collection, and the ability to perform the task unattended.

2.3   Data Preprocessing

Once the data has been downloaded through the previous phase, we proceed to clean the information. In this process, we remove unnecessary columns for our analysis. Then, we use Python to merge all the files into a single Excel file.

This resulting Excel file serves as a consolidated information repository. While the Excel file is not a database itself, it can function as a large repository that stores relevant information for our study.

The use of Python allows us to automate this data cleaning and consolidation process efficiently. Thanks to Python's data manipulation capabilities, we can perform tasks such as removing unnecessary columns and combining files quickly and accurately.

In summary, after downloading the files corresponding to all possible combinations, we use Python (Sahoo et al., 2019) to clean and merge the information into a single Excel file. This Excel file acts as a centralized repository of information for our study, facilitating the analysis and processing of the collected data.

2.4　Network Extraction and Analysis

After preprocessing to obtain the relevant information, the next step is graph analysis. To do this, the processed data is exported to a format compatible with R, such as a CSV or Excel file.

Next, the powerful igraph library in R (Valdez, 2016) is used to build a graph that represents the connections between countries and autonomous communities of Spain in terms of tourist visits. This library allows for the straightforward creation of a directed or undirected graph and the assignment of attributes to nodes and edges based on the characteristics of interest.

The generated graph, see Fig. 2a, establishes a network between the countries visiting each autonomous community, providing a clear visualization of tourist relationships and flows. Each node in the graph represents a country or autonomous community, and the edges represent the connections between them based on the number of visits.

First, the graph is opened using the VOSViewer application (Van Eck & Waltman, 2011), a utility widely used in bibliometrics and data science, which allows for navigation of the network.

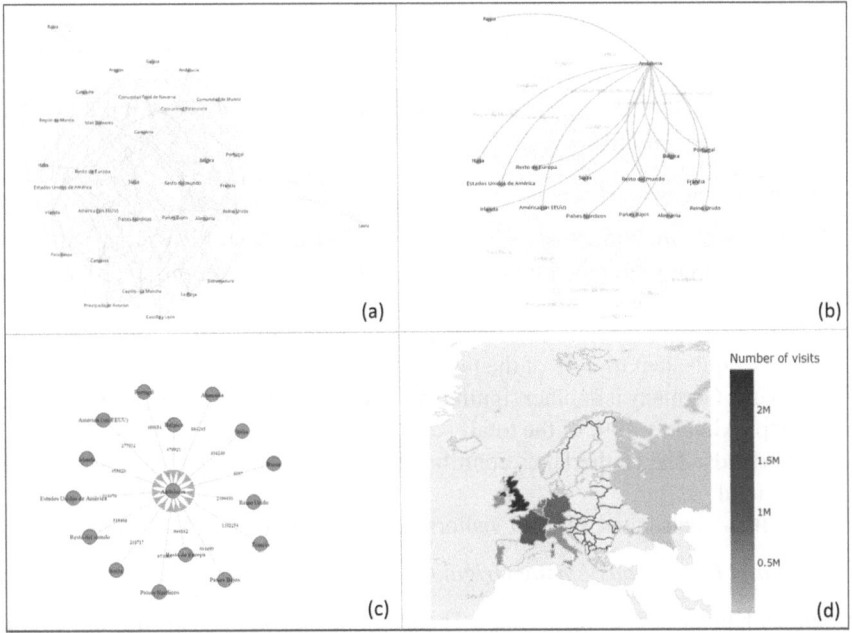

Fig. 2 Results obtained through the application of data science techniques: **a** general graph, **b** graph of Andalusia, **c** tourists heading to Andalusia, **d** number of European tourists who visited Andalusia, year 2022

Subsequently, we can focus on the specific case of Andalusia, see Fig. 2b, one of the autonomous communities that stands out in terms of receiving tourists from various countries.

Using exclusively graph theory, an analysis was conducted using the R language and the igraph library to visually represent the network of tourists visiting Andalusia, see Fig. 2c, focusing on the number of tourists per country. Using the igraph library in R, a network was constructed where each country was represented as a node (or vertex), and connections (or edges) were established between countries that had tourists visiting Andalusia in common. The strength of the connection between two countries was determined by the number of tourists they shared.

Finally, using the *pandas* and *Plotly* libraries in *Python*, a graduated color map of Europe is displayed, see Fig. 2d. You can choose the most significant countries without the need to select all of them. Visually, you can observe that darker blue represents countries with a higher number of tourists to Andalusia, while yellow represents those that provide fewer visitors to Andalusia.

2.5 Analysis Results

With the techniques performed in the previous chapter, it has been demonstrated that applying data science to the analysis of tourism-related data can be useful, providing automated and visually appealing results.

Focusing on Fig. 2d, with these results, it is possible to obtain the following analysis in a very intuitive way:

Key Tourism Sources

- United Kingdom: With a total of 2,399,433 visitors, the United Kingdom continues to be the primary source of tourism in Andalusia. This represents approximately 52% of the total visitors.
- France: France is the second most important source of tourism, with 1,102,254 visitors, equivalent to 24% of the total.
- Germany: Germany is another significant source with 864,245 visitors, accounting for approximately 19% of the total.
- Netherlands: The Netherlands contributes 694,499 visitors, which is about 15% of the total.
- Italy: Italy contributes 494,249 visitors, representing roughly 11% of the total.

Patterns and Interactions Among Origin Countries

- United Kingdom as a Key Market: The United Kingdom remains the largest and dominant market. Any tourism promotion and management strategy in Andalusia should continue to pay special attention to this market.
- Importance of European Markets: France, Germany, the Netherlands, and Italy are significant European markets and should be considered in tourism promotion and management strategies.

- Diversification Within Europe: While the United Kingdom is important, it is essential to diversify tourism sources within Europe. These European countries can be key targets for attracting more visitors.
- Emerging Markets: Russia, although representing a small proportion, may have potential for future growth. Specific strategies can be explored to attract more visitors from Russia.

Strategic Decision-Making

- Focus on the United Kingdom: Maintain and strengthen the relationship with the United Kingdom market through specific marketing and promotion campaigns.
- Key European Markets: Develop marketing strategies targeted at key European markets such as France, Germany, the Netherlands, and Italy.
- Promotion of Diversity: Highlight the diversity of experiences and attractions in Andalusia to attract visitors with different interests and preferences.
- Explore New Markets: Evaluate the feasibility of attracting more visitors from emerging markets, such as Russia, through campaigns and strategic alliances.
- Continuous Analysis: Continuously monitor tourism trends and adjust strategies to maintain competitiveness and attract visitors to Andalusia.

3   Benefits and Limitations of the Methodology Used

While there are increasingly more official data sources related to tourism, they are not always presented in a user-friendly, automatic, or unsupervised manner, and at times, they only provide data in a raw format. In such cases, having a reference methodology that equips researchers with the necessary tools to extract, process, and analyze the information can be highly beneficial.

The case presented in Sect. 2 serves as an example of data extraction from a recognized data source in the industry, which is used by many researchers without taking advantage of the proposed methodology. During this case, a data source was chosen from which data can be obtained in a user-friendly manner or via a web service. The latter method was chosen to demonstrate how information about tourist visits from a total of 15 countries and 19 autonomous communities as destinations, resulting in a total of 285 possible combinations, was successfully extracted. Manually downloading each of them would take approximately 5 min per download, totaling approximately 24 h of work and requiring constant attention. In contrast, using data science expertise within this methodology, the process only took 2 h and was entirely unsupervised.

In contrast to this methodology, a minimum level of data science knowledge and a basic understanding of programming languages are required to carry out data acquisition and processing properly. For this reason, it is likely that many researchers may choose to perform these tasks manually. However, this does not imply that this guide cannot be used, as the methodology itself serves as a guide in which each stage can be applied according to the available knowledge of each researcher.

4   Conclusions

Thanks to the methodology and visualization techniques used, it is demonstrated that a labor-intensive analysis, which would have initially required considerable effort and time, can be automated, allowing for the presentation of ready-made results for analysts to examine. This has made it possible to invest time in activities that truly add value. Thus, we can observe how a data science methodology and its associated techniques can be of great assistance in studying the tourism sector.

Through the use of data science and its techniques, the analysis process in the tourism sector has been simplified and expedited, freeing up resources and time for analysts to focus on interpreting results and generating relevant insights.

By employing graph theory, the R language, and the igraph library, we have successfully created an effective and easily interpretable visual representation of the tourist visits network to Andalusia. This tool provides valuable information for analysis and decision-making in the field of tourism, enabling us to better understand tourist flows and optimize promotion and tourism development strategies in the Andalusian region.

The proposed methodology has significant practical implications in the field of tourism. In destination management, it facilitates improved management of flows, marketing, seasonality, and predictions. For tourism businesses, it enhances decision-making in areas such as pricing, market segmentation, and service personalization. Furthermore, it underscores the growing need for data science training among the tourism sector workforce, preparing them for emerging industry challenges and promoting the acquisition of essential data analysis skills.

As indicated in the next section on future work, it will be interesting to delve deeper into the results obtained in the future. However, immediate conclusions can be drawn from the graphs obtained. During the year 2022, tourist flow between autonomous communities varied significantly. Russia and Ceuta were the territories examined with the lowest traffic. Andalusia stood out as a highly frequented destination within Spanish destinations, mainly by visitors from the United Kingdom and France, while receiving fewer visitors from Russia and Switzerland.

5   Future Work

As mentioned in the conclusions, the development of this work demonstrates how data science can assist in analyzing tourism-related data. The following are potential future works that can leverage the results:

- In-Depth Analysis of Graphs: In this future work, a comprehensive analysis of the graphs generated from tourism data would be conducted. This would involve examining the connections and relationships between different nodes, which could represent countries, regions, or specific tourist destinations. Graph analysis would help identify behavioral patterns, determine the relative importance of each node, and gain a better understanding of interactions within the tourism system. This analysis would provide valuable insights for strategic planning, identifying opportunities, and decision-making in the tourism sector.

- Comparison with Other Communities: In this work, a comparison would be made between the results obtained for the autonomous community of Andalusia and those of other communities or tourist regions. This would help identify significant differences in terms of the number of visits, the origin of tourists, behavioral patterns, etc. These comparisons could help identify relative strengths and weaknesses of each community, as well as areas for improvement.

- Analyzing Why Some Countries Receive More Visitors: This work would focus on understanding the reasons why certain countries have a higher tourist presence in the study region. Factors such as geographical location, air connectivity, trade agreements, tourism promotion, safety perception, availability of tourism infrastructure, among others, could be analyzed. By examining these factors, a deeper understanding of the motivations and preferences of tourists from different countries could be obtained, allowing for the adaptation of marketing and promotion strategies to attract more visitors from other countries.

- Applying Findings to Tourists from Other Countries: In this future work, the goal would be to apply the knowledge gained from the previous analysis to attract tourists from other countries. This could involve adapting marketing and promotion strategies, improving the customer experience to meet the specific needs and preferences of tourists from those countries, and identifying opportunities for developing customized tourism products. By better understanding the factors that attract certain countries, the acquisition of international tourists could be optimized, increasing their satisfaction, which would, in turn, benefit the tourism industry as a whole.

References

Abbasi-Moud, Z., Vahdat-Nejad, H., & Sadri, J. (2021). Tourism recommendation system based on semantic clustering and sentiment analysis. *Expert Systems with Applications, 167*, 114324.

Burbano, C., & Anderson, K. (2023). Minería de Datos para mejorar los procesos de control de la demanda turística en el Ministerio de Turismo de la Provincia del Carchi en el año 2022. UPEC.

Diezma, F. R. (2021). Estadísticas turísticas: una herramienta clave para la planificación en el sector. *Indice: Revista de Estadística y Sociedad, (81),* 33–35.

Gonzalez, P., & Moral, P. (1996). Analysis of tourism trends in Spain. *Annals of Tourism Research, 23*(4), 739–754.

Martínez, E., & Nicolás, M. Á. (2014). The construction of tourist space by public administration and institutional communication: The image of the brand Andalucía as a tourist destination. *Journal of Promotion Management, 20*(2), 181–199.

Medina-Munoz, D. R., Medina-Muñoz, R. D., & Zuniga-Collazos, A. (2013). Tourism and innovation in China and Spain: A review of innovation research on tourism. *Tourism Economics, 19*(2), 319–337.

Moral-Muñoz, J. A., Herrera-Viedma, E., Santisteban-Espejo, A., & Cobo, M. J. (2020). Software tools for conducting bibliometric analysis in science: An up-to-date review. *Profesional de la Información, 29*(1).

Moine, J. M., Haedo, A. S., & Gordillo, S. E. (2011). Estudio comparativo de metodologías para minería de datos. In *XIII Workshop de Investigadores en Ciencias de la Computación.*

Stančin, I., & Jović, A. (2019, May). An overview and comparison of free Python libraries for data mining and big data analysis. In *2019 42nd International convention on information and communication technology, electronics and microelectronics (MIPRO)* (pp. 977–982). IEEE.

Sahoo, K., Samal, A. K., Pramanik, J., & Pani, S. K. (2019). Exploratory data analysis using Python. *International Journal of Innovative Technology and Exploring Engineering (IJITEE), 8*(12), 2019.

Valdez, B. (2016). Análisis de grafos usando R e igraph. *Altamira, 1*(1), 1.

Van Eck, N. J., & Waltman, L. (2011). Text mining and visualization using VOSviewer. arXiv:1109. 2058.

Assessing Tourists' Perception of 'Smartness' in a Destination: A Case Study of Tenerife Island

Miquel Armand Mesegue-Basallo, Julia Marti-Ochoa⑩,
Berta Ferrer-Rosell⑩, and Eva Martin-Fuentes⑩

Abstract Smart Tourism Destinations (STDs) have been presented as a key element to boost the tourism sector and keep it adapted to the changing needs of governments, local inhabitants and tourists. The Spanish government launched the STDs' Network in 2013 to adapt Spanish tourist destinations to evolving needs. The program aims to create customized, accessible experiences using technology and innovation while ensuring sustainability. To be recognized as a STD, destinations must meet 80% of requirements set, classified into governance, innovation, technology, universal accessibility, and sustainability. The study aims to examine tourists' awareness of the smart characteristics of destinations, by analyzing user-generated content. The data collection focuses on Tenerife Island's top attractions and includes reviews from the English section of TripAdvisor's "things to do" category. The analysis reveals changes in tourists' comments and highlights that tourists are aware of some indicators and objectives such as accessibility. The article sheds light on the concept of STDs and their implications for the tourism industry.

Keywords Smart tourism destination · User generated content · VOS viewer · Trip Advisor · Review analysis · Destination image

M. A. Mesegue-Basallo · J. Marti-Ochoa (✉) · B. Ferrer-Rosell · E. Martin-Fuentes
Department of Economics and Business, University of Lleida, Lleida, Spain
e-mail: julia.marti@udl.cat

M. A. Mesegue-Basallo
e-mail: miquel.mesegue@udl.cat

B. Ferrer-Rosell
e-mail: berta.ferrer@udl.cat

E. Martin-Fuentes
e-mail: eva.martin@udl.cat

A. J. Guevara Plaza et al. (eds.), *Tourism and ICTs: Advances in Data Science, Artificial Intelligence and Sustainability*, Springer Proceedings in Business and Economics,
https://doi.org/10.1007/978-3-031-52607-7_5

1 Introduction

In 2013 the Spanish Industry, Commerce and Tourism Ministry together with the Spanish Tourism Secretary of State used the state company SEGITTUR to launch a program to try and adapt the Spanish touristic destinations to the new needs of tourists, since many Spanish tourism destinations were reaching the stage of maturity or even deterioration (Rodríguez-Sánchez & Conejero-Quiles, 2011). This program, the Smart Touristic Destinations' Network attempts to be a continuous synergetic process between the public sector, the private sector, and the local citizens, that uses technology and innovation to make the touristic experiences custom-made and accessible to everyone. These changes require the destination to be sustainable economically, socially, and environmentally to keep functioning in the future. This is done by collecting and processing data to anticipate possible outcomes and therefore increasing the efficiency of the destination. All of that should result in an increase in the quality of the products offered as well as an increase in the quality of life of the locals.

To become an officially recognized Smart Touristic Destination (STD) by SEGITTUR, the destination must accomplish at least 80% of the requirements proposed by the network institution, at the beginning of 2023 only six touristic destinations have reached this milestone: Benidorm, Gijón, Málaga, Tenerife Island, Santander and Donosti/San Sebastián (SEGITTUR, 2023). Becoming a STD is not just a goal to be reached, but also a process to be followed, since the aim of becoming a STD is to keep improving constantly to adapt the destination to the new needs of the market.

Additionally, all indicators and objectives can be classified into 5 axes, from which the Destination Management Organization (DMO) can work to achieve their goals, these axes are (AENOR, 2018): (1) Governance: It measures the efficacy and efficiency of the proposed measures. It also measures the transparency of the processes, the level of openness and participation of public and private entities, the coherence of the project, and the responsibilities of each participant. (2) Innovation: It evaluates the improvement of benefits and the increase of competitiveness of the introduction or improvement of new services, processes, commercialization methods and organization methods. (3) Technology: It measures the level of utility of new technologies and their degree of implementation as well as their ability to meet the needs of the tourist during all stages of the journey. In addition, technology is a key tool for data collection, but despite being an important aspect linked to the other axes, technology alone does not turn a tourism destination into a STD. (4) Universal accessibility: It measures if infrastructures allow indiscriminate access to all people, guaranteeing the right to be treated equal, so that everyone can enjoy them in an autonomous and natural way. And (5) Sustainability: it measures the present and future level of protection of the economic activities linked to the tourism sector. It also measures the level of social, environmental, and economic measures that will guarantee the development of tourism activities in the future.

For this investigation, reviews have been used to evaluate the opinion of current and past visitors. While the objective of this project is to analyse the effectiveness of the measures applied by destination managers and its impact on tourists, the main results show that there is still a lot of research to be done in the field of STDs. The results also show that while destinations, and particularly Tenerife Island, are introducing changes to increase their "smartness", tourists are aware of these changes and post smart-related reviews.

2 Literature Review

2.1 Smart Concept and Smart Tourism Destinations

The concept of "Smart" things has been around for a long time, especially since the boom of smart phones more than a decade ago, however, the concept of STDs is quite recent. Prior to STDs, there was the concept of Smart cities, which although its meaning does not have defined borders, it makes reference to many concepts linked to STDs, like the use of new technologies, the environmental concerns technologies or the need of sharing information between stakeholders (Jasrotia & Gangotia, 2018). The first attempt of turning regular tourism destinations into STDs were the eDestinations, which used the internet and communication technologies to provide information and make transactions between stakeholders, later, as tourists and destinations' interests shifted towards a higher quality and more responsible tourism, and new technologies became available, the concept of STDs was born as a way to create a common space for all stakeholders of a destination to improve this destination in aspects like sustainability or accessibility. It can be said that during this period of transition, tourists also evolved from eTourists to Smart Tourists. According to the existing literature, tourists are now more informed, demanding, independent, active, and skilled at using technologies to navigate the internet, and they also interact more online by booking, comparing, reviewing, recommending, and complaining more than ever before (Femenia-Serra & Neuhofer, 2018). These authors indicated that there are three specific behaviors linked to those smart tourists: (1) they share data with other stakeholders because they know the benefits that this can bring them and trust that their data will be protected, secured, and carefully handled. (2) as long as smart technologies are useful and easy to use, they will use these to enhance their experiences, since they have the confidence and ability to do so. And (3) they shape the experience of other tourists by being active users of the smart technology ecosystems created for smart destinations, generating and sharing content with other stakeholders as long as they feel confident. All these behaviors put the tourists at the center of STDs, since they will generate large amounts of data that will feed the DMO so that it can make better decisions about the destination.

Moreover, according to the current literature, there is proof that there are some benefits inherent to the application of smart measures. One key element that differentiates a non-STD from a smart one is that STDs make decisions based on collected data. This type of action requires the active participation of the local government along with the DMO to use the axis of governance to get the information needed from the destination, and then, plan the route to improve the destination with internet and communication technologies. Some of the benefits that come along with these policies are an improvement of the destination's image, a better connectivity network that can help tourists navigate complex scenarios, it allows for faster, more interactive, and personalized experiences and it can present more and clearer information at each stage of the trip.

Utilizing Information and Communication Technologies alongside innovative data sources under the umbrella of a Sustainable Development strategy enhances the quality of the tourist experience. It also enhances the sophistication of business intelligence for marketing efforts and promotes collaboration among stakeholders, thus strengthening the ability to manage innovation and knowledge-based processes (Soares et al., 2022).

However, some articles suggest that there are still some challenges to overcome, like having the infrastructure required to collect and analyze the data that will guide the policies, making sure that tourists know how to introduce these measures into their trip, reduce privacy invasion related concerns, avoid overexposing tourists to information, allowing the tourists to be more creative and adventurous while reducing technology dependence, avoiding overcrowded and overexploited tourist locations due to social media exposure and reducing the levels of stress that come with being constantly connected to technology between others (Femenia-Serra & Ivars-Baidal, 2021).

Nonetheless, cloud computing, mobile apps, big data analytics, geospatial services, and social media platforms are all cutting-edge instances of intelligent technologies that enhance tourism experiences and platforms (Yuan et al., 2019). Moreover, the incorporation of groundbreaking solutions into tourism planning enables visitors to perceive a destination from a fresh perspective (Shafiee et al., 2021).

2.2 Current Trends

Internet and Smart Tourism Technologies are also playing a crucial role in other parts of the world. It is the case of Indonesia, where since the start of the Covid-19 pandemic, a boom in the usage of Smart Tourism Technologies has been seen. This sharp increase in the usage of internet technologies in tourism environments can be explained because of the increase of preparation required to travel during the pandemic, having tourists check more information before their trip, but also during their trip. To bring more value to the tourist and to be more appealing, the information provided to the tourists has to be real, accessible, and comprehensive, as easier to navigate webpages help with decision-making by reducing the sense of risk (Mohseni et al., 2018). This search of more appealing information by tourists means that they normally prefer more trusted sources of information, like friends and family or comments on review platforms, there are authors that even confirm that interpersonal influence and electronic word of mouth (eWOM) are the most significant sources for tourists when making the final decision on destination choice (Chung & Buhalis, 2008).

All of this means that tourists nowadays relay more heavily on user-generated content (UGC) than other methods for obtaining the information they need, like reviews from providers of tourism services due to the level of originality and honesty of this content. This does not mean that tourists do not check the sources provided by DMOs or tourism and hospitality services' managers but, when they do it, the quality and personalization of these sources are extremely relevant to the tourist (Prihanto et al., 2022).

2.3   Hypotheses, Justification, and Objectives of Research

Since the end of the 2009 financial crisis there has been an increase in the number of Mediterranean competitors for the Spanish tourism sector, especially Italy and Greece, but also Egypt, Tunisia, and Syria with their recovery of political stability after the Arab Spring. This increasing number of competitors has been followed by a not so sharp increase of tourists, except for the years of the pandemic (Moreno-Luna et al., 2021), which has forced tourist destinations to increase their competitive advantages to stand out in the international marked and avoid staying at a standstill (Afonso-Rodríguez & Santana-Gallego, 2018). In the Spanish economy, tourism is one of the most important economic sectors. In 2022, the tourism sector, directly and indirectly, represents 12.2% of gross domestic product (GDP) (INE, 2022). The Spanish government did not fall behind in this subject, in 2013 the Spanish Industry, Commerce and Tourism Ministry together with the Spanish Tourism Secretary of State launched a program to increase these competitive advantages. This program, which is based on the concept of STDs, assists and evaluates the Spanish tourism destinations to help them grow in five different directions, called axes: governance, innovation, technology, sustainability and accessibility (SEGITTUR, 2022). According to some studies, becoming a STD can have several benefits for the public authorities and the local residents, including an improvement in economic competitiveness and a rise in the standards of living (Boes, 2015), but it can also bring improvements for the tourists including an increase in transparency from the local government, a better preserved natural environment and heritage, more efficient ways of transportation, better acceptance of tourists by the locals, better access to internet technologies, more accessible locations, or less overcrowded locations, which will jointly increase the demand for the destination, and in the long term, benefit the growth of the tourism sector in the area (INVATTUR, 2015).

Besides the fact that becoming a STD improves the quality of the tourist's experience, there are studies that also show that tourists are aware of the improvements of quality of the destinations (Medina et al., 2016), but this brings a question: To what extent are tourists aware of the "smart" characteristics that define STDs at their destination?

This study pretends to shed light on the topic of STDs and its impact on the tourist's experience, since the tourist and the information he provides will be a key instrument when shaping the destination.

3　Methodology and Data Collection

The method used in this paper to find out whether the tourist is aware of the smartness of the destination is an extraction of user generated content (UGC) from review-based platforms. Reviews are being used in this investigation because they play a crucial role to set the incoming tourists' expectations and shape their decisions, but they also serve as a method to evaluate the satisfaction of the current and the outgoing tourists. These first expectations will also greatly affect the satisfaction of the tourists, being the expectations greater than reality will result in a much worse experience for the tourist, on the contrary, if the expectations are lower than reality, it will result in a much greater experience for the tourist (Narangajavana Kaosiri et al., 2019).

Reviews are also a good method to extract data from a sample of the tourists without having to make a survey. This inexpensive method allows a wider data collection and a bigger sample, including past years but it might bring some situations that have to be considered. First of all, the analysis of individual reviews is useless for this investigation, as some of these reviews could be fake, repeated or non-representative, and second, the sample taken from different destinations' analysis will be different, which can be misleading when interpreting the results especially for those fewer known destinations that have much less reviews when compared to other more popular destinations. However, the results are still valid when taken these limitations into consideration, as studies show that when the sample is big enough, the number of fake reviews is no longer representative and does not alter results (Martin-Fuentes et al., 2018).

For this investigation, data was extracted from the English comments sections of TripAdvisor. From the destination chosen in this study, Tenerife Island, only the "things to do" section was analyzed, since it focuses more on tourism attraction and it excludes the hotels and the restaurants, and from this section, only the top 10 traveler's favorite attractions from this destination were selected. The study considers reviews from the period 2016–2021.

The data extraction was made in March of 2022, using the web scraping software program Octoparse. This program allows the extraction of each review individually, together with its publication date, the date when the user visited the attraction, the review title, the review body and the score in a scale from 1 to 5 points. The number of reviews subjected to analysis for this study is as follows: Loro Parque 1,187, Siam Park 2,317, Teide Volcano 506, Monkey Park 287, Light and Music Fountain 125, Teresitas Beach 103, Palmetum Botanical Garden 39, Market Nuestra Sra. de África

44, Duque Beach 24, Rural Park Anaga 23. The total number of reviews considered was 4,655.

4 Results

Once data have been presented, next step is to depict a graphic network map of the comments posted by users on TripAdvisor about Tenerife Island before and after becoming a Smart Tourism Destination. This analysis is a comparison of the results obtained the year before Tenerife Island became a Smart Tourism Destination with the results from the year immediately after. This gives the reader an idea of which were the most commented topics from before and after Tenerife Island became a smart destination.

In 2021 Tenerife Island registered 1,044,405 inhabitants and 168,504 tourists, from which 29% came from abroad (INE, 2022). The Island of Tenerife joined the Smart Tourism Destinations' Network (by SEGITTUR) in 2020.

4,202 reviews posted in 2019 (before Tenerife became a member of the STD Network) were downloaded and analyzed. Figure 1 shows the most commented topics that year. Green cluster refers to the public infrastructure related to the tourism sector, including transportation modes, and topics related to the volcano. Some of the most representative topics of this cluster (according to the size of the nodes) are time, hour, bus, hotel, cable car, experience, or view. Yellow cluster refers to water and theme parks. Some of the most representative topics of this cluster (according to the size of the nodes) are ride, queue, and ticket. Blue cluster refers to animal entertainment-based activities. Some of the most representative topics of this cluster (according to the size of the nodes) are park, animal, and show, most of them related to Loro Parque. Finally, red cluster refers to food, leisure, and sightseeing. Some of the most representative topics of this cluster (according to the size of the nodes) are day, slide, food, kid, siam park, and water park.

A total of 453 reviews posted in 2021 (the year after Tenerife Island became a STD) were downloaded and analyzed, from which it can be seen (Fig. 2) that the most relevant topics in the reviews were the following. Green cluster contains the topics related to Covid-19. Some of the most representative topics of this cluster (according to the size of the nodes) are person, mask, covid, and social distancing. Blue cluster includes topics related to water, mainly from the Siam Park and the beach. Some of the most representative topics of this cluster (according to the size of the nodes) are slide, Siam Park, beach, and fun. Yellow cluster contains topics related to theme parks. Some of the most representative topics of this cluster (according to the size of the nodes) are ride, queue, locker, and fast pass. Red cluster refers to topics related to infrastructure, sightseeing, leisure, and topics related to animal-based entertainment parks. Some of the most representative topics of this cluster (according to the size of the nodes) are park, day, animal, and place. Finally, purple cluster includes topics related to entrance price and timetable of the activities with words such as ticket, euro, time, or timing. This cluster is mainly in the middle of the graph, between

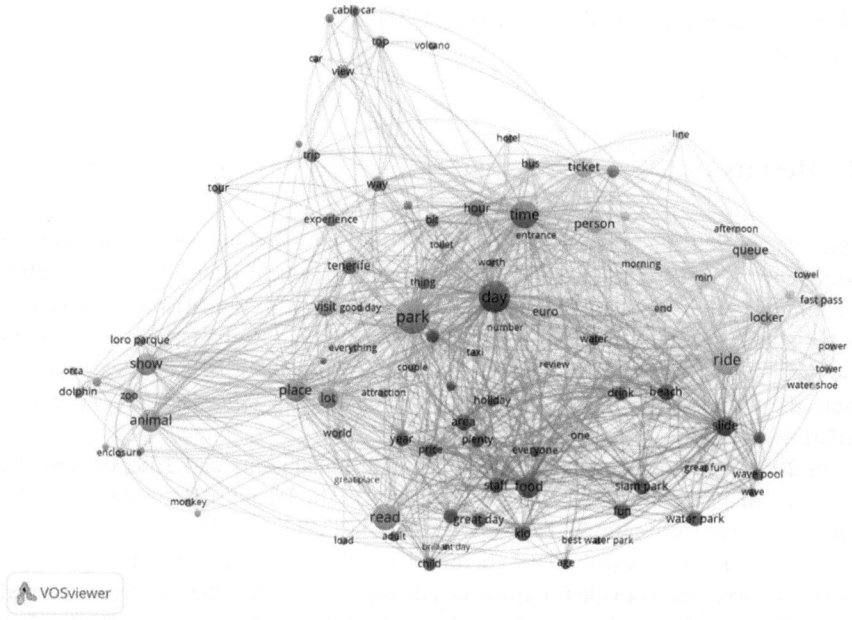

Fig. 1 Most commented topics in TripAdvisor about the Island of Tenerife's Top 10 attractions during the year 2019 (image generated by VOSviewer)

red, blue, and yellow clusters, which means that it is closely related to entertainment parks (Siam Park or animal parks).

5 Discussion and Conclusions

Tourists' experience on review-based platforms, such as TripAdvisor, has changed from before and after the destinations became smart. There have been some changes in the main topics commented by tourists in review platforms. Although some of these changes are probably motivated by other factors, like the Covid-19 pandemic, evidence shows that tourists, after a destination implemented STD policies, increased the number of comments on these policies, which shows the level of awareness of the tourists to changes in tourism policies.

As observed in the analysis of the most frequently used words by tourists in comments some new concepts about accessibility have emerged with great relevance in 2021, such as mask, social distancing, covid, security, long queue, and line, but all of them are motivated for the pandemic and not for the implementation of STD policies. Additionally, the user is placing greater importance on two intangible concepts: time and experience. Furthermore, after the implementation of STD policies, tourists did show more interest in attractions than before they were less

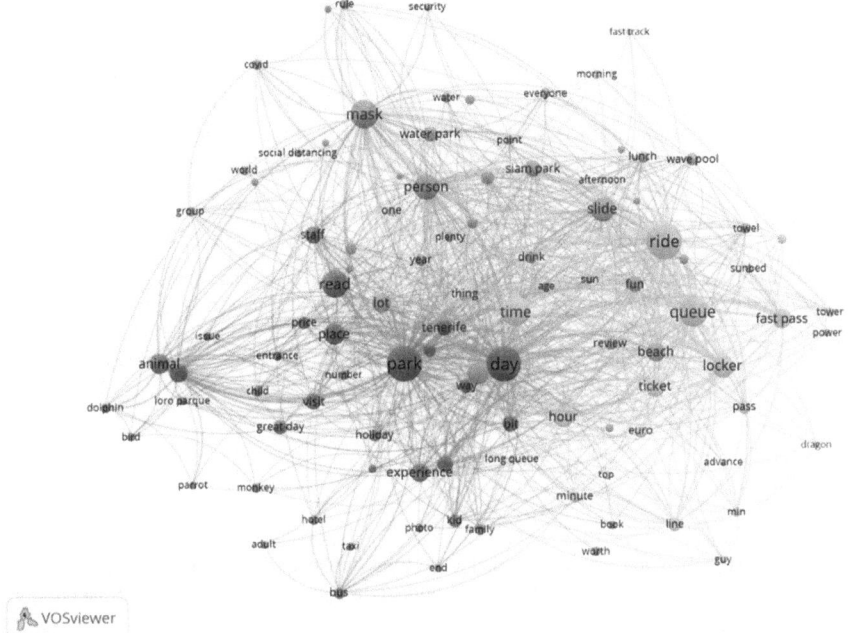

Fig. 2 Most commented topics in TripAdvisor about the Island of Tenerife's Top 10 attractions during the year 2021 (image generated by VOSviewer)

popular or known, Tenerife Island has seen an increase in interest for the few more popular attractions like the theme parks and the water parks. Even though results obtained are not ideal, they are promising, as they show that there is an intention by the authorities to implement STD policies and it also shows the acceptance of these policies by international tourists. These results also go in the same direction of other studies, pointing out that the "smart" era of tourism is still in its early ages and needs furthermore investigation to take full advantage of these new policies.

Given the fact that Tenerife Island joined the Spanish STD Network in 2020, there are some intrinsic limitations to this research. The strike of the Covid-19 crisis meant the closing of all non-essential economic activities in the Spanish territory for most of 2020 and part of 2021, which also meant the cessation of all tourism activities and the implementation of traveling restrictions.

Besides that, it should be stated that tourists not commenting on STD policies could be caused by several factors, maybe the tourists already expect the destination to be "smart" and thus do not comment on aspects that they find irrelevant, like accessibility or destination management, or maybe there are other much more interesting topics to be commented than just the ones related to the "smart" features of the destination. Moreover, not all topics related to "smart" policies stand out in the same way to tourists, while some categories like innovation or technology might be more noticeable to tourists, others like governance might be completely imperceptible to them. Furthermore, the utilization of TripAdvisor reviews may pose a limitation, as these reviews typically lack comprehensive coverage of aspects pertaining to TDI. Another limitation of this research is that it only analyzes one destination that has been awarded the distinction of STDs by SEGITTUR. A much deeper analysis of other destinations "smart" and other destinations that are currently working on implementing "smart" policies would have brought other interesting results.

Acknowledgements This research has been funded by the Spanish MCIN/AEI/https://doi.org/10. 13039/501100011033/FEDER, UE within the RevTour project Id PID2022-138564OA-I00, by the Spanish Ministry of Industry, Trade and Tourism financed by the European Union—Next Generation UE, within the Gastrotur Project Id TUR-RETOS2022-017, by the Spanish Ministry of Science and Innovation within the TradiTur project Id TED2021-129763B-I00 and by the Institute for Social and Territorial Development within the ResTur project for the call 2023CRINDESTABC.

References

AENOR. (2018). Sistema de gestión de los destinos turísticos inteligentes. Requisitos (UNE 178501). Retrieved June 21, 2023, from https://www.une.org/encuentra-tu-norma/busca-tu-norma/norma?c=N0060239

Afonso-Rodríguez, J. A., & Santana-Gallego, M. (2018). Is Spain benefiting from the Arab Spring? On the impact of terrorism on a tourist competitor country. *Quality & Quantity, 52*, 1371–1408. https://doi.org/10.1007/s11135-017-0527-2

Boes, K. (2015). Smart tourism destinations: smartness as competitive advantage. In *ENTER2015 PhD workshop research proposals* (pp. 11–15).

Chung, J. Y., & Buhalis, D. (2008). Web 2.0: A study of online travel community. In *Information and communication technologies in tourism 2008* (pp. 70–81). Springer, Vienna.

Femenia-Serra, F., & Ivars-Baidal, J. A. (2021). Do smart tourism destinations really work? The case of Benidorm. *Asia Pacific journal of tourism research, 26*(4), 365–384. https://doi.org/10.1080/10941665.2018.1561478

Femenia-Serra, F., & Neuhofer, B. (2018). Smart tourism experiences: Conceptualisation, key dimensions and research agenda. *Investigaciones Regionales-Journal of Regional Research, 42*, 129–150.

INE—Instituto Nacional de Estadística. (2022). Retrieved June 25, 2023, from https://www.ine.es

INVATTUR. (2015). Manual operativo para la configuracion de destinos turisticos inteligentes. Retrieved June 25, 2023, from https://invattur.es/uploads/entorno_37/ficheros/62690a0d5bc1 b967049880.pdf

Jasrotia, A., & Gangotia, A. (2018). Smart cities to smart tourism destinations: A review paper. *Journal of Tourism Intelligence and Smartness, 1*(1), 47–56.

Martin-Fuentes, E., Mateu, C., & Fernandez, C. (2018). Does verifying uses influence rankings? Analyzing Booking.com and TripAdvisor. *Tourism Analysis, 23*(1), 1–15. https://doi.org/10.3727/108354218X15143857349459

Medina, M. L. F., Estárico, E. H., & Marrero, S. M. (2016). Q de calidad y satisfacción del turista en el sector hotelero español. Cuadernos de turismo 203–226. https://doi.org/10.6018/turismo.37.256211

Mohseni, S., Jayashree, S., Rezaei, S., Kasim, A., & Okumus, F. (2018). Attracting tourists to travel companies' websites: The structural relationship between website brand, personal value, shopping experience, perceived risk and purchase intention. *Current Issues in Tourism, 21*(6), 616–645. https://doi.org/10.1080/13683500.2016.1200539

Moreno-Luna, L., Robina-Ramírez, R., Sánchez, M. S. O., & Castro-Serrano, J. (2021). Tourism and sustainability in times of COVID-19: The case of Spain. *International Journal of Environmental Research and Public Health, 18*(4), 1859. https://doi.org/10.3390/ijerph18041859

Narangajavana Kaosiri, Y., Callarisa Fiol, L. J., Moliner Tena, M. Á., Rodríguez Artola, R. M., & Sánchez García, J. (2019). User-generated content sources in social media: A new approach to explore tourist satisfaction. *Journal of Travel Research, 58*(2), 253–265. https://doi.org/10.1177/0047287517746014

Prihanto, Y., Samosir, J., Tampoli, D., & Manurung, S. (2022). Information searching and intention to visit tourist destination using smart tourism technologies during Covid-19. *Journal of Tianjin University Science and Technology, 55*.

Rodríguez-Sánchez, I., & Conejero-Quiles, A. M. (2011). Renovación de destinos turísticos maduros, expertos y grupos de interés, discurso global-local y escenarios de futuro: El caso de Benidorm. *Tourism & Management Studies, 1*, 969–981.

SEGITTUR. (2023). Miembros de la red. Obtenido de Red de Destinos Turísticos Inteligentes. Retrieved June 12, 2023, https://www.destinosinteligentes.es/donostia-san-sebastian-obtiene-el-distintivo-destino-turistico-inteligente/

Shafiee, S., Rajabzadeh Ghatari, A., Hasanzadeh, A., & Jahanyan, S. (2021). Smart tourism destinations: A systematic review. *Tourism Review, 76*(3), 505–528. https://doi.org/10.1108/TR-06-2019-0235

Soares, J. C., Domareski Ruiz, T. C., & Ivars Baidal, J. A. (2022). Smart destinations: A new planning and management approach? *Current Issues in Tourism, 25*(17), 2717–2732. https://doi.org/10.1080/13683500.2021.1991897

Yuan, Y., Tseng, Y. H., & Ho, C. I. (2019). Tourism information technology research trends: 1990–2016. *Tourism review, 74*(1), 5–19. https://doi.org/10.1108/TR-08-2017-0128

Analysis of the Trend in the Number of Followers on Social Networks in Spanish World Heritage Cities: A Comparative Study of Facebook, Instagram and Twitter

Marcelino Sánchez-Rivero⬤, María Cristina Rodríguez-Rangel⬤, Juan Carlos Díez-Apolo⬤, and Luis Murillo-González⬤

Abstract The presence of tourist destinations on social media has become a fundamental requirement for the success of tourism management. Virtually all tourist destinations have profiles on one or more social networks. However, their presence is not the same on all these social networks, as the existence of a profile and level of activity largely depends on the preferences of destination managers or the marketing strategy chosen by the destination. Using the weekly number of followers on the three main social networks of the 15 Spanish Cities of World Heritage (CEPH), the objective of this study is to delve into the analysis of the annual variation experienced by estimating the most appropriate trend model for the analyzed time series. The results obtained have allowed us to identify the profiles that have grown the most during the year, locate the social network in which this growth has occurred the most, and understand how this growth has occurred throughout the analyzed year. In turn, the trend analysis in time series reveals that, predominantly, the exponential model is the one that best fits the data. This implies that the highest growth rates occur in the middle and late months of the year.

Keywords Spanish cities of world heritage · Social media · Followers · Trend · Linear/logarithmic/exponential

1 Introduction

Currently, Social Media (SM) is fully integrated as an indispensable part of the commercial strategy of tourist destinations. Following the decision-making process model proposed by Goodall et al. (1991), it is known that in the final phase, the

M. Sánchez-Rivero · M. C. Rodríguez-Rangel · J. C. Díez-Apolo (✉) · L. Murillo-González
Faculty of Economics and Business Administration, University of Extremadura, Badajoz, Spain
e-mail: diezapolo@unex.es

© The Author(s) 2024
A. J. Guevara Plaza et al. (eds.), *Tourism and ICTs: Advances in Data Science, Artificial Intelligence and Sustainability*, Springer Proceedings in Business and Economics, https://doi.org/10.1007/978-3-031-52607-7_6

traveler chooses among destinations that achieve a comparative advantage among those known to them. Therefore, the mere presence of destinations on SM, while essential for a proper communication strategy, is not sufficient without an audience receiving the message, that is, without a critical mass of followers on various social media profiles. In fact, in some studies, social media presence is precisely measured through the number of followers or the level of engagement it receives from its community (Giraldo & Martínez, 2017).

Given the importance of the number of followers for the effectiveness of the social media strategy, this study aims to analyze the trend in the growth of the number of followers in the 15 cities that make up the CEPH brand. Firstly, the starting situation of each city is analyzed through a convergence ratio that allows positioning each city. Secondly, a time series trend analysis is conducted, allowing us to see which model best captures the trend in each destination and subsequently rank the 15 destinations based on the highest growth in their audience.

The results obtained through this analysis constitute an important output for management, knowing which destinations achieve better performance on social media with the benefits that this information implies for management. To achieve these results, this study conducts a literature review to frame the research problem. Subsequently, the methodology to be used is described. Chapter 4 lists the main results obtained, and finally, it concludes with a series of conclusions and recommendations for management.

2 The Presence on Social Networks of Tourist Destinations: A Strategic Objective

The importance of social media and new technologies has been growing exponentially in recent years in all areas of life, but perhaps even more so in the tourism sector. In this regard, Pan et al. (2021) conducted research in which a series of respondents had to choose a tourist destination from a list of options. They made this choice before being informed about the destination's image on social media and repeated the choice after obtaining that information. The results showed that the image of the tourist destination influenced the choice behavior of the respondents, demonstrating the importance of the social media positioning of destinations for attracting new tourists.

In the same vein, Lee et al. (2019) emphasize the importance of providing quality tourist information through social media. They see this factor as crucial for tourism growth in less-known regions of South Korea, as these regions currently do not provide adequate tourist information to meet the needs of international tourists. In a similar study, Molinillo et al. (2019) analyze ten Spanish smart cities, finding acceptable engagement results through social media such as Facebook, Twitter, and Instagram. However, they showed weaknesses related to promoting their image and brand, as well as the effectiveness with which they communicated their smart features.

On the other hand, Chopra et al. (2022) mention that the rise of social media has revolutionized the tourism industry. Currently, many people post comments about different destinations on the internet, and many others gather information about tourist destinations through these comments. In their analysis, they indicate that the quality and quantity of information offered by tourist destinations are the two most important factors for obtaining good reviews online.

Stojanovic et al. (2018) investigate the effects of the intensity of social media use on the destination brand value, analyzing how communication on social media affects the tourist's perception of the destination. They observe a positive relationship between brand awareness, destination quality, and customer value. They emphasize that tourists who obtain information about the tourist destination on social media have a better perception of it, influencing the tourist's behavior by recommending it through social media as well as outside of it.

3   The Importance of Audience Growth (New Followers) on Social Networks for Tourist Destinations

In their article, Kiralova and Pavlicek (2015) discuss the importance of social media in both tourism demand and supply. They mention that social media allows destinations to interact directly with visitors through various online platforms. They emphasize the positive relationship between destination visitors on social media (followers) and tourists who directly experience the destination. They indicate that a higher number of followers on social media increases the chances of the destination boosting its tourism demand.

On the other hand, Song et al. (2021) point out that in the context of tourism marketing, it is essential to establish effective strategies for engaging with social media followers and strengthening relationships. They highlight the role of social media image and how it influences tourists' destination choices. In this regard, the increase in the number of followers is crucial for better destination promotion.

Regarding the analysis of social media data, Linnes et al. (2021) stress the importance of reviewing the behaviors and interests of social media followers, as it provides a wealth of information and valuable data for tourism organizations. They emphasize that a higher number of followers on social media means more data available for analysis, enabling better insights to help tourism companies market their products. In their study on the city of Fredikstad in Norway, they use Facebook data to understand the needs of local tourists. This allows tourism businesses to be prepared to meet those needs. The study is also valuable for understanding the evolution of tourists' preferences and needs, enabling quick adaptation to them.

4 Analysis of the Audience on Social Networks in Spanish World Heritage Cities

4.1 Data

The data used in this study were obtained from the Application Programming Interface (API) of Optimizadata's barometer (www.optimizadata.com). Specifically, various daily metrics were obtained from the profiles of the 15 Spanish Cities of World Heritage (CEPH) on the social media platforms Facebook, Twitter, and Instagram throughout the year 2022. Among all the metrics obtained, the only one utilized in this study is the number of followers on these three social media platforms.

Given that the number of followers is likely to be a metric that changes less from day to day (unlike the number of posts, comments, or impressions), it has been considered that the most suitable temporal unit of analysis in this case is the week, rather than the day. For this reason, a weekly metric of the number of followers has been generated by averaging the daily information generated by the API. In this way, we have worked with a time series of 52 weeks, all corresponding to the year 2022.

4.2 Methodology

Firstly, we aimed to analyze, from a purely descriptive perspective, the starting point of the audience on social media for the 15 Spanish Cities of World Heritage (CEPH). To do this, the number of followers on the three analyzed social media platforms as of January 1, 2022, was considered, and a convergence/divergence ratio was constructed with respect to the maximum audience of the studied group. This ratio (calculated as the quotient between the number of followers of a CEPH and the maximum number of followers among all of them) generates a variable with a maximum value of 1 (corresponding to the CEPH with the maximum number of followers on the social media platform), and where the rest of the values are always less than 1.

Secondly, also with a purely descriptive intention, the distribution of followers for the profiles of each CEPH on each social media platform was calculated. This was done by simply dividing the number of followers on each social media platform by the sum of followers on the three analyzed platforms. This simple descriptive analysis will reveal which social media platform is preferred by CEPH for promotion, to showcase their activities, etc.

Finally, leveraging the weekly information on the audience of CEPH on social media, and given that the primary interest of this study is to understand how the growth of this audience has been distributed throughout the year 2022, we have resorted to statistical time series analysis, specifically, the analysis of the trend in the number of followers. Among the different trend modelings of a time series, three have been considered in this study, as they, in most cases, explain it better:

Linear trend:

$$Y_t = \beta_0 + \beta_1 t + e_t \tag{1}$$

Logarithmic trend:

$$Y_t = \beta_0 + \beta_1 \ln t + e_t \tag{2}$$

Exponential trend:

$$Y_t = \alpha_0 exp^{\alpha_1 t} u_t \tag{3}$$

Model (3) can also be expressed, alternatively, in the following way:

$$\ln Y_y = \beta_0 + \beta_1 t + e_t \tag{3b}$$

where $\beta_0 = \ln\alpha_0$; $\beta_1 = \alpha_1$ and $e_t = \ln u_t$

The first of these models (linear) assumes that the growth of the audience on social media occurs more or less steadily throughout the entire year. The second trend model (logarithmic) assumes that audience growth is concentrated mainly in the early months of the year and that afterward, this growth is much smoother (or even non-existent). Finally, the third model (exponential) presupposes that during the early months of the year, the growth in the number of followers is very modest, and as the year progresses, this growth becomes increasingly pronounced, to the point that the majority of the increase in the audience occurs in the later months of the year.

To determine which of these trend models best fits the evolution of the audience on social media for the CEPH, these models have been estimated for each of the three social media platforms using the statistical package "stats" (version 3.6.2) of the R software. The model with the highest coefficient of determination (R^2) was chosen. Subsequently, it was verified whether the corresponding parameter β_1 is statistically significant or not (at 5%). Finally, the value of this parameter was recorded as an estimate of the average weekly increase in the number of followers on the analyzed social media platform. This was done to rank the 15 CEPH studied based on the greater or lesser growth of their audience throughout the year 2022.

4.3   Results

Table 1 presents the convergence ratio to the maximum audience on the three considered social media platforms for the 15 Spanish Cities of World Heritage (CEPH). In the case of Facebook, the city with the highest number of followers is San Cristóbal de la Laguna, and only four cities have more than 75% of the followers of this city.

Table 1 Ratio of convergence to the maximum audience on CEPH social networks as of January 1, 2022

CEPH	Facebook	Instagram	Twitter
Alcalá de Henares	0,151	0,089	0,319
Ávila	0,399	0,079	0,526
Baeza	0,149	0,040	0,083
Cáceres	0,075	0,033	0,018
Córdoba	0,760	0,124	**1,000**
Cuenca	0,064	0,080	0,165
Ibiza	0,133	0,348	0,201
Mérida	0,310	0,069	0,056
Salamanca	0,915	0,144	0,047
San Cristóbal de la Laguna	**1,000**	0,091	0,309
Santiago de Compostela	0,728	0,637	0,901
Segovia	0,374	0,148	0,406
Tarragona	0,572	**1,000**	0,764
Toledo	0,780	0,384	0,485
Úbeda	0,780	0,028	0,374

Source Own elaboration based on data from Optimizadata.com

These cities are Salamanca, the city that comes closest to the number of followers of San Cristóbal de la Laguna (0.915), Toledo (0.780), Úbeda (0.780), and Córdoba.

On the other hand, Tarragona has the highest number of followers on Instagram, and it seems to be the only CEPH clearly investing in this social media platform. With the sole exception of Santiago de Compostela (0.637), the other cities have a convergence ratio below 0.4. In the case of the social media platform Twitter, Córdoba leads in the number of followers, with Santiago de Compostela (with 10% fewer followers than Córdoba; ratio equal to 0.901) and Tarragona (with 23.6% fewer followers than Córdoba; ratio equal to 0.764) following in the ranking behind the Andalusian capital.

At the opposite end of the cities leading in audiences on the three analyzed social media platforms are the cities with the fewest followers. Therefore, they should express some concern about their limited social media audience compared to the rest of the CEPH. Among these cities, whose average convergence ratio on the three social media platforms does not exceed 15%, are Mérida (average ratio of 0.145), Cuenca (0.103), Baeza (0.090), and Cáceres (0.042).

Table 2 presents the distribution of the total audience for each Spanish City of World Heritage (CEPH) across social media platforms. In this table, the focus is on each social media platform, and it is possible that the same person follows a CEPH on more than one social media platform. Therefore, the percentages in Table 2 do not account for possible duplications or triplications of the same user following a CEPH on multiple social media platforms. It is evident that Facebook is the preferred social media platform for these 15 CEPH, as the majority of their followers are

Table 2 Distribution of the number of followers on Facebook, Instagram and Twitter of the CEPH as of January 1, 2022

CEPH	Facebook	Instagram	Twitter
Alcalá de Henares	37,5%	20,8%	41,7%
Ávila	53,3%	9,9%	36,8%
Baeza	64,8%	16,4%	18,8%
Cáceres	65,3%	26,6%	8,1%
Córdoba	54,2%	8,3%	37,4%
Cuenca	28,4%	33,2%	38,3%
Ibiza	23,5%	57,9%	18,6%
Mérida	76,7%	16,0%	7,3%
Salamanca	85,2%	12,5%	2,3%
San Cristóbal de la Laguna	80,1%	6,9%	13,0%
Santiago de Compostela	40,5%	33,2%	26,3%
Segovia	51,5%	19,2%	29,3%
Tarragona	29,9%	49,1%	21,0%
Toledo	55,9%	25,8%	18,2%
Úbeda	77,8%	2,6%	19,5%

Source Own elaboration based on data from Optimizadata.com

located on this platform. This is the case for Ávila (53.3% of its followers are on Facebook), Baeza (64.8%), Cáceres (65.3%), Córdoba (54.2%), Toledo (55.9%), and, especially, Mérida (76.7%), Úbeda (77.8%), San Cristóbal de la Laguna (80.1%), and Salamanca (85.2%). However, there are some exceptions to this majority preference for Facebook. Instagram leads in online audience for Ibiza (57.9%) and Tarragona (49.1%), while Twitter is the social media platform with the highest percentage of followers for Alcalá de Henares (41.7%) and Cuenca (38.3%).

Moving on to the analysis of the observed trends in the evolution of social media audiences for the Spanish Cities of World Heritage (CEPH), and after estimating the three aforementioned models (1), (2), and (3b) for each city and the three considered social media platforms, it is observed that, in most cases, the model that best fits the analyzed data is the exponential trend model (3b), whose estimations are presented in Table 3. The only exceptions to this general behavior occur with the linear trend model (1), which provides the best fit for 7 CEPH on Instagram and for the cities of Ávila and Baeza on Twitter (Table 4).

Focusing on the exponential trend model (Table 3), the adjustments made result in high values of the coefficient of determination, and thus, with β_1 parameters statistically significant at 1%, with only exceptions for Alcalá de Henares on Facebook and Baeza on Instagram. In model (3), the parameter β_1 represents the estimation of the expected weekly growth of the natural logarithm of the number of followers of the CEPH on the social media platform. Analyzing the estimates from Table 3, it can be observed that the highest growths in the Facebook audience are recorded in Cáceres and Cuenca, followed at a great distance by Ávila and Mérida. In the case of

Table 3 Estimation of the exponential trend of the audience (number of followers) on Facebook, Instagram and Twitter of the CEPH during 2022

CEPH	Facebook	Instagram	Twitter
Alcalá de Henares	$R^2 = 0,0084$ $\beta_1 = -0,02$		$R^2 = 0,4314$ $\beta_1 = 0,0255**$
Ávila	$R^2 = 0,7566$ $\beta_1 = 0,1730**$		
Baeza	$R^2 = 0,6299$ $\beta_1 = 0,0057**$	$R^2 = 0,0618$ $\beta_1 = 0,0598$	
Cáceres	$R^2 = 0,6896$ $\beta_1 = 0,4416**$	$R^2 = 0,8658$ $\beta_1 = 0,6412**$	$R^2 = 0,7941$ $\beta_1 = 0,1867**$
Córdoba	$R^2 = 0,9034$ $\beta_1 = 0,0072**$	$R^2 = 0,9774$ $\beta_1 = 0,5252**$	$R^2 = 0,3980$ $\beta_1 = 0,0135**$
Cuenca	$R^2 = 0,7733$ $\beta_1 = 0,4214**$	$R^2 = 0,7391$ $\beta_1 = 1,1020**$	$R^2 = 0,7085$ $\beta_1 = 0,0277**$
Ibiza	$R^2 = 0,8789$ $\beta_1 = 0,0509**$		$R^2 = 0,8142$ $\beta_1 = 0,0131**$
Mérida	$R^2 = 0,7701$ $\beta_1 = 0,1726$	$R^2 = 0,9847$ $\beta_1 = 0,4251**$	$R^2 = 0,5596$ $\beta_1 = 0,0644**$
Salamanca	$R^2 = 0,8913$ $\beta_1 = 0,0019**$		$R^2 = 0,5782$ $\beta_1 = 0,1573**$
San Cristóbal de la Laguna	$R^2 = 0,842$ $\beta_1 = 0,0065**$	$R^2 = 0,9409$ $\beta_1 = 0,2061**$	$R^2 = 0,7835$ $\beta_1 = 0,0130**$
Santiago de Compostela	$R^2 = 0,6307$ $\beta_1 = 0,0442**$		$R^2 = 0,7876$ $\beta_1 = 0,0027**$
Segovia	$R^2 = 0,2963$ $\beta_1 = 0,0552**$	$R^2 = 0,9722$ $\beta_1 = 0,3529**$	$R^2 = 0,6793$ $\beta_1 = 0,0244**$
Tarragona	$R^2 = 0,5434$ $\beta_1 = 0,0901**$		$R^2 = 0,5506$ $\beta_1 = 0,0173**$
Toledo	$R^2 = 0,3802$ $\beta_1 = 0,0263**$	$R^2 = 0,9726$ $\beta_1 = 0,2442**$	$R^2 = 0,5009$ $\beta_1 = 0,0225**$
Úbeda	$R^2 = 0\ 7503$ $\beta_1 = 0,0389**$		$R^2 = 0,5879$ $\beta_1 = 0,0068**$

** Significant parameter at 1%. * Significant parameter at 5%
Note R^2 represents the coefficient of determination of the estimated model
Source Own elaboration based on data from Optimizadata.com

Instagram, audiences have grown mainly in Cuenca, although Cáceres, Córdoba, and Mérida have also recorded truly significant weekly increases in their audiences. On the other hand, on the Twitter social media platform, the most significant estimated weekly growths have been recorded in Cáceres and Salamanca. As can be easily observed, the highest audience growths have been recorded in the CEPH with fewer followers on these three social media platforms (especially notable in the cases of Cáceres and Mérida). Furthermore, it is also clear that the highest audience growths

Table 4 Estimation of the linear trend of the audience (number of followers) on Instagram and Twitter of the CEPH during 2022

CEPH	Instagram	Twitter
Alcalá de Henares	$R^2 = 0,5766$ $\beta_1 = 10,360**$	
Ávila	$R^2 = 0,9655$ $\beta_1 = 22,320**$	$R^2 = 0,5312$ $\beta_1 = 10,720**$
Baeza		$R^2 = 0,4431$ $\beta_1 = 9,930**$
Ibiza	$R^2 = 0,6669$ $\beta_1 = 20,501**$	
Salamanca	$R^2 = 0,9772$ $\beta_1 = 26,210**$	
Santiago de Compostela	$R^2 = 0,9816$ $\beta_1 = 10,010**$	
Tarragona	$R^2 = 0,9889$ $\beta_1 = 47,810**$	
Úbeda	$R^2 = 0,9770$ $\beta_1 = 18,99**$	

** Significant parameter at 1%. * Significant parameter at 5%

Note R^2 represents the coefficient of determination of the estimated model

Source Own elaboration based on data from Optimizadata.com

are recorded on Instagram, as the estimated β_1 parameter for this social media platform is higher than the one estimated for Facebook and Twitter. This can be clearly seen in the 7 CEPH where the best model is the exponential trend for all three studied social media platforms.

Finally, considering the estimates of the linear trend model presented in Table 4 (referring only to Instagram and Twitter), it is observed that the β_1 parameter (representing, in this case, the estimation of the expected weekly growth of the number of followers) reaches the highest estimated values on the Instagram social media platform in the city of Tarragona, and to a lesser extent, in the cities of Ávila, Salamanca, and Ibiza. In the case of the Twitter social media platform, for which the linear trend model is the best fit for the evolution of followers in only two cities (Ávila and Baeza), it is observed that the estimate of weekly growth is very similar in these cities (around 10 more followers per week on average).

5 Discussion and Conclusions

Tourist destinations are obligated to provide sufficient information for travelers to make informed decisions, utilizing all available means, including their presence on social media. This level of presence can be measured by the number of followers a profile has. Therefore, monitoring and comparing the evolution of the number of followers becomes essential for proper management of this important communication tool.

This study aims to analyze the trend of the number of followers in a designation that acts as a brand for tourist destinations, the distinction as a Spanish City of World Heritage (CEPH).

The results have identified which CEPHs lead in terms of their number of followers on each of the analyzed social media platforms. This information allows the identification of cities whose social media marketing strategies are yielding better results and provides a relative perspective on the distance between them. This information can be used to guide benchmarking strategies, especially useful for destinations identified as distant from leading positions on each platform.

Regarding the ongoing competition for leadership in different social media platforms, there is a clear preference for the most established network, Facebook. While San Cristóbal de la Laguna is the best-positioned, many other cities show convergence rates close to each other. In contrast, despite the favorable growth trend of Instagram, which has become a popular photographic platform for promoting cultural tourism, CEPHs show some stagnation. Only Tarragona and Santiago de Compostela seem to be successful on this platform, with convergence ratios for the rest of the cities below 50%.

Finally, the analysis of trend in time series reveals that, for the most part, the exponential model is the best fit for the data. This implies that the highest growth rates occur in the middle and late months of the year. This result makes sense as most trips and events concentrate during this time.

It is noteworthy that the linear model is the best fit in some cities, both on Instagram and Twitter. This could reflect that strategies on these platforms are more stagnant, failing to increase the number of followers despite increased activity on the accounts. Destinations should reflect on the effectiveness of strategies developed on these platforms.

As a future line of research, it would be interesting to expand both the geographical scope of the study to see if the pattern is similar in cultural destinations internationally and to continue introducing metrics from new social media platforms, such as TikTok.

Similarly, one of the main weaknesses of this study is represented by the use of a single variable to explain a concept as multivariate as the evolution of the number of followers. Therefore, adding new metrics from the analyzed social media platforms would be useful to identify factors that may help explain the identified trend.

References

Giraldo, C. C, M., & Martínez, M. D. S. M. (2017). Análisis de la actividad y presencia en facebook y otras redes sociales de los portales turísticos de las Comunidades Autónomas españolas. *Cuadernos de turismo, 39*, 239–264. https://doi.org/10.6018/turismo.39.290521

Chopra, I. P., Lim, W. M., & Jain, T. (2022). Electronic word of mouth on social networking sites: What inspires travelers to engage in opinion seeking, opinion passing, and opinion giving? *Tourism Recreation Research.* https://doi.org/10.1080/02508281.2022.2088007

Goodall, B., et al. (1991). Understanding holiday choice 58–77. https://www.statista.com/statistics/272014/global-social-networks-ranked-by-nu

Kiralova, A., & Pavliceka, A. (2015). Development of social media strategies in tourism destination. *Procedia- Social and Behavioral Sciences, 175,* 358–366. https://doi.org/10.1016/j.sbspro.2015.01.1211

Lee, H., Chung, N., & Nam, Y. (2019). Do online information sources really make tourists visit more diverse places?: Base don the social networking analysis. *Information Processing & Management, 56*(4), 1376–1390. https://doi.org/10.1016/j.ipm.2018.01.005mber-of-users/&sa=D&source=docs&ust=1648380888249801&usg=AOvVaw37

Linnes, C., Itoga, H., Agrusa, J., & Lema, J. (2021). Sustainable tourism empowered by social network analysis to gain a competitive edge at a historic site. *Tourism and Hospitality, 2*(4), 332–346. https://doi.org/10.3390/tourhosp2040022

Molinillo, S., Anaya-Sánchez, R., Morrison, A., & Coca-Stefaniak, J. A. (2019). Smart city communication via social media: Analysing residents and visitors engagement. *Cities, 94,* 247–255. https://doi.org/10.1016/j.cities.2019.06.003

Pan, X., Rasouli, S., & Timmermans, H. (2021). Investigating tourist destination choice: Effect of destination image from social network. *Tourism Management, 83.* https://doi.org/10.1016/j.tourman.2020.104217

Song, S., Park, S., & Park, K. (2021). Thematic analysis of destination images for social media engagement marketing. *Industrial Management & Data Systems, 121*(6), 1375–1397. https://doi.org/10.1108/IMDS-12-2019-0667

Stojanovic, I., Andreu, L., & Curras-Perez, R. (2018). Effects of the intensity of use of social media on brand equity. *European Journal of Management and Business Economics, 27*(1).

Assessment of Functional and Emotional Factors in the Hotel Experience Through UGC

Elena Sánchez-Vargas⬤, **José Manuel Hernández-Mogollón**⬤,
Sergio López-Salas⬤, **Bárbara Sofía Pasaco-González**⬤,
and Ana Moreno-Lobato⬤

Abstract User Generated Content (UGC) is a valuable source of information that allows us to know what are the attributes that tourists value the most. In the hotel context, user reviews are useful for knowing tourists' opinions. There are two forms of UGC: functional and emotional. The first is to analyse messages with practical information, while the second is composed of messages that show feelings. This paper aims to identify the differences between the functional and emotional factors assessed positively and negatively by tourists about the hotels in Trujillo (Cáceres, Spain). A content analysis of Booking.com reviews of Trujillo hotels is carried out. The hotels are divided into two groups demonstrating the differences in services and prices: 1 and 2-stars and 3 and 4-stars hotels. The results show that guests evaluated functional and emotional factors positively and negatively in both groups. According to the attributes identified, to increase the positive hotel experience, the factors that should be considered are those that include emotional dimension; while to minimise the negative experience, functional factors should be considered to cover the basic hotel experience. As a main conclusion, it is outstanding that the emotional value of the hotel experience is not exclusive to the higher categories, as it is present in both groupings.

This research is funded by the European Regional Development Fund (ERDF) and the Regional Government of Extremadura (Regional Ministry of Economy, Science and Digital Agenda) through a GR23 grant.

 **Financiado por la Unión Europea**

JUNTA DE EXTREMADURA
Consejería de Economía, Ciencia y Agenda Digital

E. Sánchez-Vargas (✉) · J. M. Hernández-Mogollón · S. López-Salas · B. S. Pasaco-González · A. Moreno-Lobato
Universidad de Extremadura, Badajoz, Spain
e-mail: elenasv@unex.es

B. S. Pasaco-González
Universidad de Beira Interior, NECE-UBI, Covilhã, Portugal

A. J. Guevara Plaza et al. (eds.), *Tourism and ICTs: Advances in Data Science, Artificial Intelligence and Sustainability*, Springer Proceedings in Business and Economics, https://doi.org/10.1007/978-3-031-52607-7_7

Keywords UGC · Hotels · Tourism experience · Nvivo · Tourism marketing

1 Introduction

In recent years, websites, platforms, and social media have evolved, making it easier for tourists to exchange information through User Generated Content (UGC) (Mariné-Roig, 2022). In the hotel context, reviews are useful for knowing the preferences of guests (Sánchez-Franco et al., 2018). When tourists share their emotional experiences, this information have a greater influence on the choice of service (Xu et al., 2021). Hotels, according to their category, have different types of customers, prices, and service qualities. Thus, knowing the positive and negative ratings of tourists stays in hotels of different categories allows to understand their preferences and it helps to adapt marketing strategies, considering that the category of the hotel can be observed by the tourist before booking, acting as a marketing element (Xu, 2019). Higher-category hotels have higher prices, and this causes customer expectations to increase (Choi and Mattila, 2004). On the other hand, Xu et al. (2021) showed that UGC can be functional (linked to knowing the destination, such as history or means of transport) and emotional (linked to psychological tourist´s attitudes) and both types were positively associated with the destination. This paper locates its analysis in the town of Trujillo (Cáceres, Extremadura, Spain), which is an inland cultural destination which is increasingly developing as a tourist destination in Extremadura, and that stands out for its central position in terms of the relevant cultural and natural resources in the region. This study uses content analysis, based on reviews of tourists that have stayed in different hotels in the town, to find out the most frequently mentioned themes. Since experiences that produce satisfaction or dissatisfaction are described differently (Cassar et al., 2020), it is relevant to analyse positive and negative reviews separately. For this purpose, data were downloaded from the Booking.com platform. Therefore, it is useful to know if there are differences between the elements most tourists assess according to higher and lower hotel categories. This study aims to determine the differences between the factors most positively and negatively evaluated by tourists according to higher and lower hotel categories.

2 Hotel Experience and UGC

Following Nguyen and Tong (2022), content based on UGC attracts potential travellers. UGC is rich in content because it allows tourists to respond freely by focusing on the emotions that they have experienced and allows hotels to adapt supply to demand and discover new markets and activities (Bigné et al., 2020). It is a data source that allows for consider in-depth research on the tourism experience and a deeper understanding of tourists' perceptions and feelings (Chiu & Cho, 2020). Through the reviews, tourists describe service attributes in detail to help future customers make decisions (Xu, 2019). Gebbels et al. (2021) highlighted that those who enjoyed their experiences, then, commented in detail and recommended them to others.

Furthermore, UGC can be functional or emotional. Functional reviews are those related to practical information such as price, room design or bed size, while emotional reviews refer to messages based on feelings produced by the service (Cheung et al., 2021). Thus, as a source of information, UGC helps to find positive and negative aspects of the tourism experience and reveal emotions (Yan et al., 2022). Following Sthapit et al. (2021), in the hotel context, negative experiences are mainly those based on negative room conditions, while positive experiences are referred to location, socialisation, and bonding. In the current context of services´ digitisation, hotels that offer interaction with staff are more likely to offer a memorable experience than those with digitised functions (Sthapit, 2017). Xu (2019) founds the role of independent hotels and chain hotels and hotels with different star ratings in influencing positive and negative attributes perceived by customers. Therefore, knowing which attributes are evaluated as functional and emotional according to hotel categories is necessary. Thus, an emotional factor could be the friendly attitude of the hotel staff, which could also contribute to the memorability of the experience (Sthapit, 2017). This paper divides the sampled hotels into two categories: 1 and 2-star and 3 and 4-star, as following Ren et al. (2016) the former is considered in the budget category as they offer fewer services and features and good value for money compared to mid-level, 3 and 4-star hotels. In this sense, guests in higher-category hotels may prefer different service-related issues in contrast to those staying in more affordable categories (Heo & Hyun, 2015).

3 Methodology

The methodological approach is based on two steps. The first step consists of downloading data from the online reviews, and the second step is based on analysing them using NVIVO software. The research setting is the town of Trujillo (Cáceres, Extremadura). It has great historical and monumental heritage and proximity to the "World Heritage Triangle"; Cáceres, Mérida and Guadalupe, which have been declared World Heritage Sites by UNESCO. Trujillo is also located close to important natural resources such as the Monfragüe National Park and the Villuercas-Ibores-Jara Geopark, which makes this destination a privileged enclave for visiting other places of interest in Extremadura (Disfrutando Trujillo, 2022). Trujillo is a booming inland cultural destination that played an important role in the discovery of America. Because of this, it has palaces and historic buildings of great value, some of which were converted into hotels that are present in the sample analysed.

Booking.com platform was selected for downloading the data because it contains more hotel reviews for the selected sample compared to the other major platform, Tripadvisor. One of the advantages of this platform is that guests can give separate

Table 1 Characterisation of
the sample

	1 and 2-star hotels	3 and 4-star hotels
Number of hotels	3	7
Hotel places	128	563
Positive reviews	972	3166
Negative reviews	643	2524

Source Own elaboration

positive and negative reviews of their stay, which allows separate attribute evaluations. The period contained in the review download has been from September 2019
to September 2022 and the language selected for the reviews was Spanish because
it was the language most frequently used in the comments. During this period, there
is a change in the platform; since 2019–2020, Booking.com has kept the reviews for
3 years instead of 2 years (Mellinas & Martín-Fuentes, 2021). Also, the COVID-19
pandemic occurred in the period analysed. The web scraping technique has been used
to collect the data, as it allows large amounts of data to be collected and converted
into structured data for subsequent analysis (Khder, 2021). Subsequently, content
analysis is used because it can identify the main topics guests discuss and the relationships between the most frequently mentioned words (Krippendor, 2004). The sample
consists of 10 hotels in the locality, and as previously mentioned, they have been categorised into two groups: 1 and 2-star and 3 and 4-star. These groupings reveal the
effect of the difference in characteristics and prices. A total of 7305 reviews were
downloaded and categorised into positive (4138) and negative (3167). Those with
no content were removed. For the total sample analysed, 56.65% were positive, and
43.35% were negative reviews. Regarding the first group, 3 hotels were analysed,
with 128 hotel beds, 972 positive and 643 negative reviews. In the second group,
7 hotels were analysed, with 563 hotel beds and 3166 positive and 2524 negative
reviews (Table 1).

4 Results

The results are presented and divided according to the two hotel categories and
according to positive and negative comments. The hierarchical map shows the most
frequently mentioned themes and their relationships for each analysis. The functional
and emotional factors associated with the most prominent themes in each hierarchical
map are analysed. In some cases, examples of reviews are shown to aid understanding.

4.1   1 and 2-Star Hotels

In the hierarchical map (see Fig. 1), three themes stand out positively: location, staff treatment and the characterisation of the hotel. Concerning the functional factors, the location. The central location and, in some cases, the fact that it is located away from the centre to avoid noise are appreciated. The location of the accommodation is assessed with respect to the main attributes of the destination. The treatment of the staff is rated very positively. In terms of the characterisation of the hotel, different elements of the building are mentioned.

Regarding the emotional factors, the location has an added value when the accommodation is in the historic centre, i.e.: *"The stay has been wonderful to be able to stay in a place that transports you to the essence of the sixteenth century, very much in keeping with the rest of the historic centre"*. The reviews mention the names of those staff members who facilitated their stay or what it meant for the whole stay, i.e.: *"The hotel staff was amazing in every aspect and contributed without a doubt to the trip's success"*. About the characterisation of the hotel, it also highlights the hotel sensations, such as "relaxation" and positive value judgements, the "historical" value of the building or elements that surprise and exceed guests' expectations. The "special" category contains reviews of what the guests' stay at the hotel has meant

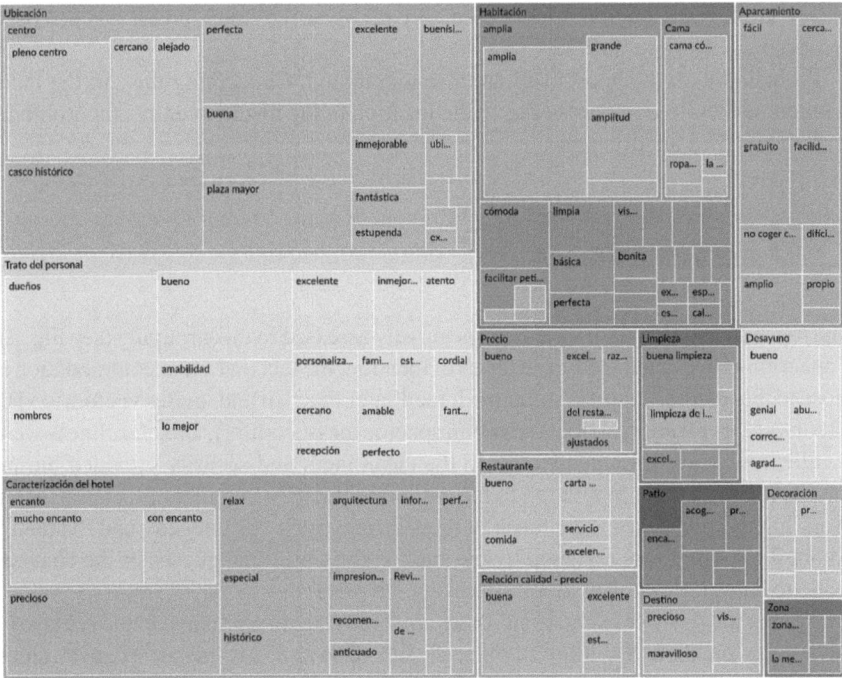

Fig. 1 Hierarchical map of positive comments 1- and 2- stars. *Source* Nvivo 12

to them, demonstrating what is of value to the tourist, i.e.: "*Spending a night in a 16th-century palace in such a comfortable bed, in an unbeatable location for visiting the historic centre and with the kindness and recommendations of [staff name] ...will always remain in our memory*".

The room is also an important element. In addition to its size or comfort, the category "facilitate requests" refers to those that the staff fulfils, such as changing the room if there is a problem. A small section refers to the destination, with positive reviews about the destination and recommendations to other users. When the experience at the destination is satisfactory, tourists link it to the hotel through the reviews.

The main elements that users evaluated negatively were room, bathroom, and bed. Regarding functional factors, the room was rated for its equipment, size, and age. The TV stands out as an element in the room contributing to dissatisfaction. The window is another of the elements mentioned. In the bathroom, different issues are associated with the lack of amenities, the age of the furniture, the lack of cleanliness, or incidents with the water and pressure. As for the bed, whether it is small, hard, or uncomfortable. Concerning the emotional factors of the room, complaints have been made with respect to requesting changes and the staff not acceding to specific requests or characteristics. In the bathroom, expectations regarding the shower and, in some cases, its functions, such as the hydromassage. Regarding the bed, it is worth mentioning the request made by users before their arrival regarding the type of bed they want. Dissatisfaction arises when they arrive at the hotel, and it has not been provided the things requested.

Problems with the hotel itself are also mentioned. Concerning the car, the main problem is the difficult access due to the location in the historic centre and problems with the GPS in historic areas.

4.2   3 and 4-Star Hotels

The location and the room have been positively assessed in this grouping (see Fig. 2). Concerning functional factors, in terms of location, the fact that the accommodation is close to the historic centre is valued as it facilitates the visit and invites visitors to visit it thanks to its location. About the room, spaciousness, comfort, and cleanliness were highlighted. Some comments refer to the cleanliness and security provided during the COVID-19 stage. In relation to the emotional factors, in terms of location, some users highly value their stay through the subcategories "privileged" and "valued". About the room, those assigned by the staff, surprising some guests, or the changes made to superior rooms without increasing the price.

Among the positive evaluations, there are three categories related to the enclave of the hotel, which are "Building", "Palace", and "Convent", as the guests have valued very positively staying in this type of establishment, expressing their satisfaction, i.e.: "*Sleeping under a 16th-century vault is a real pleasure, and touring the palace and its libraries is quite an experience*".

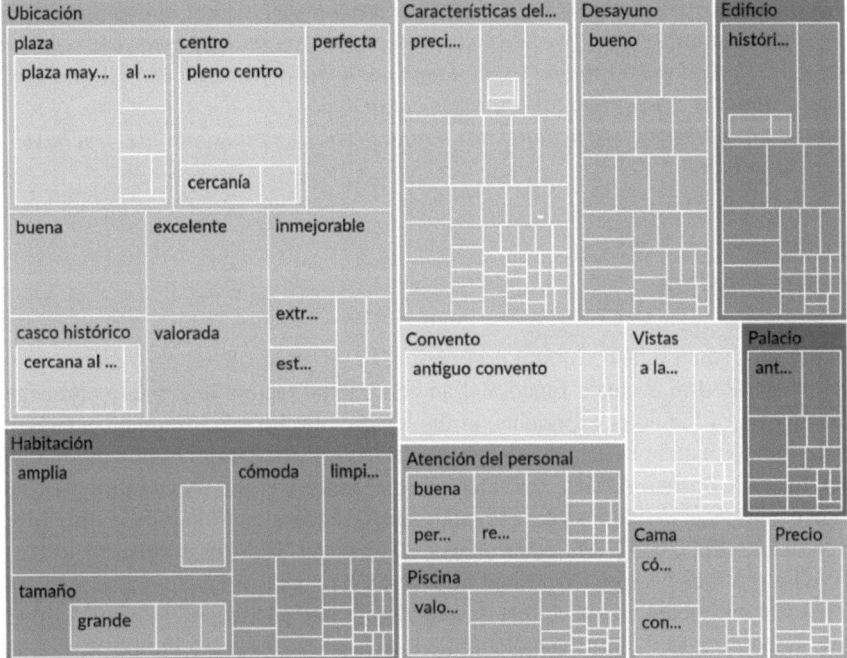

Fig. 2 Hierarchical map of positive comments 3- and 4-stars. *Source* Nvivo 12

The main elements negatively rated in this grouping are the hotel, the room, and the bed. Concerning the functional factors in the hotel, reference is made to its category, comparing it with other similar hotels. General dissatisfaction with the stay is also shown, i.e.: "*From the photos, I expected something better in general, I will not come back*". Also, the lack of maintenance of common areas, the need for renovation, and problems with accessibility lead to negative comments. Regarding the room, complaints about the furniture (if it is old or worn out), lighting, maintenance, cleanliness, location, and the view appeared. With respect to the bed, complaints were found about the hardness of the mattress, pillow, bedding, and discomfort.

In relation to the emotional factors in the hotel, it was mentioned whether the expectations of the guests and complaints regarding the staff were not met, i.e.: "*I am very sorry for [staff name], as their attention has been the only memorable part of my stay, but there are certain limits that should not be crossed*". Attention to detail is valued, as this differentiates these hotel categories according to users. In addition, they made some suggestions such as: "*As it is a hotel in a historic building, it would be great if reception at some time of the day at a specific time offered a short tour of the building commenting on its history and characteristics*". From the room, the incorrect soundproofing, the lack of cleanliness, requests not covered, or problems not solved correctly were highlighted. Regarding the bed, the availability of the type of bed is requested.

It is worth noting that these hotel categories are considered more demanding, as the following examples show: "*We had a cleaning problem in the bathroom, although the reception staff solved it promptly, this should not happen in a hotel of this category*". "*I think there is much room for improvement and many details to take care of for a hotel of this category.*" "*The hotel has a high price, and based on this, you have to demand from it.*"

5 Conclusions

Trujillo is a small inland cultural destination. In this study, hotel customer reviews have been used to evaluate functional and emotional factors in positive and negative aspects of the hotel experience in the locality. In the two groupings analysed, it was found that the most positively rated factor is the location. Following Sthapit and Jiménez-Barreto (2018), this element contributes to the memorability of the hotel experience. Locations near the main tourist attractions benefit the entire travel experience (Xu, 2019). After the analysis, it can be said that tourists who have stayed in both categories have rated both positively and negatively different functional and emotional elements that have added or detracted from the value of their stay. According to the attributes identified by users, to increase the positive hotel experience, the factors that should be considered are the emotional ones. Thus, 1 and 2-star hotels should promote their location, the friendliness of the staff and the general characteristics of the hotel as promotional elements, while 3 and 4-star hotels should promote their location and the characteristics and details of the rooms in their communications. On the contrary, to minimise the negative experience, functional factors should be considered to cover the basic hotel experience. In 1 and 2-star hotels, aspects of the room, bathroom and bed should be considered, while in 3 and 4-star hotels, the focus should be on the characteristics of the hotel or the stay as a whole, emphasising the details that differentiate them from other categories, as well as taking into account elements of the room and the bed. Although the staff's treatment has positive ratings in both groupings, it stands out more in the 1 and 2-star category. Likewise, the staff is one of the reasons for dissatisfaction in the 3 and 4-star categories, while in the 1 and 2-star categories, there is not a high volume of complaints, which could be because guests consider staff treatment as a basic element in higher categories, while in lower categories it is an added value. These results are in line with the study by Ren et al. (2016), which highlights that staff attitude is also an important factor for guests in lower hotel categories. In both categories, there was dissatisfaction with the price paid, although this was higher in the 3 and 4-star categories, which may be because the higher price increases expectations and that customers travelling for leisure on weekends are more price-sensitive (Choi & Mattila, 2004). Also, in both categories, recommendation and revisit intentions have been mentioned, following Bigné et al. (2020), memorable experiences are linked to these positive behavioural intentions. Analysing the categories separately helps hoteliers to better understand what customers assess when staying in their establishments, meeting the tourists' needs, so it could enhance the appropriate implementation of some marketing strategies. As a main conclusion, the emotional value of the hotel experience is not exclusive to the higher categories. The main limitation of this work is that having resorted to grouping into two categories, information details may have been lost. As future lines of research, it is proposed to deepen the analysis of emotional and functional factors of the different hotel attributes and their relevance to overall satisfaction. Segmentation can also be studied according to whether the hotel belongs to a chain or independent hotel.

References

Bigné, E., Fuentes-Medina, M. L., & Morini-Marrero, S. (2020). Memorable tourist experiences versus ordinary tourist experiences analysed through user-generated content. *International Journal of Hospitality Management, 45*, 309–318.

Cassar, M. L., Caruana, A., & Konietzny, J. (2020). Wine and satisfaction with fine dining restaurants: An analysis of tourist experiences from user generated content on TripAdvisor. *Journal of Wine Research, 31*(2), 85–100.

Cheung, M. L., Leung, W. K., Cheah, J. H., & Ting, H. (2021). Exploring the effectiveness of emotional and rational user-generated contents in digital tourism platforms. *Journal of Vacation Marketing, 28*(2), 152–170.

Chiu, W., & Cho, H. (2020). Mapping aboriginal tourism experiences in Taiwan: A case of the Formosan Aboriginal Culture Village. *Journal of Vacation Marketing, 27*, 17–31.

Choi, S., & Mattila, A. S. (2004). Hotel revenue management and its impact on customers' perceptions of fairness. *Journal of Revenue and Pricing Management, 2*, 303–314.

Disfrutando Trujillo. (2022). *Datos para turoperadores*. Retrieved from https://disfrutandotrujillo.com/datos/

Gebbels, M., McIntosh, A., & Harkison, T. (2021). Fine-dining in prisons: Online tripadvisor reviews of the clink training restaurants. *International Journal of Hospitality Management, 95*, 102937.

Heo, C. Y., & Hyun, S. S. (2015). Do luxury room amenities affect guests' willingness to pay? *International Journal of Hospitality Management, 46*, 161–168.

Khder, M. A. (2021). Web scraping or web crawling: State of art, techniques, approaches and application. *International Journal of Advances in Soft Computing & Its Applications, 13*(3), 145–168.

Krippendor, K. (2004). Measuring the reliability of qualitative text analysis data. *Quality and Quantity, 38*, 787–800.

Mariné-Roig, E. (2022). Content analysis of online travel reviews. *Handbook of e-Tourism* (pp. 1–26). Springer International Publishing.

Mellinas, J. P., & Martín-Fuentes, E. (2021). Effects of Booking.com's new scoring system. *Tourism Management, 85*, 104280.

Nguyen, T. T. T., & Tong, S. (2022). The impact of user-generated content on intention to select a travel destination. *Journal of Marketing Analytics*, 1–15.

Ren, L., Qiu, H., Wang, P., & Lin, P. M. C. (2016). Exploring customer experience with budget hotels: Dimensionality and satisfaction. *International Journal of Hospitality Management, 52*, 13–23.

Sánchez-Franco, M. J., Cepeda-Carrion, G., & Roldan, J. L. (2018). Understanding relationship quality in hospitality services: A study based on text analytics and partial least squares. *Internet Research, 29*(3), 478–503.

Sthapit, E. (2017). A netnographic examination of tourists' memorable hotel experiences. *Anatolia, 29*(1), 108–128.

Sthapit, E., Björk, P., Coudounaris, D. N., & Stone, M. J. (2021). A new conceptual framework for memorable Airbnb experiences: Guests' perspectives. *International Journal of Culture, Tourism and Hospitality Research, 16*(1), 75–86.

Sthapit, E., & Jiménez-Barreto, J. (2018). Exploring tourists' memorable hospitality experiences: An Airbnb perspective. *Tourism Management Perspectives, 28*, 83–92.

Xu, X. (2019). Examining the relevance of online customer textual reviews on hotels' product and service attributes. *Journal of Hospitality & Tourism Research, 43*(1), 141–163.

Xu, H., Cheung, L. T., Lovett, J., Duan, X., Pei, Q., & Liang, D. (2021). Understanding the influence of user-generated content on tourist loyalty behavior in a cultural World Heritage Site. *Tourism Recreation Research, 48*(2), 173–187.

Yan, Q., Jiang, T., Zhou, S., & Zhang, X. (2022). Exploring tourist interaction from user-generated content: Topic analysis and content analysis. *Journal of Vacation Marketing*.

Analysis of the Opinions of Users of the Tripadvisor Web Platform on the Cultural Tourism Resources of Málaga

Marco Antonio Soto-Rumiche and **José Luis Caro**

Abstract This study analyses the experiences of visitors to cultural tourism resources in the municipality of Malaga (Spain) through sentiment analysis. The online reviews shared by visitors on TripAdvisor and other platforms are relevant to know the valuation of users, being an influencing factor in decision-making by other users. The aim of this research work is to shed light on the online reputation of the cultural heritage of the city of Málaga through reviews on social networks or TripAdvisor opinion web platforms. The basis of the study were the reviews issued by TripAdvisor users, expressing the satisfaction and emotions experienced in the experiences at the destination, focusing interest on museum exhibitions, and highlighting the architectural spaces that complement the visit. Likewise, our results highlight that the emotions and feelings experienced are mostly positive in visits to heritage monuments, highlighting the historical value and the synergy with green areas as an ideal complement that make up the urban landscape of the city of Malaga. The findings of this study will not only contribute to the existing literature on consumer behaviour towards online reviews but may also provide valuable information for organisations involved in the cultural tourism sector.

Keywords Online reputation · Online reviews · Cultural tourism · Data mining · Museums

M. A. Soto-Rumiche (✉) · J. L. Caro
Universidad de Málaga, Málaga, Spain
e-mail: marco.soto91@uma.es

J. L. Caro
e-mail: jlcaro@uma.es

© The Author(s) 2024
A. J. Guevara Plaza et al. (eds.), *Tourism and ICTs: Advances in Data Science, Artificial Intelligence and Sustainability*, Springer Proceedings in Business and Economics,
https://doi.org/10.1007/978-3-031-52607-7_8

1 Introduction

The impact of online reviews, which are part of electronic word-of-mouth or *eWOM*, through user-generated content (UGC), has significance because of the large-scale accessibility and versatility of content across communities with diverse interests (Verma & Dewani, 2021), serving as indicators of the quality of tourism services (Yang et al., 2018). Such reviews have become an integral part of users' decision-making process towards experiential goods (Chu et al., 2022), which have denoted an influencing factor in consumer behaviour (Cox et al., 2009), generating a bond of trust towards the experiences conveyed on review web platforms.

This research analyses the state of mind of TripAdvisor reviews, referring to the cultural tourist resources that configure the tourist offer of Malaga, which are ideal for the current study, through data mining, as they are unstructured texts. For this purpose, a qualitative analysis is carried out, examining the content, the themes of the reviews, and the feelings expressed by the users. By delving into the qualitative aspects of the reviews, this research aims to provide a deeper understanding of the impact of the reviews on the image of Málaga as a destination.

2 Literature Review and Research Background

2.1 *Cultural Tourism in Málaga*

The tourist destination of the municipality of Málaga, which is primary constructed on the "sun and beach" binomial, is one of the references that has positioned Málaga as one of the relevant points of the tourist offer of the Costa del Sol. However, over the last few decades, Malaga has undergone considerable progress in the cultural sphere, and the revaluation of heritage monuments, whose interventions have placed cultural tourism as the second reason for visits (Costa del Sol Málaga, 2021).

The search for diversification of opportunities in tourism development is accompanied by the initiatives established in the various tourism plans that Málaga has, the latest being the Málaga 2030 Strategic Plan, which shows the commitment to cultural tourism in the last decade, generating the development of other segments such as meetings and congresses (Fundación CIEDES, 2023). The presence of cultural spaces that form part of Malaga's tourist offer has placed it in third place among Spanish cities, corresponding to the cultural offer in 2021, with 53.6%, behind the cities of Madrid, with 88.9% and Barcelona, with 66.3% (Fundación Contemporánea, 2022).

2.2 TripAdvisor, Relevance of Reviews for the Tourism Sector and Sentiment Analysis

TripAdvisor is one of the social networks for travellers, containing more than 1 billion comments and reviews from almost 8 million businesses affiliated with the platform (TripAdvisor, 2021). This platform is considered one of the early adopters of Web 2.0, as its information and advice indexes are simultaneously built from accumulated opinions (Valdivia et al., 2019).

Experiences, transmitted through opinions and reviews shared by users of the TripAdvisor web platform, are part of online reputation, highlighting the connectivity between users without pre-existing associations (Baggio et al., 2008); whose only connections are based on sharing reviews of experiences. These interrelated connections, through online dialogue, are a factor that influences decision-making by other users (Rubio Gil et al., 2017); highlighting the values of credibility in the face of unbiased opinions and, in addition, reliability causing an increase in the prominence of options towards decision-making (Gavilan et al., 2018).

In a report by TripAdvisor, (2022), the users reported recognition of the value of reviews as descriptive and useful, as well as the accuracy of the content across a wide range of travel information. These qualities have granted trust to the qualitative content of the reviews, whose distinctiveness is part of the image of a collaborative digital tool that is useful for tourism (Minkwitz, 2018) and popular among tourism users and researchers (Taecharungroj & Mathayomchan, 2019).

2.3 Social Media Sentiment Analysis

The opinions issued on review web platforms reflect quality on a certain scale, being sufficient to capture sentiment (TripAdvisor, 2021); they are complemented by the sentiment of trust through indicators that provide veracity in the comments, ranging from personal information to actual images, locations, and dates of access to the website (Lee et al., 2018).Through qualitative interpretation, based on text mining or sentiment analysis, they can be developed into two types of studies: the word-level study, in which the analysis relies on the detection of keywords and lexical affinity (Poria et al., 2012), and the concept-level study, which considers the expressions coming from different words (Qazi et al., 2016).

Currently, there are several proposals in the current study and analysis of sentiment that cover the qualitative aspect, ranging from the search for keywords to verifying correlations between terms that can generate terminological guidelines (Delvizio, 2018). The aim of the conducted studies on sentiment analysis is to determine the emotions and personality of the wording on specific topics (Ray et al., 2021). Obtaining results through sentiment analysis has been useful in the formulation of various recommendations and predictions, such as the proposal made by Hu et al.

(2017) formulating a multi-text summarisation technique to identify the most reiterative phrases in hotel reviews. Likewise, the results obtained can be oriented towards the determination of predictions, through the usefulness of the opinions and resorting to the classification technique (Lee et al., 2018). However, the authors Farhadloo et al. (2016) determine that one of the challenges in the qualitative study of reviews lies in understanding the aspects and determining a relationship between the feelings associated with the aspects found or the state of mind of tourists (Li et al., 2018).

3 Data and Methods

This study has considered the reviews transmitted on the TripAdvisor web platform, popularly accepted by tourists and managers (Valdivia al., 2017); and whose information has significant effects on decision-making by other users (Seok et al., 2020). For this purpose, online reviews have been analysed in Spanish using the phrase "cultural tourism in Málaga" on *TripAdvisor.es* to understand the perception of users towards the cultural tourism resources that form part of the tourism offer of the municipality of Málaga, from 2017 to 2022, compiling a total of 18.227 reviews. In terms of user ratings, 83% were positive (excellent and very good); 11% corresponded to neutral opinions (normal) and 3% to negative ratings (bad and very bad), demonstrating the high level of acceptance and satisfaction in the users' experiences.

For the treatment of the extracted texts in a crude manner, far from any formal structure, the data structuring has been employed, as proposed by the authors Farhadloo et al. (2016), intending to obtain semi-structured data, following the interest of the analysis of the sentiments of the reviews on TripAdvisor.

The first step was to analyse the TripAdvisor ratings quantitatively, segmenting them into positive (excellent and very good), neutral (normal), and negative (bad and very bad) ratings according to the categories of the cultural tourism resources, as shown in Table 1. The findings show that most of the users' opinions are positive, which indicates a high level of satisfaction in visiting these cultural resources.

Demonstration through visualisation of sentiment analysis data from reviews, as an important part of the analysis of the macro data, as observed by Cheng and Jin (2019), has been implemented through the *KH Coder* software, a programme that enables qualitative content analysis or text mining, employed in this research, responding correctly to tourism-related texts (Povilanskas et al., 2016; Jurkus et al., 2022).

4 Results

Based on word frequency analysis using the *KH Coder* software, as shown in Table 2, seeds of sentiments are visible, which are the nouns that place us in the positive or negative context of the image of cultural tourism resources. The positive terms with

Table 1 Percentage evaluation of the reviews according to the categories of cultural tourism resources in the municipality of Malaga

Categories	Positive (%)	Neutral (%)	Negative (%)
Wineries and vineyards	90.1	6.1	3.8
Castles	86.1	11.4	2,6
Civic centres	97.7	0.0	2.3
Churches and cathedrals	88.4	9.1	2.5
Architectural interest	79.5	13.7	6.8
Gardens	85.7	9.1	5.2
Art museums	78.9	15.4	5.8
History museums	91.2	7.7	1.1
Specialised museums	91.3	5.7	2.9
Landmarks and points of interest	81.6	15.2	3.2
Archaeological sites	79.7	18.8	1.5
Theatres and performances	89.1	5.8	5.1

Source Own elaboration based on the results of this research, 2023

the highest number of frequencies are the following: *good* (1063), *interesting* (934), *nice* (859), *best* (566), *great* (548) and *recommended* (542); which convey positive and favourable feelings about the image of the resources analysed. In addition, these expressions reflect the level of satisfaction of visitors to the cultural spaces, with the comments being overwhelmingly positive, emphasising the positive feeling towards the museum spaces in a more proportional manner.

However, terms also have been detected that attribute a negative sentiment status with less than 200 recurrences, referring to the terms *full* (147) and *expensive* (126); in direct relation to the categories of wineries and vineyards and churches and cathedrals. Another group of comments expressed the following terms in relation to the rest of the cultural tourism resources, such as *bad* (122), *incomplete* (29), *poor* (27) and, finally, the term *scarce* (26).

In Fig. 1, the co-occurrence network graph of the reviews is presented, emphasising the semantic aspect and the high degrees between the terms. The result, using the limit of 120 co-occurrences, has shown a relationship between 57 words (N), with a density of 0.075. Based on the co-occurrence study, 7 subgraphs could be detected, the first one being museums, linking the expressions *interesting, *great, *good, *art. Likewise, the terms *car, *collection, *building and *old, are associated with the Automobile and Fashion Museum, as it is one of the spaces with a high index of positive valuation and favourable reviews, giving favourable recognition to the permanent collection it hosts and the architectural value of the space, in relation to the old building of the Royal Tobacco Factory or locally known as "la tabacalera".

The second sub-graph corresponds to the image of historical monuments, which have been related to the feelings of *recommendable, *worthwhile, *best, *precious, *impressive; highlighting the places of Gibralfaro and Alcazaba, obtaining a higher

Table 2 The most common words for cultural tourism resources in the municipality of Malaga, found in TripAdvisor reviews

Positive	Frequency	Positive	Frequency	Negative	Frequency
Good	1063	Malagueño	221	Full	147
Interesting	934	Wonderful	202	Expensive	126
Nice	859	Incredible	173	Bad	122
Best	566	Great	167	Incomplete	29
Great	548	Unique	162	Poor	27
Recommended	542	Magnificent	161	Scarce	26
Beautiful	438	Pretty	157	Worse	23
Impressive	343	Important	156	Unpleasant	22
Old	332	Permanent	148	Dirty	21
Spectacular	310	Curious	147	Indifferent	14
Excellent	302	Cultural	136	Horrible	10
Pleasant	300	Different	131	Uncomfortable	9
Essential	274	Wide	123	Rare	9
Free	271	Greater	117	Nefarious	8
Large	260	Complete	116	Dark	8
Roman	250	Lovely	115	Terrible	8
Temporary	237	Friendly	101	Terrifying	8
Historical	223	Original	101	Embarrassing	8

Source Own elaboration based on the results of this research, 2023

degree of correlation coefficient with the terms *spectacular and *views. The terms theatre and Roman, appear as another sub-graph; however, they have a strong link of co-occurrence with the historical monuments, which is why they have been included in this segment.

Subsequently, the third sub-graph corresponds to the state of feelings of the most emblematic resources that compose the spaces of the historic centre, having a direct co-occurrence with the terms *historic, *street, *plaza; in addition, the Cathedral is related to the terms *palace and *nice. The term Picasso has a high rate of co-occurrence with *nice, which alludes to the Picasso Museum in Málaga, followed by the expressions *house and *square in relation to the geographical location of the Málaga artist's house-museum.

The fourth sub-graph corresponds to visits to monuments, where the term *entrance ticket* is highly correlated with the terms *opinion, *free, *Sunday, *time and *price. Such expressions demonstrate an interest in the time slot of free visits to museums and historical monuments.

The fifth sub-graph is related to the favourable comments on the satisfaction of visiting cultural tourism resources with the expressions of *staff, *rooms and *children. It is worth specifying the didactic factor of these resources in relation to

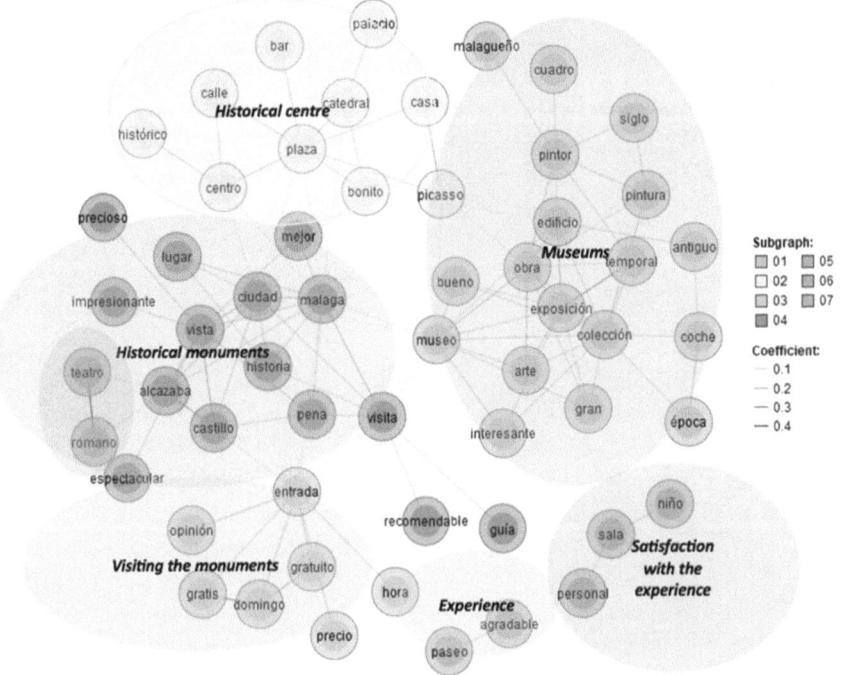

Fig. 1 Network of co-occurrences of reviews issued on TripAdvisor

the experience of children. Lastly, there are the terms *walk and *pleasant, which demonstrate the high rate of satisfaction on the part of the users.

Finally, a correspondence analysis was carried out, as shown in Fig. 2, to visualise the relationships between the dimensions of the reviews, through the experiences towards the cultural tourism resources of the municipality of Málaga, where the expressions that accompany the experience of museums, are characterised by *exhibition, *interesting, *great. As far as historical monuments are concerned, we can see that Alcazaba, the Roman theatre, the Castle and Gardens of Gibralfaro are related to the experiences of *views and *wonderful, *spectacular and *walking; in addition, there is a valuation in the correspondence between the terms of the city with the expression of *impressive.

Likewise, about the historic centre, experiences are characterised by the terms *precious and *beautiful; and churches and cathedrals, together with the expressions *essential and *impressive. In reference to the words emitted towards the museum spaces in Málaga, they are: *art, *great, *collection, *work, *interesting, *great, *painter.

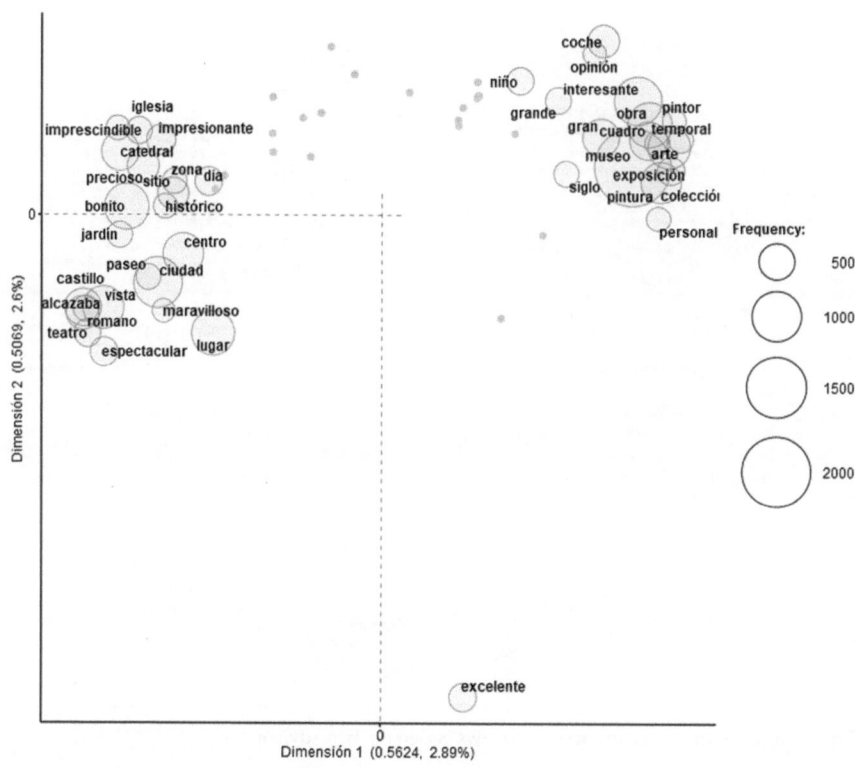

Fig. 2 Correspondence analysis between the experiences and the cultural tourism resources of the municipality of Málaga

5 Conclusions

The study and sentiment analysis of the reviews transmitted on TripAdvisor towards the cultural tourism resources that form part of the tourism offer in the municipality of Málaga, based on a qualitative study, have shown the high approval and high level of satisfaction of visitors, whose reviews demonstrate that users tend to evaluate the experiences globally, confirming the conclusion of Valdivia et al. (2019).

The opinions reflected the interest in the monumental heritage assets distributed throughout the city of Málaga, expressing admiration and appreciation for the symbolic connection (historical), demonstrating the visitor's empathy towards the cultural heritage, and, in addition, appreciation for the state of conservation of these monuments. The reviews issued towards the museums recognise the variety of the collections they host, both permanent and itinerant, highlighting the works of local artists (such is the case of the Museum of Málaga and the Picasso Museum), adding the textual emphasis of "good and interesting exhibitions". Likewise, there is a group of visitors who emphasise the architectural value of the museums as an added value of the tourist resource, as is the case of the Automobile and Fashion Museum, recognising good practices in the conservation of an industrial monument for museum purposes. Similarly, the comments show a high rate of appreciation for the environmental component (gardens), in complementarity with the monumental cultural heritage, reflecting a positive assessment of destinations committed to sustainability, through the protection of green areas. This conclusion ratifies the research of authors Nowacki and Niezgoda (2023); on visitors' interest in nature, possibilities of contemplation and connection with the environment, and intangible values concerning nature tourism (Teles da Mota & Pickering, 2020).

There is also an emphasis on enquiries about the economic value of tickets for cultural tourism resources, confirming the research carried out by TripAdvisor (2021), which stipulates that 44% of visitors resort to the description of places and 36% to enquiries about the cost of tickets, as elements prior to trip planning, with the aim of making a more precise budget.

Another point to highlight is the recognition of the pedagogical factor in the management of cultural tourism monuments, which continue to disseminate content in a didactic manner for a diverse public, with appropriate information and, in the case of museums, with recreational activities for the attention of the younger public.

Overall, online reviews on TripAdvisor and other opinion platforms are relevant for a better understanding of the language of reviews and are indispensable for the tourism sector, as stated by authors Bridges and Vasquez (2018). Online reviews not only have an impact on the decision-making of other tourists but also influence how the entities in charge manage their offers. Similarly, reviews can provide insights into initiatives to promote authentic and enriching experiences, with the aim of preserving cultural heritage and encouraging sustainable practices.

The current study reveals several research topics. Firstly, comparative studies using machine learning. Secondly, using variables such as descriptions, the responsibility of the resource management bodies towards users and the sustainability of resources, with special attention to the divergences that exist between the information considered relevant by users and that prioritised by the TripAdvisor web platform. In addition, linguistic and semantic analyses of the use of different languages in tourism social networks.

References

Baggio, R., Costa, C., Miguéns, J., & Costa, C. (2008). Social media and tourism destinations: TripAdvisor case study. *Advances in Tourism Research*, 1–6.

Bridges, J., & Vásquez, C. (2018). If nearly all Airbnb reviews are positive, does that make them meaningless? *Current Issues in Tourism, 21*(18), 2065–2083. https://doi.org/10.1080/13683500. 2016.1267113

Cheng, M., & Jin, X. (2019). What do Airbnb users care about? An analysis of online review comments. *International Journal of Hospitality Management, 76*, 58–70. https://doi.org/10. 1016/j.ijhm.2018.04.004

Chu, M., Chen, Y., Yang, L., & Wang, J. (2022). Language interpretation in travel guidance platform: Text mining and sentiment analysis of TripAdvisor reviews. *Frontiers in Psychology, 13*, 1029945. https://doi.org/10.3389/fpsyg.2022.1029945

Costa del Sol Málaga. (2021). Observatorio Turístico de la Costa del Sol—2021. Retrieved from https://www.costadelsolmalaga.org/base/descargas/377961/observatorio-turistico-2021

Cox, C., Burgess, S., Sellitto, C., & Buultjens, J. (2009). The role of user-generated content in tourists' travel planning behavior. *Journal of Hospitality and Leisure Marketing, 18*(8), 743–764. https://doi.org/10.1080/19368620903235753

Delvizio, I. A. (2018). Directrices para la elaboración de definiciones terminológicas: una aplicación a los términos del turismo An application to terms of tourism. *Revista Digital Internacional de Lexicología, Lexicografía y Terminología, 1*(1).

Farhadloo, M., Patterson, R. A., & Rolland, E. (2016). Modeling customer satisfaction from unstructured data using a Bayesian approach. *Decision Support Systems, 90*, 1–11. https://doi.org/10.1016/j.dss.2016.06.010

Fundación CIEDES. (2023). Plan estratégico Málaga 2030. Fundación CIEDES. Retrieved from https://ciedes.es/images/Plan2030/Plan_Estrategico_Malaga_2030.pdf

Fundación Contemporánea. (2022). Observatorio de la cultura: Lo mejor de la cultura 2021. Retrieved from https://www.lafabrica.com/observatorio-de-la-cultura/

Gavilan, D., Avello, M., & Martinez-Navarro, G. (2018). The influence of online ratings and reviews on hotel booking consideration. *Tourism Management, 66*, 53–61. https://doi.org/10.1016/j.tourman.2017.10.018

Hu, Y. H., Chen, Y. L., & Chou, H. L. (2017). Opinion mining from online hotel reviews—A text summarization approach. *Information Processing and Management, 53*(2), 436–449. https://doi.org/10.1016/j.ipm.2016.12.002

Jurkus, E., Povilanskas, R., & Taminskas, J. (2022). Current trends and issues in research on biodiversity conservation and tourism sustainability. *Sustainability, 14*(6), 3342. https://doi.org/10.3390/su14063342

Lee, P. J., Hu, Y. H., & Lu, K. T. (2018). Assessing the helpfulness of online hotel reviews: A classification-based approach. *Telematics and Informatics, 35*(2), 436–445. https://doi.org/10.1016/j.tele.2018.01.001

Li, J., Xu, L., Tang, L., Wang, S., & Li, L. (2018). Big data in tourism research: A literature review. *Tourism Management, 68*, 301–323. https://doi.org/10.1016/j.tourman.2018.03.009

Minkwitz, A. (2018). TripAdvisor as a source of data in the planning process of tourism development on a local scale. *Turyzm/Tourism, 28*(2), 49–55. https://doi.org/10.2478/tour-2018-0014

Nowacki, M., & Niezgoda, A. (2023). What experiences do tourists seek in national parks? Analysis of Tripadvisor reviews. *Economics and Environment, 84*(1), 341–359. https://doi.org/10.34659/eis.2023.84.1.538

Poria, S., Gelbukh, A., Cambria, E., Yang, P., Hussain, A., & Durrani, T. (2012). Merging SenticNet and WordNet-Affect emotion lists for sentiment analysis. In *ICSP 2012 - 2012 11th International Conference on Signal Processing, Proceedings* (Vol. 2, pp. 1251–1255). https://doi.org/10.1109/ICoSP.2012.6491803

Povilanskas, R., Armaitiene, A., Dyack, B., & Jurkus, E. (2016). Islands of prescription and islands of negotiation. *Journal of Destination Marketing and Management, 5*(3), 260–274. https://doi.org/10.1016/j.jdmm.2016.01.004

Qazi, A., Shah Syed, K. B., Raj, R. G., Cambria, E., Tahir, M., & Alghazzawi, D. (2016). A concept-level approach to the analysis of online review helpfulness. *Computers in Human Behavior, 58*, 75–81. https://doi.org/10.1016/j.chb.2015.12.028

Ray, B., Garain, A., & Sarkar, R. (2021). An ensemble-based hotel recommender system using sentiment analysis and aspect categorization of hotel reviews. *Applied Soft Computing, 98*. https://doi.org/10.1016/j.asoc.2020.106935

Rubio Gil, Á., Jiménez Barandalla, I. C., & Mercado Idoeta, C. (2017). Reputación corporativa online en la hotelería: el caso TripAdvisor. *ESIC Market, 48*(158), 595–608. https://doi.org/10.7200/esicm.158.0483.4e

Seok, H., Joo, Y., & Nam, Y. (2020). An analysis of the sustainable tourism value of graffiti tours through social media: Focusing on TripAdvisor reviews of graffiti tours in Bogota, Colombia. *Sustainability, 12*(11). https://doi.org/10.3390/su12114426

Taecharungroj, V., & Mathayomchan, B. (2019). Analysing TripAdvisor reviews of tourist attractions in Phuket, Thailand. *Tourism Management, 75*, 550–568. https://doi.org/10.1016/j.tourman.2019.06.020

Teles da Mota, V., & Pickering, C. (2020). Using social media to assess nature-based tourism: Current research and future trends. *Journal of Outdoor Recreation and Tourism, 30*. https://doi.org/10.1016/j.jort.2020.100295

TripAdvisor. (2021). The power of reviews how TripAdvisor reviews lead to bookings and better travel experiences. Retrieved from https://www.tripadvisor.com/powerofreviews.pdf

TripAdvisor. (2022). Travel in 2022. A look head. IPSOS Mori. Retrieved from https://www.TripAdvisor.com/TravelTrendsReportJan2022

Valdivia, A., Hrabova, E., Chaturvedi, I., Luzón, M. V., Troiano, L., Cambria, E., & Herrera, F. (2019). Inconsistencies on TripAdvisor reviews: A unified index between users and sentiment analysis methods. *Neurocomputing, 353*, 3–16. https://doi.org/10.1016/j.neucom.2018.09.096

Valdivia, A., Luzón, M. V., & Herrera, F. (2017). Sentiment analysis in TripAdvisor. *IEEE Intelligent Systems, 32*(4), 72–77. https://doi.org/10.1109/MIS.2017.3121555

Verma, D., & Dewani, P. P. (2021). EWOM credibility: A comprehensive framework and literature review. *Online Information Review, 45*(3), 481–500. https://doi.org/10.1108/OIR-06-2020-0263

Yang, Y., Park, S., & Hu, X. (2018). Electronic word of mouth and hotel performance: A meta-analysis. *Tourism Management, 67*, 248–260. https://doi.org/10.1016/j.tourman.2018.01.015

Rise and Fall of TripAdvisor: The Lack of Participation and Its Causes

José Luis Ximénez de Sandoval◉

Abstract TripAdvisor's remarkable growth since its launch is undeniable, with over 859 million reviews covering 8.6 million businesses by 2023. However, recent years have seen a noticeable stagnation, if not a decline, raising pertinent questions from both a business and academic perspective about its future as a key player in the tourism industry. Our research, launched in 2016, tracks monthly reviews of restaurants and hotels on TripAdvisor and Booking. It covers global destinations. It focuses on four well-known tourist hubs - Madrid, London, Paris and Rome - and covers the period from 2016 to 2022. The results show an initial phase (2017–2019) with a decrease in the annual growth rate of reviews in all destinations. The subsequent phase (2020–2021), influenced by pandemic-induced inactivity, showed minimal annual variation. The third phase shows a slight recovery, but no destination has exceeded a year-on-year variation of 4%. To counter this downward trend, TripAdvisor needs to implement innovative strategies and adapt its business model and user interaction processes. Such proactive measures are essential to overcome current challenges, ensure its relevance and maintain a pivotal role in the evolving tourism industry.

Keywords TripAdvisor · Rankings · Hotels · Reviews

1 Introduction

TripAdvisor has revolutionized the travel and tourism industry by becoming the largest online travel guide platform in just a few years (Filieri et al., 2021). For hotels, TripAdvisor serves as a benchmark for their online presence (Xie et al., 2014), and hotel revenues are influenced by reviews on aspects such as staff or facilities (Nieto-García et al., 2019). Furthermore, tourism experiences shared online have a significant impact on the decisions of other travellers (Stoleriu et al., 2019).

J. L. X. de Sandoval (✉)
University of Málaga, Málaga, Spain
e-mail: joseluis.xs@uma.es

© The Author(s) 2024
A. J. Guevara Plaza et al. (eds.), *Tourism and ICTs: Advances in Data Science, Artificial Intelligence and Sustainability*, Springer Proceedings in Business and Economics, https://doi.org/10.1007/978-3-031-52607-7_9

93

Reading user reviews before making a purchase has become a habit for many consumers (Filieri et al., 2021), making e-WOM a crucial source of information for decision-making in the tourism sector (Reyes-Menéndez et al., 2019).

TripAdvisor's growth since its launch in 1999 has been remarkable. In 2006, just six years after it was founded, it already had over 5 million reviews for 220,000 hotels and attractions. By 2013, they surpassed 100 million reviews for 2.5 million businesses. By 2023, they will have more than 859 million reviews for over 8.6 million businesses.

However, in recent years, there has been a noticeable stagnation or even decline in its development as an industry leader. TripAdvisor's average monthly unique users have been declining in recent years (Dedeoğlu et al., 2020).

Following Filieri et al. (2021), we consider it relevant to analyse the evolution of this influential platform in recent years from both a business and academic perspective and to determine whether it will continue to be a prominent player in the tourism industry in the future.

2 Background: The Success Model of TripAdvisor

TripAdvisor's great success is based on its ability to develop two production processes that, when combined, create synergies that generate significant added value that is recognized by tourists.

Firstly, it has the ability to capture a large number of user comments and opinions that are useful to those looking for a hotel or restaurant. Second, it uses these opinions to rank the set of hotels and restaurants in a destination, creating a ranking that helps users make decisions in an information-saturated world.

This powerful combination of processes (capture and classification) feeds off each other. The ability to generate reviews and opinions is the result of a mechanism we call the TripAdvisor virtuous circle, where the three players (hotel, customer and TripAdvisor) benefit from each other as long as they all work together. (Illustration 1).

Illustration 1 The Virtuous Circle of TripAdvisor.
Sources All diagrams, graphs and tables were prepared by the author

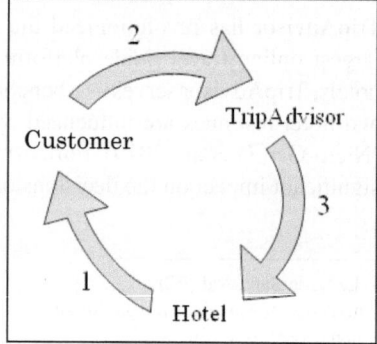

> ## About Tripadvisor
>
> Tripadvisor, the world's largest travel guidance platform*, helps hundreds of millions of people each month** become better travelers, from planning to booking to taking a trip. Travelers across the globe use the Tripadvisor site and app to discover where to stay, what to do and where to eat based on guidance from those who have been there before. With more than 1 billion reviews and opinions of nearly 8 million businesses, travelers turn to Tripadvisor to find deals on accommodations, book experiences, reserve tables at delicious restaurants and discover great places nearby. As a travel guidance company available in 43 markets and 22 languages, Tripadvisor makes planning easy no matter the trip type. The subsidiaries of Tripadvisor, Inc. (Nasdaq: TRIP), own and operate a portfolio of travel media brands and businesses, operating under various websites and apps, including the following:
>
> www.bokun.io, www.cruisecritic.com, www.flipkey.com, www.thefork.com, www.helloreco.com, www.holidaylettings.co.uk, www.jetsetter.com, www.niumba.com, www.seatguru.com, www.singleplatform.com, www.vacationhomerentals.com, www.viator.com.
>
> * Source: SimilarWeb, unique users de-duplicated monthly, September 2023
>
> ** Source: Tripadvisor internal log files

Illustration 2 TripAdvisor and the importance of volume. *Source* https://tripadvisor.mediaroom. com/US-about-us (oct-2023)

TripAdvisor has achieved these impressive figures thanks to the invaluable cooperation of establishments (hotels and restaurants) who have promoted the platform free of charge.

Ensuring that this virtuous circle continues is TripAdvisor's main goal, as can be seen in Illustration 2, which states that TripAdvisor is "the world's largest travel guidance platform".

Much of their promotional communication is based on the volume of information available, i.e., the quantity of comments, rather than their quality.

The main objective of this study is to test whether this virtuous circle continues after the pandemic. In order to do this, we want to answer the following question Do users still trust TripAdvisor to publish their comments, opinions and reviews?

3 Methodology

Since 2016, we have been tracking the number of comments and ratings for restaurants and hotels published on both TripAdvisor and Booking in destinations around the world on a monthly basis. All this information (business name, address, number of reviews, overall average rating, etc.) has been stored in a database.

For this study, we analyzed the evolution of the number of comments published on TripAdvisor between 2016 and 2022 in four internationally renowned tourist destinations: Madrid, London, Paris and Rome. By collecting information on all hotels listed on TripAdvisor in these four cities, there was no need for sampling.

4 Results

Table 1 shows the total number of hotel establishments (with at least one review) in the four selected cities.

Table 2 shows the total number of comments at the end of the year in hotels in the four selected cities.

Based on the total number of reviews, and in order to determine the evolution of user participation through their comments, Table 3 was obtained, which shows the annual variation in the number of reviews.

Finally, the number of reviews received by hotels (on average) by year is shown in Table 4.

Table 1 Number of hotels (with reviews)

	Madrid	London	Paris	Rome
2016	425	1.047	1.774	1.208
2017	420	1.054	1.764	1.193
2018	430	1.065	1.784	1.205
2019	441	1.087	1.799	1.221
2020	442	1.102	1.799	1.232
2021	449	1.127	1.818	1.247
2022	458	1.132	1.824	1.260

Table 2 Total number of comments in hotels

	Madrid	London	Paris	Rome
2016	227.769	915.678	682.303	483.817
2017	287.334	1.134.717	797.389	560.301
2018	333.462	1.275.741	901.947	627.077
2019	370.736	1.368.103	996.253	673.447
2020	374.512	1.403.711	1.009.621	683.820
2021	377.680	1.405.631	1.014.081	682.643
2022	391.882	1.448.464	1.049.600	686.343

Table 3 Variation (%) in the number of comments

%	Madrid	London	Paris	Rome
2017	26,15	23,92	16,87	15,81
2018	16,05	12,43	13,11	11,92
2019	11,18	7,24	10,46	7,39
2020	1,02	2,60	1,34	1,54
2021	0,85	0,14	0,44	−0,17
2022	3,76	3,05	3,50	0,54

Table 4 New comments per hotel (average)

	Madrid	London	Paris	Rome
2017	142	208	65	64
2018	107	132	59	55
2019	85	85	52	38
2020	9	32	7	8
2021	7	2	2	−1
2022	31	38	19	3

5 Discussion

If we analyze the data from Table 1 on a graph, we can see that the evolution of the four destinations is very similar over the period analyzed (Fig. 3).

A first phase (2017–2019) is characterised by a significant decrease in the annual growth of the number of comments for all destinations.

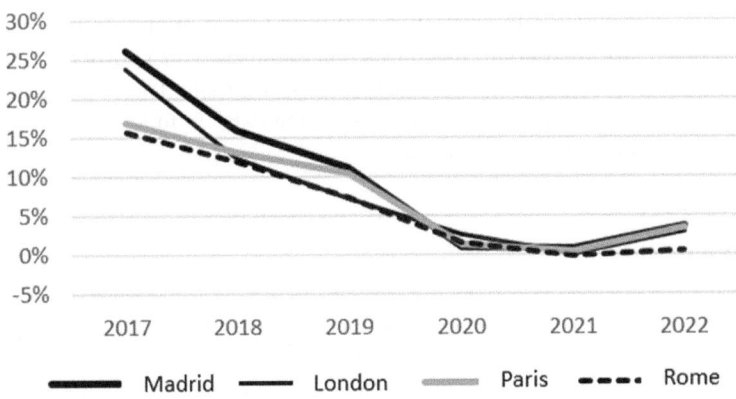

Fig. 3 Annual variation (%) in the total number of comments

A second phase (2020–2021) shows an annual variation close to zero for all destinations, due to the lack of activity caused by the pandemic.

A third phase shows a slight recovery in the activity of users posting comments, but it does not exceed 4% per year in any destination.

Finally, looking at the number of new comments per hotel, it can be seen that in Madrid and London, hotels received an average of 31 and 38 comments respectively in 2022, which corresponds to around 3 new comments per month.

In Paris, the figures are lower (19 comments over the year). Finally, the negative annual variation in Rome's data is due to the closure of some hotels with a high number of comments.

6 Causes of the Decline in the Number of Reviews

Encouraging customers to share their reviews has been identified as a major challenge for review sites for several years (Bishop, 2007). Johnson et al. (2012) suggested that in the absence of motivations to share opinions, tourists may receive some form of micropayment or other remuneration for their contributions in the not-too-distant future.

The issue of declining user participation that these authors anticipated is now a reality on TripAdvisor. The causes of this declining engagement can be found in the academic literature:

1. Competition from Google: Gaining a significant number of comments, especially through mobile devices (Singh, 2019).
2. Loss of credibility: TripAdvisor has experienced a loss of credibility due to controversies in the media about fake reviews (Filieri, 2016).
3. The "gift economy" (Kollok, 1999): This concept refers to a situation where individuals contribute without expecting an immediate return. However, for this altruistic collaboration to occur, five motivational conditions are necessary: (i) reciprocity, (ii) appropriate incentives, (iii) efficacy, (iv) knowledge of other users' needs, and (v) a sense of belonging to a group. The absence of these five motivations would explain the low or non-existent motivation of users to post new comments on TripAdvisor.

7 Conclusion

The success of TripAdvisor in attracting tourists and customers to share their opinions has been undeniable.

However, the credit for the large number of comments is equally distributed among TripAdvisor, hotels, and tourists. We have termed this process of generating comments and opinions the "Virtuous Circle of TripAdvisor," where the three protagonists (hotel, customer, and TripAdvisor) benefit when all cooperate: (i) the hotel cooperates with TripAdvisor by encouraging customers to write comments, (ii) the customer cooperates with TripAdvisor by writing a comment on its platform, and (iii) TripAdvisor cooperates with the hotel by improving its position in the ranking, provided the comments are positive, current, and numerous.

This paper has provided evidence of the quasi-paralysis of this process of generating new comments.

The reasons for this growing disinterest of users in sharing their opinions on TripAdvisor can be explained by the following factors: (1) Competition from another technological giant like Google, (2) the reputational deterioration of TripAdvisor due to numerous cases of fraudulent reviews in the media and social networks, and (3) the lack of incentives, efficacy, and reciprocity.

To reverse this clear declining trend in the acquisition of opinions and ratings, TripAdvisor will have to react by developing new strategies involving profound changes in its business model and interaction process with users.

Only then can it survive current threats and challenges and continue to be a key player in the tourism industry.

References

Bishop, J. (2007). Increasing participation in online communities: A framework for human–computer interaction. *Computers in Human Behavior, 23*(4), 1881–1893.

Dedeoğlu, B. B., Taheri, B., Okumus, F., & Gannon, M. (2020). Understanding the importance that consumers attach to social media sharing (ISMS): Scale development and validation. *Tourism Management, 76*, 103954.

Filieri, R., Acikgoz, F., Ndou, V., & Dwivedi, Y. (2021). Is TripAdvisor still relevant? The influence of review credibility, review usefulness, and ease of use on consumers' continuance intention. *International Journal of Contemporary Hospitality Management, 33*(1), 199–223.

Filieri, R. (2016). What makes an online consumer review trustworthy? *Annals of Tourism Research, 58*, 46–64.

Singh, V. (2019). How google reviews is crushing TripAdvisor. Hospitalitynet, 10 Mayo 2023. Disponible en https://www.hospitalitynet.org/opinion/4092845.html.

Johnson, P., Sieber, R., & Magnien, N. (2012). Automated web harvesting to collect and analyse user-generated content for tourism. *Current Issues in Tourism, 15*(3), 293–299.

Kollock, P. (1999). The economies ol online cooperation.*Communities in Cyberspace, 220.*

Nieto-Garcia, M., Resce, G., Ishizaka, A., Occhiocupo, N., & Viglia, G. (2019). The dimensions of hotel customer ratings that boost RevPAR. *International Journal of Hospitality Management, 77*, 583–592.

Reyes-Menendez, A., Saura, J. R., & Martinez-Navalon, J. G. (2019). The impact of e-WOM on hotels management reputation: Exploring tripadvisor review credibility with the ELM model. *Ieee Access, 7*, 68868–68877.

Stoleriu, O. M., Brochado, A., Rusu, A., & Lupu, C. (2019). Analyses of visitors' experiences in a natural world heritage site based on TripAdvisor reviews. *Visitor Studies, 22*(2), 192–212.

Xie, K. L., Zhang, Z., & Zhang, Z. (2014). The business value of online consumer reviews and management response to hotel performance. *International Journal of Hospitality Management, 43*, 1–12.

Artificial Intelligence and Tourism

Data Platform for a Data-Driven Tourism Organization. A Conceptual Architecture

Juan Vidal-Gil⊙, Ramón Alberto Carrasco-González⊙, and María Francisca Blasco-López⊙

Abstract The tourism sector is one of the sectors that has undergone most changes in recent years due to digital transformation. One of the pillars of this transformation is the management of organizations based on data-driven decision making. The raw material for these data-driven strategies is, of course, the sources of information used, which have changed and grown significantly in recent years. This article attempts to provide a conceptual architecture for a modern data platform that effectively manages and analyses these information sources and facilitates data-driven decision-making in tourism organizations.

Keywords Tourism destinations · Smart destinations · Data-driven organizations · Tourism digitalization · Tourism data-platform

1 Introduction

Data-driven decision making is an area of crucial importance in the digital transformation in which many organizations are immersed. These decision-making methodologies allow organizations to be truly market-oriented, enabling them to focus on customers in order to build customer loyalty in a more cost-effective way (Moreno et al., 2019). Of course, the tourism sector is no exception to this situation and is undergoing a major transformation in which this type of management will be predominant (Camilleri, 2020).

The raw material for these data-driven strategies is data and its correct management, storage and use within an organization is crucial. The aim of this study is to propose a conceptual architecture for a data platform for an organization in the

J. Vidal-Gil (✉) · M. F. Blasco-López
Facultad de Comercio y Turismo, Universidad Complutense de Madrid, Madrid, Spain
e-mail: juavid01@ucm.es

R. A. Carrasco-González
Facultad de Estudios Estadísticos. Departamento de Marketing, Universidad Complutense de Madrid, Madrid, España

© The Author(s) 2024
A. J. Guevara Plaza et al. (eds.), *Tourism and ICTs: Advances in Data Science, Artificial Intelligence and Sustainability*, Springer Proceedings in Business and Economics, https://doi.org/10.1007/978-3-031-52607-7_10

tourism sector that helps companies to better manage and use data in order to implement data-driven strategies. There are studies in the literature that propose a conceptual architecture for market-oriented organizations (Moreno et al., 2019) in our case this architecture focuses on the type of data and analysis requirements of organizations in the tourism sector. In the field of tourism itself we find studies that propose data architecture of different types and scope in terms of the variety of the type of data used (Navarro & Rubio, 2000; Abdulaziz et al, 2015; Bustamante et al, 2020). In our study we extend this scope to the entire spectrum of possible types of data in the tourism sector. Due to the digitization of products and services, the types of data handled in the tourism sector have grown significantly in variety and quantity. A modern architecture such as the one we propose, in line with current standards in data platforms, is required for their management.

2 Conceptual Architecture for a Tourism Organization Data Platform

As mentioned above, the objective of this study is to propose a conceptual architecture for the data platform of an organization in the tourism sector. A good starting point for this architecture is the one proposed by Moreno et al (2019) for a market-oriented organization. This architecture proposes several layers:

- Data Sources
- Data Management for analytics
- Analytical techniques and Business Intelligence
- Business insights

In our approach we will start with an initial analysis of the types of data sources currently existing in the tourism sector and, based on these types, the following layers of information management and analysis will be proposed, reaching a final layer in which applications are proposed for the most common analysis needs of the tourism sector. In the following sections, the characteristics of each layer are detailed and, finally, the complete conceptual architecture is proposed.

2.1 Data Sources

Data sources are the raw material on which all analysis that will enable data-driven decisions to be made is based. There is a wide variety of types of data sources. The different types of data sources should be well identified as their typology will determine how they are stored, managed and analysed. In the tourism sector, a very interesting classification is made by Li et al. (2018), in which three large blocks are defined as can be seen in Fig. 1:

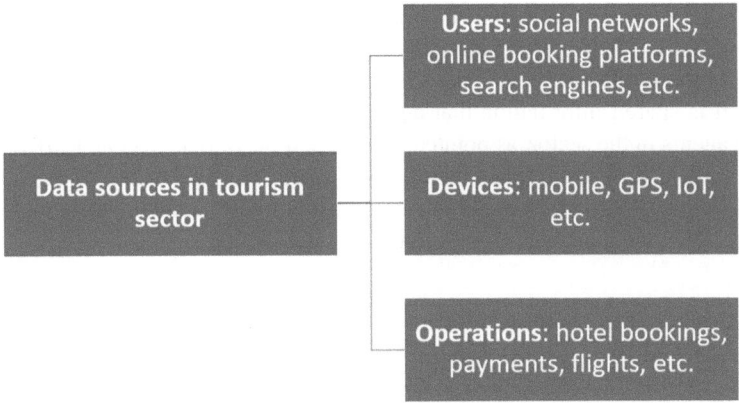

Fig. 1 Data sources classification in tourism research. Adapted from on Li et al. (2018)

- **Operations**: data from transactions or operations such as hotel bookings, payments, flights, transport (flights, cruises, rail transport), website visits, etc.
- **Devices**: data coming from devices: mainly mobile data, but also IoT (Internet of Things) data from sensors or other devices.
- **Users**: data generated by tourists themselves: comments on social networks, online booking platforms, search engines, virtual communities, co-creation of tourist experiences, etc. This type of data is often referred to as User Generated Content (UGC).

There are interesting application cases in the literature for each of these types of data sources; if we focus on operations, we see applications in payment data (Ramos & Murta, 2022) or air flights (Gallego & Font, 2020). In terms of data from devices, we find applications in mobile data (Zaragozi et al., 2021), generally with georeferenced information, as well as data from IoT (Cha et al., 2017). In the third block concerning UGC-type data we also find applications of social network data (Gunter et al., 2019) or data from online booking platforms (Liu et al., 2021; Van der Zee & Bertocchi, 2018). In this last block we have a type of information that is worth highlighting, namely data from emerging co-creation models (Mohammadi et al, 2020). This data is data collected on travel booking platforms that allows consumers to co-design their own travel experiences. It should be noted that while in the first block (operations) the data are structured (standard format and well-defined structure), in the other two blocks (devices and users) we can find semi-structured or unstructured data, which should be taken into account in their management and storage. The last two blocks are those that have experienced the greatest growth in the last decade and those that require the greatest need for real-time management (Ranganathan et al., 2020).

In addition to the three blocks of data mentioned above, we can add data generated by public institutions. Here we find statistical data generated by specialized institutions or open data provided by local or state administrations or international organizations. For example, information on the level of occupancy of a destination, origin of tourists, expenditure and others. This type of open data has grown significantly in the last decade and is used in multiple applications (Bratucu & Cismaru, 2015). It is shared information that democratizes access to data for all public and private agents in the sector, as pointed out by Celdran-Bernabeu et al. (2018). In the tourism sector, different tourism intelligence systems have been developed in the last decade (Gajdosik, 2019), some at state administration level and others at local level, which collect and generate information of great interest.

2.2 Data Management for Analytics

These different types of data sources must be stored and managed in order to apply analytical techniques to obtain insights. For this data management and storage layer we propose to use a Data Lakehouse architecture. This architecture was introduced by Armbrust et al. (2021) and is an architecture that combines the transactions and data governance of enterprise data warehouses with the flexibility and cost-efficiency of data lakes to enable business intelligence and machine learning. This architecture is currently being adopted by many companies and we believe that the flexibility it provides is appropriate for the diversity of data sources we have identified in the previous section. A Data Lakehouse is the natural evolution of the Data Warehouse and Data Lake (Harby & Zulkernine, 2022). Data Warehouses have been widely used in the tourism sector (Navarro & Rubio, 2000; Abdulaziz et al., 2015) and more recently so have Data Lakes (Sankaranarayanan & Lalchandani, 2017; Raju et al., 2018). One of the characteristics of a Data Lakehouse architecture is scalability, which is very useful given the significant growth rate of UGC or IoT sources in the tourism sector. On the other hand, the flexibility of this type of architectures is suitable for storing structured, semi-structured or unstructured data sources, which are typologies of source structure identified in the previous section. The data sources managed in the Data Lakehouse will pass through different storage areas. These areas are differentiated by the degree of elaboration of the data and there will be areas with raw information and areas with highly elaborated information, which will facilitate different types of data analysis. The processes that ingest the information into the Data Lakehouse from the original sources and that carry out the treatment of the different data areas are the ETL (Extract, Load and Transform) processes. These processes must support batch data ingestion processes with the periodicity defined (daily, weekly, monthly) and others closer to real-time. This will depend on the type of source we are working with, for example, UGC data has a very high generation speed and will require ingestion close to real-time, while if we are working with open data information published by an organization, this information will have a specific publication frequency, for example, monthly, and will be ingested in a monthly batch process. In terms of infrastructure, this type of architecture can be implemented in the company's own servers or in a cloud infrastructure. We consider a cloud infrastructure to be appropriate in our case, as it allows companies to better adapt to market changes and therefore to the data to be managed, as well as to improve cost efficiency.

Finally, it should be noted that the storage and management of data in an organization must follow the rules, policies and processes defined at the Data Governance level. A Data Lakehouse type architecture will facilitate Data Governance tasks. Moreover, these governance processes will facilitate the cataloguing of data and its sharing with third parties where necessary, using a semantic model as standard as possible with that used in the tourism sector. This feature may be of relevance if a company wants to integrate into the Gaia-X digital ecosystem (Gaia-X; Braud et al, 2021). This European initiative proposes an open and secure data infrastructure, complying with the highest standards of digital sovereignty while promoting innovation that can be of enormous interest to a company in the tourism sector. Thus, we consider that a management and storage architecture such as the one proposed allows a company to be prepared to integrate into the Gaia-X ecosystem in the future. In terms of good practices, data standards and interoperability, consideration should also be given to the Tourism Data Space project (Tourism Data Spaces), which proposes a data marketplace for sharing and accessing data at European level. Similarly, we have the European Data Spaces for Tourism project (DATES) that focuses on the development of governance and business models, while providing a shared roadmap that will ensure the coordination of the tourism ecosystem stakeholders. Finally, another interesting reference to consider is the EU guide on data for tourist destinations (Smart Tourism Destination).

2.3 Analytical Techniques and Business Intelligence

The Data Lakehouse architecture outlined in the previous section allows the use of different types of analytical techniques from Business Intelligence (BI) to Machine Learning, each technique will use the most appropriate data areas of the Data Lakehouse depending on whether it requires raw information or more elaborated information. Within the wide range of possible data analysis techniques that can be applied in the tourism sector, the following are the most commonly used. There are multiple BI use cases in the tourism sector, such as the BI architecture proposed by Bustamante et al. (2020), which integrates information from four collaborative sources (Twitter, Openstreetmap, Tripadvisor and Airbnb) and is an example of an architecture focused only on BI and certain sources, but similar to the one proposed in this article. Complementary to classic BI we have the techniques of Data Discovery and self-service BI that give greater freedom when exploring the data. When tourist behaviour is analysed, another widely used analytical technique is clustering (Rodríguez et al., 2018). As mentioned in Sect. 2.1, an important block of data are those coming from mobile devices generally with geo-referenced information that allows the application of geospatial analytics techniques (Yang et al., 2012), as well as the block related to UGC type data are becoming increasingly important and are data in which techniques are applied to analyse texts such as Natural Language Processing techniques

(Guerrero-Rodríguez et al., 2023). More advanced analytical techniques such as Machine Learning (Peng et al., 2020) or Deep Learning (Essien & Chukwukelu, 2022) are increasingly used in the tourism sector. In the field of Machine Learning techniques, one of the most widely used in the tourism sector is recommender systems (Esmaeili et al., 2020). Finally, it is worth mentioning the recent applications of Generative AI techniques to the tourism sector, in particular ChatGPT (Carvalho & Ivanov, 2023).

2.4 Business Insights

The final objective of the entire data cycle carried out in the previous sections is to obtain relevant insights in the different use cases of the tourism sector. The knowledge obtained has multiple uses in the tourism sector, we highlight the most frequent cases. Lv et al. (2021) differentiate two main levels of business insights: individual level (consumer behaviour and attitude) and organizational level (marketing management and performance analysis of tourism organizations). Using this division, we first find that there are many studies that put tourists at the center and analyse their behaviour (Miah et al., 2017), their perception (Nave et al., 2018) and their satisfaction (Li et al., 2020). Similarly, with regard to tourism supply, other areas of research are the personalization or recommendation (Esmaeili et al., 2020) of products and services and the co-creation of experiences (Mohammadi et al., 2020). All these use cases try to cover the different phases of the travel lifecycle (before, during and after) and mostly use UGC type data. On the other hand, at the organizational level, we find use cases at the level of tourism destination management such as demand forecasting (Li & Jiao, 2020), planning and development, value proposition, resource management, sustainability management (De Marchi et al. 2022) or reputation analysis (Cillo et al., 2019), as well as multiple use cases in the field of tourism companies such as marketing management or performance analysis (Bi et al., 2018) and pricing (Sánchez-Lozano et al., 2021) of products and services.

2.5 Conceptual Architecture of the Data Platform

Once the different layers of the data platform have been defined, Fig. 2 shows the complete conceptual architecture:

As a practical example, with a similar scope to the proposed data platform, we have the case of the Destination Data Platform within smart tourism ecosystem of the city of Gothenburg (Jansson et al, 2022).

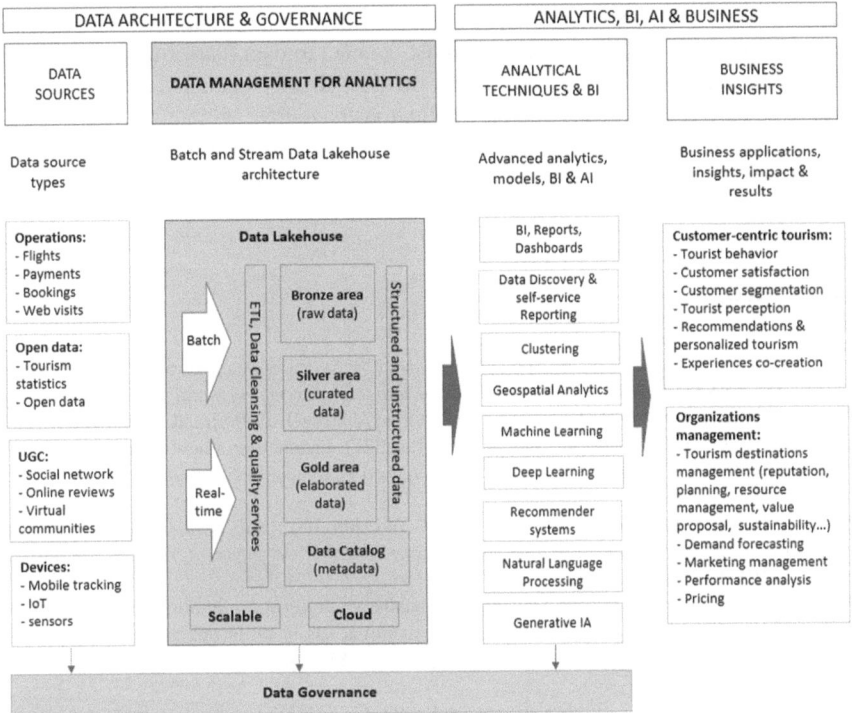

Fig. 2 Conceptual architecture for a tourism organization data platform

3 Conclusions

In this study we have proposed a conceptual architecture for a data-driven data platform of a tourism organization. We believe that this architecture can help tourism organizations in their digital transformation and in making data-driven decisions. The proposed architecture is based on modern and flexible architectures and facilitates the management, storage and governance of data, taking into account the variety and growth of data types that currently exist in the tourism sector. In addition, this architecture also enables organizations to be prepared to integrate into data ecosystems such as those proposed in the Gaia-X initiative, this will enable both the integration of data from the ecosystem into the organization and the sharing of the organization's own data in the ecosystem in a simple and governed way. Finally, it should be made clear that the proposed architecture is an ambitious one and probably not within the reach of all players in the tourism value chain. Large companies in the hotel or transport sector or public institutions, for example, may be able to tackle this type of architecture, but it may be beyond the reach of other smaller companies in the restaurant and leisure sector, for example. The latter must approach their work with data in a different way. In terms of analytical techniques, these companies should consider Business Intelligence and those advanced analytical techniques that apply to them. In terms of data management, in order to avoid having to generate and maintain a costly architecture, these smaller companies must connect to data platforms generated by public institutions that offer a lot of information already managed, organized and with open data access. Many tourist destinations have tourism intelligence systems or smart destination platforms that generate a lot of useful information for all agents in the tourism value chain, regardless of the size of the company.

References

Abdulaziz, T. A., Moawad, I. F., & Abu-Alam, W. M. (2015). Building data warehouse system for the tourism sector. In *2015 IEEE Seventh International Conference on Intelligent Computing and Information Systems (ICICIS)* (pp. 410–417). https://doi.org/10.1109/IntelCIS.2015.7397253

Armbrust, M., Ghodsi, A., Xin, R., & Zaharia, M. (2021). Lakehouse: a new generation of open platforms that unify data warehousing and advanced analytics. In *Proceedings of CIDR* (Vol. 8).

Bi, J. W., Liu, Y., Fan, Z. P., & Zhang, J. (2018). Wisdom of crowds: Conducting importance-performance analysis (IPA) through online reviews. *Tourism Management, 70,* 460–478. https://doi.org/10.1016/j.tourman.2018.09.010

Bratucu, G., & Cismaru, L. (2015). Developing a business intelligence planning tool for managing ecotourism destinations based on indicators existing at EU level. In *International Multidisciplinary Scientific Geo Conference-SGEM,* (pp. 181–188). https://doi.org/10.5593/SGEM2015/B53/S21.023

Braud, A., Fromentoux, G., Radier, B., & Le Grand, O. (2021). The road to European digital sovereignty with GAIA-X and IDSA. *IEEE Network, 35*(2), 4–5. https://doi.org/10.1109/MNET.2021.9387709

Bustamante, A., Sebastia, L., & Onaindia, E. (2020). BITOUR: A business intelligence platform for tourism analysis. *ISPRS International Journal of Geo-information, 9*(11). https://doi.org/10.3390/ijgi9110671

Camilleri, M.A. (2020). The use of data-driven technologies in tourism marketing. In *Entrepreneurship, innovation and inequality: exploring territorial dynamics and development* (pp. 182–194). https://doi.org/10.4324/9780429292583-11

Carvalho, I., & Ivanov, S. (2023). ChatGPT for tourism: Applications, benefits and risks. *Tourism Review.* https://doi.org/10.1108/TR-02-2023-0088

Celdran-Bernabeu, M. A., Mazon, J. N., & Sanchez, D. G. (2018). Open Data and tourism. Implications for tourism management in Smart Cities and Smart Tourism Destinations. *Investigaciones Turísticas, 15,* 49–78. https://doi.org/10.14198/INTURI2018.15.03

Cha, S., Ruiz, M. P., Wachowicz, M., Tran, L. H., Cao, H., & Maduako, I. (2017). The role of an IoT platform in the design of real-time recommender systems. In *IEEE 3RD World Forum on Internet of Things (WF-IOT),* (pp. 448–453). https://doi.org/10.1109/WF-IoT.2016.7845469

Cillo, V., Rialti, R., Del Giudice, M., & Usai, A (2019). Niche tourism destinations' online reputation management and competitiveness in big data era: Evidence from three Italian cases. *Current Issues in Tourism, 24*(2), 177–191. https://doi.org/10.1080/13683500.2019.1608918

DATES (last consulted 2023, Sept). https://www.tourismdataspace-csa.eu/

De Marchi, D., Becarelli, R., & Di Sarli, L. (2022). Tourism sustainability index: Measuring tourism sustainability based on the ETIS toolkit, by exploring tourist satisfaction via sentiment analysis. *Sustainability, 14*(13). https://doi.org/10.3390/su14138049

Esmaeili, L., Mardani, S., Golpayegani, S. A. H., & Madar, Z. Z. (2020). A novel tourism recommender system in the context of social commerce. *Experts Systems with Applications, 149.* https://doi.org/10.1016/j.eswa.2020.113301

Essien, A., & Chukwukelu, G. (2022). Deep learning in hospitality and tourism: A research framework agenda for future research. *International Journal of Contemporary Hospitality Management, 34*(12), 4480–4515. https://doi.org/10.1108/IJCHM-09-2021-1176

Gaia-X: Gaia-X Hub (last consulted 2023, May). https://www.gaiax.es/

Gajdosik, T. (2019). Towards a conceptual model of intelligent information system for smart tourism destinations. *Software Engineering and Algorithms in Intelligent Systems, 763*, 66–74. https://doi.org/10.1007/978-3-319-91186-1_8

Gallego, I., & Font, X. (2020). Changes in air passenger demand as a result of the COVID-19 crisis: Using Big Data to inform tourism policy. *Journal of Sustainable Tourism, 29*(9), 1470–1489. https://doi.org/10.1080/09669582.2020.1773476

Guerrero-Rodríguez, R., Álvarez-Carmona, M. A., Aranda, R., & López-Monroy, A. P. (2023). Studying Online Travel Reviews related to tourist attractions using NLP methods: The case of Guanajuato, Mexico. *Current Issues in Tourism, 26*(2), 289–304. https://doi.org/10.1080/13683500.2021.2007227

Gunter, U., Onder, I., & Gindl, S. (2019). Exploring the predictive ability of LIKES of posts on the Facebook pages of four major city DMOs in Austria. *Tourism Economics, 25*(3), 375–401. https://doi.org/10.1177/1354816618793765

Harby, A., & Zulkernine, F. (2022). From data warehouse to Lakehouse: A comparative review. In *Proceedings-2022 IEEE International Conference on Big Data, Big Data 2022* (pp. 389–395). https://doi.org/10.1109/BigData55660.2022.10020719

Jansson, J., Johansson, O., & Roshan, M. (2022). Initiating a smart tourism ecosystem: A public actor perspective. In *Proceedings of the 55th Hawaii International Conference on System Sciences.* https://doi.org/10.24251/HICSS.2022.335

Miah, S. J., Vu, H. Q., Gammack, J., & McGrath, M. (2017). A big data analytics method for tourist behaviour analysis. *Information & Management, 54*(6), 771–785. https://doi.org/10.1016/j.im.2016.11.011

Li, G., & Jiao, X. Y. (2020). Tourism forecasting research: A perspective article. *Tourism Review, 75*(1), 263–266. https://doi.org/10.1108/TR-09-2019-0382

Li, H. X., Liu, Y., Tan, C. W., & Hu, F. (2020). Comprehending customer satisfaction with hotels Data analysis of consumer-generated reviews. *International Journal of Contemporary Hospitality Management, 32*(5), 1713–1735. https://doi.org/10.1108/IJCHM-06-2019-0581

Li, J. J., Xu, L. Z., Tang, L., Wang, S. Y., & Li, L. (2018). Big data in tourism research: A literature review. *Tourism Management, 68*, 301–323. https://doi.org/10.1016/j.tourman.2018.03.009

Liu, T., Zhang, Y., Zhang, H., & Yang, X. P. (2021). A methodological workflow for deriving the association of tourist destinations based on online travel reviews: A case study of Yunnan Province, China. *Sustainability, 13*(9). https://doi.org/10.3390/su13094720

Lv, H., Shi, S., & Gursoy, D. (2021). A look back and a leap forward: A review and synthesis of big data and artificial intelligence literature in hospitality and tourism. *Journal of Hospitality Marketing & Management, 31*(2), 145–175. https://doi.org/10.1080/19368623.2021.1937434

Mohammadi, F., Yazdani, H. R., Pour, M. J., & Soltanee, M. (2020). Co-creation in tourism: a systematic mapping study. *Tourism Review, 76*(2), 305–343. https://doi.org/10.1108/TR-10-2019-0425

Moreno, C., Carrasco, R. A., & Herrera-Viedma, E. (2019). Data and artificial intelligence strategy: A conceptual enterprise big data cloud architecture to enable market-oriented organizations. *International Journal of Interactive Multimedia and Artificial Intelligence, 5*(6), 7–14. https://doi.org/10.9781/ijimai.2019.06.003

Navarro, J. R., & Rubio, J. Q. (2000). DATATUR: Tourism statistics information system-the experience of Spain. *Information and Communication Technologies in Tourism, 2000*, 126–146. https://doi.org/10.1007/978-3-7091-6291-0_12

Nave, M., Rita, P., & Guerreiro, J. (2018). A decision support system framework to track consumer sentiments in social media. *Journal of Hospitality Marketing & Management, 27*(6), 693–700. https://doi.org/10.1080/19368623.2018.1435327

Peng, R. Q., Lou, Y. X., Kadoch, M., & Cheriet, M. (2020). A Human-guided machine learning approach for 5G smart tourism IoT. *Electronics, 9*(6). https://doi.org/10.3390/electronics9 060947

Raju, R., Mital, R., & Finkelsztein, D. (2018). Data lake architecture for air traffic management. In *2018 IEEE/AIAA 37TH Digital Avionics Systems Conference (DASC)* (pp. 604–609). https://doi.org/10.1109/DASC.2018.8569361

Ramos, L. M., & Murta, F. S. (2022). Tourism seasonality management strategies-what can we learn from payment data. *Journal of Hospitality End Tourism Insights*. https://doi.org/10.1108/JHTI-12-2021-0337

Ranganathan, I., Thangamuthu, P., Palanimuthu, S., & Balusamy, B. (2020). The growing role of integrated and insightful big and real-time data analytics platforms. *Advances in Computers, 117*, 165–186. https://doi.org/10.1016/bs.adcom.2019.09.009

Rodríguez, J., Semanjski, I., Gautama, S., Van de Weghe, N., & Ochoa, D. (2018). Unsupervised hierarchical clustering approach for tourism market segmentation based on crowdsourced mobile phone data. *Sensors, 18*(9). https://doi.org/10.3390/s18092972

Sanchez-Lozano, G., Pereira, L. N., & Chavez-Miranda, E. (2021). Big data hedonic pricing: Econometric insights into room rates' determinants by hotel category. *Tourism Management, 85*. https://doi.org/10.1016/j.tourman.2021.104308.

Sankaranarayanan, H. B., & Lalchandani, J. (2017). Passenger reviews reference architecture using big data lakes. In *Proceedings of the 7th International Conference Confluence 2017 on Cloud Computing, Data Science and Engineering* (pp. 204–209). https://doi.org/10.1109/CONFLU ENCE.2017.7943150

Smart Tourism Destination (last consulted 2023, Sept). https://smarttourismdestinations.eu/

Tourism Data Space (last consulted 2023, Sept). https://dsft.modul.ac.at/tourism-data-inventory/

Van der Zee, E., & Bertocchi, D. (2018). Finding patterns in urban tourist behaviour: A social network analysis approach based on TripAdvisor reviews. *Information Technology & Tourism, 20*(1–4), 153–180. https://doi.org/10.1007/s40558-018-0128-5

Yang, B., Madden, M., Kim, J., & Jordan, T. R. (2012). Geospatial analysis of barrier island beach availability to tourists. *Tourism Management, 33*(4), 840–854. https://doi.org/10.1016/j.tourman.2011.08.013

Zaragozi, B., Trilles, S., & Gutierrez, A. (2021). Passive mobile data for studying seasonal tourism mobilities: An application in a mediterranean coastal destination. *ISPRS International Journal of Geo-Information, 10*(2). https://doi.org/10.3390/ijgi10020098

Innovation and AI: An Opportunity for Spanish Tourism in the Post COVID-19 Era

Aimée Torres-Penalva ⓘ **and Luis Moreno-Izquierdo** ⓘ

Abstract The value of innovation in economic activity is undeniable, as is the importance of tourism in the Spanish economy. However, tourism has traditionally been considered less innovative than other sectors, which has led to less attention being paid to research in this area. With the arrival of the pandemic and its destructive impact on tourism, interest in new technologies applied to the sector has reached its peak. For this reason, this paper seeks to determine whether the use of these technologies, and specifically AI, represents an opportunity for the Spanish tourism sector in the post-COVID-19 crisis. To this end, a descriptive analysis of several successful cases of the application of this technology in the sector is carried out, as well as a solution to one of the problems arising from this new situation: the use of face masks.

Keywords Tourism · Innovation · IA · COVID-19

1 Introduction

Innovation has proved to be one of the main drivers of economic development, which has led to a great deal of research in this area, in order to respond to changing market needs and trends. In recent years, technological advances have been made in various sectors of the economy. Among these, the "emergence" of Artificial Intelligence (hereinafter AI) stands out. Although its discovery dates back to the 1950s, it is only in recent decades that there has been a growing interest in this technology, due to the possibility of accessing data, the appearance of new and powerful hardware and software for generating algorithms, and so on. In this context, and despite the fact that the tourism sector is presented as a very traditional industry, it is one of the

A. Torres-Penalva (✉) · L. Moreno-Izquierdo
University of Alicante, Alicante, España
e-mail: atp39@gcloud.ua.es

L. Moreno-Izquierdo
e-mail: luis.moreno@gcloud.ua.es

© The Author(s) 2024
A. J. Guevara Plaza et al. (eds.), *Tourism and ICTs: Advances in Data Science, Artificial Intelligence and Sustainability*, Springer Proceedings in Business and Economics, https://doi.org/10.1007/978-3-031-52607-7_11

sectors with the greatest need and capacity for innovation. However, research on the technology in question has paid less attention to its application in the service sector than, for example, in the manufacturing industry. As a result, a large part of tourism research focuses on the study of other variables, such as the number of arrivals, employment in tourism or the seasonality that characterises this activity, which means that those studies that refer to the application of AI in the sector are more recent.

The arrival of COVID-19 plunged the economy and society into a period of great uncertainty. This uncertainty has had disastrous consequences for the tourism sector. The negative impact of the pandemic has also been exacerbated in countries that are highly dependent on tourism, such as Spain. According to the National Statistics Institute tourism ended 2019 with a contribution of 14.6% to Spain's GDP. As a result of the pandemic, this percentage will fall to 5.5% of GDP by 2020, representing an economic loss of more than ninety million euros (Instituto Nacional de Estadística, 2020).

This unexpected and unfortunate situation has necessitated the implementation of ongoing restrictions as a means of combating the virus. These include the compulsory use of masks, the limitation and control of capacity and the maintenance of safety distances. All of this, together with restrictions on the free movement of travellers, has had a significant impact on tourist activity. To this end, technology, and in particular AI, has helped to overcome many of these obstacles, leading to an acceleration of the innovation race in tourism.

2 Theorical Background

2.1 Innovation Trends

Towards service innovation: from the Oslo manual to the new wave of technology

The concept of innovation as a factor of development and economic growth has been studied over time and has been the subject of numerous economic theories. Until 2005, the most classic definitions of innovation, by authors such as Smith (1776), Schumpeter (1934), Drucker (1985) and Porter (1991), were developed with the industrial sector in mind and were used indifferently for the services sector, despite the specificities of this sector. With the publication of the third edition of the Oslo Manual this year, an important difference for our field of study was introduced: the inclusion of the service sector. This was not the case in previous editions. Two ideas emerge from this fact. The first is that studies on innovation in services are becoming increasingly interesting. Secondly, as the OECD notes, the lack of economic literature on innovation in tourism prevents the existence of a handbook, such as the Oslo Handbook, which collects comparable and generally accepted data on innovative activities in the sector (OECD and EUROSTAT, 2005).

The Spanish economy is currently showing a strong and growing commitment to new technologies. Within this framework, a new paradigm is emerging. These are tools that work with large volumes of data, which are ultimately transformed into highly valuable information for decision-making. Within these new trends, and given the recent interest it has generated in the tourism sector, this paper focuses on AI. Although it was born as a discipline of computer science, its study and application are generating a growing interest in the tourism sector.

2.2 AI in the Tourism Sector

Innovation and AI in tourism

There has often been a tendency to think that this sector requires little innovative activity. However, as the tertiarization of the economy progresses, this idea is beginning to be invalidated, confirming the need for the production and application of innovation in this sector (Mullo Romero et al., 2019). Thus, in 2011, tourism activity was declared as increasingly defined by innovation (UNWTO, 2011), defending a tourism strategy based on data. Likewise, an increasing number of experts consider AI as a fundamental part of strengthening Spain's leadership and competitiveness as a tourist destination, highlighting its strengths and trying to mitigate its weaknesses (Pedreño and Ramón, 2019).

An overview of the tourism sector

In order to understand the context in which the sector operates, it is worth recalling the specific characteristics of the tourism product, which are different from those of the industrial product and which partly explain the lower level of adoption of this technology compared to other sectors. The tourism product is intangible, heterogeneous, perishable, highly seasonal (Middleton and Clarke, 2001) and subject to constant change. It therefore not only requires innovation, but it does so in a dynamic, uncertain, complex and changing environment. It is not easy to operate in such an environment. That is why the tourism sector, in such a delicate period where the only certainty is uncertainty, needs tools such as AI to facilitate decision making.

Measuring AI in tourism

In the report "Realidad y perspectivas de la IA en España" by PwC and Microsoft (2018), the tourism sector is one of the twelve sectors in which AI will have the greatest impact. In this sense, it would be interesting to measure the real impact of this technology on the sector.

However, there are still no tourism-specific indicators to measure this [Aires and Varum, 2018]. Some experts in the sector have already warned that this will require "an evolution in digitalisation in order to work well in this new sector" (Mario Villar, 2021). In the meantime, various indicators and general reports can be used. For example, the "AI Index Report" (Stanford University, 2021) or the dossier "Indicadores de uso de Inteligencia Artificial en las empresas españolas" by the Spanish government, prepared with data from Eurostat, which shows that Spain's AI performance is below the global average, ranking 23rd out of 26 countries considered, although it has improved its position in several of the indicators included in the index, such as the rate of AI hiring, the number of LA companies created or the total private investment in this technology. At the EU level, "Indicators of the use of artificial intelligence in Spanish companies" is published, which concludes that Spain is among the EU-27 countries with the lowest level of adoption of AI in companies.

Evolution of interest and investment in AI for Spanish tourism

Despite the boom in interest and use of AI in Spain, its performance is still below average. In 2020, the Secretary of State for Digitalisation and Artificial Intelligence promoted the National Strategy for Artificial Intelligence (ENIA), with an investment of more than 600 million euros for the period 2021–2023. In parallel, some autonomous communities-such as the Valencian Community, Galicia or the Basque Country are presenting their own AI strategy (Gobierno de España, 2020).

In the field of tourism, the Secretary of State for Tourism is promoting the network of smart tourist destinations through SEGITTUR (2021). Likewise, several municipalities are already launching their own initiatives, such as the Digital District of the Community, which is leading conferences on innovative solutions for tourism (Business Insider, 2021).

A stumbling block: AI ethics and regulation

Many experts agree that the Spanish tourism sector has what it takes to continue growing with AI. "We have the opportunity to lead artificial intelligence in Europe from Spain", so says Reyes Maroto, Minister of Industry, Trade and Tourism of the Spanish government. However, it has been proven that Spain is currently far from being considered a leader in the application of this technology. The idea of global leadership, with competitors such as the United States and China, may be too ambitious. One of the obstacles is "ethics", and when it comes to personal data, this becomes an essential factor to be taken into account. In addition to the White Paper on AI, the European Commission (2021) has recently approved the first regulation on AI. In the specific case of Spain, the General Law on Data Protection (LGPD) has been added. In some autonomous communities, such as the Valencian Community, there is even a specific regulation.

3 Aims and Hypotheses

The main objective of this paper is to study the role of innovation, and specifically AI, in the post-pandemic future of the Spanish tourism sector. In this sense, a series of specific objectives have been set. Firstly, to study the evolution of the concept of innovation in the tourism sector. Secondly, to identify the new trends that are currently shaping the tourism sector. In addition, to identify a series of cases in which AI offers a solution to the problems caused by the pandemic in the tourism sector. Finally, to propose its own solution to one of the problems arising from this new situation, the use of masks. Based on these objectives, the following hypothesis is formulated Does the use of innovation, and specifically AI, represent an opportunity for the Spanish tourism sector in the post-COVID-19 era?

4 Methodology

This study presents an analysis of the opportunities introduced by innovation, especially AI, to the Spanish tourism industry since the onset of the pandemic and the potential opportunities for the future. The study is divided into three stages.

First stage: Collection of AI application cases as a solution for post-COVID-19 tourism. A search for AI-based technological solutions for tourism recovery was carried out in various written sources, all of which are cited in the bibliography of the paper. We also attended the masterclass "IA en el día a día", organised by Spain AI, and several webinars, including "VIII Thinktur Technology Transfer", by Thinktur, and "Aplicación de la Inteligencia Artificial al turismo tras el COVID-19", organised by Turisme Comunitat Valenciana.

Second stage: A selection and study of successful cases was conducted for each of the five segments, building on an accurate classification of typologies of AI solutions for the sector as defined by Thinktur and also including an additional segment for sustainability.

Third stage: A proprietary solution was proposed using Teachable Machine. Finally, a proprietary solution has been suggested utilising Teachable Machine–an AI tool crafted by Google which simplifies the creation of models- in response to a recurring predicament in this contemporary era: regulating the correct usage of masks within enclosed surroundings.

5 Results. Case Studies and Proposals

5.1 Tourism and COVID-19

In 2019, Spain reclaimed its position as the top global leader in tourism competitiveness, as reported by the World Economic Forum (2019). Regrettably, the high hopes for growth in the sector for the year 2020 were hindered by the emergence of a new virus. Aena's (2020) revealed a sharp decrease in air transport passengers from 275,247,387 to 76,064,322, representing a staggering decline of 72.4%. Undoubtedly, the pandemic has had a significant impact on bars, restaurants and other catering establishments, resulting in intermittent activity interruptions due to restrictions on opening hours and capacity. These restrictions have forced such businesses to temporarily cease their activities and, in the worst cases, to shut down. The Bank of Spain has reported that 50,000 tourism businesses were closed in 2020 due to the pandemic (Ministerio de Trabajo y Economía Social, 2021). The state of the tourism industry has raised concerns about the effectiveness of the Spanish tourism model. A key priority now is to modernise and revamp the sector. Accordingly, the Spanish Government (2021) has emphasised the crucial requirement for "a modernisation and enhanced competitiveness strategy to prepare the industry for significant changes, particularly in the areas of digitalisation and sustainability." There is an opportunity to promote a data-driven strategy, in which innovation, especially AI, is crucial.

5.2   Cases of Application of AI in Tourism COVID-19

In the arena of industry resizing, solutions like BiOnTrend have surfaced. BiOn-Trend is a collaborative data analytics tool for hotels designed to address the sector's dearth of a proprietary tool that is competent in scrutinizing authentic data on tourist accommodation and destinations (HOSBEC and Turisme Comunitat Valenciana, 2020). Tools have been developed to ensure compliance with minimum interpersonal distancing in real time (Landing AI, 2020). Additionally, measurement and control of beach capacities has been achieved through the use of technology (Alicante Plaza, 2020; Konica Minolta, 2020).

For communication and transparency, Intelligent Virtual Assistants (AVI) or chat-bots are particularly noteworthy. A noteworthy accomplishment is the Carina chatbot, created by the technology firm 1MillionBot based in Alicante. The chatbot can respond to inquiries about over 300 subjects regarding the COVID-19 outbreak with a success rate of 91.70% (1MillionBot, 2020). Concerning health, thermographic cameras permit swift detection of fever without direct contact with the person (Tecon Group, 2020). Finally, in regard to sustainability, Substrate AI and the Poseidon hotel chain have initiated a project with the aim of reducing their hotel energy consumption by 10% through the application of AI (Hosteltur, 2021).

5.3   An Own Case Study: Mask Control with Teachable Machine.

Several companies are dedicated to developing advanced technologies and making them widely accessible to the public. Google, a technology leader, offers the Teach-able Machine tool that enables the creation of automatic learning models in a straight-forward, user-friendly manner. In the following section, we will showcase an applied case study that addresses one of the most significant changes resulting from the pandemic: the mandatory use of face masks. The proposed AI-based solution is capable of detecting correct and incorrect mask usage.

Upon accessing the tool, users must select one of three project types: audio, posture or image (in this instance, image has been selected). The model follows a five-phase structure that includes learning, preparation (or training), evaluation, parameter reconfiguration and model export.

Phase (1) Learning. Two classes of data will be created, with different labels, namely "mask" and "no mask." Subsequently, pictures will be entered via webcam. The initial phase involves gathering data, which is crucial to a large degree for the model's success. The device will learn from the samples provided to it. The user will capture a collection of photographs depicting themselves wearing a mask. The first sample consists of 31 images in total.

To obtain the "no mask" class, the previous procedure will be duplicated, but without utilizing the mask accessory shown in the other class. As a result, the ensuing sample consists of 27 photos. By doing so, the primary fundamental data will have been provided to initiate model learning. It is not desirable to consider practices such as wearing a mask without covering the nose, mouth or holding it on the chin as acceptable. As a result, a new collection of images will be included in the "no mask" set, demonstrated as follows.

Now that the datasets have been defined and supplied, the training or model preparation phase will commence.

Phase (2) Preparation or Training. Once the "prepare mode-lo" option is selected, the mode-lo will commence processing the data. Essentially, the program will amalgamate all the given data to generate algorithms, which subsequently can be employed to automatically detect if a person is wearing a mask appropriately or not from an image. Following the completion of the model, a "Preview" block will manifest on the right-hand side of the page. This is the result of the model's evaluation phase.

Phase (3) Evaluation. If everything has functioned properly, it should be possible for the model to identify, from an image, whether or not the individual in the picture is equipped with a mask. Figure 1 demonstrates the model's accurate identification of the case in question. Additionally, it effectively discerns instances where the mask is not securely fastened.

However, the model may also present faults. If the user swaps their surgical mask for an FFP2 mask, the model fails to detect accurately. The same issue may arise if a woman wears Niqab as the model detects the presence of a mask, even when there isn't one. This occurs due to the fact that we haven't educated the model on the

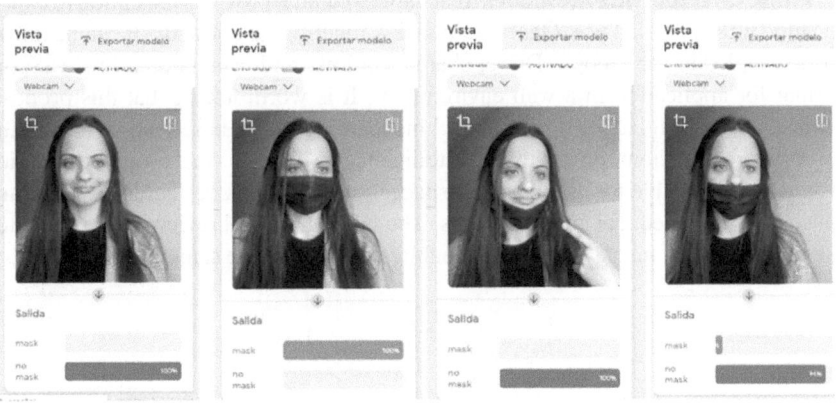

Fig. 1 Correct detection of mask use/non-use. *Source* Screenshot from the Teachable Machine website, 2022

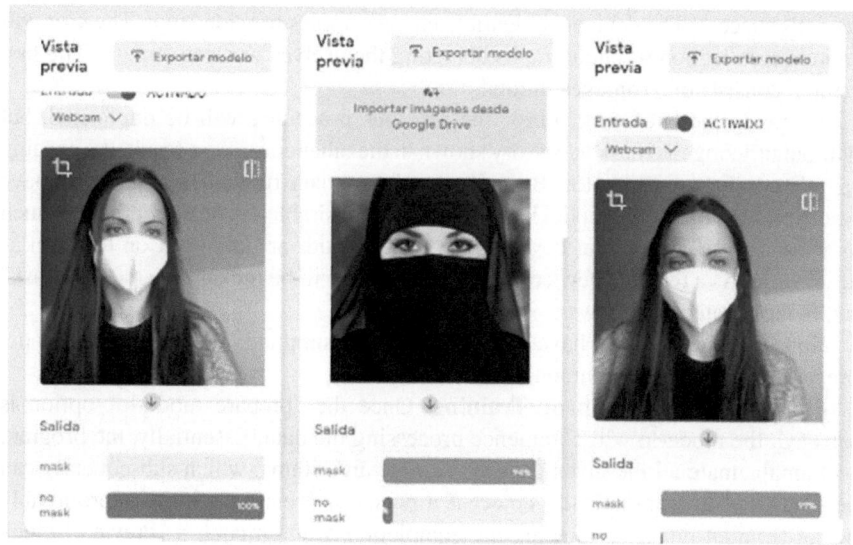

Fig. 2 Failure of the model when using another mask or Niqab, and new model corrections. *Source* Screenshot from the Teachable Machine website, 2022

difference Here is a further indication of the significance of the preparatory stage for the model to acquire and develop knowledge to the fullest extent feasible.

Phase (4) Parameters Reconfiguration. The issues identified during the evaluation phase will be resolved in this stage. The model will be continually fed to fine-tune the results. As the model is currently unable to accurately recognise the FFP2 mask, additional images will be added to the "mask" label, featuring users wearing FFP2 masks. After this step, the model will be re-run, and the updated results will be examined. Figure 2 depicts that the FFP2 mask is now successfully detected.

Phase (5) Exporting the model. Teachable Machine provides the option to export the model for personal use. Once the model is functioning correctly, it can be downloaded, uploaded to Google Drive, shared via link, and even copied in JavaScript format for application in a web environment. It is worth noting that this proposal represents a simplified version of a machine learning model based on AI. According to current regulations on Artificial Intelligence in Europe, the proposed solution would only be viable for use in private spaces, such as hotels, restaurants, shops, and museums, due to ethical considerations. The bibliographical review has highlighted the prohibition of image recording in public areas under the same legislation.

6 Conclusions

All in all, it is concluded that there are reasons to believe that AI represents an opportunity for the country's post-COVID-19 tourism. However, in order for the sector to benefit from these opportunities, a number of challenges need to be addressed, which are detailed below.

- AI measurement system for tourism. Regardless of the variable under study, measuring and evaluating the results is an essential step in order to move forward. At present, AI does not have a measurement system that makes use of tourism-only indicators, which makes it difficult to establish corrective actions that seek to improve the sector's results.
- AI ethical framework for tourism. The lack (or sometimes over-regulation) of AI regulation can be a disadvantage in the race for innovation. Although the European Union is making progress in this area, work must continue on the construction of an ethical framework that adapts to the specific needs of this sector, avoiding leaving behind countries with great tourism potential, such as Spain.
- AI Education and Training. There are individuals in our society who are hesitant to implement this new technology, likely due to fear or lack of knowledge. Therefore, it is critical to educate and provide training on AI to the population, allowing them to comprehend the benefits it offers. By doing so, utilising AI in the tourism industry could lead to the development of higher quality employment, a reduced workload, and overall enhance the service provided to visitors. A clear example is the case study proposed in the results section.

Is it wise to invest in a technology that lacks public trust? This is a valid question. To mitigate this issue, there should be a focus on creating new job opportunities and facilitating reskilling for those who lack technological proficiency.

References

Aena. (2020). Informe de Gestión Consolidado 2020.

Aires, J. D. M., & Varum, C. A. (2018). La investigación sobre la medición de la innovación en las empresas de turismo. Revisión de la literatura. *Estudios y perspectivas en turismo, 27* (1), 102–120.

Alicante Plaza. (2020). Dinapsis analiza la implantación de la IA en el turismo post Covid-19y avisa: habrá fraudes.

Business Insider. (2021). Sensorización, inteligencia artificial, realidad virtual…: Distrito Digital ofrece nuevas soluciones para el Turismo.

Drucker, P. F. (1985). Innovation and entrepreneurship: Practice and principles.

Gobierno de España. (2020). Estrategia Nacional de Inteligencia Artificial.

HOSBEC y Turisme Comunitat Valenciana. (2020). BIONTREND-Herramienta colaborativa de analítica de datos para hoteles.

Hosteltur. (2021). Substrate AI reducirá un 10% el gasto energético de los hoteles Poseidón con la IA.

Instituto Nacional de Estadística. (2020). Cuenta Satélite del Turismo de España (CSTE).

Konica Minolta. (2020). Konica Minolta lanza un sistema de control de aforo con inteligencia artificial.

Landing AI. (2020). Landing AI creates an AI tool to help customers monitor social distancing in the workplace.

Ministerio de Trabajo y Economía Social. (2021). Estadística de empresas inscritas en la Seguridad Social.

Mullo Romero, E. D. C., Castro Salceso, J. P., & Guillén Herrera, S. R. (2019). Innovación y desarrollo turístico. Reflexiones y desafíos. *Revista Universidad y Sociedad, 11*(4), 394–399.

OECD y EUROSTAT. (2005). Manual de Oslo. Guía para la recogida e interpretación de datos sobre innovación. (3ra ed). Grupo Tragsa.

1MillionBot. (2020). Chatbot Carina - Coronavirus.

Pedreño, A., & Ramón, A. (2019). Por qué el turismo necesita imperiosamente la Inteligencia Artificial (y mucha tecnología digital).

Porter, M. E. (1991). La ventaja competitiva de las naciones.

PwC y Microsoft. (2018). Bots, Machine Learning, Servicios Cognitivos. Realidad y perspectivas de la Inteligencia Artificial en España, 2018.

Schumpeter, J. A. (1934). The theory of economic development: An inquiry into profit capital, credit, interest, and the business cycle.

SEGITTUR. (2021). Catálogo de soluciones tecnológicas para destinos turísticos inteligentes.

Smith, A. (1776). La riqueza de las naciones.

Stanford University. (2021). The AI Index 2021 Annual Report.

UNWTO. (2021). Evaluación del impacto de la COVID-19 en el turismo internacional.

World Economic Forum. (2019). The Travel & Tourism Competitiveness Report 2019.

Tourism Intelligence, Key to Reviving the Sector

Carlos Hernández-White⬤, Beatriz Rodríguez-Díaz⬤, and Alfonso Expósito-García⬤

Summary The crisis caused by the COVID-19 pandemic has hit the tourism sector hard, causing an unprecedented drop in activity. This has accentuated the need for robust tourism knowledge systems that provide intelligence, improvements in competitiveness and greater efficiency in the sector, taking advantage of its potential through more collaborative and digital processes. The added value of this work is to define, based on existing literature and experience in different territories, the main aspects to be taken into account in the design of an integrated tourism knowledge and intelligence system. We are at a stage of recovery of tourism activity after the pandemic where digitalisation processes are key factors in the structural changes. Tourism intelligence systems must be based on collaboration between all the agents in the sector, on the consolidation and integration of information from different sources, on the application of technology and business intelligence techniques to provide high-value knowledge, on the contribution of the tourism sector to the development of the territories and on the improvement of competitiveness based on knowledge management.

Keywords Tourism intelligence · Collaboration · Knowledge · Digitisation · Tourism

1 Introduction

The tourism sector, which is currently in a period of reactivation, needs robust tourism knowledge systems that provide intelligence, improvements in competitiveness and greater efficiency in the sector, taking advantage of its potential through more collaborative and digital processes, which are key to structural changes in the sector.

C. Hernández-White (✉) · B. Rodríguez-Díaz · A. Expósito-García
Universidad de Málaga, Malaga, Spain
e-mail: carloshw@uma.es

© The Author(s) 2024
A. J. Guevara Plaza et al. (eds.), *Tourism and ICTs: Advances in Data Science, Artificial Intelligence and Sustainability*, Springer Proceedings in Business and Economics, https://doi.org/10.1007/978-3-031-52607-7_12

The added value of this work is to define, based on existing literature and experience in different territories, which are the main aspects to be taken into account in the design of an integrated tourism knowledge and intelligence system.

At this point, intelligence systems in the tourism sector are key. They must be based on collaboration between all agents in the sector, on the consolidation and integration of information from different sources, on the application of technology and business intelligence tools to provide high-value knowledge, on the contribution of the tourism sector to the development of territories and on the improvement of competitiveness based on knowledge management.

2 Tourism Intelligence

Intelligence means the ability to understand, to learn from experience and to acquire knowledge from it in order to make decisions in an agile way. The term "tourism intelligence" is approached from different perspectives, although all of them are complementary in that they lead to improvements in knowledge and help to make well-informed decisions.

From the visitor's point of view, tourism intelligence is associated with a set of information resources that provide value through new technologies: points of interest, transport, activities, leisure, culture, etc.... All this provides information for a better-informed visit by tourists.

In this regard, Spain has had a pioneering development with smart tourism destinations (STD) which began with the National and Integral Tourism Plan 2012–2015. This involves a certification process for destinations so that municipalities can be declared as STD based on requirements related to technology, innovation, accessibility and sustainability.

The term tourism intelligence has also been developed from the point of view of destinations, integrating it into the field of development and territorial intelligence. As tourism is a key sector for economic development, tourism intelligence is an important tool for increasing economic dynamism and growth, incorporating governance and collaboration in the integrated management of the territory.

In this analysis we focus on the term tourism intelligence from the point of view of the agents. In other words, tourism intelligence as an information system for decision-making in the tourism sector, both in public and private agents, who are the real protagonists.

Intelligence does not necessarily imply knowledge. It requires a series of elements that make up a system and that respond to the needs of the agents with real knowledge that facilitates their decision-making. In this sense, Valdés et al. (2011) developed the idea that a Tourism Information System should collect the information provided by other entities, thus allowing the analysis and dissemination of knowledge. Collaboration therefore also comes into play.

The design of an intelligence system is applicable to any territory that aims to improve information processes within the sector. Furthermore, it supports decision-making in private companies and in the public management of tourist destinations, improving the competitive position of the sector as a whole and its economic viability. They are based on public and private innovation criteria. The generation of new innovative forms of management influences the quality of the tourism offer.

In this sense, Bigné et al. (2000) defined the tourism information system as a permanent and systematised process of collection, treatment, organisation and distribution of the information necessary for the objectives of tourism planning, action and evaluation for the different public and business tourism agents of a destination.

The generation, collection and capture of information consists of creating or acquiring knowledge that is needed at the sectoral level and involves organising, validating and verifying the knowledge, and then disseminating it to the members of the organisation.

The implementation of knowledge systems in the tourism sector is supported by tools and technologies. Depending on the territories and tourist destinations, there is great variability in the existence of tourism information and intelligence systems.

Information systems in the tourism sector have been evolving and must meet the demands of all types of agents, who have different information needs (Valdés et al., 2011). In this sense, appropriate tools and close collaboration are essential for decision-making.

Since the World Tourism Organisation (UNWTO) highlighted the need for tourism statistics systems and promoted Tourism Satellite Accounts, many systems have been implemented in destinations around the world. The Management Information Systems for Tourism (MIST) are made up of a set of statistical operations that are carried out in a country in order to have a better and greater knowledge of the reality of the tourism sector UNWTO (2001).

The objective of these systems, as mentioned by Massieu (2000), is to facilitate decision-making by social agents, to serve international comparisons and to enable research. However, in many cases, statistical systems do not meet all the information needs of the various actors in the sector, both public and private. Since then, technologies and information systems have evolved a great deal, but with varying degrees of intensity in the management of tourism destinations.

The main objective of this work is to analyse integrated tourism intelligence systems and the creation of knowledge for decision-making in the sector, in both the public and private spheres.

3 Research Objectives

We are currently in a period of tourism reactivation. If we also take into account the relevance of ICT advances, we consider it an appropriate time to carry out research on tourism intelligence systems.

In this research, firstly, an analysis of the existing literature is carried out in order to find common ground in relation to the contributions, limitations and challenges of its application.

The research questions posed in this paper are:

- What are the characteristics and advantages of integrated tourism intelligence systems?
- What are the challenges and limitations of applying intelligence systems in the tourism sector?

On the other hand, a specific tourist destination was analysed by means of interviews with agents in the sector. In this analysis, an in-depth analysis was carried out on how tourism intelligence systems respond to the needs of public and private agents in their territory.

4   Results and Discussion

After the study and analysis of the works identified as optimal for the achievement of the objective of this research, it has been observed that, despite the fact that knowledge and tourism intelligence is an important topic for a sector as competitive as the tourism sector, the research is recent, focusing especially on the period from 2016 to 2022.

In the works analysed, a series of lines of argument can be observed that are reproduced repeatedly and that make up the basic attributes that characterise tourism intelligence systems. The challenges for tourism information and intelligence systems can be deduced from them.

These lines of argument are discussed in more detail.

- Collaboration between actors.
- Consolidation and integration of information.
- Technology, Business Intelligence (BI) and Competitive Intelligence (CI).
- Territories and destinations.
- Knowledge, efficiency and competitiveness.

5   Collaboration

Collaboration is a fundamental attribute of tourism intelligence systems and is a term that is present in much of the literature. There is a need to create collaborative environments in tourism destinations that are conducive to the implementation of knowledge creation systems.

The creation of synergies between stakeholders is analysed by Mariani et al. (2018) and Pérez-Guilarte (2015), which also includes research groups among the agents and also studies the need for public sector leadership in collaborative structures.

Tulungen et al. (2021) also discusses the creation of a framework for reviving the tourism industry based on public sector leadership and technological innovation.

Sheehan et al. (2016) studied the integration and collaboration between stakeholders in the tourism sector, assigning the coordination function to destination managers (DMOs). The need for a new governance model, implementing a learning culture and establishing knowledge networks were his contributions in terms of collaboration in tourism intelligence systems.

But there is a wide variety of actors operating in the sector, and not all of them need the same type of information. Valdés et al. (2011) pointed to the different needs of all actors. In many cases, statistical tools are not able to respond to all the needs of the different actors. Each user requires some specific type of information that is different from the rest, even if there is a common core of information that is of interest to all. Pérez Guilarte (2015) and (Morales and Hernandez, 2011).

The use of information for decision-making is not only exclusive to large tour operators. Also small enterprises can analyse their environment with the resources at their disposal and use the information to develop their business (Vizjak et al., 2010).

Sepúlveda and Plumed (2018) studied a defined structure for the centralisation and transfer of knowledge between all public and private spheres of tourism. These authors propose the creation of a National System of Knowledge and Tourism Intelligence, leaving as a future line of research the possibility of designing and implementing their proposal in a practical way.

In this sense, as Pérez Guilarte (2015) points out when analysing a comprehensive tourism analysis system for heritage destinations, the availability of tools is key to decision-making in the public and private spheres, as well as collaboration between agents.

6   Consolidation and Integration of Information

An information system must collect and synthesise qualitative and quantitative data in a way that allows for the analysis and dissemination of knowledge to the different actors. This information must be consistent, durable and comparable over time and across territories. It must be accurate and enable tourism stakeholders, both public and private, to understand the tourism phenomenon in terms of its activity and economic impact (Valdés et al., 2011). It should also facilitate decision-making by social agents, generate comparable data and promote research (Massieu, 2000).

The main concept of this research is the tourism intelligence system, which is analysed in some of the reviewed publications. These systems should collect data and information from visitors in a systematic and structured way, translating them into knowledge, analysis and publications accessible to tourism stakeholders (Pérez Guilarte, 2015).

There is a great complexity in the collection and consolidation of data, being necessary to synthesise information from all tourism entities (Valdés et al., 2011).

Diverse public and private agents coexist, operating in territories with different levels of competence (Morales and Hernandez et al., 2011).

There are a wide range of tourism stakeholders, public administrations at different territorial and competence levels, private stakeholders, specialised researchers, training professionals, consultants, service companies, media, etc.

On many occasions, official statistical systems that provide tourism information do not respond to the needs of all stakeholders. They do not generate real knowledge. More comprehensive, ambitious and dynamic systems that are useful to all stakeholders are increasingly in demand.

The knowledge that is generated among all the agents must be transferred in the form of communiqués, graphics, presentations, or periodic reports (Marshall et al., 1996). The management of this knowledge and its dissemination are key to the development of tourism sector.

Adopting the best strategies, making the best decisions based on the best information, is fundamental for destinations and all the agents involved. Tourism information systems must have a broad and dynamic vision, providing answers to all needs (Valdés et al., 2011).

7 Technology, BI and CI

A fundamental aspect of intelligence systems is the technological factor. It clearly determines the strategy and competitiveness of the actors operating in the sector. Smart environments transform structures, linking tourism service ecosystems. Information and technology are fundamental to drive innovation in tourism marketing and management (Buhalis, 2020).

At this stage, there are new challenges that the tourism sector is addressing. Digitalisation, technology and business process integration are the challenges facing the sector to address this post-pandemic stage (Tulungen et al., 2021).

Big data has evolved a lot in recent years in general. In the tourism sector it is clearly palpable, when analysing the increasing literature on the application of Business Intelligence and Big Data to tourism management. There is a need for greater integration between management and data science and a conceptual framework to help identify tourism business management problems (Mariani et al., 2018).

There is a great deal of fragmentation in the literature on intelligence applied to the tourism sector, both in scope and in the methodologies applied. But in all cases the ultimate goal is knowledge as an innovative process. In an environment such as tourism, which is characterised by high levels of competition, uncertainty, change and rapid customer decisions, Competitive Intelligence practices are crucial for the competitiveness of the sector. Knowledge enables well-informed decisions about the market and the competitive environment (Köseoglu et al., 2019).

8 Territories and Destinations

Business intelligence and knowledge transfer models in the tourism sector are of fundamental use in projecting regions and generating new market positioning, responding to the new demands of visitors. Decision-making supported by information systems and efficient knowledge transfer is growing and playing an increasingly important role (Barrera-Narváez et al., 2020; Valeri & Baggio, 2022).

In addition to the existence of tourism information systems, and in parallel to the growth of the sector, tourism observatories have been created in various territories for this purpose. The sector is evolving and with it, so are the needs for studies and information. From an organisational point of view, tourism observatories are in charge of compiling supply and demand data to structure them in analyses and publications for tourism stakeholders in a specific territory Pérez Guilarte (2015).

From a territorial point of view, geographic information systems have also contributed significantly to the development of tourism products and are already a fundamental part of many business models. In this way, the tourism sector has fostered growth and socio-economic development in various regions. Tourism continues to be a growing economic activity that contributes significantly to socio-economic development in many territories around the world Barrera-Narváez et al. (2020).

9 Knowledge, Efficiency and Competitiveness

Innovation in knowledge management must continue to be the fundamental vector for growth in the tourism sector, providing valuable information that improves its competitiveness and quality with positive effects on the territory and the inhabitants of tourist areas. The application of intelligence and the integration of knowledge is a form of innovation in a very important sector for the economy and with greater impact in certain territories.

The future of the sector necessarily involves the adoption of BI and DB tools, given the high level of competition in the sector. High levels of efficiency and competitiveness require increasingly innovative information tools. The industry continues to benefit from innovative developments that drive its growth (Nyanga et al., 2020).

The evolution of academic research on tourism activity is parallel to the continuous development of the sector. An example of this is the growth in the number of doctoral theses defended in tourism in recent years (Sepúlveda & Plumed, 2018) (Table 1).

Table 1 Reviewed publications on tourism intelligence systems

	Contributions	Challenges	Limitations
Mariani et al. (2018). Business intelligence and big data in hospitality and tourism: a systematic literature review	Data analysis. Customer centric	Collaboration. Real-time data	Fragmentation of the research field. Lack of conceptual framework. Official data
Buhalis (2020). Technology in tourism-from information communication technologies to eTourism and smart tourism towards ambient intelligence tourism: a perspective article	The net balance of the technology must be positive	Interconnecting all actors through technology	Inefficiency, digital exclusion and loss of information
Nyanga et al. (2020). Enhancing competitiveness in the tourism industry through the use of business intelligence: a literature review	Advantages of BI. Improvements in competitiveness	Business Intelligence (BI) is the key to greater efficiency	Future research should be quantitative Extensive field of application of BI in tourism
Köseoglu et al. (2019). Competitive intelligence in hospitality and tourism: a perspective article	Knowledge is an asset to gain competitiveness	CI practices are crucial for the tourism sector	Competitive environment characterised by uncertainty
Valdés et al. (2011). Knowledge of tourism at regional level	Decision-making by actors,	Different information needs	Administrative decentralisation. Tourist profile. Breakdown of data
Vizjak et al. (2010). Using business intelligence in economics in view of tourism	Effective information for decision making. BI	Reorganisation of tourist agents. New knowledge	
Barrera-Narváez et al. (2020). Decision-making in the tourism sector through the use of Geographic Information Systems and business intelligence	Growing trend in GIS research in tourism		Lack of studies incorporating business intelligence in the GIS framework
Pérez Guilarte (2015). Design of an Integrated Tourism Analysis System (SIAT) in heritage destinations	Tools for integrated analysis. Indicators	Collaboration. Public sector leadership. Tourist profile	Lack of primary data collection in most observatories in Spain
Tulungen et al. (2021). Competitive intelligence approach for developing an e-tourism strategy post COVID-19	Solutions to reactivate tourism. Technological	Framework for reviving the tourism industry. Public sector	5C strategy based on: Campaigns, Content, Community, Cooperation and Competitiveness
Salguero et al. (2017). Proposal of an assessment scale in competitive intelligence applied to the tourism sector	Internal and external data, competitive advantages	CI helps to implement technology. Model applicable to hotels	Uncertain and complex environment to maintain competitive advantage

(continued)

Table 1 (continued)

	Contributions	Challenges	Limitations
Sheehan et al. (2016). The Use of Intelligence in Tourism Destination Management: An Emerging Role for DMOs	Collaboration of destinations. *Stakeholders*	Coordination. Knowledge network. Governance	Different competences of the administrations on tourism activities
Bustamante et al. (2020). Bitour: A business intelligence platform for tourism analysis	Collaborative data. Tourist profile	Official UNWTO data source to be explored	Quality of information collected in the absence of a supervisory body
Höpken et al. (2015). Business intelligence for cross-process knowledge extraction at tourism destinations	Data model for tourist destinations	Real-time knowledge of tourist profiles	More complex data mining models
Abdullah et al. (2009). Collaborative knowledge management system for eco-tourism sector: a technical perspective	Technological opportunities, collaboration	Complementing technological developments	
Silva et al. (2018). Influence of business intelligence on tourism marketing	Increased revenues from implementing BI	Data unification and analytics	
Parrilla-González et al. (2017). Territorial intelligence and tourism: Towards the integration of an economic transformation model	Balanced scorecard with management variables	Apply the model to territories with less dynamic tourism	
Madyatmadja et al. (2021). The positive impact of implementation business intelligence and big data in hospitality and tourism sector	BD and BI can respond to the needs of the tourism industry	Competitive advantages, efficiency and strategies	
Wöber (2002). Information supply in tourism management by marketing decision support systems	Marketing decision support system. Added value	Utilisation levels. Standardisation of information	
Pérez Rives & Echarri, (2021). Challenges and perspectives of information systems in tourism destinations	Decision-making. international comparisons	Need to change the traditional management model	
Fuchs et al. (2013). A knowledge destination framework for tourism sustainability: A business intelligence application from Sweden	Data with different needs of the actors. Collaboration and information exchange	Integration of new indicators into the information system (DMIS)	Non-explicit consideration of sustainability indicators aligned with the WTO

(continued)

Table 1 (continued)

	Contributions	Challenges	Limitations
Lemelin (2006). The tourism intelligence network: The quebec source for information on the evolving tourism industry	Collaborative network within the destination	Long-term maintenance of the system	Uncertainty of the system as it comes from public funds
Fantoni et al. (2020). Network of tourism observatories towards tourism intelligence: the case of Brazil	National observatory to coordinate methodologies	Consolidation of information. Role of stakeholders	Lack of continuity of investigations. High dependence on public resources
Vajirakachorn and Chongwatpol (2017). Application of business intelligence in the tourism industry: A case study of a local food festival in Thailand	Tourist profiling, to improve visitor retention	Integration of data model development. Evolving from descriptive to predictive models	Leadership for such projects must come from top management and local governments. Development of BI is new in tourism
Godnov and Redek (2019). The use of user-generated content for business intelligence in tourism: insights from an analysis of Croatian hotels	Transforming text generated by tourists into knowledge	Improve the study with financial data. Take advantage of the wealth of information available	Lack of demographic data and customer profile
Valeri and Baggio (2022). Increasing the efficiency of knowledge transfer in an Italian tourism system: a network approach	Tourism SMEs	Knowledge and tourism activity	To know the dimensions of the transferred knowledge, its characteristics and essence
Casado and Jimenez (2016). Competitive intelligence in the tourism sector, with special focus on Southern Europe	Well-informed decisions	Internal hotel information is not sufficient. Need for staff in CI	Need to improve the low levels of CI implementation in hotels on the Costa del Sol
Munas and Chandrasekaran (2021). Impact of Covid-19 and the importance of seamless integration of information technology in tourism industrial business processes in Sri Lanka	Structures interconnected through technology to create advantages	Tourism intelligence techniques and strategies to meet the challenges	Survey conducted on Sri Lankan hotel guests only
Bravo et al. (2020). Corporate governance as a strategic factor for competitive intelligence development in the tourism industry: The case of Puerto Vallarta, Jalisco	72.6% of tourism companies use data to generate new knowledge	Data management in tourism companies is not integrated in the business strategy	Low response in the process of interviewing managers of tourism service companies

Source Own elaboration

10 Tourist Intelligence in the Costa Del Sol Destination

During this research, meetings and interviews were held with agents from the sector within the Costa del Sol destination (Malaga, Spain) and a high degree of coincidence was found with the lines of argument put forward in the publications analysed.

In this sense, this tourist destination has a system of collaboration within the Costa del Sol Tourist Board, which exercises the leadership and coordination function.

There is also a system that consolidates information from different sources, generating an integrated database, with indicators and graphs displayed in a web environment. This provides useful information for agents accessing an application adding value, efficiency and competitiveness to the sector.

The next step for future lines of research will be to apply this methodology in different territories and to analyse the levels of coincidence with the conclusions of this research. In addition, the sector's assessment of tourism intelligence systems, their contributions, proposals for improvement and the aspects and attributes they consider most important will be studied.

11 Conclusions

The future of tourism lies in making the most of data, transforming it into knowledge through tools and collaboration between all the agents in the sector. After the Covid-19 pandemic, digitalisation and process optimisation will be part of many sectors, especially the tourism sector. Intelligence systems as an innovative process in the tourism sector are key in this stage after the biggest crisis that tourism has ever suffered. The following key aspects are identified with respect to tourism information systems, based on the tourism intelligence systems analysed:

– Collaboration between all the agents in the sector: administrations, companies, research centres, tourism observatories, travel agencies, tour operators, etc.... The participation of the agents in the knowledge management process, through collaborative structures, is key. Some authors mention the leadership of the administrations.
– Consolidation and integration of information from different sources. The data must be integrated and its processing managed in a unified database. The origin can be internal data, external sources, etc....
– Application of technology and business intelligence techniques to provide high-value knowledge, defining information systems architecture frameworks best suited to the circumstances of each destination. The use of techniques such as big data is increasingly common.
– Contribution to territorial and economic development by the tourism sector, being the main driver and multiplier of economic activity in many territories. An important part of the studies analysed focus on a specific territory.

– Improving the efficiency and competitiveness of the sector requires knowledge management. The collection of data on tourism supply and demand, in order to structure, analyse and disseminate them, transforming them into regular and rigorous analyses and publications, involves the creation of a flow of knowledge that provides valuable information to the sector as a whole.

References

Abdullah, R., Zamli, K., & Selamat, M. (2009, February). Collaborative knowledge management system for eco-tourism sector: A technical perspective. *International Journal of Computer Science and Network Security, 9* (2).

Barrera-Narváez, C. F., González-Sanabria, J.S., & Cáceres-Castellanos, G. (2020). Geographic information systems and business intelligence in decision making in the tourism sector. *Revista Científica, 38*(2).

Bigné, J., Font, X., & Andreu, L. (2000). *Marketing de Destinos Turísticos: Análisis y Estrategias de Desarrollo.* ESIC.

Buhalis, D. (2020). Technology in tourism-from information communication technologies to eTourism and smart tourism towards ambient intelligence tourism: a perspective article. *Tourism Review. 75*(1), 267–272.

Bustamante, A., Sebastia, L., & Onaindia, E. (2020). Bitour: A business intelligence platform for tourism analysis. *International Journal of Geo-Information, 9,* 671

Casado, G., & Jiménez, J. A. (2016). Competitive Intelligence in the Tourism Sector, with special focus on Southern Europe. *Tourism & Management Studies, 12*(1), 136–144.

Fantoni Alvares, D., Ribeiro dos Santos, S., & Costa Perinotto, A. (2020). Network of tourism observatories toward tourism intelligence: The case of Brazil. *Enlightening Tourism. 10*(2), 140–178.

Fuchs, M., Abadzhiev, A., Svensson, B., Höpken, W., & Lexhagen, M. (2013). A knowledge destination framework for tourism sustainability: A business intelligence application from Sweden. *Tourism* (13327461). *61*(2), 121–148.

Godnov, U., & Redek, T. (2019). The use of user-generated content for business intelligence in tourism: Insights from an analysis of Croatian hotels. *Economic Research., 32*(1), 2455–2480.

Höpken, W., Fuchs, M., Keil, D., & Lexhagen, M. (2015). Business intelligence for cross-process knowledge extraction at tourism destinations. *Information Technology & Tourism, 15,* 101–130.

Köseoglu, M. A., Morvillo, A., Altin, M., De Martino, M., & Okumus, F. (2019). Competitive intelligence in hospitality and tourism: A perspective article. *Tourism Review., 75*(1), 239–242.

Lemelin, S. (2006). The tourism intelligence network: the Quebec source for information on the evolving tourism industry. *Knowledge Sharing & Quality Assurance in Hospitality & Tourism., 2006,* 147–159.

Madyatmadja, E., Nur Aulia Adiba, C., Jumpa Malem, D., Pristinella, D., & Madyana, A. (2021, June). The positive impact of implementation business intelligence and big data in hospitality and tourism sector. *International Journal of Emerging Technology and Advanced Engineering, 11,* (06).

Mariani, M., Baggio, R., Fuchs, M., & Höepken, W. (2018). Business intelligence and big data in hospitality and tourism: A systematic literature review. *International Journal of Contemporary Hospitality Management., 30*(12), 3514–3554.

MarshallShpilberg, P. (1996). Financial risk and the need for superior knowledge management. In L. Prusak (Ed.), *Knowledge in organizations* (pp. 227–251). US, Butterworth-Heinemann.

Massieu, A. (2000). System of tourism statistics. *Statistical Sources, 45,* 6-7.

Morales, G., & Hernández, J. M. (2011). Tourism stakeholders. book of proceedings. In *International conference on tourism and management studies* (Vol. I). Algarve.

Munas, M., & Chandrasekaran, K. (2021). Impact of Covid-19 and the importance of seamless integration of information technology in tourism industrial business processes in Sri Lanka. *Journal of Applied Technology and Innovation* (e-ISSN: 2600–7304) *5*(1).

Nonaka, I. (1994). A dynamic theory of organizational knowledge creation. *Organization Science, 5*(1), 14–37.

Nyanga, C., Panrisi, J., & Chatibura, D. (2020). Enhancing competitiveness in the tourism industry through the use of business intelligence: A literature review. *Journal of Tourism Futures., 6,* 139–151.

Pérez Guilarte, Y. (2015). *Design of an integrated tourism analysis system (SIAT) in heritage destinations.*

Pérez Rives, L., & Echarri, M. (2021). Retos y perspectivas de los Sistemas de Información en Destinos Turísticos. *Revista Internacional de Turismo, Empresa y Territorio N°9*, enero-junio de 2021 (pp. 125–146).

Sepúlveda, A., & Plumed, M. (2018). Research and statistical information in Tourism in Spain: towards a system of knowledge and tourism intelligence. *Estudios Turísticos.* (215), 101–120.

Salguero, G. C., Resende, P. C., & Fernández, I. A. (2017). Proposal of an assessment scale in competitive intelligence applied to the tourism sector. *Journal of Intelligence Studies in Business, 7*(2), 38–47.

Sheehan, L., Vargas-Sanchez, A., Presenza, A., & Abbate, T. (2016). The use of intelligence in tourism destination management: An emerging role for DMOs. *International Journal of Tourism Research, 18*, 549–557.

Silva Idrovo, R. R., Pino Morán, F. N., & Alejo Machado, O. J. (2018). Influencia de la inteligencia de negocio en el marketing turístico. *Universidad y Sociedad, 10*(1), 326–330.

Tulungen, F., Batmetan, J. R., Komansilan, T., & Kumajas, S. (2021). Competitive intelligence approach for developing an e-tourism strategy post COVID-19. *Journal of Intelligence Studies in Business., 11*(1), 48–56.

United Nations. (2001). *Tourism satellite account: Recommended methodological framework.*

Vajirakachorn, T., & Chongwatpol, J. (2017). Application of business intelligence in the tourism industry: A case study of a local festival in Thailand. *Tourism Management Perspectives, 23*(2017), 75–86.

Valdés, L., Del Valle, E., & Sustacha, I. (2011). Knowledge of tourism at the regional level. *Cuadernos de Turismo, 27*, 931–952.

Valeri, M., & Baggio, R. (2022). Increasing the efficiency of knowledge transfer in an Italian tourism system: A network approach. *Current Issues in Tourism, 25*(13), 2127–2142.

Vizjak, A., Vizjak, M., & Ivančić, I. Using Business intelligence in tourism. In *Tourism & hospitality management 2010, Conference Proceedings* (pp. 1318–1331)

Wöber, K. (2002). Information supply in tourism management by marketing decision support systems. *Tourism Management, 24* (2003), 241–255.

Big Data in Real Time for the Management of Tourist Destinations: The TOURETHOS Platform Technological Model

José Juan Hernández-Cabrera⊙, Ana María Plácido-Castro⊙, and Jacques Bulchand-Gidumal⊙

Abstract Big data is one of the main existing promises for improving the management of tourist destinations. The acquisition of large amounts of data from different sources, their consolidation and exploitation by means of artificial intelligence algorithms will allow the achievement of various objectives for destination management, such as understanding tourist flows, an increase and better distribution of tourist spending, improving the quality of life of residents and achieving better sustainability. Additional benefits could even be obtained if this big data were to be managed in real time. To achieve these objectives, it is necessary to have high quality and reliable data sources. This article describes a technological platform called Tourethos, which allows active collaboration between different stakeholders to collect data on the movements of tourists in the territory based on their connections to Wi-Fi networks in the area. This data source has interesting and valuable characteristics: it is relatively simple to collect, it can be easily anonymized and it offers a sufficient level of precision to draw valuable conclusions for the management of tourist destinations in real time.

Keywords Big data · Software architecture · Smart destination

1 Introduction

In general, there is an expectation that big data will help improve the management of tourist destinations (Ardito et al., 2019). Obtaining massive data from different sources, consolidating it and exploiting it by means of artificial intelligence algorithms will make it possible to achieve various goals for improving destination

J. J. Hernández-Cabrera · A. M. Plácido-Castro · J. Bulchand-Gidumal (✉)
University of Las Palmas de Gran Canaria, Campus Universitario de Tafira, 35017 Las Palmas, Spain
e-mail: jacques.bulchand@ulpgc.es

A. J. Guevara Plaza et al. (eds.), *Tourism and ICTs: Advances in Data Science, Artificial Intelligence and Sustainability*, Springer Proceedings in Business and Economics, https://doi.org/10.1007/978-3-031-52607-7_13

137

management. For example, improving the flow of tourists, enabling a better distribution and an increase of spending, improving the quality of life of residents and increasing sustainability. Big data is considered one of the foundations of smart tourist destinations (Shafiee et al., 2021).

There are numerous definitions and characteristics of big data. But an analysis of them allows us to summarize its differential characteristics into two main ones: volume and variety (Xu et al., 2020). In other words, we can say that we have big data when we consolidate different data sources, some of which are massive ones. Numerous data sources are mentioned in the literature to create big data, such as social networks, tourist movements captured based on their phones or their spending, and online traces in the search and booking process (Li et al., 2018), among many others.

An alternative that allows to complement the previous sources is the monitoring of the movements of tourists in the destination based on the Wi-Fi points to which they connect. This article describes a technological platform called Tourethos, which has been developed within the international Welcome2 project. This platform allows active collaboration between different participants, public administrations and private companies, to collect connection data to a series of Wi-Fi hotspots, as well as other additional functionalities that are part of the strategy of a smart tourist destination: the cross-selling of products and the creation of destination intelligence in real time based on the collected data.

2   Literature Review

Smart Tourist Destination. The concept of Smart Tourist Destinations (STD) is usually based on that of smart cities (Gretzel, 2018). A smart city is a city that is able to improve the quality of life of its residents while making the city more competitive (Boes et al., 2015). One of the main authors in the field of smart cities, Cohen (2014), mentions six dimensions that characterize them: smart governance, smart environment, smart mobility, smart economy, smart people and smart life.

Based on this, an STD can be defined as a destination that leverages on technology to improve the sustainability of the tourism that takes place at the destination, to improve the quality of life of residents of the destination, and that promotes accessibility and integrates visitors with residents. An STD must consider multiple domains and perspectives. For example, Bulchand-Gidumal (2022) proposes an integrated model for STD development based on Cohen's (2014) model for smart cities. Bulchand-Gidumal's (2022) model consists of 18 dimensions grouped into 6 main domains: smart economy, smart sustainability, smart residents, smart mobility, smart tourists and smart governance.

Definition of big data. The term big data usually refers to two concepts. On the one hand, to the data, to the databases that build big data and that must present some differential characteristics to be qualified as such. On the other hand, big data platforms, that is, flexible and scalable software that processes and analyzes the data, usually with artificial intelligence techniques, and that makes it possible to explain and predict the behavior of a population or the operation of an infrastructure, among many others.

There are several definitions of big data in the literature. These definitions usually mention different characteristics that allow qualifying big data. Attributes beginning with the letter 'v' are sometimes mentioned. Among others, volume, variety, velocity, variation, validity and value are cited (Kitchin, 2013). Among all of them, we believe that it is possible to summarize the differential features of big data into two: volume and variety (Xu et al., 2020). These two features implicitly include many of the other ones often mentioned. For example, volume is usually associated with a high velocity of data generation.

In terms of what distinguishes big data platforms, it is the computational load required to process this data. Big data belongs to the group computational problems whose resolution time is exponential to the size of the problem. From this point of view, what determines whether software is big data is the architecture that supports the processing of the data. The software must be able to adapt to changes in data growth, depending on the processing requirements. At present, there are already architectures (e.g., Lambda) and computing paradigms (e.g., Map Reduce) that are adapted to this type of need.

Big data sources. The review by Li et al. (2018) classifies big data sources in tourism into three main categories: user-generated content (UGC), device data, and transaction data. UGC is found on social media, which in turn includes social networks, review sites such as TripAdvisor, and blogs. Device data, on the other hand, comes from users' cell phones, which leave traces of their movements at the destination, and from other traces derived from Bluetooth and Wi-Fi connections (Lee et al., 2023; Xu et al., 2020), either from the cell phones themselves or from other types of devices. This last type of connection is the focus of this article. Finally, transaction data refers to the operations that the user performs online, both before and during the trip, such as searches, bookings and purchases.

Other data sources can be added to these three. First of all, the data that can be obtained through classical research methodologies (for example, interviews, questionnaires and focus groups) and that can help to qualify the previous sources. Second, the databases of public administrations (for example, urban planning permits or vehicles in circulation), of companies operating in the tourism sector (for example, customer consumption in hotels), and open databases that may exist.

3 Objective

It has been suggested in the literature that mobile phones can be one of the sources of big data, since these devices leave a trace when they connect to Wi-Fi points, Bluetooth devices, and the antennas that provide the cellular signal. In the specific case of Wi-Fi points, in a geographical area, each point usually belongs to a different business operating in that area, which makes the collection and integration of data almost impossible. The objective of this contribution is to describe the technological architecture of a system designed to create a common Wi-Fi network in a territory in order to integrate the information generated by the devices in the territories when connected to this common Wi-Fi network.

4   The Welcome2 Project and the TOURETHOS Platform

As described above, there are different data sources that can be part of the big data of an STD. One of these sources that has not yet received much attention, either from an academic or a business point of view, is the acquisition of data on the flow of tourists in the destination based on their connections to existing Wi-Fi points while at the destination (Lee et al., 2023). The Welcome2 project, officially called *MAC2/1.1b/ 374: Welcome2, Destination Intelligence: A Strategy to Analyze Tourist Behavior in Tourist Destinations*, was developed to take advantage of this opportunity. This project obtained funding in the MAC call for territorial cooperation between Madeira, the Azores and the Canary Islands, as well as a number of third countries: Cape Verde, Senegal and Mauritania.

The Welcome2 project is part of the joint smart tourism strategy of three munici-palities in the Canary Islands: Mogán, Teguise and Granadilla de Abona, whose main objective is to generate intelligence through digital technologies. The three African territories admitted to the MAC projects also participate in this project: Cape Verde, Senegal and Mauritania. In turn, the project was born thanks to the encouragement and support of the consulting firm EPC, specialized in innovation for the public sector and the network economy. Finally, in addition to the three municipalities mentioned above, there are a number of partners involved in the project. The Fundación Canaria Universitaria de La Palmas is involved in the development of the platform. On the business side, different orgnaizations are part of the project: the Lanzarote Tourism Federation; the Federation of Hospitality and Tourism of Las Palmas (FEHT); the Business Association of El Médano (ASEC El Médano); the Operational Nucleus of Information Societies (NOSI) of Cape Verde; the Agence de l'Informatique de l'Etat (ADIE) and the Senegal Office of Organization and Method (BOM) of Senegal; and the General Directorate of Information and Communication Technologies (DGTICS) and the National Tourist Office (ONT) of Mauritania.

Finally, the scientific part of the project is led by the University of Las Palmas de Gran Canaria, with the collaboration of the Piaget University of Cape Verde, the Faculty of Sciences and Techniques of the Cheikh Anta Diop University of Senegal, the Assane Seck University of Ziguinchor of Senegal and the University of Nouakchott Al Aasriya of Mauritania.

For the development of the Welcome2 project, a technological platform called Tourethos (*tourism + ethos*, behavior in Greek) has been created. This technological platform allows the collaboration between the different municipalities to implement an intelligence strategy in the destination. In turn, it allows the development of a public–private cooperation strategy with companies that provide tourist services.

4.1 Description of the TOURETHOS Platform

The Tourethos architecture consists of sensors that collect data about the presence of a tourist in an area. The hardware of these sensors is a Wi-Fi access point. This Wi-Fi access point is installed on top of the Internet access that the establishments (e.g., accommodations, restaurants, cafes, hairdressers, stores) in the tourist area already have and creates a Wi-Fi network that has the same network identifier for all the access points in the area, thus allowing the tourist's device to connect directly to the Wi-Fi network when entering a new establishment. For example, a tourist may connect to the network created by the project when they arrive at the destination, in the first establishment they go to, as could be the hotel in which they will stay. Later, while moving around the destination, their device would automatically connect to the Wi-Fi network at the restaurant they may go to or in a store they may enter, without having to perform any validation operation. Given the project in which the action is framed, in each tourist destination in which the points are installed a different Wi-Fi network identification will be generated, with names such as Welcome2Mogán, Welcome2Teguise and so on.

In a pilot phase, 200 access points were deployed in each territory, using the existing internet connections of shops, hotels, restaurants and tourist offices. With more than 1,000 devices deployed, the first functionality offered by the platform is device control. This is, remote monitoring and diagnosis. For example, devices need to be monitored to know how long they have been running and if they are online or offline. It must also be possible to update the firmware of the devices to guarantee security. To this end, the Tourethos platform includes a management tool (Fig. 1) in which all the access points that are deployed in the territory are registered. With this tool, each territory has an inventory of all devices with their serial number, model, brand and installed firmware version. In addition, it is possible to remotely update the firmware or manage the captive portal that is displayed to users when they connect.

At the locations where the Wi-Fi access points are installed, two subnets connected to the Internet Service Provider's (ISP) router are created: a corporate subnet and a guest subnet. This separates network traffic into corporate and guest traffic, allowing businesses to achieve greater security. This allows organizations to offer Wi-Fi to their customers without compromising the security of internal traffic because the corporate subnet cannot be accessed from the guest subnet. This configuration prevents corporate traffic from being seen by guests. In addition to improving security, it also improves network speed and performance by reducing network congestion and load (Fig. 2).

As already mentioned, the main characteristic of the deployment of these access points in the territory is that they all offer the same SSID, that is, they all have a Wi-Fi network with the same name. It is enough for the user to connect to one of the access

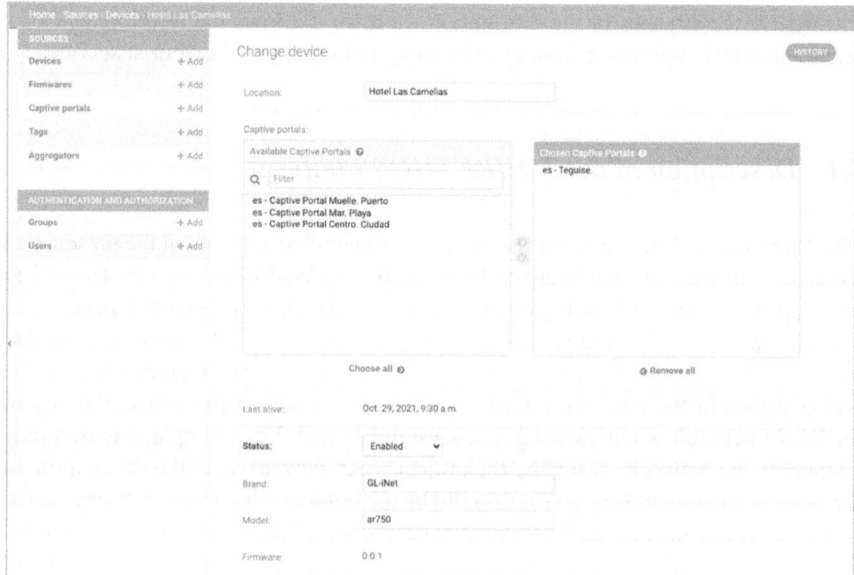

Fig. 1 Device control in the Tourethos platform

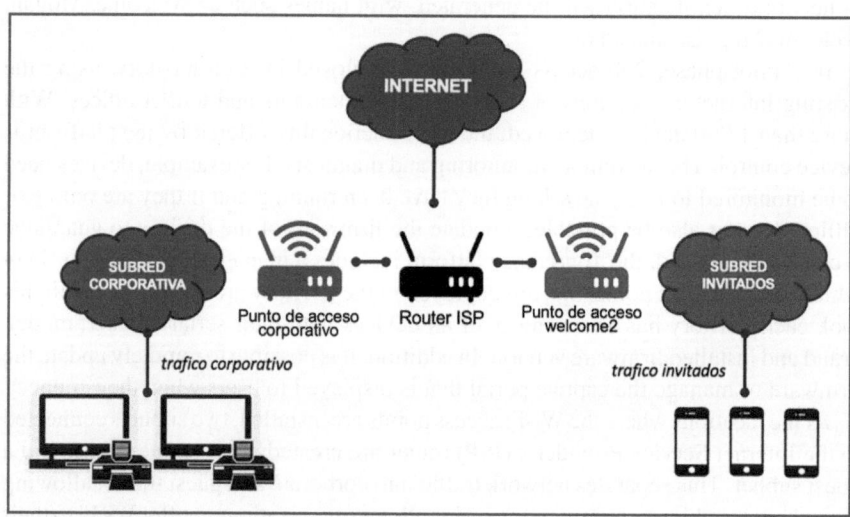

Fig. 2 Installation of Wi-Fi access points on ISP routers

points in order to have automatic access to any of the other access points. This is due to the fact that when a device has the Wi-Fi connection enabled, it will automatically connect to a network with an SSID that it has already connected to before. In this way, it is possible to offer a Wi-Fi service to tourists and citizens, taking advantage of the internet connections that the businesses have already contracted. Many authors point out the importance of free Wi-Fi access in a tourist destination (Magasic & Gretzel, 2020; Noorhaiza et al., 2017).

In the access points a software is installed to monitor the connections: *tourethos-monitor*. This possibility of installing software in the access point is one of the advantages of the operating system that the installed devices include by default (OpenWrt). In addition, it allows access to the MAC addresses of the connecting device, through which a user can be uniquely identified. The function of *tourethos-monitor* is to generate a message (event) and send it to a cloud server when a user connects to the access point. This message contains the time, the MAC address of the connected device and the geographic location in the form of a label from which the geographic coordinates can be obtained. The *tourethos-sensor* module is in charge of this functionality. The events generated by the sensor are sent to the cloud, where a service, *tourethos-datahub*, records them. *Tourethos-datahub* is a fully managed service that can send both real-time and batch data streams for processing.

This process of integrating data from different devices, while keeping the data conceptually separated on the platform and, when appropriate, between different platforms, is one of the strengths of the system and one is of great importance. In this way, each participant in the project can be offered a data analysis tailored to their needs, while respecting the confidentiality and use of the data. The different businesses participating in the project will have access to a dashboard that will allow them to see the (anonymous) behavior of those who have connected to the point/points of their establishment/establishments. In addition, they will have access to aggregated data on the behavior of other businesses so that they can make comparisons. For example, the total time the person spends in the establishment or the rate of repeat customers.

In turn, and in the same way, the tourist offices participating in the project will have a control panel that will allow them to observe the behavior of tourists in the destination, from routes in it to other data derived from questions that can be asked to tourists connected to the network. Where appropriate, it will be possible to make aggregate comparisons regarding the behavior in other destinations of the project.

In Tourethos, data is stored redundantly and protected against unauthorized access. Each of the countries involved in the project has its own set of restrictions regarding data storage and access. For example, in the case of Senegal there is the restriction that the data can only be stored in the country's own data centers. The configuration of the project respects this type of restrictions.

Tourethos data storage services can be deployed independently, so that each territory has the possibility of storing data in compliance with current legislation. In other words, each territory has the power to deploy an independent storage service so that it can autonomously protect its own data, without prejudice to the fact that they can also cooperate to have a shared data infrastructure.

However, there may be scenarios in which these data may be used by third parties other than the organizations that collect them. In fact, in the Welcome2 project, the transnational research network ACODE is formed by the aforementioned University of Las Palmas de Gran Canaria, University of Piaget, Cheikh Anta Diop University, Assane Seck University of Ziguinchor and University of Nouakchott Al Aasriya. One of the commitments of this research network is the sharing of data with the aim of carrying out joint publications in scientific journals.

To this end, a component was added to the Tourethos architecture that allows the aggregation of data from the territories. This component allows consolidated data to be analyzed in research papers. In this way, the Tourethos platform also becomes a vehicle for collaborative research, involving the territories themselves in research that can contribute to better management of their destinations. This functionality is specified in the management environment of the Tourethos platform through an operation that allows the sharing of data with other organizations. One of the characteristics of this functionality is that what data is shared and for how long is under control.

5   Results and Discussion

The implementation and development process of STD presents many challenges for destinations. The STD concept is complex and involves multiple dimensions and domains. This project touches on several of these dimensions. First and foremost, as mentioned above, and following Bulchand-Gidumal's (2022) model, it touches the IT and data dimension. Indeed, the data sources for big data are multiple and diverse, and the richer and more diverse they are, the more valuable and interesting information can be obtained from their processing.

So far, connections to Wi-Fi hotspots have been mentioned in the literature as a possible source of data (Li et al., 2018), although they have not been studied in detail. The main reason is that in an area, each Wi-Fi access point usually belongs to a different network, so obtaining joint information from these connections would be extremely difficult. This project proposes the creation of a common Wi-Fi network at the destination that, by analogy with cellular networks and antennas, allows devices to connect to the different points of the network in a seamless manner, without user intervention.

Compared to a typical situation, the proposal is very advantageous for tourists, since it allows them to connect to Wi-Fi networks in a similar way as they do with the mobile phone network. In this sense, it must be taken into account that a certain part of the tourists who go to the destinations participating in the project (Canary Islands, Cape Verde, Senegal, Mauritania) come from areas where there is no international roaming agreement. Tourists arriving in the Canary Islands from the European Union have access to this international roaming, but those arriving from the United Kingdom after Brexit or from third countries such as Russia or Asian countries do not. This situation extends to all international tourists arriving in Cape Verde, Senegal and

Mauritania. Therefore, for these tourists, the smooth use of this Wi-Fi network can be extremely convenient.

For the companies participating in the project, the main advantage is that they will have access to real-time information on what tourists are doing at the destination. All companies that participate in the project and therefore contribute data to the platform will have access to processed and anonymized information on the behavior of tourists. For example, where tourists come from when they arrive at a particular establishment, what their next visits are, or what kind of consumption they make at the destination. In addition, in the connection to the Wi-Fi network a welcome webpage is shown, in which a cross-selling of products can take place.

From the point of view of the participating universities, the project represents a qualified data source with valuable characteristics. First, it has not been discussed in the literature. Secondly, it allows to obtain data in a simple and anonymous way, which has not been possible until now. As we know, data is generally owned by the companies that generate it, and therefore access to data based on mobile phone movements or purchasing behavior has been possible, but extremely expensive. In this case, data that is generated in a distributed way in each company, is then consolidated anonymously and can be exploited at the research level by universities.

In short, and as can be verified, what the project allows is the cooperation between different stakeholders operating in the destination in a distributed way, generating data sources of great value and interest to understand the behavior of tourists and, based on this, to offer them products and services better adapted to their interests. Thus, and although we have already commented that this project is mainly oriented towards the IT and data dimension of the model of STD presented, we see that it also affects other dimensions: Marketing and promotion. Facilities and experiences, Sustainable tourism economy and Support services.

Even the generation and development of the type of data proposed in this project will allow the development of actions that would be part of the Entrepreneurship and innovation dimension, by having data on tourist behavior that will subsequently allow the development of new actions in this area.

One aspect that has been particularly relevant in the development of the project is that of privacy. To this aim, the user agreements that are presented to tourists have been thoroughly analyzed, taking into account the specificities of the participating countries. In addition, all the necessary precautions have been taken to mask the data stored in the databases, so that it is possible to have a profile of the movements of a tourist in the destination, but without being possible to follow the reverse path of identifying the tourist starting from these data on movements and connections.

As mentioned above, the proposed solution has been experimentally tested in a pilot study based on the development of both sensors and services for public administrations, tourism companies and academia. Collaterally, it has been possible to provide universal Wi-Fi access to tourists in destinations where it has been implemented. The user experience is that of feeling at home, with Wi-Fi access always available wherever they are.

This research shows a new source of data that can be used by tourism stakeholders (destinations, researchers, businesses) in order to better understand the behavior of tourists while at the destination.

6 Conclusions

In the process of developing smart tourist destinations, a key issue is the availability of high quality and diverse data sources for the creation of destination big data. So far, different data sources have been mentioned in the literature. One of them is device related, although in general it is more associated with the use of mobile phones or GPS devices. In this manuscript, the Welcom2 project is presented in which data is generated through the connections of tourists to the Wi-Fi hotspots available in the destination thanks to the Welcome2 project and the TOURETHOS platform. The project and the platform are developing a common Wi-Fi network for all the establishments in the destination. This allows tourists to connect continuously and frictionless to every participating Wi-Fi hotspot. At the same time, data is generated and consolidated in the destination's big data database. In addition, with the presented platform, this data can be exploited in real time. What has been developed in this project is a first pilot that will be strengthened in the coming years with the integration of other types of data already available in the different destinations, with the aim of better understanding the behavior of the tourist and thus improving the management of the destination, moving towards the concept of smart tourist destinations.

References

Ardito, L., Cerchione, R., Del Vecchio, P., & Raguseo, E. (2019). Big data in smart tourism: Challenges, issues and opportunities. *Current Issues in Tourism, 22*(15), 1805–1809.

Boes, K., Buhalis, D., & Inversini, A. (2015). Conceptualising smart tourism destination dimensions. In I. Tussyadiah & A. Inversini (Eds.), *Information and communication technologies in tourism 2015* (pp. 391–403). Springer.

Bulchand-Gidumal, J. (2022). Post-COVID-19 recovery of island tourism using a smart tourism destination framework. *Journal of Destination Marketing & Management, 23*, 100689.

Cohen, B. (2014). *The smartest cities in the world 2015: Methodology.* Disponible en. Retrieved February 2, 2023, from https://www.fastcompany.com/3038818/the-smartest-cities-in-the-world-2015-methodology.

Gretzel, U. (2018). From smart destinations to smart tourism regions. *Investigaciones Regionales –Journal of Regional Research, 42*, 171–184.

Kitchin, R. (2013). Big data and human geography: Opportunities, challenges and risks. *Dialogues in Human Geography, 3*(3), 262–267.

Lee, S., Sung, B., & Kitin, J. (2023). The watchful eye: investigating tourist perceptions of different wireless tracking technologies at a travel destination. *Current Issues in Tourism*, 1–17.

Li, J., Xu, L., Tang, L., Wang, S., & Li, L. (2018). Big data in tourism research: A literature review. *Tourism Management, 68*, 301–323.

Magasic, M., & Gretzel, U. (2020). Travel connectivity. *Tourist Studies, 20*(1), 3–26.

Noorhaiza, M., Faiz, I. A., & Astri, Y. (2017). Influence of Wi-Fi service quality towards tourists' satisfaction and dissemination of tourism experience. *Journal of Tourism, Hospitality and Culinary Arts, 9*(2), 383–397.

Shafiee, S., Ghatari, A. R., Hasanzadeh, A., & Jahanyan, S. (2021). Smart tourism destinations: A systematic review. *Tourism Review, 76*(3), 505–528.

Xu, F., Nash, N., & Whitmarsh, L. (2020). Big data or small data? A methodological review of sustainable tourism. *Journal of Sustainable Tourism, 28*(2), 144–163.

Big Data and Business Intelligence in Cruise Destinations

Josep Maria Espinet⑩, Carles Mulet-Forteza⑩, and Berta Ferrer-Rosell⑩

Abstract The aim of this research is to analyse the potential of Big Data and Business Intelligence in cruise destinations. This potentiality is faced from a managerial view management but also from a sustainable view management. Although the cruise industry is very small in relation to all tourism activity, in the places where ships embark/disembark or in the ports of call it has a large economic impact. The study focuses on the challenges and opportunities of big data and Business Intelligence differentiating between ports of embarkation/disembarkation and ports of call. This is conceptual research that makes a set of proposals for the application of Big Data and Business Intelligence based on the information that a cruise destination may have available.

Keywords Artificial Intelligence · Big data · Business Intelligence · Cruises · Data bases · Home port · Port of call

1 Introduction

The cruise industry is a segment of tourism activity with high levels of growth in spite of their limited supply worldwide: 272 ships with an average capacity of 2,126 passengers in 2022 (CLIA, 2023). In the ports where cruise ships dock, they generate a high economic and environmental impact. In fact, it is estimated that cruisers spend an average of $750 USD per passenger in port cities over the course of a typical seven-day cruise (CLIA, 2023). However, there are high differences when the port acts as

J. M. Espinet
Universitat de Girona, Girona, Spain

C. Mulet-Forteza
Universitat de Les Illes Balears, Palma de Mallorca, Spain
e-mail: carles.mulet@uib.es

B. Ferrer-Rosell (✉)
Universitat de Lleida, Lleida, Spain
e-mail: berta.ferrer@udl.cat

A. J. Guevara Plaza et al. (eds.), *Tourism and ICTs: Advances in Data Science, Artificial Intelligence and Sustainability*, Springer Proceedings in Business and Economics,
https://doi.org/10.1007/978-3-031-52607-7_14

a home port (embarkation or disembarkation) or when the port is a port-of-call. The passenger spending in port before boarding a cruise is $376 and the passenger spending in port while visiting during a cruise is $101. Despite the economic impact associated with the ever-growing arrival of cruise ships, the sector is accused of not being sustainable, especially in environmental terms, which is why associations and political parties are increasingly appearing to limit the arrival of cruise ships. This is the case, for example, in Barcelona and Palma de Mallorca in Spain. In fact, sustainability and responsible tourism is the biggest challenge facing the sector today (CLIA, 2023).

The aim of this research is to analyse the potential of Big Data and Business Intelligence in cruise destinations. This potentiality is faced from a managerial view management but also from a sustainable view management. The average time spent in a port of call in Spain is 7.95 h–6.50 h in terms of useful time (Espinet Rius et al., 2020). In this sense, the authors consider relevant to differentiate the challenges and opportunities of big data and business intelligence depending on the use of the port as a homeport or only as a port-of-call.

This conceptual research is part of a larger project that aims to be of use in both the applied–public and private–and academic spheres. This project brings together academics and practitioners from the sector to achieve more useful results in both areas.

2 Literature Review

Although the literature on Big Data and Business Intelligence in the tourism sector is relatively extensive (Li et al., 2018; Grundner & Neuhofer, 2021; Knani et al., 2022; Lyu et al., 2022), in the case of the cruise industry is scarce. Indeed, the search in the Web of Science (WOS), in which in the Topic there are both concepts: "cruise" and the terms: "Big Data", "Business Intelligence" or "Artificial Intelligence" in tourism ("hospitality") or transportation ("transportation") journals, written in English, in SSCI and ESCI indexes, returns 17 articles that have been analysed in detail. There 6 articles completely technics and go beyond the aims of this study. Weng & Yang (2015) collect several data to analyse shipping accident injury severity and mortality, splitting the specific impact of the cruise ships. Park et al. (2016) use the information available from twitter to assess opinions about the cruise sector. Pallis et al. (2018) analyze private entry strategies and internationalization patterns in the cruise terminal industry in the Mediterranean. Tao and Kim (2019) assess cruise experience and satisfaction through online reviews. Tham et al. (2021) use several data sources to analyse recreational cruise sustainability. Wu et al. (2020) assess the impact of cruise image on Chinese passengers' satisfaction and purchase intent. Xie et al. (2021) use the possibilities of Big Data to predict Chinese cruise tourism demand. Calatayud et al. (2022) use Big Data to analyse the relationship between traffic congestion and cruise activity using more than 80 million observations. Carvache-Franco et al. (2022) analysed the discussion topics in the popular Twitter's tourism hashtags during the

COVID-19 crisis related to coastal and marine tourism. Finally, Muritala et al. (2022) analyse the perception of cruise ships in the wake of COVID-19 through almost 140,000 tweets. Buhalis et al. (2022) is the only work found whose objective is more conceptual and broader and they propose a conceptual model that is a benchmark for the sector, although with a more technical perspective than the one proposed in this study.

3   Methodology

As this is a theoretical research, methodologically this study is carried out according to the existing literature and at the same time with the managerial experience of the authors. Given that the existing literature on this topic is very limited, the methodological approach is based on what has been obtained from the literature and the authors' extensive professional experience and knowledge of Big Data. This is undoubtedly a limitation that will need to be complemented in future studies with some qualitative and quantitative empirical research. Espinet Rius et al. (2022) propose a process of collecting and managing cruise data after defining the aims of the research. First, it is necessary to identify the necessary data. Second, to search where to find the necessary information (assessing the cost and benefit of obtaining it and dismissing it if deemed appropriate). With the information that it is finally decided to collect, it will be necessary to proceed to its integration and processing, ensuring the quality of the data so that the results derived from the analyses carried out cannot lead to erroneous decisions. Finally, statistic and econometric development will be carried out using all available tools (including artificial intelligence and virtual reality). Other relevant issues to be considered are the technical requirements for capturing, integrating and analyzing the information, as well as the frequency of updating the information.

In the case of the present research, in order to make the most of Big Data and Business Intelligence in the cruise industry, the authors will focus on identifying which information from the point of view of ports is available and their specific characteristics and proposing a model that allows the different information to be linked together. Then, some potential studies from a managerial view but also from a sustainable view are suggested.

4   Results

In order to manage the possibilities of Big Data and Business Intelligence in cruise destinations as efficiently as possible, it is important to differentiate when the port acts as an embarkation and/or disembarkation port or when the port acts as a port of call. There are ports that, due to their size or due to operational decisions, they only act as a port of call. To be a port of embarkation/disembarkation an additional set of very strict requirements must be met, apart from the high economic investment. In all cases, the number of ships and their characteristics that dock at each port are also very important, especially for managing economic and sustainable issues.

When the port is a port of embarkation and/or disembarkation, some passengers are residents of the area (for example, some of the passengers of cruises embarking and/or disembarking in Barcelona live in their surroundings), so that these passengers must be considered in a different way that the rest of passengers (from now on, passengers living in the vicinity of the port of embarkation/disembarkation will be considered as "natives" and the rest as "tourists"). For the purposes of our study, we are interested in tourists. In the case of tourists, it is important to be able to trace what they do during their stay (if this is the case) and also to be able to know all their spending behavior at the destination. The impact on destination and surroundings is completely different when tourist arrive directly to embark or leave directly upon disembarking, that when they decide to spend any night at the destination.

When the port acts as a port of call, all persons disembarking–passengers and crew–can be considered "tourists". The first key element is the number of hours that these people will stay at the destination, which is limited as already indicated in the introduction. From here it is relevant to know the number of people who disembark - on a cruise ship there are always passengers who do not disembark–and therefore have no impact on the destination–and the traceability of what they do and the expenditure they incur–always differentiating between passengers and crew (the latter are often underestimated).

Another relevant issue to consider is not only the port where the ship docks, but also the excursions and activities that take place, which can go beyond the port itself and can lead to tourism development.

Figure 1 presents an outline of the stages of a cruiser and from which we will define what information can be obtained that can be useful for efficient destination management in terms of Big Data and Business Intelligence. From here it is explained what information may be available from each stage and how it could be used to make the most of the potential of Big Data. The study does not consider the information and steps taken by cruise passengers prior to travelling to the port of embarkation, which can also be a useful source of information. For reasons of space limitation, basic approaches are made, although in another version of the study it is more detailed and precise. It is not the aim of this study to go into the analytical part.

It is important to note that the planning of cruise itineraries is done at least 2–3 years in advance, and is only changed in exceptional situations, so that destinations can know much of the information in advance and therefore prepare their destination and sustainability strategies in advance.

4.1 Embark/Disembark Destination

As mentioned above, some passengers arrive at the port of embarkation destination a day before the departure of the cruise, either because of tourist interest or transport logistics. The same happens when disembarking. It is therefore very important to

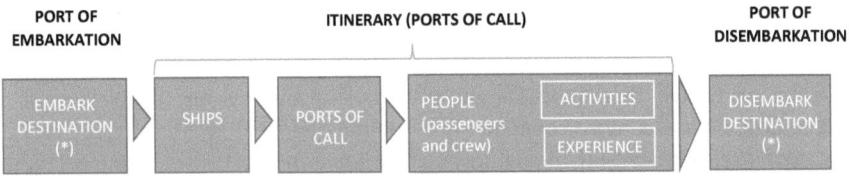

PORT OF EMBARKATION   ITINERARY (PORTS OF CALL)   PORT OF DISEMBARKATION

(*) Cruise passengers who take advantage of embarking / disembarking at a port to complete their visit to the destination and surroundings.

Fig. 1 Stages of a cruiser in defining an efficient Big Data and Business Intelligence model. (*) Cruise passengers who take advantage of embarking / disembarking at a port to complete their visit to the destination and surroundings. *Source* own elaboration

have traceability of what these passengers do. This includes where they stay, what activities they do and the expenditure they incur, as well as their socio-demographic data that allows the visitor profile to be defined. The most efficient way to obtain this information would be at the time of embarkation through a survey reflecting all information needs, but without tiring the interviewee. This should be complemented by qualitative surveys. Traceability is much more difficult once disembarked, and in this sense, it could be asked in the embarkation questionnaire or at the end of the cruise, but it will always be an estimate, but not definitive.

This information is very relevant for destination purposes as it can help a lot to define the impact of the sector and to propose strategies to convince cruise passengers to return to the destination.

4.2 Ports

In this section we refer specifically to the location and technical characteristics of the ports. The growth of cruise activity has led in many cases to having to move the ports of embarkation to the surrounding area, which is an inconvenience for many cruise passengers as it implies a greater loss of time, although it is more sustainable at the destination level. This is more common in embarkation/disembarkation ports than in ports of call (for example, from the cruise terminal in Barcelona-to-Barcelona City Hall is a 42-min walk). Again, traceability to get to/move from this location is very relevant here and can help efficient destination management, both in terms of passenger satisfaction and sustainability. This information can be collected by the port or the shipping company and shared.

In relation to the technical characteristics of the ports, the most relevant for the purposes of this study are all the measures that are being taken to guarantee sustainability and which, to a large extent, involve electrification. Unlike the previous ones, these are characteristics that are fixed for a period of time, and which are apparently easier to obtain and, therefore, susceptible to more precise analysis.

4.3 Ships

Information on the characteristics and attributes of ships is one of the keys to a destination, both at a more economic and commercial level, as well as in terms of sustainability. For each ship, they may be of particular interest: size, tonnage, length, beam, total crew, passengers, passenger space ratio, passenger crew ratio, total of cabins by each type of cabin...

This information can be obtained at a very precise level from the cruise company and in many cases is stable over time (size, tonnage, capacity... do not change often). In any case, an annual review is recommended. It is public information, so the maximum cost of obtaining it is its capture, which can be done through web scraping techniques. It anticipates knowing roughly the profile of the cruise passengers who will arrive in port and who will therefore visit nearby destinations. It is also the most important part of assessing sustainability.

4.4 Destinations of Ports of Call

In the field of port of call destinations, the first thing to know is how long the ship will stay in port and how much time passengers have to get to know the port destination and its surroundings. This information as indicated above is known 2–3 years in advance.

4.5 People: Passengers and Crew

Undoubtedly, the key to a destination is the profile of the people who disembark at its port, the activities they undertake and the degree of satisfaction they derive from these activities. This includes both passengers and crew, although the latter have far fewer opportunities.

In relation to the profile of cruise passengers, this refers to the socio-demographic characteristics, but also to the motivational and behavioural characteristics of the cruise passenger during the itinerary. For example: age; gender; academic training; professional activity; range of family income; motivations for taking the cruise; indicator of the number of cruises taken... These data are accurately recorded by the shipping companies, as are the data on the crew members, which should be shared with the destination. This information is very useful at the destination level to know the profile of the people who visit them and to be able to adapt to their needs and preferences.

In relation to the activities, they carry out, it is relevant to have the traceability of what passengers/crew members do when they arrive at the port, as indicated in Sect. 4.1 above. As an example, it is important to know how many passengers and crew move around the destination, as in some cases they do not move from the ship, which does not bring any benefit to the destination. Since in some cases passengers contract excursions with the ship itself, they may be able to provide information on this. Therefore, the source of information to obtain this information is through surveys and the shipping company itself. In any case, this information is not precise.

The last part of the analysis of disembarking persons corresponds to the analysis of the customer experience rating. This is undoubtedly one of the broadest fields, with more possibilities from the point of view of Big Data and business intelligence. In this field, there are different websites that provide precise information on the rating (for example, www.cruisecritic.com or www.logitravel.com), not only quantitatively but also qualitatively through the comments made, which can be captured by web scraping techniques at an acceptable economic cost. In addition, it is common for both shipping companies and destinations to carry out their own evaluation surveys, which they can make available if they consider it appropriate, but it is not common for them to do so. It is advisable to carry out surveys periodically since it is very important to see the evolution of satisfaction so that appropriate decisions can be made. Information on quality and satisfaction is very useful for the image, reputation and loyalty of both shipping companies and destinations, and is of special interest when it can be cross-referenced with other variables such as ship characteristics, itineraries, prices and the profile of the cruiser.

4.6   An Application to Cruise Destinations

With everything seen in the previous sections, ports could take advantage of Big Data and Business Intelligence in different areas. First, it is very important to remember that itineraries are planned 2–3 years in advance, making it much easier to anticipate measures, both from a public and private perspective.

- To know the profile of cruise ship passengers. This would allow comparison with other types of tourism arriving to the destination, and help to define the strategy as a tourist destination.
- To know the traceability of what cruise passengers, do when they arrive at port so that their priorities can be identified and adapted to achieve an excellent customer experience.
- Precise analysis of the economic, social and sustainable impact of the cruise sector, which will help to take measures in both the public and private sectors.
- Given the limitations on the number of ships that can dock at the destination, help to choose the type of shipping companies / ships that are most recommendable for the destination in the economic, social and sustainable spheres as a whole.
- Assess the possibility that cruise tourism could reduce the seasonal nature of tourism and promote longer stays when the destination is the port of embarkation/disembarkation.

In terms of requirements for the efficient application of Big Data and Business Intelligence, we consider that they are not very demanding. On the one hand, at a technical level, it is a matter of having technical equipment without great sophistication. On the other hand, at the human level, it is very convenient to have a multidisciplinary team that can identify data needs, obtaining them, integrating them in computerized form and managing them through statistical and econometric analyses that result in reports that facilitate decision-making in the economic, social and sustainability fields. Depending on the speed of implementation of measures, results could begin to be observed in the short term. In any case, a more in-depth analysis is needed.

5   Conclusions

This study aims to analyse the potential of Big Data and Business Intelligence applied to cruise destinations at a conceptual level. In this sense, the study clearly differentiates between destinations that are embarkation/disembarkation destinations and those that are ports of call, where cruise passengers spend a very limited time at the destination. This is a conceptual investigation based on the authors' experience and the scarce existing literature, and is therefore new in its field.

A very relevant issue compared to other types of tourism is that destinations can anticipate the passenger profile, given that the planning of cruises is carried out 2–3 years in advance, which means that they can adapt more to the passengers' priorities. This is particularly relevant at a time when the cruise sector is being questioned because of the overcrowding it entails-we insist, which is well known in advance-and because of its impact in social and sustainability terms.

The main sources of information for an adequate use of Big Data and Intelligence in cruise destinations are the cruise lines themselves and what the destinations have been able to identify from the traceability of what cruise passengers do. It is therefore very important that there is close collaboration between destinations and cruise lines in order to have integrated databases which should allow decisions to be made that benefit destinations and cruise lines, both economically, socially and in terms of sustainability. These databases should be maintained over time to identify trends and adapt to changes in demand as well as social and sustainability requirements.

In terms of applicability this is very diverse: to know the profile of cruise ship passengers and the traceability of what they do in destinations; to precise analysis of the economic, social and sustainable impact of the cruise sector; to help to choose the type of shipping companies/ships that are most recommendable for the destination in the economic, social and sustainable spheres as a whole; or to assess the possibility that cruise tourism could reduce the seasonal nature of tourism.

This work is a summary of extensive research that looks precisely at each of the fields that could be useful, the difficulties in obtaining them, their cost and how they could be used.

To the best of our knowledge, this study is pioneering in its field because there is very little research on the subject in the cruise sector. The main limitation of the study is that there is hardly any literature or previous experience. Therefore, it is recommended that this study be extended with a literature review in other tourism areas, and an empirical analysis in different cruise destinations, distinguishing those which are ports of embarkation/disembarkation from those which are only ports of call.

Acknowledgements This communication is part of the project "Retos para la transición digital en turismo: análisis de la inteligencia turística y propuestas normativas", approved by the Ministry of Science and Innovation Order CIN/1360/2021, reference TED2021-129763B-I00.

References

Buhalis, D., Papathanassis, A., & Vafeidou, M. (2022). Smart cruising: smart technology applications and their diffusion in cruise tourism. *Journal of Hospitality and Tourism Technology*, (ahead-of-print).

Calatayud, A., Sánchez González, S., & Marquez, J. M. (2022). Using big data to estimate the impact of cruise activity on congestion in port cities. *Maritime Economics & Logistics*, 1–18.

Carvache-Franco, O., Carvache-Franco, M., & Carvache-Franco, W. (2022). Coastal and marine topics and destinations during the COVID-19 pandemic in Twitter's tourism hashtags. *Tourism and Hospitality Research, 22*(1), 32–41. https://doi.org/10.1177/1467358421993882

Cruise Lines International Association. (2023). 2023 State of the cruise industry. Retrieved May 7, 2023, from https://cruising.org/-/media/clia-media/research/2023/2023-clia-state-of-the-cruise-industry-report_low-res.ashx.

Espinet Rius, J. M., Gassiot, A., & Rigall-I-Torrent, R. (2020). El Mercado de Cruceros: un análisis desde la perspectiva de la Oferta. Finalista Premio Fitur 2020.

Espinet Rius, J. M., Gassoit, A., & Rigall-I-Torrent, R. (2022). World ranking of cruise homeports from a customer pricing perspective. *Research in Transportation Business & Management, 43*, 100796.

Grundner, L., & Neuhofer, B. (2021). The bright and dark sides of artificial intelligence: A futures perspective on tourist destination experiences. *Journal of Destination Marketing & Management, 19*, 100511.

Knani, M., Echchakoui, S., & Ladhari, R. (2022). Artificial intelligence in tourism and hospitality: Bibliometric analysis and research agenda. *International Journal of Hospitality Management, 107*, 103317.

Li, J., Xu, L., Tang, L., Wang, S., & Li, L. (2018). Big data in tourism research: A literature review. *Tourism Management, 68*, 301–323.

Lyu, J., Khan, A., Bibi, S., Chan, J. H., & Qi, X. (2022). Big data in action: An overview of big data studies in tourism and hospitality literature. *Journal of Hospitality and Tourism Management, 51*, 346–360.

Muritala, B. A., Hernández-Lara, A. B., Sánchez-Rebull, M. V., & Perera-Lluna, A. (2022). #CoronavirusCruise: Impact and implications of the COVID-19 outbreaks on the perception of cruise tourism. *Tourism Management Perspectives, 41*, 100948.

Pallis, A. A., Parola, F., Satta, G., & Notteboom, T. E. (2018). Private entry in cruise terminal operations in the mediterranean sea. *Maritime Economics & Logistics, 20*, 1–28.

Park, S. B., Ok, C. M., & Chae, B. K. (2016). Using Twitter data for cruise tourism marketing and research. *Journal of Travel & Tourism Marketing, 33*(6), 885–898.

Tao, S., & Kim, H. S. (2019). Cruising in Asia: What can we dig from online cruiser reviews to understand their experience and satisfaction. *Asia Pacific Journal of Tourism Research, 24*(6), 514–528.

Tham, A., Waldron, R., McCallum, A., & Srivastava, S. K. (2021). Eclectic approaches to analyze recreational cruise sustainability. *Journal of Park & Recreation Administration, 39*(2).

Weng, J., & Yang, D. (2015). Investigation of shipping accident injury severity and mortality. *Accident Analysis & Prevention, 76*, 92–101.

Wu, L., Dong, C., & Xiong, G. (2020). A big-data–based analysis on the impact of cruise tourism image on Chinese tourist satisfaction and behavioral intentions. *Journal of Coastal Research, 106*(SI), 314–318.

Xie, G., Qian, Y., & Wang, S. (2021). Forecasting Chinese cruise tourism demand with big data: An optimized machine learning approach. *Tourism Management, 82*, 104208.

Big Data in Restaurant Management: Unsupervised Modelling of Ticket Data and Environmental Variables for Sales Forecasting

Ismael Gómez-Talal⬤, Lydia González-Serrano⬤, Pilar Talón-Ballestero⬤, and José Luis Rojo-Álvarez⬤

Abstract Revenue Management (RM) is one of the challenges facing the restaurant industry, mainly due to the lack of technology in this sector and the lack of data. Forecasting is the most valuable input of RM. For this reason, the main objective of this research is the proposal of a sales forecasting model based on the data provided by the tickets of a restaurant to extract information that allows the correct management of price and capacity. A system based on an unsupervised Machine Learning (ML) model was implemented to analyze the information and visualize the relationships between dishes and temperatures. The developed system uses unsupervised ML techniques, such as multicomponent analysis and bootstrap sampling, to identify and visualize statistically relevant relationships between data. This study provides a simple and understandable solution to improve management and maximize profits to support restaurant managers' decision-making.

Keywords Revenue management · Big data · Machine learning · Sales forecasting

1 Introduction

Revenue Management (RM) is a critical new approach in the food service industry in order to improve profitability and operational efficiency. The food service industry, unlike the hotel industry, collects little business data, so databases for customer relationship management are scarce (Moreno & Tejada, 2019). This limitation means that the research analyzes consumer behavior in restaurants is limited (Cavusoglu, 2019).

Sales tickets are the most common type of information available in restaurants; these data as such do not identify specific customer characteristics, making it difficult

I. Gómez-Talal (✉) · L. González-Serrano · P. Talón-Ballestero · J. L. Rojo-Álvarez
Rey Juan Carlos University, Madrid, Spain
e-mail: ismael.gomez.talal@urjc.es

© The Author(s) 2024

A. J. Guevara Plaza et al. (eds.), *Tourism and ICTs: Advances in Data Science, Artificial Intelligence and Sustainability*, Springer Proceedings in Business and Economics, https://doi.org/10.1007/978-3-031-52607-7_15

to forecast demand. However, these tickets provide valuable insight into customer consumption behavior in restaurants, allowing for sales forecasting, as demonstrated in this study.

Conventional forecasting methods sometimes fail to meet the current and future challenges associated with implementing strategies to optimize restaurant management (Jiao et al., 2018). On the contrary, Big Data (BD) technologies provide tools to manage and process large amounts of data (Samara et al., 2020). This allows the study of the restaurant's sales behavior, which facilitates optimal management through the implementation of strategies that increase operational and financial efficiency (Tao et al., 2020).

Sales predictive capabilities are essential in many industries, and various models have been developed for their application (Mariani et al., 2018). Several studies have adopted different models to forecast customer consumption, including linear autoregressive and nonlinear models (Tanizaki et al., 2019).

This study aims to obtain consumption predictions through unsupervised modeling to increase knowledge of customer consumption, leading to more efficient procurement of restaurant supplies. Sales forecasting also helps make short- and long-term decisions, reducing costs and increasing sales. Today, it must be supported by computer systems that can play the role of a good purchasing manager (Tsoumakas, 2019). Forecasting restaurant sales is a complex task, as several external factors, such as weather or economic factors (Lasek et al., 2016). The effect of meteorological factors has been demonstrated in other studies using data from a hotel restaurant and employing a regression model categorizing dishes into 4 types (Bujisic et al., 2017).

To this end, a series of experiments have been conducted by applying DB techniques to data from 367,527 restaurant tickets in 2019 through Dynameat. The startup Dynameat aims to optimize restaurant profitability using Artificial Intelligence models based on RM and Menu Engineering strategies. Dynameat was born before Covid-19 to offer restaurants a "dynamic menu pricing" depending on demand, providing the restaurant manager with a recommendation system based on customer behavior. The selected dishes are perishable foods, which are the most critical in catering. This type of food with poor forecasting can lead to food waste and high costs for companies (Lasek et al., 2016).

Multiple Correspondence Analysis (MCA) technique used in this study focuses on finding relationships between the variables that are stored in the restaurant tickets. (Pouyanfar et al., 2019). To better represent the variables, Support Vector Domain Description (SVDD) is applied to generate clouds representing the relationships in a three-dimensional latent variable space (Talón-Ballestero et al., 2018). This allows us to obtain relationships between each category (such as dishes and temperatures) using an unsupervised model without prior information about the data.

This paper introduces an innovative approach to Machine Learning (ML) based models by applying an unsupervised ML method and implementing MCA. This allows our model to employ ML in a novel way, with the potential to pioneer a new paradigm in sales forecasting.

2 Theoretical Framework and Literature Review

Restaurant sales forecasting has typically relied on techniques based on intuitive forecasting based on the manager's experience. However, forecasting restaurant sales is a complex process since it is influenced by a number of factors such as weather conditions and economic factors (Lasek et al., 2016). Alternatively, ticket data can be exploited to develop sales forecasts using ML models. This process is more straightforward, apart from being unbiased and dynamic, because it can adapt to changes (Tsoumakas, 2019).

Longitudinal data sets often manifest trends such as seasonality and linearity, which can be effectively managed with linear deterministic models. This set of methodologies includes models based on moving averages, presenting a wide range of variants, including the autoregressive (AR) model, the autoregressive moving average (ARMA) model, or the autoregressive moving average integrated autoregressive (ARIMA) model (Lasek et al., 2016).

There is a growing trend to employ supervised algorithms in food service studies using time series models. Supervised learning models use training and test data to predict a specific variable. Depending on the type of variable forecast, these models can be classified into classification or regression models (Jeong-Gil et al., 2022). Supervised models offer significant advantages, such as allowing predictions of study variables and handling larger volumes of data, but one of the drawbacks of these models is their low interpretability. These models are often referred to as black boxes since it is unknown which variables affect the prediction (Apley & Zhu, 2020).

Therefore, the study conducted in this paper focuses on extracting the characteristics provided by the restaurant ticket data, starting from the assumptions of unsupervised models. In this work, the statistical model approach is based on dimensionality reduction.

3 Methodology

In this study, the database used is configured from the ticket information of a restaurant in Madrid extracted from the Point-of-Sale terminal (POS). The company Dynameat provided us with the data and supervised access to the information from the POS systems per table. The database consists of 367 527 tickets extracted from 3 POS systems during 2019. An example of a ticket is seen in Table 1. The study uses two main variables, which are the daily temperatures and the dishes sold in the restaurant, associating the date information of the ticket with the data time stored in the temperature sensor located in the same district of the restaurant.

In order to perform the filtering, the "family" variable has been used, which allows us to discern between different families of dishes. The filtering of perishable dishes is

Table 1 Example of a ticket extracted from POS systems

Company information		
Contact in the company	Date	01/03/19
	Number #	T/017792
Company name	TPV	TPV 1
Address	Location	Terrace
City, Province 00000	Employee	Waiter's name
(00) 22 22 22 22	Table	n7

Number	Major group	Family	Product	Unit price	Amount
1	Drink	WINE GLASSES	MARQ DE VARGAS	4,00 €	4,00 €
1	Food	FISH	BLUEFIN TUNA TARTAR	24,00 €	24,00 €
2	Drink	REFRESHMENTS	WATHER 0.5	2,50 €	2,50 €
1	Food	FISH	Cantabrian hake	24,00 €	24,00 €
Subtotal					54,50 €

	10%VAT	5,45
	Total	59,95 €

Comments:

based on the different selected families ('cheese', 'fish', 'meats', 'seafood', 'vegetables and mushrooms', 'smoked and sauces', 'sausages') based on the consideration of perishable dishes in the literature (Terpstra et al., 2005).

In this study, the State Meteorological Agency (AEMET) database has been used for the collection of temperature provided by the same district of Madrid where the restaurant of the tickets of the study is located (Luna Rico et al., 2008). In order to aggregate each of the databases, it is necessary to cross both databases by comparing the same date formats of the AEMET data with the database of the restaurant tickets. The extraction of the data was done using Python code by collecting the response information from the URL where the AEMET data is stored in JSON format. The subsequent step, using the two databases, is to correlate the temperature value with the field of the dish sold on the ticket, using the date when the temperature sensor records that value and the date of the sold ticket as a key. To achieve this, we have developed a program in MATLAB. This program compares the same formats and iterates through each of the fields, comparing each of the rows.

Figure 1 shows the diagram of this study, where the first two blocks show the loading of the two mentioned databases and their preprocessing to prepare the dataset for the unsupervised model (MCA). In addition to exploring the statistical variability and the distribution of the data information, the bootstrap resampling method is added. This technique is based on the idea of generating multiple (replacement) data samples from the original sample and then calculating the statistic of interest for each of the samples (Hesterberg, 2011). In our study, the statistic of interest is the confidence interval of the weights of each of the eigenvectors obtained by MCA, where the information of each category is represented, and it is determined whether that category is statistically significant or not (which corresponds to the red vertical lines shown in the block of eigenvectors in Fig. 1).

After the bootstrap resampling, the next step is to observe the confidence volume using the SVDD method, where the bootstrap resamples considered within the hypersphere are accumulated. Another tool used is the amplitude of the Gaussian kernel from the probability density. This method is an assiduously used tool based on the central limit theorem (Wang et al., 2019). The interpretation of the latent space of the categories through the MCA is viewed as a probability mass function. In this context, centered samples represent larger values, indicating more significant repetition within the statistical range. Conversely, less repetitive samples are not centrally located. In terms of relationships between categories, closer samples show greater affinity. On the other hand, samples farther imply a lower association.

The three-dimensional representation sometimes does not allow a clear and summarized view of the relationships between the categories. Therefore, this information is transferred as a distance table, which compares all clouds and their respective distances. On the other hand, this distance table is, in turn, modified by normalizing the distances and adding a color (based on an inverted heat map) to each table cell. The heat map represents that a cold color cell represents larger distances where categories have a lower affinity and warm colors represent smaller distances and thus higher affinity between categories.

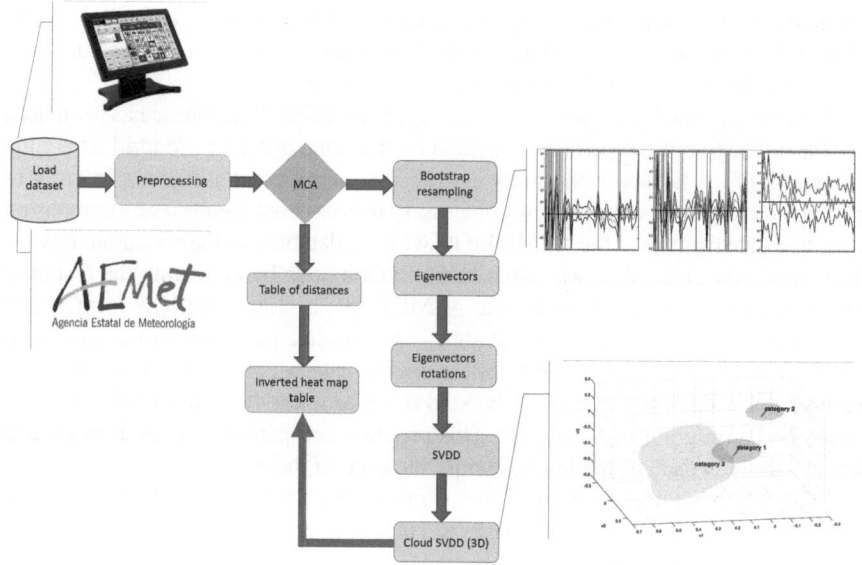

Fig. 1 Diagram of the research framework

4 Experiments and Results

In this case, the data included are the temperature values obtained from the average value published by AEMET and the dishes sold and invoiced in the tickets (considering perishable foods). Figure 2a shows the three principal eigenvectors together with the confidence intervals of each category, where the red vertical lines mean that these categories have a confidence interval higher than 95%. These three principal eigenvectors are plotted in three-dimensional space, as shown in Fig. 2b, where the clouds of temperatures and dishes are denoted. Closer clouds represent higher statistical affinity and lower affinity in the case of categories farther away from each other. On the one hand, the categories represented in the center of the three-dimensional representation are the categories with the highest representation or frequency in the data.

On the other hand, the categories farther away from the center have a lower representation in the data in the form of a Gaussian. Many categories of both variables (dishes and temperatures) do not allow us to visualize the relationships correctly. Therefore, we transferred this information to a table of distances.

We calculate a distance table using the center of the confidence volume between the categories. This table is a square matrix whose dimensions are the number of dishes and the total temperatures. Since this matrix is large and complex, we have simplified it. To do this, we have divided the temperatures into 7 categories: extremely high, very high, high, medium, low, very low, and extremely low. To decide which

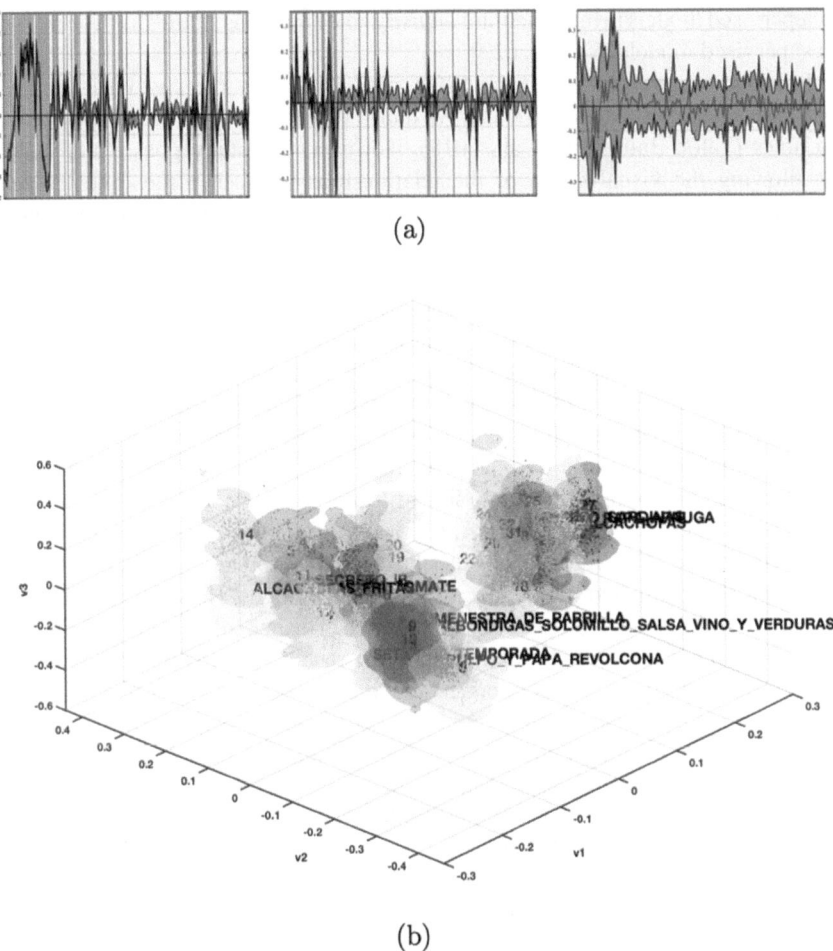

(a)

(b)

Fig. 2 The three principal eigenvectors (**a**) and the bootstrap sample representation together with the confidence volumes (**b**)

temperature goes into each category, we have used quartiles. In this way, we have summarized all the information of the matrix in a form that is easier to understand.

5 Conclusions

The present work has employed tickets from a restaurant in Madrid together with weather data from AEMET to identify relationships and improve sales forecasting. On the other hand, this study represents an important starting point for implementing unsupervised models in the restaurant industry since previous studies have been based on supervised models (Sakib, 2023).

Previous research has used the MCA model to study the customer profile in the hotel industry, which allows us to visualize the statistical relationships between variables (Talón-Ballestero et al., 2018). However, this study goes a step further by allowing the visualization of the relationships between dishes and temperatures in an inverted heat map, which provides a more complete and comprehensive representation of sales patterns.

These results reveal information that the restaurateur should investigate. On the one hand, the similar consumption of some dishes may indicate that customers tend to order them together, which opens the possibility of promoting their joint sale through techniques such as cross-selling. On the other hand, the presence of dishes consumed at the most extreme temperatures may indicate seasonal dishes or dishes that have been introduced to the menu for specific periods. Thus, these sales patterns provide valuable information to the restaurant manager to accurate sales forecasts and improve the restaurant's operational efficiency.

Although these results are promising, it is essential to consider some limitations. For example, the MCA method reveals statistically solid relationships, but its effectiveness may be affected by the size of the study samples. However, despite these limitations, this model shows relationships between dishes sold regularly throughout the year. Another important limitation is that the results refer to the "dishes" and not to the restaurant inputs (all the products that make up the dish), for which it would be necessary for restaurants to computerize the standard recipes of all the dishes, and this is still a pending issue in the restaurant industry. With this information, it would be possible to carry out forecasting of inputs and solve the problem of stock forecasting. However, if the restaurants collected this information, this could open up a promising future line of research.

The proposed methodology could be applied to other variables such as months, days of the week, and hours to know the consumption pattern. On the other hand, another study is the relationships of sales to the composition of the restaurant tables to know the behavior of the different types of segments (single, couple, family, among others). Similarly, it would also allow us to see the productivity of workers through the relationship of employees or areas of the restaurant with sales. In this line of research, there is still a long way to go as sales transaction data collected by restaurants improve their operations and product management. This increases the quality of food service, assessing the impact of promotional activities on sales and applying RM techniques such as dynamic pricing or menu engineering to maximize profits and improve customer satisfaction.

Acknowledgements This work was partly supported by the State Research Agency of the Ministry of Science and Innovation with reference code AEI/https://doi.org/10.13039/501100011033 and PID2022-140786NB-C31. We would like to especially thank Dynameat for providing the data used in this work and for the useful discussions.

References

Apley, D. W., & Zhu, J. (2020). Visualizing the effects of predictor variables in black box supervised learning models. *Journal of the Royal Statistical Society Series B: Statistical Methodology, 82*(4), 1059–1086.

Bujisic, M., Bogicevic, V., & Parsa, H. G. (2017). The effect of weather factors on restaurant sales. *Journal of Foodservice Business Research, 20*(3), 350–370.

Cavusoglu, M. (2019). An analysis of technology applications in the restaurant industry. *Journal of Hospitality and Tourism Technology, 10*(1), 45–72.

Hesterberg, T. (2011). Bootstrap. *Wiley Interdisciplinary Reviews: Computational Statistics, 3*(6), 497–526.

Jeong-Gil, C., Yi-Wei, Z., & Nadzri, N. I. B. M. (2022). A review of forecasting studies for the restaurant industry: Focusing on results, contributions and limitations. *Global Business & Finance Review, 27*(2), 61.

Jiao, R., Zhang, T., Jiang, Y., & He, H. (2018). Short-term non-residential load forecasting based on multiple sequences LSTM recurrent neural network. *IEEE Access, 6*, 59438–59448.

Lasek, A., Cercone, N., & Saunders, J. (2016). Restaurant sales and customer demand forecasting: Literature survey and categorization of methods. In *Smart City 360°: First EAI International Summit, Smart City 360°, Bratislava, Slovakia and Toronto, Canada, October 13–16, 2015. Revised Selected Papers* (Vol. 1, pp. 479–491).

Luna Rico, Y., Morata Gasca, A., Martín Pérez, M. L., Santos Muñoz, D., & Cruz, J. D. L. (2008). Validación de la base de datos reticular de la AEMET: Temperatura diaria máxima y mínima.

Mariani, M., Baggio, R., Fuchs, M., & Höepken, W. (2018). Business intelligence and big data in hospitality and tourism: A systematic literature review. *International Journal of Contemporary Hospitality Management, 30*(12), 3514–3554.

Moreno, P., & Tejada, P. (2019). Reviewing the progress of information and communication technology in the restaurant industry. *Journal of Hospitality and Tourism Technology, 10*(4), 673–688.

Pouyanfar, S., Tao, Y., Tian, H., Chen, S. C., & Shyu, M. L. (2019). Multimodal deep learning based on multiple correspondence analysis for disaster management. *World Wide Web, 22*, 1893–1911.

Sakib, S. N. (2023). Restaurant sales prediction using machine learning. In *Handbook of research on AI and machine learning applications in customer support and analytics* (pp. 202–226). IGI Global.

Samara, D., Magnisalis, I., & Peristeras, V. (2020). Artificial intelligence and big data in tourism: A systematic literature review. *Journal of Hospitality and Tourism Technology, 11*(2), 343–367.

Talón-Ballestero, P., González-Serrano, L., Soguero-Ruiz, C., Muñoz-Romero, S., & Rojo-Álvarez, J. L. (2018). Using big data from customer relationship management information systems to determine the client profile in the hotel sector. *Tourism Management, 68*, 187–197.

Tanizaki, T., Hoshino, T., Shimmura, T., & Takenaka, T. (2019). Demand forecasting in restaurants using machine learning and statistical analysis. *Procedia CIRP, 79*, 679–683.

Tao, D., Yang, P., & Feng, H. (2020). Utilization of text mining as a big data analysis tool for food science and nutrition. *Comprehensive Reviews in Food Science and Food Safety, 19*(2), 875–894.

Terpstra, M. J., Steenbekkers, L. P. A., De Maertelaere, N. C. M., & Nijhuis, S. (2005). Food storage and disposal: Consumer practices and knowledge. *British Food Journal*.

Tsoumakas, G. (2019). A survey of machine learning techniques for food sales prediction. *Artificial Intelligence Review, 52*(1), 441–447.

Wang, J., Liu, W., Qiu, K., Xiong, H., & Zhao, L. (2019). Dynamic hypersphere SVDD without describing boundary for one-class classification. *Neural Computing and Applications, 31*, 3295–3305.

Predictors of the Success of Yacht Charter in Andalusia from a Leading P2P Platform Using Machine Learning

Amor Jiménez-Jiménez⓪, Pilar Sancha⓪, Juan Manuel Martín-Álvarez⓪, and Ana Gessa⓪

Abstract Research related to the sharing economy in yacht charter is scarce compared to other tourism services such as accommodation, so more contributions are needed. Yacht rental has become essential in the tourist services of coastal destinations, providing important benefits. The vertiginous growth of the boat rental offer hosted on p2p platforms requires analysis, characterization, and search for product patterns that allow a better knowledge of it. The data obtained, based on machine learning techniques, can be used as predictors to detect which products are suitable for the growth and development of the sector in each Andalusian marina. The results provide a relevant contribution to the sector and the enrichment of the literature.

Keywords Sharing economy · Yacht charter · Nautical tourism · Machine learning · Cluster

1 Introduction

Today, the sharing economy, also known as the collaborative economy or peer-to-peer (p2p) economy (Krok, 2019), acts as a disruptive force and a crucial ally in the transformation of tourism, providing tourists options beyond traditional tourism services it provides. Tourist destinations require a wide range of services to support tourists' experiences among which are those related to aquatic leisure and boat rentals, in particular. In recent years, yacht charter has experienced a significant increase, in socializing navigation and becoming essential for the present and future of coastal tourism, being the tourism with the highest spending in some destinations qualified as a premium product that can contribute to maintaining tourist activity, increase average tourist spending, and change the image of destinations (Alcover et al., 2011).

A. Jiménez-Jiménez (✉) · P. Sancha · A. Gessa
Universidad de Huelva, Huelva, Spain
e-mail: amor.jimenez@decd.uhu.es

J. M. Martín-Álvarez
Universidad Internacional de la Rioja (UNIR), Logroño, Spain

© The Author(s) 2024
A. J. Guevara Plaza et al. (eds.), *Tourism and ICTs: Advances in Data Science, Artificial Intelligence and Sustainability*, Springer Proceedings in Business and Economics, https://doi.org/10.1007/978-3-031-52607-7_16

Andalusia has a privileged geographical location in south Spain, 910 km of coastline, 45 marinas, and an exceptional climate, which makes it an ideal destination for nautical tourism. In 2022, more than 30 million tourists visited it, which represents an inter-annual variation of 53.6% (IECA, 2023). The yachting sector offers many new opportunities and developments that Andalusia has integrated to continue ensuring a tourist service with high added value.

In this context, like the accommodation industry, the activity of p2p platforms for the intermediation of tourist services contributes to the expansion of tourist boat rentals and makes a wider range of products available to users. Due to the great diversity of products hosted on these platforms, it is necessary to dedicate efforts to their analysis and characterization to better understand them. The objective is to determine patterns to group products and facilitate the study of their offer and consumption behavior, providing values of the rates of the offered and chartered vessels that will be used as predictors to make tailor-made decisions, according to the type of product and destination.

2 Theoretical Framework

There is no universally agreed definition of the sharing economy (Höfner & Rosegger, 2022). We will adopt the definition established by the European Commission in 2016, which refers to *"commercial models where activities are facilitated by collaborative platforms that create an open market for the temporary use of goods or services, often provided by individuals"* (EC, 2016). Undoubtedly, the collaborative economy interests companies in its ability to create economic opportunities for all parties involved (Hamari et al., 2016). This has fuelled research on the sharing economy to examine how it has transformed specific sectors, as well as new opportunities and challenges brought about by it. In this sense, some studies analyze key sectors of the sharing economy in Europe (Vaughan & Daverio, 2016; Akbari et al., 2022), with the transportation sector being the most influential in terms of revenue. This sector enables the connection of drivers and passengers to save on travel costs and share rental vehicles (De Miguel-Molina et al., 2021; Ghorbani et al., 2023; Nerinckx, 2016; Akbari et al. 2020). On the other hand, the largest sector in terms of total transaction value is the peer-to-peer accommodation sector, which provides access to various rental modalities and includes rental platforms, vacation rentals, and home exchanges (Dredge et al., 2016; Milone et al., 2023).

Focusing on the tourism sector, several reasons are established that highlight the importance and growth of the collaborative economy, providing benefits for both companies and consumers. Among others, the following are fundamental: greater access to accommodation and tourism services, income generation for the local communities where these shared services are located, and the promotion of sustainable tourism (Dredge & Gyimóthy, 2017; Gössling & Michaei Hall, 2019; Hossain, 2020; Vila-Lopez & Küster-Boluda, 2022).

Yacht charter is an important subsector of the tourism industry in general. European Commission (2017), estimates that the global recreational boat rental market is expected to grow by 7.1% per year until 2026. Applying this growth rate assumes that the boat rental market could double in size by 2026. Unlike the rest of tourist activities, nautical tourism is recovering faster and better than expected. Yacht charter has experienced an increase of more than 80% in the years after covid19 (Click&Boat, 2023), becoming an important asset with a high economic return for the regions where they operate (Luković, 2012), being a tourist option that is gaining more and more prominence as a trend among tourists whom they choose the Spanish coasts. The main motivations of the nautical tourist in normal conditions are to enjoy the most beautiful beaches in the country, relax and live an original experience on board (Nexotur, 2023). In addition, the offer through p2p platforms has triggered access to these products and more and more marinas are promoting this rental, also producing a significant increase in the fleet of rental boats.

Even though, in the literature, extensive research has been conducted on digital business models for hotel reservations (Dredge et al., 2016; Zentner et al., 2022), little attention has been given to other areas of the tourism industry, such as yacht rentals (Seraphin and Maingi, 2023; Wilhelms et al., 2017). This justifies the convenience of conducting studies on this sector. For this, we consider it necessary to start by determining the characterization and behavior of the offer and consumption of these products hosted on the p2p platform.

This study focuses on a leading p2p yacht charter platform, Click&Boat, founded in 2013 and based in France. This company focused on expanding its international market and has experienced fast growth by acquiring the main competitors in France (Sailsharing in 2016, Oceans Evasion in 2019), Germany (Scansail in 2020), and Spain (Nautal in 2020). It has become the largest boat rental service in Europe, operating in more than 50 countries and 600 destinations, being considered the Airbnb of the sea. With the acquisition of Nautal, Click&Boat reinforces its position in Spain, considered one of its most important markets.

It connects boat owners with individuals interested in renting boats for recreational use. It operates similarly to other collaborative economy models. Boat owners can register on the platform and offer their boats for rent, setting their rates, conditions, and availability. The platform offers a wide range of rental options with options that adapt to all budgets and needs, allowing users to choose the boats, in the different Andalusian marinas distributed along the coast.

3   Methodology

3.1   Data Collection

Automated web scraping techniques were used to collect web data from the Click&Boat website applying a filter to Andalusian provinces. The dataset consists of information from 365 offered nautical products in March 2023 and 11 attributes (Province, location, boat, captain, license, fuel, passengers, deposit, price, beds, and users). Apart from these variables, we also incorporate the binary variable Rented (yes/no) that defines whether the boat was ever chartered depending on whether the user variable had a value or not.

The nautical charter dataset, with the total of products offered, presents the following descriptive characteristics:

The vast majority of the boat is offered in Malaga province (52.60%) followed by Cadiz (21.64%) and Huelva (14.79%). In the range of boats available, mostly launches and sailboats are offered with 66,58% and 23,29% respectively. The high-light of the charter offer is the skipper onboard service (67.67%), no license require-ments (63.84%), and no fuel supply (73.15%). Regarding capacity, the most common offer is boats with capacity for a large number of people (more than six less than thir-teen) (65.75%) instead of smaller boats (less than seven people) (34.25%), usually doing not have beds. Finally, almost 45% of charters do not require a deposit. The price per day depends on the type of boat but dataset analysis led us to conclude that the cheapest option are water scooters and sailboats, this last with a median price similar to launches and versus yachts as the most expensive option.

3.2   Clustering Yacht Charter

Clustering is a widely used statistical tool in determining a data set that groups items that are close enough to each other and far enough from other items (Rokach & Maimon, 2005), i.e., has the highest intra-class similarity and minimal inter-class similarity. The clustering technique has been extensively studied in many fields such as pattern recognition, customer segmentation similarity search, and trend analysis of products (Akay & Yüksel, 2018; Lan et al., 2023). These groups are useful for exploring data, identifying anomalies, and making predictions (Sun et al., 2008; Van Steenbergen & Mes, 2020). This method is an unsupervised machine-learning technique used to identify groups of data objects based on similar characteristics (Asensio et al., 2022; Nedyalkova et al., 2021; Rojas-Torres et al., 2022). Useful patterns may be extracted by analyzing each cluster. For this reason, clustering with an R language package software is utilized for grouping the boat rental offer. The scripts were created using the R programming language, which was set up in the RStudio environment, to accomplish the goal mentioned in this study (R Core Team, 2021; RStudio Team, 2020). The tidyverse and cluster libraries have also been used to clean the data, estimates, and graphic representations (Maechler et al., 2022; Wickham et al., 2019). In this paper, a classification of the behavior of the offer of boats for rent is given. We provide visually attractive groups to predict the preferences of the nautical offer of the users from an analyzed data set. In this way, we offer a detailed inspection of the data collected to facilitate the understanding of their behavior regarding the possibility of being rented.

Clustering mixed-type data is important for the areas such as knowledge discovery and machine learning (Li et al. 2022) although it is difficult for applying traditional clustering algorithms directly to these kinds of data. Our boat dataset contains both numeric and categorical attributes where traditional clustering (k-means or hierarchical) is not valid. We have used Gower´s distance during the clustering process, which allows giving weight for each variable as a combination of absolute distance and 0–1 distance (Gower, 1971). This means that the distance calculated for two individuals includes mixed attributes (d(i,j)). The Partitioning Around Medoids (PAM) algorithm was selected to group data points around the most centrally located object of the cluster (medoid) with a minimum sum of distances to other points rather than using the mean point as the center of a cluster as k-means method. Once the optimal number of clusters is identified (e.g. k value), the first medoid is assigned as the data point that has the smallest distance to all other data points, so it is in the center of the data set. The subsequent medoid is introduced such that the total distance of each data point to their nearest medoid is reduced. All subsequent medoids in the building phase follow a similar cycle. Then, different data points are tested as medoids, and if a different point reduces the total within-cluster distance the PAM method swaps the medoid with that point (Botyarov & Miller, 2022). All possible combinations in the given data set are tested, therefore only one solution is possible.

The optimal number of clusters is selected by silhouette width method, best used with the PAM method, which measures the similarity between each point in a cluster and compares it to the closest point in the neighboring cluster. The value $K = 2$ corresponds to the optimal number of clusters for the given data set using the silhouette width. It means that segmenting the data set into 2 groups maximizes the similarity within the groups and the difference between the groups. However, using $k = 2$ produces useful results.

4   Results

After applying the k-medoids machine learning algorithm for clustering our boat datasets, two clusters with 157 and 209 objects respectively were obtained. This section presents an analysis of cluster characteristics to help define the type of boats offered and give light on the nautical charter to increase the success of boat-marketed. Furthermore, it is so significant to provide key information regarding the proportion offered and chartered boats by location (associated with a marina). It would lead to establishing a suited offer to meet the particular needs of tourists in different places from the Andalusian region.

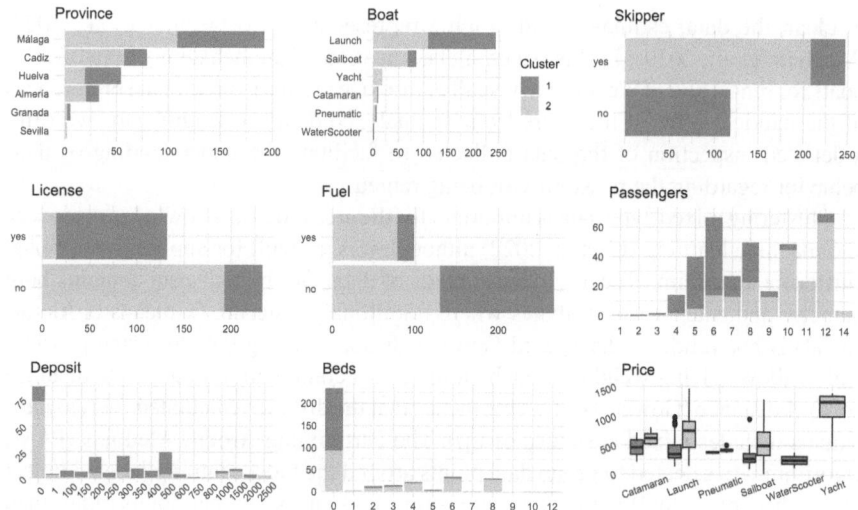

Fig. 1 Representation of the composition of each cluster

Firstly, the proportion of boats ever were chartered or not by cluster is 68.15% and 31.85% respectively in cluster 1 and 54.32% and 45.67% in cluster 2. This data is relevant to get knowledge of how the characteristics of each cluster affect to chartered rate.

Subsequently, we graph the variables by cluster to find differences between them and to be able to recognize discriminatory variables and construct patterns in the boats offered in the two clusters (see Fig. 1).

Cluster 1 presents less diversity of types of boats. It is mainly formed by launches (85.35%), although it also contains sailboats (10.83%) and other boats (3.81%). The services and equipment are linked to charter boats without skippers intended for people who own a boat license, with a maximum capacity of 4–6 passengers on board (64%), normally without beds (89.17%) or fuel included in the trip (87.26%). The fleet of boats is characterized by low prices per day that usually require a deposit. The boats chartered rate belong this cluster is 68.15%.

Cluster 2 involves a lower chartered rate than Cluster 1 (54.32%). Mostly, it contains more sophisticated boats such as yachts, sailboats, catamarans, or launches with skippers included (100%). It is common in this group, boats provide capacity on board for more passengers, in addition to being equipped with beds more frequently. Thus, it includes higher-priced boats in which a deposit is not normally required and there is optionality regarding the inclusion of fuel.

Once patterns had been identified, it can be helpful to have a better understanding of what yacht charter offer and, as such, to be able to determine the matching between boats offered and demand for complements or services for users, who are mostly tourists spending their holidays in coastal areas. The data obtained can enable a suitable product for the growth and development of the sector. In addition, being able to predict the most appropriate type of chartered boat according to the location, based on machine learning technique, is a relevant contribution of this paper.

For this, an in-depth and detailed analysis by location is required to prevent general diagnoses and achieve a positive impact based on the boat-chartered needs of each area. To do this, we compute and compare the proportion of boats available (total offer) and the rate of boats ever chartered, specifically by cluster and location. Using the variable *Rented*, previously defined, and the segmentation by clustering obtained, we calculate the proportion of boats chartered in each location. Table 1 shows a comparison between the total available (offer) and total chartered (consume), detailing the cluster and the location. We observe imbalances in some places caused by:

- Higher interest in Cluster 1 boats.

In the marinas of the towns of Garrucha, El Puerto de Santa María, San Roque, Ayamonte, El Rompido, Isla Cristina, Punta Umbría, Benalmádena, or Nerja, the rental of boats grouped in Cluster 1 is more likely.

- Higher interest in Cluster 2 boats.

In Almería, Carboneras, Cádiz, Sotogrande, Fuengirola, Málaga, and Marbella, the probability of renting a boat classified in cluster 2 is higher.

- Lack of interest in cluster products

There are marinas where boats from two patterns defined in clusters 1 and 2 are offered, but the probability of success of being rented is low or null for one of them. These are the cases of the marinas of Almería and Carboneras, where cluster 1-boats have not ever been chartered. All charter transactions have been with cluster 2-boats.

The opposite occurs in the marinas of San Roque, Isla Cristina, Mazagón, or Torre del Mar, where cluster-2-boats have uninteresting in that area.

For their part, the boats offered in Almerimar are not successful in the market, such as boats in Isla Canela or Sanlucar de Guadiana.

In addition, by province, we observe more concentration of cluster-2-boats in Cadiz and Malaga, perhaps according to the purchasing power of tourists from those areas. Nevertheless, Malaga diversifies its offer more than Cadiz, with an acceptable demand for both products. However, Huelva and Almeria have the strongest presence of cluster-1-boats. Despite this, boat rentals in Cluster 2 are more successful in Almeria. For its part, Huelva, like Malaga, shows a high acceptance of rentals in both clusters.

Table 1 Proportion of boats that have ever been chartered, by cluster and location

Province	Location	Cluster 1	Cluster 2	Cluster 1	Cluster 2
		Offered		Chartered	
Almeria	Adra	–	100%	–	0%
	Aguilas	–	100%	–	0%
	Almería	33.33%	66.67%	0%	100%
	Almerimar	33.33%	66.67%	0%	0%
	Carboneras	50%	50%	0%	100%
	Garrucha	40%	60%	**55.56%**	44.44%
	Mojacar	100%	–	100%	–
	San Juan de los Terreros	50%	50%	50%	50%
Cadiz	Algeciras	–	100%	–	0%
	Cadiz	17.65%	82.35%	23.08%	76.92%
	Chiclana de la Frontera	–	100%	–	100%
	Chipiona	–	100%	–	100%
	El Puerto de Santa María	44.83%	55.17%	**52.63%**	47.37%
	Gibraltar	–	100%	–	100%
	Línea de la Concepción	–	100%	–	100%
	Rota	–	100%	–	100%
	San Roque	66.67%	33.33%	**100%**	0%
	Sotogrande	23.53%	76.47%	25%	75%
Granada	Almuñecar	75%	25%	66.67%	33.33%
	Costa Tropical	–	100%	–	100%
Huelva	Ayamonte	50%	50%	**75%**	25%
	El Portil	–	100%	–	100%
	El Rompido	56.52%	43.48%	**73.33%**	26.67%
	Huelva	–	100%	–	100%
	Isla Canela	100%	–	0%	–
	Isla Cristina	66.67%	33.33%	**100%**	0%
	La Antilla	100%	–	100%	–
	Lepe	100%	–	100%	–
	Mazagon	–	100%	–	0%
	Punta Umbria	75%	25%	**66.67%**	33.33%
	Sanlucar de Guadiana	100%	–	0%	–
Malaga	Benalmadena	75%	25%	72%	28%
	Caleta de Vélez	–	100%	–	100%
	Estepona	–	100%	–	100%
	Fuengirola	44%	56%	47.06%	52.94%
	Málaga	44%	56%	45%	55%

(continued)

Table 1 (continued)

Province	Location	Cluster 1	Cluster 2	Cluster 1	Cluster 2
		Offered		Chartered	
	Marbella	30.12%	69.88%	34.04%	65.96%
	Nerja	87.50%	12.50%	80%	20%
	Puerto Banus	–	100%	–	100%
	Torre del Mar	–	100%	–	0%
Sevilla	Sevilla	–	100%	–	0%

5 Conclusions

Nautical tourism has recorded one of the highest development rates in the tourism industry. Tourism values water resources and activities related to marine leisure. The yacht charter provides a nautical experience that can be enjoyed by anyone, regardless of their purchasing power, breaking with the thought associated exclusively with high purchasing power people. In this way, the nautical charter is established as an asset for local tourism.

Spain ranks fifth among the top ten countries with the largest offer of boats on Click&Boat. This boat rental platform confirms a growing trend in bookings by Spanish users and offers an increasingly complete offer that responds to the plans and budgets of boaters. The expansion of this offer along the Spanish coast and, more specifically, along the Andalusian coast, is destined to play an important role in the economy and the tourist development of Andalusia. The enclaves such as those in the province of Malaga, which concentrate the largest offer of the community, stand out.

Searching for patterns of yacht charter product offerings has yielded good results by identifying two groups. The first with simpler boats and the second with more complete and sophisticated boats. In the aggregate data for Andalusia, we find that the yacht charter offer has a slight tendency towards cluster-2-boats. However, the chartered boat rate in Andalusia is higher for cluster-1. This can be visualized in Cadiz province, where cluster-1-boats are accepted by demand but the offer is low. In this sense, it would be advisable to expand the supply of more affordable boats to tourists with basic equipment to meet the profile of the boats assigned to cluster-1.

However, interesting findings emerged when the cluster-provided segmentation is performed in each locality or municipality, based solely on the rate of ever-chartered vessels compared to the total offer. As for the groups obtained, significant differences are observed depending on the locality, probably conditioned by the type of tourism in the area. This study contributes to a better understanding of the behavior of the nautical charter on the p2p platform by providing a characterization of the nautical products that affect the consumption trends of tourists in each location. Likewise, the providers obtain information on the profile of the most accepted or most needed boats in the town where they wish to moor their boats. In this way, it will be possible to improve the boat-chartering offer, the visitor experience, and the tourist development of the different localities in Andalusia.

While data-driven boat rental management is offered as a solution to improve promotional strategy design, we also saw some limitations in our case study. These are mainly related to the particular context studied. At the same time, it becomes an opportunity to expand it in future research.

References

Akay, Ö., & Yüksel, G. (2018). Clustering the mixed panel dataset using Gower's distance and k-prototypes algorithms. *Communications in Statistics-Simulation and Computation, 47*(10), 3031–3041. https://doi.org/10.1080/03610918.2017.1367806

Akbari, M., Moradi, A., SeyyedAmiri, N., Zúniga, M. A., Rahmani, Z., & Padash, H. (2020). Consumers' intentions to use ridesharing services in Iran. *Research in Transportation Business & Management.* https://doi.org/10.1016/j.rtbm.2020.100616

Akbari, M., Foroudi, P., Khodayari, M., Fashami, R. Z., & Shahriari, E. (2022). Sharing your assets: A holistic review of sharing economy. *Journal of Business Research, 140*, 604–625.

Alcover, A., Alemany, M., Jacob, M., Payeras, M., García, A., & Martínez-Ribes, L. (2011). The economic impact of yacht charter tourism on the Balearic economy. *Tourism Economics, 17*(3), 625–638. https://doi.org/10.5367/te.2011.0045

Asensio, E., Almeida, A., Galiano, A., & Martín-Álvarez, J. M. (2022). Using customer knowledge surveys to explain sales of postgraduate programs: A machine learning approach. *International Journal of Interactive Multimedia and Artificial Intelligence, 17*(3). https://doi.org/10.9781/iji mai.2022.01.008

Botyarov, M., & Miller, E. E. (2022). Partitioning around medoids as a systematic approach to generative design solution space reduction. *Results in Engineering, 15*, 100544. https://doi.org/ 10.1016/j.rineng.2022.100544

Click&Boat. (2023). https://www.clickandboat.com/

Comisión Europea. (2016). Comunicación de la Comisión al Parlamento Europeo, al Consejo, al Comité Económico y Social Europeo y al Comité de las Regiones. Una Agenda Europea para la Economía Colaborativa. Bruselas, 2.6.2016 COM(2016) 356 final. https://eur-lex.europa.eu/ legal-content/ES/TXT/PDF/?uri=CELEX:52016DC0356&from=GA

De-Miguel-Molina, M., de-Miguel-Molina, B., & Catalá-Pérez, D. (2021). The collaborative economy and taxi services: Moving towards new business models in Spain. *Research in Transportation Business & Management, 39*, 100503. https://doi.org/10.1016/j.rtbm.2020. 100503

Dredge, D., & Gyimóthy, S. (Eds.). (2017). *Collaborative economy and tourism: Perspectives, politics, policies and prospects.* Springer.

Dredge, D., Gyimóthy, S., Birkbak, A., Elgaard Jensen, T., & Madsen, A. (2016). The impact of regulatory approaches targeting collaborative economy in the tourism accommodation sector: Barcelona, Berlin, Amsterdam and Paris. Impulse Paper, 9.

European Commission. (2017). Assessment of the impact of business development improvements around nautical tourism. ISBN 978-92-79-67732-8. https://doi.org/10.2771/26485

Ghorbani, E., Fluechter, T., Calvet, L., Ammouriova, M., Panadero, J., & Juan, A. A. (2023). Optimizing energy consumption in smart cities' mobility: Electric vehicles, algorithms, and collaborative economy. *Energies, 16*(3), 1268. https://doi.org/10.3390/en16031268

Gössling, S., & Michael Hall, C. (2019). Sharing versus collaborative economy: How to align ICT developments and the SDGs in tourism? *Journal of Sustainable Tourism, 27*(1), 74–96. https:// doi.org/10.1080/09669582.2018.1560455

Gower, J. C. (1971). A general coefficient of similarity and some of its properties. *Biometrics*, 857–871. https://doi.org/10.2307/2528823.

Hamari, J., Sjöklint, M., & Ukkonen, A. (2016). The sharing economy: Why people participate in collaborative consumption. *Journal of the Association for Information Science and Technology, 67*(9), 2047–2059. https://doi.org/10.1002/asi.23552

Höfner, M., & Rosegger, R. (2022). A critical perspective on the sharing economy in tourism using examples of the accommodation sector in Austria. In *The sharing economy in Europe: Developments, practices, and contradictions* (pp. 285-303). Springer International Publishing.

Hossain, M. (2020). Sharing economy: A comprehensive literature review. *International Journal of Hospitality Management, 87*, 102470. https://doi.org/10.1016/j.ijhm.2020.102470

Instituto de Estadística y Cartografía de Andalucía, IECA. (2023). Encuesta de Coyuntura Turística de Andalucía. https://www.juntadeandalucia.es/institutodeestadisticaycartografia/turismo/visualizacion-anual.htm

Krok, E. (2019). Collaborative consumption in a sharing economy. Zeszyty Naukowe. Organizacja i Zarządzanie/Politechnika Śląska. https://doi.org/10.29119/1641-3466.2019.135.8

Lan, R., Tian, D., Wu, Q., & Li, M. (2023). An improved collaborative filtering model based on time weighted correlation coefficient and inter-cluster separation. *International Journal of Machine Learning and Cybernetics*, 1–18. https://doi.org/10.1007/s13042-023-01849-y

Li, F., Qian, Y., Wang, J., Peng, F., & Liang, J. (2022). Clustering mixed type data: A space structure-based approach. *International Journal of Machine Learning and Cybernetics, 13*(9), 2799–2812. https://doi.org/10.1007/s13042-022-01602-x

Luković, T. (2012). Nautical tourism and its function in the economic development of Europe. In *Visions for global tourism industry–creating and sustaining competitive strategies* (pp. 1304637622).

Maechler, M., Rousseeuw, P., Struyf, A., Hubert, M., & Hornik, K. (2022). Cluster Analysis Basics and Extensions. R package version 2.1.4—For new features, see the 'Changelog' file (in the package source). https://CRAN.R-project.org/package=cluster

Milone, F. L., Gunter, U., & Zekan, B. (2023). The pricing of European Airbnb listings during the pandemic: A difference-in-differences approach employing COVID-19 response strategies as a continuous treatment. *Tourism Management, 97*, 104738.

Nedyalkova, M., Madurga, S., & Simeonov, V. (2021). Combinatorial k-means clustering as a machine learning tool applied to diabetes mellitus type 2. *International Journal of Environmental Research and Public Health, 18*(4), 1919. https://doi.org/10.3390/ijerph18041919

Nerinckx, S. (2016). The 'Uberization' of the labour market: some thoughts from an employment law perspective on the collaborative economy. *Era Forum, 17*(2), 245–265. https://doi.org/10.1007/s12027-016-0439-y. (Springer Berlin Heidelberg).

Nexotur. (2023). https://www.nexotur.com/

R Core Team. (2021). R: A language and environment for statistical computing. R Foundation for Statistical Computing, Vienna, Austria. www.R-project.org/

Rojas-Torres, I. L., Ahmad, M., Martín Álvarez, J. M., Golpe, A. A., & Gil Herrera, R. D. J. (2022). Mental health, suicide attempt, and family function for adolescents' primary health care during the COVID-19 pandemic. F1000Research, 11, 529.

Rokach, L., & Maimon, O. (2005). *"Clustering methods" in data mining and knowledge discovery handbook* (pp. 321–352). Springer.

RStudio Team. (2020). RStudio: Integrated Development for R. RStudio, PBC, Boston, MA. http://www.rstudio.com/

Seraphin, H., & Maingi, S. W. (2023). The luxury yacht charter market and sustainable brand image: the case of Sunreef. Worldwide Hospitality and Tourism Themes. 0.1108/WHATT-03-2023-0045.

Sun, Z. L., Choi, T. M., Au, K. F., & Yu, Y. (2008). Sales forecasting using extreme learning machine with applications in fashion retailing. *Decision Support Systems, 46*(1), 411–419. https://doi.org/10.1016/j.dss.2008.07.009

Van Steenbergen, R. M., & Mes, M. R. (2020). Forecasting demand profiles of new products. *Decision Support Systems, 139*, 113401. https://doi.org/10.1016/j.dss.2020.113401

Vaughan, R., & Daverio, R. (2016). *Assessing the size and presence of the collaborative economy in Europe.* Publications Office of the European Union.

Vila-Lopez, N., & Küster-Boluda, I. (2022). Sharing-collaborative economy in tourism: A bibliometric analysis and perspectives for the post-pandemic era. *Tourism Economics, 28*(1), 272–288. https://doi.org/10.1177/13548166211035712

Wickham, H., Averick, M., Bryan, J., Chang, W., McGowan, L. D., François, R., Grolemund, G., Hayes, A., Henry, L., Hester, J., Kuhn, M., Pedersen, T. L., Miller, E., Bache, S. M., Müller, K., Ooms, J., Robinson, D., Seidel, D. P., Spinu, V., Takahashi, K., Vaughan, D., Wilke, C., Woo, K., Yutani, H. (2019). Welcome to the tidyverse. *Journal of Open Source Software, 4*(43), 1686. https://doi.org/10.21105/joss.01686

Wilhelms, M. P., Merfeld, K., & Henkel, S. (2017). Yours, mine, and ours: A user-centric analysis of opportunities and challenges in peer-to-peer asset sharing. *Business Horizons, 60*(6), 771–781. https://doi.org/10.1016/j.bushor.2017.07.004

Zentner, H., Gračan, D., & Barkiđija Sotošek, M. (2022). Digital business models in the hospitality sector: Comparing hotel bookings with yacht charter bookings. *Sustainability, 14*(19), 12755. https://doi.org/10.3390/su141912755

Last Tendencies in Acquiring Text Competence in the Field of Tourism. The Case of Chatbots and AI

María Dolores Fernández de la Torre Madueño

Abstract Our aim is to propose the usage of generative Artificial Intelligence, hereafter AI, while lecturing, as a complement to the traditional methodology, to ease technological skills acquisition in the related AI. Widely spread in all aspects of cultural life and professional praxis worldwide, it is of key importance in the training of our professional to be. In Malaga University's Degree of Tourism, in subjects dealing with English for tourism management, we shall concentrate on chatbots aided by AI, in order to make a literary review to see the state of the question and to reflect on the needed changes to implement these tools. We shall try to outline the characteristics, possibilities, advantages and disadvantages, and the influence on both students and lecturers alike of the usage of AI in chatbots to deal with outcoming texts. Direct interaction with the tools will be highlighted. Of key importance is training lecturers in the productive use of "prompt engineering". To conclude, handling specialised texts in the field of tourism by means of chatbots might help lecturers' awareness and responsibility for right use to obtain semi-specialised and specialised texts in the field of tourism in order to understand, extract and evaluate its pertinence.

Keywords Generative AI · English applied to tourism · Chatbots · Training · Prompt engineering

1 Introduction

AI chatbots have emerged as versatile tools with applications in various fields, showcasing their potential to revolutionize communication and generate possibilities through the use of generative AI. The emergence of chatbots has brought about a new way of viewing communication, especially when considering the possibilities that can be unleashed using generative AI tools. The introduction of ChatGPT in November 2022, as well as the access to other chatbots such as Perplexity, Bing, or

M. D. F. de la Torre Madueño (✉)
University of Málaga, Málaga, Spain
e-mail: mdfernandez@uma.es

© The Author(s) 2024
A. J. Guevara Plaza et al. (eds.), *Tourism and ICTs: Advances in Data Science, Artificial Intelligence and Sustainability*, Springer Proceedings in Business and Economics, https://doi.org/10.1007/978-3-031-52607-7_17

Bard, has sparked numerous perspectives and proposals for its application in various fields, including education, professional settings, creative endeavours, or the arts, among many others.

Chatbots can prove especially valuable as consultation channels for managing critical situations in a professional environment. These situations can arise in various contexts such as handling complaints, offering apologies, resolving conflicts, facilitating brainstorming sessions, discussing key aspects of a project, negotiating, designing, or conducting a marketing campaign. The amalgamation of personal creativity with the information provided by chatbots undoubtedly enhances the outcome, leading to a more comprehensive and effective work.

2   Context and State of the Art. A Review of the Literature on Generative AI and Chatbots for Language Learning

The utilization of chatbots in lecturing presents both advantages and limitations that should be considered. We need to convey to our students that their interaction with AI tools goes beyond simply receiving the output of their request through a prompt. Instead, we take on the role of reviewers and validators of the generated text. Therefore, it is essential for tourism students to understand the specific requirements of the text they need. These generative AI apps continuously improve through feedback and training provided by users and developers, allowing the generated texts to surpass previous limitations and shortcomings. However, it is important to note that the outputs or results produced by these apps are not to be automatically accepted. Hence, we stress the importance of verifying every outcome, drawing on our own knowledge of the required material.

In essence, while generative AI apps provide aid, we hold the ultimate authority in confirming and approving the result. Schmidt and Strasser (2022) highlight that some students may lack access to digital technology, or even have limited literacy; they also point out a risk that technology could replace or reduce real human interaction and opportunities to speak and listen. Lecturers will adapt technology to their own methods to ensure that the experience is being effective and stimulating.

2.1   Enhancing Language Learning. Tailoring Chatbot Usage for Language Tourism Education

To fully capitalize on the potential benefits for students, it is essential to foster self-learning automated processes. By instilling such habits in graduating students, they will be better equipped to continue their professional development beyond the academic setting. Li et al. (2022) highlight the need for conversational skills and support the lack of access to qualified native instructors with large-conversational data set, grammar correction, and reinforcing the system to make it more adaptive to individual user profiles. An experiment using online language learning tools showed an 84% feeling more confidence after the interactions. This may support the recognition of chatbots for increasing self-confidence in individual habits of improving fluency, as there are apps that contributes to these individual habits of learning and improving second language performance. Thus, Nykon (2023) mentions Duolingo, Rosetta Stone, Babbel, Busuu, Mondly, Memrise, or ChatGPT. AI models can replicate real speech and conversations with increasing accuracy, and language learning chatbots can respond to messages with personalized, relevant information.

The importance of considering lecturers' feelings on their use of AI apps, in addition to learners' perceptions, may be overlooked in specialised English learning. The need for greater attention to users experience in educational settings should be highlighted, mainly when the experience is still in progress with the newest chatbots. Belda-Medina and Calvo-Ferrer (2022) state that knowledge, level of satisfaction and perceptions are to be examined among educators, as there are practical implications for future educators, given for granted the need for good information about different chatbots and their benefits and limitations in language learning. It is pointed out a gap between the preparation of language lecturer candidates and the recent advancements in AI application to language learning, highlighting the need for improved training in the curriculum of English as a Foreign Language, hereafter EFL. Chatbots can be effectively utilized in the subjects of English for specific purposes, hereafter ESP, in tourism to enhance learning outcomes and facilitate engagement among students. Chatbots have shown effectiveness in providing personalized and interactive language learning experiences, offering immediate feedback and support in various language context, as chatbots can support self-directed learning, allowing individuals to improve their reading competence and develop skills such as questioning, answering, conversing, quizzing, and generating ideas or narratives (Dokukina & Gumanova, 2020). However, it is important to acknowledge the limitation of communication and potential challenges that may arise during interaction.

Training tailored chatbots to specific purposes and proficiency levels of students may enable structured interactions; these chatbots could be referred to as "intelligent tutoring systems" (Dokukiva & Gumanova, 2020). Given that the subject of English taught in the program of Bachelor's Degree in Tourism is one of the language for specific purposes subjects, there is a need for specifically designed chatbots, appropriately trained to support effective progress in self-learning English for the tourism industry, as well as their adequate utilization in the lesson setting.

Consideration should be given to the intercultural contexts in which students at Malaga University typically engage in their professional lives. Malaga is widely recognized as an internationally sought-after tourist destination, and this characteristic extends to other places in Spain and many other international destinations. Given the prevalence of intercultural interactions, it is crucial to incorporate this aspect into the data used for chatbot consultations. Zhao (2023) emphasizes the significance of incorporating courses on culture and global competence, highlighting the importance of a multi-dimensional education that encompasses knowledge, skills, attitudes, and values, which proves successful when tackling global issues or navigating intercultural situations. By including a diverse range of cultures in the database, the motivation of tourism students can be enhanced, as it allows them to develop the necessary skills for effective performance in cross-cultural contexts.

2.2 Overcoming the Lack of Experience in Using This Technology in Teaching

This knowledge gap in the EFL curriculum regarding the integration of AI in language lecturing, particularly in preparing language lecturers, highlights the need for better training in the EFL curriculum to bridge the disconnection between the preparation of language lecturers and the recent advances in AI application to language learning. AI chatbots may improve EFL learners' mastery, fluency, and skills. Therefore, lecturers must face AI-powered technologies in foreign language to ensure their students receive the best education experience.

Support and training are also required to enhance willingness and self-reliability for effective use in lessons. For Dittmeyer (2023) AI offers a significant advantage as it enables the system to determine the appropriateness of tasks efficiently and systematically for individual learners based on their respective skill levels and learning trajectories. AI can also assist lecturers and textbook writers in selecting and customizing educational materials; this capability allows lecturers to identify suitable texts, modify them as needed, or even generate entirely new texts to offer students a range of linguistically suitable resources for skill development. The potential for personalized learning afforded by AI technology is a transformative advancement in the field.[1]

Thus, to effectively leverage the potential of chatbots for English for specific purposes learners, prioritizing lecturer training on AI integration in lessons is a must. Wahyuni (2022) proposes the integration of chatbots in the lessons as an alternative and collaborative solution for English language learners, and highlights the benefits of incorporating chatbots in English language learning, particularly in terms of providing feedback and obtaining responses during interaction. The impact of chatbots on learners' confidence and specific language acquisition is in close relationship with enhanced fluency levels and conversational support.

Recognizing the potential risks involved in heavily relying on ChatGPT should be emphasized; both students and instructors must exercise caution when incorporating AI tools for learning purposes. Jalil et al. (2023) focus on ChatGPT and its performance in answering curriculum-based questions. The study reveals that while the responses generated by ChatGPT were not always 100% accurate, they did provide valuable insights; the framing of the problem significantly influences the accuracy of the responses and explanations. By providing additional information, the answers

---

[1] See also Jiang (2022), Pokrivcakova (2019), Dupuy and Grosbois (2020), Sumakul et al. (2022), Lorentzen and Bonner (2023).

improved progressively, showcasing a trajectory from initial incorrect responses to modified versions until the desired answer was achieved.

2.3 Chatbots as Collaborative Solutions for English Language Learning

Prompt engineering is a relatively new discipline that refers to the practice of developing and optimizing prompts to effectively utilize large language models, particularly in natural language processing tasks (Giray, 2023). Prompt engineering has shown potential in enhancing the performance of chatbots withing educational environments. For achieving optimal outcomes in tourism ESP subjects, the inclusion of prompt engineering as a component of competence training content is recommended. Following with Jalil et al. (2023), incorrect responses were characterized by the chatbot's lack of knowledge (due to its database only covering until 2021 in version 3.5). This lack of information led to a lack of definitions for certain terms or a misunderstanding of certain concepts. In other instances, ChatGPT incorrectly focused on irrelevant aspects of the question instead of addressing what was important. There were also cases where ChatGPT made erroneous assumptions due to a lack of understanding of the requested information. In these situations, ChatGPT's responses were incorrect. This research warns us about the need to make our students aware of these limitations and emphasize the use of chatbots as assistants, and insist on good prompting engineering training, as said above. Given the possibility of obtaining incomplete or incorrect answers, our students should develop the ability to make the most of these tools without taking unnecessary risks. They should also be cautious about relying on limited, stereotyped, or non-inclusive responses.

ChatGPT can perform effectively in tasks that involve reasoning, which can lead to an improvement in learners' reasoning abilities, ultimately reflecting in their conversational skills. However, the way the prompt is framed remains one of the main challenges, and the impact of prompt engineering needs to be taken into account. For Qin et al. (2023) the datasets encompass a wide range of tasks including reasoning, natural language inference, question answering, dialogue, summarization, named entity recognition, and sentiment analysis. Topsakal and Topsakal (2022) have specifically evaluated the performance of ChatGPT in generating dialogues for language learning purposes; they have leveraged the capabilities of ChatGPT to generate interactive dialogues that can be integrated with platforms like Google DialogFlow, successfully testing ChatGPT's ability to create dialogues in a format compatible with DialogFlow, which facilitates its practical usage.

Hallucination problems may arise, and reasoning is not reliable. However, ChatGPT performance can be enhanced through interactive engagement with users; other possibilities, such as multitasks capacities, are still under study.

2.4 Ensuring Ethical Uses and Integrity in Professional Competences

These statements suggest the need to provide students with training in crafting suitable prompts to enhance ChatGPT's performance. To enable language models to showcase their abilities, sophisticated prompt engineering is required. However, previous language models only allow for a single exploration, meaning that the target outcome can vary significantly with minor changes in the prompt instruction.

The practical implications of conversational AI models such as ChatGPT extend to various industries, offering the potential to enhance customer service, improve language translation, and generate creative content. However, their deployment also raises significant ethical and social concerns, including the potential perpetuation of biases and stereotypes as well as their impact on employment. To address these issues, it is crucial to develop these systems in an ethical and socially responsible manner, which involves utilizing diverse and representative training data and conducting regular bias testing (Mattas, 2023). Moreover, the incorporation of gamification elements and surprise rewards can enhance the engagement and enjoyment of the learning process. These elements can also encourage learners to explore different features of the software and participate in new activities, promoting a more interactive and immersive learning experience.

Susnjak (2022) highlights ChatGPT's ability to mimic human-like text generation and perform complex cognitive tasks. However, this raises concerns about the potential threat it poses to the integrity of online exams. The paper suggests solutions such as invigilated and oral exams, advanced proctoring techniques, and AI-text output detectors, although they are not foolproof. Further research is needed to fully understand the implications of large language models like ChatGPT and develop effective strategies to prevent cheating. Educators and institutions must be aware of the possibility of ChatGPT being used for cheating and take measures to ensure fairness and validity in online exams for all students.

The potential adverse societal consequences of ChatGPT, including the propagation of fake news, plagiarism, and concerns regarding social security are emphasized by Guo et al. (2023). To assess these impacts, the authors gathered a substantial dataset consisting of tens of thousands of comparison responses encompassing a wide range of topics, including open-domain, financial, medical, legal, and psychological domains. Through comprehensive human evaluations and linguistic analyses, the study aims to elucidate the inherent disparities between human-generated content and that generated by ChatGPT.

Humans can understand hidden meanings based on their common sense and knowledge, while ChatGPT relies solely on the literal words of the question. In terms of objectivity, ChatGPT provides objective answers, whereas humans often express subjective opinions. In terms of safety and neutrality, ChatGPT tends to generate safer, more balanced, and neutral texts compared to humans. When it comes to specificity, human answers are often more detailed and include citations from sources like legal provisions, books, and papers, particularly in fields such as medicine, law, and technology. For instance, Kung et al. (2023)'s exam of the implications of qualitative and quantitative feedback on ChatGPT's performance and clinical reasoning abilities. AI models like ChatGPt show potential in assisting with text production, but cannot replace human grading and evaluation.

ChatGPT's responses are typically more formal, while humans may use more colloquial language. Finally, ChatGPT's responses are less expressive in terms of emotion, whereas humans often convey their feelings using punctuation and grammar features. These differences underscore the unique characteristics of human and ChatGPT responses across various dimensions. However, further development is needed to overcome limitations and enhance the model's capabilities.

3 Methodology. Literature Review and Bibliometric Analysis

Prior to this study, there is a notable dearth of original contributions concerning the practical implementation of these technologies within the realm of tourism education. The existing body of literature lacks substantive empirical data to substantiate the efficacy and utility of chatbots and AI in the pedagogical context, particularly within the unique context of English learning in tourism studies.

Recognizing the conspicuous gaps in the literature regarding the application of chatbots and AI in the field of education, this deficiency is especially pertinent within the domain of tourism. Our methodology for this contribution commences with an exhaustive review of the existing literature in the field. This literature review aims to elucidate the theoretical underpinnings and potential benefits of integrating chatbots and AI in educational settings within the specific context of tourism studies.

In addition to our comprehensive literature review, we employ a bibliometric analysis as a crucial methodological approach. Bibliometric analysis is instrumental in identifying the most influential authors, institutions, and publications within the field of chatbots and AI in education. By integrating bibliometric analysis into our methodology, we seek to enhance our understanding of the current state of research, although we still require adequate feedback to refine our objectives in the present article.

This bibliometric analysis serves as the cornerstone upon which we construct our research framework and proposal for the incorporation of chatbots as a valuable tool to provide insights into the prevailing trends in English language education within the tourism context.

It is essential to highlight the notable absence of original contributions by the author in terms of personal publications, practical experience, and empirical findings related to the integration of chatbots and AI in English language education in the context of tourism. However, through this study, we aim to address this gap and contribute to a more comprehensive and data-driven assessment of the integration of chatbots and AI in the unique field of English for tourism education.

4   Results. Innovating English Lessons with AI Chatbots: Challenges and Opportunities

With the advent of generative AI, the landscape in which university graduates will embark on their future professions is being reconsidered. It is necessary to reassess lecturing methods, taking this situation into account, and integrating the use of these tools during the lesson, aiming to anticipate situations that require the use of the English language, occasionally incorporating generative AI tools.

By leveraging the educational framework offered by the Bachelor's Degree in Tourism at Malaga University, a novel perspective on engaging in the professional realm of tourism is introduced, as the subjects on English are focused on acquiring a high level of proficiency in a specialised and demanding context, serving as a bridge between the academic realm and the graduates' future professional lives. While these subjects must adhere to the parameters outlined in the degree verification report, the delivery of its contents allows for the integration of cutting-edge technology, hereby enhancing the effectiveness of the learning process and, above all, improving the future English proficiency of the graduates in their professional tourism environments.

5   Conclusions

The importance of incorporating technology in lecturing English in the field of tourism at the University cannot be overstated. University lecturing involves developing our students' competencies as well as their knowledge of content so that they can effectively perform the professional tasks they will face. The use of chatbots and generative AI apps enables the application of these new tools to focus on the competencies taught in university degrees. The English lecturing team specialised in tourism at the University of Malaga is aware of this new paradigm and is actively exploring the integration of these tools, while considering specific criteria:

1. The professional trajectory of students in the field of tourism can experience substantial enhancements through the utilization of applications aimed at assisting them in its design. Websites such as Europassport have emerged as indispensable platforms for personal promotion, enabling the creation of curriculum vitae and the generation of accompanying documents including cover letters, interview preparation materials, language passports, and more. Professional social networks like LinkedIn also serve as highly effective platforms for candidate and company interaction, service promotion, and more. In recent years, applications like Canvas or Trello have contributed to enhancing professional performance. In addition to these existing tools, uncoded generative AI has emerged, allowing professionals to rely on them as assistants for generating content such as text, images, videos, audio, and more. These apps require proper handling when requesting information through descriptors or prompts, especially when dealing with conversational chatbots. Lesson training

for proficient and professional utilization of these prompts is essential for adapting to the latest technologies and achieving optimal professional performance.

2. In the tourism industry, the texts generated are characterized by their technical nature, whether in marketing, commercial letters (complaints, apologies, information, confirmation, etc.), reports, memos, minutes, etc. As a textual typology, technical discourse is recognized for its clear messaging, use of specific formulas, concise sentences, or the incorporation of bullet points, among other features. If a tourism professional utilizes a chatbot like ChatGPT, Bing, Bard, Perplexity, etc. they must ensure that the resulting text maintains the specific characteristics required for that type of text generation. This is one of the reasons for which we must convey to our students that chatbots are not substitutes for our work. Consistently using this type of tool will gradually alleviate the more tedious and repetitive aspects of certain functions, such as generating technical documents.

3. The potential of integrating AI chatbots in these ESP subjects is worth exploring. Students in the Bachelor's Degree in Tourism, particularly in their English subjects that cover tourism management content and skills, can explore various applications of AI in their respective contexts. One such application involves the use of AI apps to comprehend user profiles and, subsequently, provide tailored products, services, or content based on their individual needs, interests, and preferences.

For tourism professionals, it is crucial to utilize appropriate prompts to gather user profile information that aligns with the specific demands of each situation, being, in fact a matter of highly competent communication skills. It may be emphasized that the present contribution represents one of the pioneering efforts in this area, with limited prior feedback or experiences documented by the author herself.

Apps of AI Used for Researching and Editing

Bing for All Browser (extension)
 Chat Gpt (www.chat.openai.com)
 ChatPDF (www.chatpdf.com)
 Consensus (consensus.app)
 EditGPT (extension)
 Elicit (elicit.org)
 SciSpace (typeset.io)

References

Belda-Medina, J., & Calvo-Ferrer, J. R. (2022). Using chatbots as AI conversational partners in language learning. *Applied Sciences, 12*, 8427. https://doi.org/10.3390/app12178427

Dittmeyer, M. (2023) How is the role of teachers changing as a result of the application of Artificial Intelligence? Interview to Prof Dr. Torben Schmidt. Goethe-Institut e. V., Redaktion Magazin Sprache. Retrieved from https://www.goethe.de/en/spr/mag/zuk/24515785.html

Dokukiva, I., & Gumanova, J. (2020). The rise of chatbots–New personal assistants in foreign language learning. *Procedia Computer Science (Elsevier), 169*(10), 542–546. https://doi.org/10.1016/j.procs.2020.02.212

Dupuy, B., & Grosbois, M. (Coords.). (2020). Language learning and professionalization in higher education: Pathways to preparing learners and teachers in/for the 21st century. Research Publishing. https://doi.org/10.14705/rpnet.2020.44.9782490057757

Giray, L. (2023). Prompt engineering with ChatGPT: A guide for academic writers. *Annals of Biomedical Engineering.* https://doi.org/10.1007/s10439-023-03272-4

Guo, B., Zhang, X., Wang, Z., Jiang, M., Nie, J., Ding, Y., Yue, J., & and Wu, Y. (2023). How close is ChatGPT to human experts? Comparison corpus, evaluation, and detection. arXiv:2301.07597. https://doi.org/10.48550/arXiv.2301.07597

Jalil, S., Rafi, S., LaToza, T. D., Moran, K., & Lam, W. (2023). ChatGPT and software testing education: Promises & Perils. arXiv:2302.03287. https://doi.org/10.1109/ICSTW58534.2023.00078

Jiang, R. (2022). How does artificial intelligence empower EFL teaching and learning nowadays? A review on artificial intelligence in the EFL context. *Frontiers in Psychology. Section Educational Psychology.* https://doi.org/10.3389/fpsyg.2022.1049401

Kung, T. H., Cheatham, M., Medenilla, A., Sillos, C., De Leon, L., Elepaño, C., Madriaga, M., Aggabao, R., Diaz-Candido, G., Maningo, J., & Tseng, V. (2023). Performance of ChatGPT on USMLE: Potential for AI-assisted medical education using large language models. *PLOS Digital Health, 2(2).* https://doi.org/10.1371/journal.pdig.0000198

Li, Y., Chen, C., Yu, D., Davidson, S., Hou, R., Yuan, X., Tan, Y., Pham, D., & Yu, Z. (2022). Using Chatbots to teach languages. In *L@S '22: Proceedings of the Ninth ACM Conference on Learning @ Scale* (pp. 451–455). https://doi.org/10.1145/3491140.3528329

Lorentzen, A., & Bonner, E. (2023). Customizable ChatGPT AI Chatbots for Conversation Practice. In *The FLTMAG. IALLT's free language technology magazine.* Retrieved from https://fltmag.com/customizable-chatgpt-ai-chatbots-for-conversation-practice/

Mattas, P. S. (2023). ChatGPT: A study of AI language processing and its implications. In *International Journal of Research Publication and Reviews, 4*(2), 435–440. https://doi.org/10.55248/gengpi.2023.4218

Nykon, Y. (2023). Essentials of artificial intelligence for language learning. Retrieved from https://intellias.com/how-ai-helps-crack-a-new-language/

Pokrivcakova, S. (2019). Preparing lecturerrs for the application of AI-powered technologies in foreign language education. *Journal of Language and Cultural Education, 7*(3), 135–153. https://doi.org/10.2478/jolace-2019-0025

Qin, C., Zhang, A., Zhang, Z., Chen, J., Yasunaga, M., & Yang, D. (2023). Is ChatGPT a general-purpose natural language processing task solver? arXiv:2302.06476. 10.48550

Schmidt, T., & Strasser, T. (2022). Artificial intelligence in foreign language learning and teaching. *Anglistik, 33*(1), 165–184. https://doi.org/10.33675/ANGL/2022/1/14

Sumakul, D. T., Hamied, F. A., & Sukyadi, D. (2022). Artificial intelligence in EFL classrooms: Friend or Foe? In *LEARN Journal: Language Education and Acquisition Research Network, 15*(1), 232–256. Retrieved from https://so04.tci-thaijo.org/index.php/LEARN/article/view/256723

Susnjak, T. (2022). ChatGPT: The end of online exam integrity? https://doi.org/10.48550/arxiv.2212.09292. (ArXiv).

Topsakal, O., & Topsakal, E. (2022). Framework for a foreign language teaching software for children utilizing AR, Voicebots and ChatGPT (Large Language Models). *The Journal of Cognitive Systems, 7*(2), 33–38. https://doi.org/10.52876/jcs.1227392

Wahyuni, D. S. (2022). Integrated classroom-chatbot experience: An alternative solution for English as foreign language learners. *English Language Education and Current Trends (ELECT)*, *1*(1), 63–68. https://doi.org/10.37301/elect.v1i1.36

Zhao, Y. (2023). AI means a rethink of teaching foreign languages. Retrieved from https://pursuit. unimelb.edu.au/articles/ai-means-a-rethink-of-teaching-foreign-languages

Sustainability, Platform Economies and New Realities

Digital Transition, Innovation and Business Models in Airbnb: A Bibliometric Analysis

Ana María Barrera-Martínez and Eduardo Parra-López

Abstract The process of digital transition often involves disruptive innovations in the ways we work, processes and how we understand firms. These flexible processes and their ability to be innovative require mechanisms of collective knowledge and uniqueness. Similarly, the application of business models and the management of Airbnb is another field of study, which has not been explored in sufficient depth in the academic literature. However, the applications and possible derivatives of their impact need to be clarified. To this end, a bibliometric analysis is carried out through the *VOSviewer* and *Bibliometrix* software's, grouping the aforementioned constructs and resulting in a total analysis of 4729 published works, 97 countries and 2872 authors. After this process, the reality that links the phenomena of digital transition, innovation, business models and Airbnb will be known and future lines of research are proposed to complete this conclusion.

Keywords Digital transition · Innovation · Business models · Airbnb · Bibliometric analysis

1 Introduction

Firms create value and commercialize their products and ideas through their business models. As the foundation of any venture, business models are responsible for manifesting as a final product every idea initially proposed. It is essential for a company to know every of its element in order to have a wider perspective towards the digital transition and other type of innovation other than that of products or processes. As a consequence, markets are transformed or even new ones are born, thus demonstrating the value of business model innovation. In this way, incorporating a digital

A. M. Barrera-Martínez (✉) · E. Parra-López
Universidad de La Laguna, San Cristóbal de La Laguna, Spain
e-mail: alu0101350042@ull.edu.es

E. Parra-López
e-mail: EPARRA@ULL.EDU.ES

A. J. Guevara Plaza et al. (eds.), *Tourism and ICTs: Advances in Data Science, Artificial Intelligence and Sustainability*, Springer Proceedings in Business and Economics, https://doi.org/10.1007/978-3-031-52607-7_18

transition into business models is, in addition to an opportunity for growth, a necessity to maintain competitiveness and permanence in the tourism market. In contrast to the above, the Airbnb may have been more impregnated with the phenomena of innovation and digitalisation. Therefore, this study aims to respond to this debate by identifying research trends, topics, journals, influential authors and methodologies through a review of the literature using the methodology of bibliometric analysis. Along these lines, the answers to the questions raised will be defined in the different sections of the work.

2 Theoretical Framework

2.1 How to Turn the Digital Transition into Innovation?

While it is true that digitalization and its transition are concepts that are broadly applicable to any industry, their meaning may vary depending on the perspective of application and the objectives pursued. In this way, the tourism industry focuses on the use of technologies that allow them to transit, transform and improve the way in which generate value and exchange it with the market (Matarazzo et al., 2021). In addition, the application of technology and digitalization in this industry means not only new modifications in the labour structure and in the service sector, but it also enables opportunities in terms of management of the collection and analysis of information and data on tourism supply and demand (OECD, 2020).

Along with the digital transition, new opportunities have been generated leading to the other construct of analysis of this study, innovation. It can be said that one of the main objectives of innovation is the implementation of new production processes or the improvement of current ones, thus increasing the productivity and competitiveness of the company. Today, the tourism industry is increasingly characterized by its immense capacity for innovation. Thus, as part of the service sector, has inevitably been associated with the evolution of new technologies and organizational and structural innovations. It also faces new challenges that require new perspectives, such as the diffusion of information and communication technologies, with an effect on the creation, production and consumption of tourism products.

2.2 Business Model and Airbnb

With the rise of entrepreneurship, the determination of a business plan is considered the key and main element to propose innovation and business creation initiatives. In this way, a business model is understood as the foundations that allow companies to create, provide and capture value (Osterwalder & Pigneur, 2010). Tourism activity, as dependent on environmental factors, requires an adaptation of business models. In this way, and considering the trends in the sector, it is essential to commit to a tourism development model that incorporates the principles of innovation, technology and sustainability into its business models (Segittur, 2021).

Over the last few decades, the tourism sector has experienced one of the biggest changes and challenges in terms of the business model related to the operation and marketing of non-hotel accommodation units, known as *"holiday tourist housing"*. Since then, this tourist phenomenon has revolutionized the sector, as it has been the choice of accommodation for millions of tourists every year. At the same time, and due to its social implication, it has been the subject of multiple analyses and studies that cover both its organization and regulation, as well as its advantages and disadvantages. It is important to note that in addition to the intrinsic characteristics of the Airbnb as a reason for its expansion, the development of the internet and social networks has played a fundamental role in its current positioning.

3 Methodology

This paper performed a bibliometric analysis to review and classify the studies published on Digital Transition, innovation, business models and Airbnb, in order to identify the main themes and sub-themes that emerged in the existing literature (Donthu et al., 2020). Bibliometrics involves the application of mathematical and statistical methods to analyze and evaluate the quantity and quality of publications within a given scientific field (Durieux & Genevan, 2010). Therefore, it is a very useful methodology to develop a global view of the main trends affecting a research area, journal or country (Hood & Wilson, 2001), and to help identify the main researchers in an area (Bjork et al., 2014).

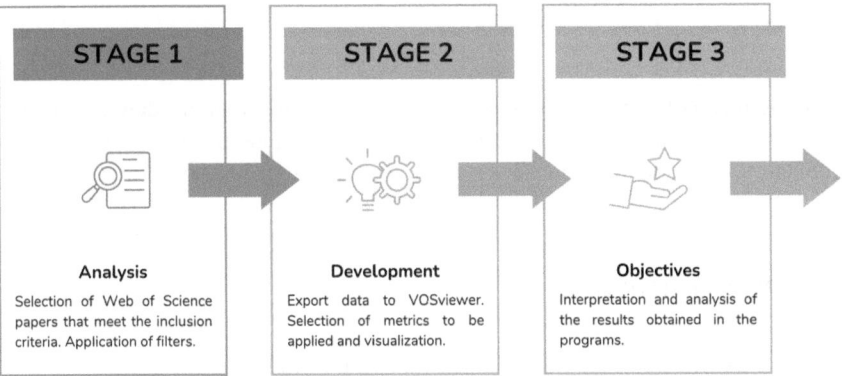

Fig. 1 Methodological stages of bibliometric analysis. *Source* Authors' own elaboration based on the analysis of the literature

Vos-viewer and *Bibliometric software* were used to carry out the bibliometric analysis, as contain a broader set of techniques and provide analyses and graphs for the metrics of the sources (journals, documents and authors) and the structures (conceptual, intellectual and social) of knowledge (Moral-Muñoz et al., 2020). In this work, three stages were carried out, identified in the following illustration. (Fig. 1).

3.1 Data Collection

The database of this study corresponds to the Web platform of Science (Wos), the world's leading academic multidisciplinary database for published articles and citations (Castillo-Vergara et al., 2018; Goyal & Kumar, 2021), in addition to its high compatibility with the Vosviewer and Bibliometrix. To identify the published studies on the concepts to be analyzed, the following was used Search Equation (EC):

EB = ("digital transition" AND "innovation") y ("business model" AND "airbnb")

The keyword search provided a large number of articles, obtaining a total of 4,729 and 123 results respectively. Several filters were used to narrow the search field, improve the operability of the analysis and focus the specific area of study. To this end, a time limit of 10 years was established and the search was limited to studies published in the categories "Business", "Economics", "Hospitality and Leisure" and "Management". The last filter was applied to identify empirical studies published in peer-reviewed journals and excluded proceedings, book chapters, review articles and editorial material, resulting in the identification of 399 articles on digitalization and innovation and 65 articles on business models and vacation homes.

3.2 Data Analysis

Once the data collection process is completed, the indicators are defined, such as the concurrence of keywords, the density of publications per year, the scientific production and collaborations between countries and the analysis of citations.

3.3 Data Visualization

This work complemented the bibliometric analysis with *Vosviewer and Bibliometrix* software to outline the existing knowledge on the domain of digitalization, innovation, business model and vacation home. These programs are increasingly used for this type of analysis, as they provide a graphical representation of biblio-metric networks and, specifically, establish network maps that relate keywords, cited authors, or cited journals. In addition, they highlight the most common terms in the defined description of a bibliographic record, highlight the cluster groups of the concepts analyzed, and identify the citation intensity of the highlighted concepts (Lulewicz-Sas, 2017).

4 Analysis of Results

4.1 Keywords

Figure 2 presents the network of co-occurrence relationships between keywords in the titles, digitization and innovation, with the aim of subsequently classifying them by topic. For the analysis, it was indicated that the minimum frequency of occurrence of the terms was 20 times, resulting in a total of 31 words distributed among 3 clusters. The most repeated word per cluster is "digitization" (red cluster), "innovation" (green cluster), "dynamic capabilities" (blue cluster).

Continuing with the same analysis, Fig. 3 shows the relationships between keywords in the titles business model and Airbnb. For this analysis, the minimum frequency of occurrence was limited to 4 times, resulting in a total of 28 words distributed in 3 clusters. The most repeated words per cluster are "*sharing economy*" (red cluster), "*business model*" (green cluster) and "*trust*" (blue cluster).

4.2 Scientific Production by Country and Collaborations Between Countries

After analysing the articles published according to their respective countries, a graph is established to indicates the geographical dispersion of the topic discussed, as well as the existing links in relation to research on the subject at an international level. In this way, the importance of a topic in different countries and at a global level is shown.

On the one hand, the binomial "*digital transition*" and "*innovation*" are terms that are widespread internationally, since there is at least one article in up to 64 different countries, showing that the 5 countries (USA, China, Germany, Spain and Italy) with the most articles published on this topic and their respective frequency (15.02;14,1;12,9;7,8 and 6.4%). In relation to the international collaborations of the documents studied. The countries with the most collaboration are Sweden and Finland, with a total of 10 articles, followed by the United States and China with 9 articles.

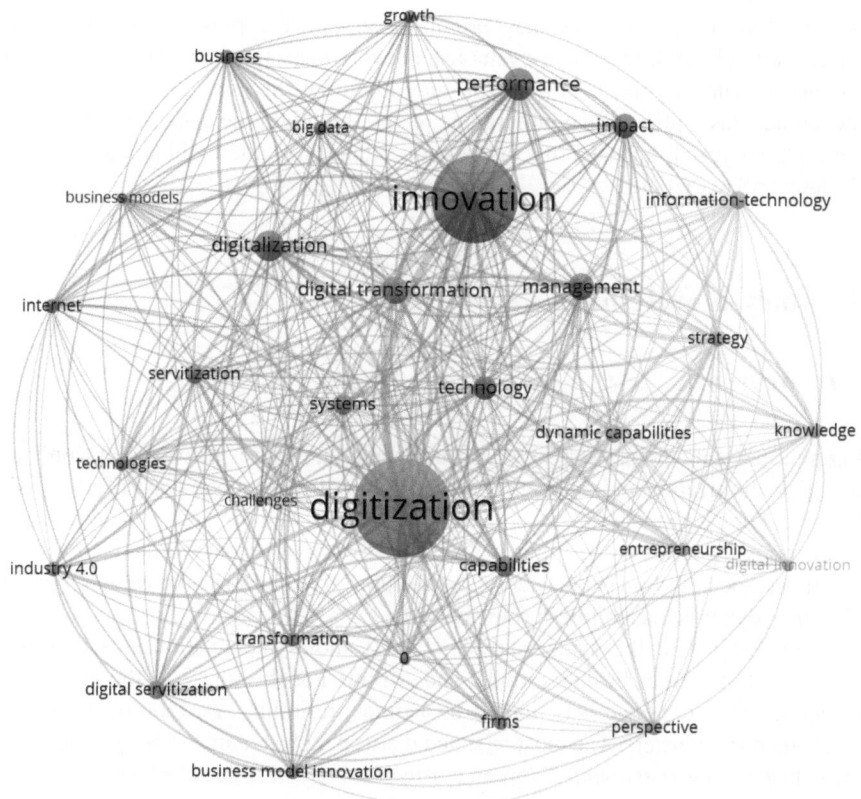

Fig. 2 Network of co-occurrence of keywords in articles on digital transition and innovation. *Source* Authors' own elaboration based on VOSViewer's analysis

On the other hand, for the binomial *"business model"* and "Airbnb", the number of articles is relatively low with respect to the analysis of the previous binomial, but they share the main countries producing articles. Furthermore, the network of collaborations between countries of the concepts analysed is significantly smaller than in terms of digitalisation and innovation. Thus, the countries with the highest number of collaborative works are the United States and China with a total of 4 articles, followed by the United Kingdom and China with 2 articles.

4.3 Analysis of the Most Cited Documents and Authors

The analysis of cited articles is one of the most widely used tools when it comes to establishing the importance of the various authors, journals and articles, since it enables to define the key publications in terms of a specific topic (Calvacante,

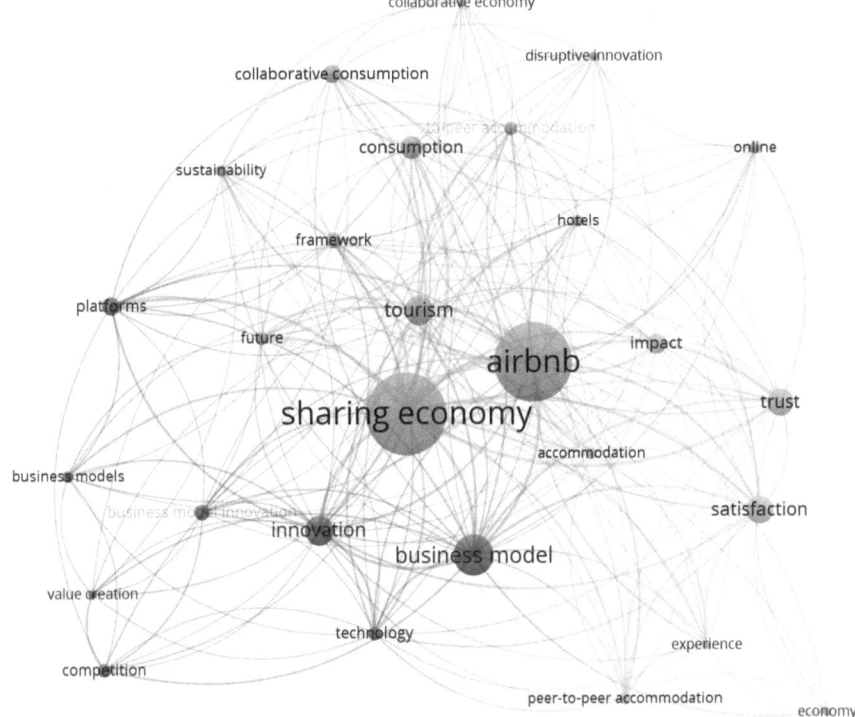

Fig. 3 Network of co-occurrence of keywords in articles on business model and vacation home. *Source* Authors' own elaboration based on VOS Viewer's analysis

2021). In this sense, we establish a detailed analysis of which are the 5 most cited publications within the framework "*digital* transition" and "*innovation*", establishing a minimum of 500 citations. Likewise, citations by authors are studied, analysing the number of times they have been cited through the development of a graph that shows the relationships between citations and authors.

- The New Organizing Logic of Digital Innovation: An Agenda for Information Systems Research Yoo, Youngjin; Henfridsson, Ola; Lyytinen, Kalle Information Systems Research. 2010, citations 1194
- Digital Innovation Management: Reinventing innovation management research in a digital world Nambisan, Satish; Lyytinen, Kalle; Majchrzak, Ann; Song, Michael. *With Quarterly.* 2017, citations 937
- Digital transformation: A multidisciplinary reflection and research agenda. Verhoef, Peter; Broekhuizen, Thijs; Bart, Yakov; Bhattacgarya, Abhi; Dong, John; Fabian, Nicolai; Haenlein, *Michael Journal of Business Research.* 2021, citations 748
- The expected contribution of Industry 4.0 technologies for industrial performance Dalenogare, Lucas Santos; Benitez, Guilherme Brittes; Ayala, Nestor Fabian;

Frank, Alejandro German *International Journal of Production Economics*. 2018, citations 747.

- The digital transformation of innovation and entrepeneurship: progress, challenges and key themes Nambisan, Satish; Wright, Mike; Feldman, Maryann. *Research Policy*. 2019, citations, 594.

In order to obtain a complete analysis of the citations, it is crucial to continue with the analysis of the second binomial, "*business model*" and "Airbnb". To this end, 65 selected articles were selected, which identifies the 5 most cited documents worldwide on this subject, establishing a minimum of 100 citations.

- Airbnb: disruptive innovation and the rise of an informal tourism accommodation sector (2015). Guttentag, D. *Current Issues in Tourism*. 2015, citations 934.
- Understanding platform business models: A mixed methods study of marketplaces Deceiver, Karl; Laudien, Sven M. European Management Journal. 2018, citations 220.
- Platforms in the peer—to—peer sharing economy. Wirtz, Jochen; So, Kevin Kam Fung; Mody, Makarand Amrish; Liu,Stephanie Q.; Chun, HaeEun Helen Journal of Service Management. 2019, citations 176.
- What managers should know about the sharing economy Habibi, Mohammad Reza; Davidson, Alexander; Laroche, Michel Business Horizons. 2017, citations 142.
- Data—Driven Business Model Innovation Sorescu, A Journal of Product Innovation Management. 2017, Citations 128.

4.4 Institutions with the Highest Academic Production

Next, the different institutions to which the analysed documents are ascribed are analysed. The analysis of the different organizations from which the selected documents were published establishes an approximation of the specific location of the productions or how they relate to others through the authors of the different documents. That is, the longer the length, the more documents are published by this organization.

After studying the binomial of "*digital transition and innovation*", a total of 576 organizations are detected that have at least one document and one citation per organization. Among Spanish universities, the University of Granada has the highest number of publications, with a total of 10 articles on the subject studied. However, some organizations as: Bucharest University Economy Studies; Lulea University; ST. Gallen University; Hanke Economics; Vaasa University; Copenhagen University. Etc, that have the most articles on these terms, with Alexandru Ioan Cuza University being the first with a total of 19 documents.

Continuing with the same analysis, in the case of the binomial "*business model and Airbnb*", a total of 113 organisations have been detected that have at least one document and citation per organisation. Among the Spanish universities, the University of the Basque Country and the University of Malaga stand out, with a total of 4 articles on business model and holiday housing. In the same way as the previous binomial, others institutions with the highest production in this area are: Oklahoma University; South Carolina Univrsity; Central Florida University; Bston University or Cornell Univerties, etc. Within this topic, the institution with the highest academic production is the University of Oklahoma with a total of 6 documents.

5 Conclusions, Future Lines of Work and Limitations

This study contributes to the literature on digital transition, innovation, business models and Airbnb by conducting a bibliometric analysis of 464 publications in total, from 2013 to 2023. The bibliometric analysis carried out makes it necessary to adopt a digital integration approach in order to minimise the possible impacts on tourism. The relevance of the digital transition in innovation processes is evidenced throughout the work, given that the annual publication trends identified in this area increase rapidly every year. Digital platforms, along with other factors such as artificial intelligence, the Internet of Things and the cloud, are having a significant impact on the value chain. It is therefore necessary to adapt in order to strengthen sovereignty in this area and to establish defined rules, as set out by the European Union in its programme "*Europe's Digital Decade 2030*". This programme covers specific goals and purposes in areas such as skills, secure and sustainable digital infrastructures, digital transformation of companies and the digitalisation of public services.

However, it has been determined, in contrast to what was initially proposed, that the management of Airbnb lacks, according to articles published on the subject, a defined business model. Thus, it is concluded that an innovation process for the Airbnb phenomenon should start from the implementation of a structured and solid business model. That is why this paper propose a future line of research that encompasses the implementation of a business model in Airbnb supported by digitalization as a path to innovation.

In view of the limitations found in this work, it is emphasized that, although it is a bibliometric analysis around 4 terms already mentioned above, from the beginning the study of them as a whole was discarded due to the scarcity of documents that resulted in this search. And, consequently, a result would be obtained with a low number of entries, poor results and without much academic interest, so it was decided to establish an analysis by pairs of terms. Finally, another limitation is related to carrying out a bibliometric analysis following only one database, in this case WoS, so it is recommended in future research to carry out a more complete bibliometric review by establishing comparisons with other databases to complete the information.

Bibliography

Bjork, S., Offer, A., & Söderberg, G. (2014). Time series citation data: The Nobel prize in economics. *Scientometrics, 98*(1), 185–196. https://doi.org/10.1007/s11192-013-0989-5.

Castillo-Vergara, M., Alvarez-Marin, A., & Placencio-Hidalgo, D. (2018). A bibliometric analysis of creativity in the field of business economics. *Journal of Business Research, 85,* 1–9. https://doi.org/10.1016/j.jbusres.2017.12.011.

Cavalcante, W. Q. de F., Coelho, A., & Bairrada, C. M. (2021). Sustainability and tourism marketing: a bibliometric analysis of publications between 1997 and 2020 using VOSviewer software. *Sustainability, 13*(9), 4987, https://doi.org/10.3390/su13094987.

Donthu, N., Kumar, S., Mukherjee, D., Pandey, N., & Lim, W.M. (2021). How to conduct a bibliometric analysis: An overview and guidelines. *Journal of Business Research, 133,* 285–296. https://doi.org/10.1016/j.jbusres.2021.04.070.

Durieux, V., & Gevenois, P. A. (2010). Bibliometric indicators: quality measurements of scientific publication. *Radiology, 255*(2), 342–351. https://doi.org/10.1148/radiol.09090626.

Goyal, K., Kumar, S. (2021). Financial literacy: A systematic review and bibliometric analysis. *International Journal of Consumer Studies, 45*(1), 80–105. https://doi.org/10.1111/ijcs.12605.

Hood, W., & Wilson, C. (2001). The literature of bibliometrics, scientometrics, and informetrics. *Scientometrics, 52*(2), 291–314. https://doi.org/10.1023/A:1017919924342.

Lulewicz-Sas, A. (2017). Corporate social responsibility in the light of management science—bibliometric analysis. *Procedia Engineering, 182,* 412–417. https://doi.org/10.1016/j.proeng.2017.03.124.

Matarazzo, M., Penco, L., Profumo, G., & Quaglia, R. (2021). Digital transformation and customer value creation in Made in Italy SMEs: A dynamic capabilities perspective. *Journal of Business Research, 123,* 642-656. https://doi.org/10.1016/j.jbusres.2020.10.033.

Moral-Muñoz, J.A., Herrera-Viedma, E., Santisteban-Espejo, A., & Cobo, M.J. (2020). Software tools for conducting bibliometric analysis in science: An up-to-date review. *El profesional de la información, 29*(1). https://doi.org/10.3145/epi.2020.ene.03.

OECD. (2020). OECD tourism trends and policies 2020. *OECD iLibrary.* https://doi.org/10.1787/6b47b985-en.

Osterwalder, A., & Pigneur, Y. (2010). *Business model generation.* John Wiley & Sons Limited.

Segittur. Tourism and Innovation. (2021). *Competitiveness, sustainability, digitalization and tourism resilience in Spain.* Ministry of Industry, Trade and Tourism. https://www.segittur.es/wp-content/uploads/2021/12/Informe.pdf.

The Impact of the Pandemic on the P2P Market for Tourist Accommodation

Beatriz Benítez-Aurioles(iD)

Abstract This paper examines the impact of the COVID-19 pandemic, which was declared in March 2020, on the peer-to-peer (P2P) market for tourist accommodation, focusing on supply, demand, and prices. By analyzing monthly data between February 2019 to February 2021 from 15 cities across Europe, North America and Australia, the study provides insights into the changes experienced in the P2P market during the pandemic. The ensuing findings indicate a significant decline in both supply and demand. The number of reviews, serving as a proxy for demand, shows a clear downward trend that reflects the reduced travel activity during the pandemic. In parallel, the number of listings decreases, highlighting the adaptability of supply to demand shocks. The pandemic also led to a notable decrease in prices, as observed in the analysis of price data and backed by previous studies. Professional hosts demonstrate their capacity to adapt by adjusting prices and minimum stays to attract a stable demand. This finding aligns with previous research that displays the strategic responses of professional hosts to market conditions. Furthermore, the results contribute to the existing literature by providing empirical evidence of the simultaneous decline in supply and demand, leading to lower prices and income for hosts. The strategic responses of professional hosts make evident their adaptability in the P2P market.

Keywords Airbnb · COVID-19 · Tourist demand · Entry and exit barriers · Housing rentals

1 Introduction

Airbnb has experienced remarkable growth since 2018 and became a dominant player in the peer-to-peer (P2P) tourist accommodation market. By 2017, Airbnb featured 4 million accommodations—more than the collective capacity of

B. Benítez-Aurioles (✉)
Malaga, Spain
e-mail: bbaurioles@uma.es

A. J. Guevara Plaza et al. (eds.), *Tourism and ICTs: Advances in Data Science, Artificial Intelligence and Sustainability*, Springer Proceedings in Business and Economics, https://doi.org/10.1007/978-3-031-52607-7_19

the world's top five hotel chains (Hartmans, 2017). As a disruptive innovation, Airbnb revolutionized the accommodation market, particularly in urban centers, and triggered negative externalities (Bugalski, 2020).

However, in March 2020, the trajectory of Airbnb and the entire global tourism industry faced an abrupt disruption due to the transmission of COVID-19, as declared by the World Health Organization (WHO, 2022). Shortly thereafter, Brian Chesky, the CEO and co-founder of Airbnb, acknowledged the devastating impact of the preceding months in a letter to the platform's hosts (Airbnb, 2020), outlining measures such as allowing reservation cancellations, full fee refunds, and various host assistance programs.

Given the evolving context, we ask the following question: Has the pandemic redefined the P2P market for tourist accommodation? We focus on supply, demand, and prices. We begin by outlining a microeconomic model of consumer choice, the empirical methodology and the pertinent data to answer our questions. Later, we compare recent results with our perceived trends using economic arguments, specifically the overall decrease in demand, the impacts of the pandemic's dual supply and demand shocks on hosts' prices and income. Finally, the conclusions are exposed.

2 Conceptual Framework

Based on the quasi-linear utility derived from homothetic preferences (Varian, 1983) and on the Hotelling model of horizontally differentiated competition (Hotelling, 1929), a consumer's dilemma can be seen as the choice among various alternatives: an Airbnb, a hotel room, and the outside option (staying home). Individual preferences are distributed among a continuum in $[(0, V_1), (0, V_2)]$ where $v > 0$, with a joint cumulative distribution function F. u_{i1}, being the utility of Airbnb, will increase with i's value for social factors such as befriending the host or living like a local. If i values professionality more, then $u_{i2} > u_{i1}$. Prices p_1 and p_2 are equal for all consumers.

$$\max_{D_{i1}, D_{i2}} \{u_{i1} - p_1, u_{i2} - p_2, 0\} | D_{i1} + D_{i2} \leq 1, (D_{i1}, D_{i2}) \in \{0, 1\}^2$$

where D_{i1}, D_{i2} are dichotomic variables that equal 1 when the decision is to go to the option 1, 2 respectively (if both are 0, the outside option is chosen). x_{i1} and x_{i2} vary by consumer according to certain cumulative distribution function $(x_{i1}, x_{i2})\sim$F. Therefore,

$$Pr.(x_{i1} > x_{i2} \cap x_{i1} > 0) = \int \int [1 - F(x_{i2}, x_{i1})]f(x_{i1})dx_{i1}dx_{i2}$$

where $f(x_{i1})$ is the probability density function (PDF) of x_{i1}, as the share of potential consumers in the market that book Airbnb. A shock, such as the pandemic, negatively affects x_{i1} and x_{i2} for all, but does not change the outside option. So what we expect is a decrease of the total share of Airbnb and hotels, but their relative share varies ambiguously if the effect varies by option. As for the hosts, they may initially enjoy a markup in pricing due to this differentiation but now will lose part of it due to the fall in demand. And if the pandemic were to affect the marginal cost of supply, total occupancy could further contract.

We use data the unofficial database InsideAirbnb (2022), extensively utilized in previous P2P accommodation research (Dann et al., 2019), which offers metrics such as city-specific listings, guest reviews, and host pricing. Our sample features Amsterdam, Austin, Barcelona, Bordeaux, Dublin, Florence, Los Angeles, London, Lyon, Madrid, New York, Paris, Sydney, Toronto, and Vienna selected based on the completeness of monthly data between February 2019 and 2021. We measured supply by counting the number of listings, thereby quantifying the availability of accommodations in each city. For approximating occupancy, we employed the number of reviews as a lower-bound, reflecting confirmed guest activity. Assuming the pandemic did not significantly alter the behavior of guests refraining from leaving reviews, we can reliably employ this variable as a proxy for occupancy in our study. Additionally, we calculated the average prices for each city. To obtain the global average across the 15 cities, we weighed them proportionally according to their number of listings.

We suggest the following hypotheses: the pandemic might have caused (1) decrease in the number of stays; (2) a transformation in the type of accommodations offered (a shift towards entire homes due to isolation measures, reinforcing prior trends against the "shared" nature of P2P); (3) a reduction in supply and/or pricing; and (4) resilience of the P2P accommodation market because it has shown adaptability to shocks in the past.

3   Results

To answer our questions, we compare results to those of prior studies. Airbnb's growth resulted in vast literature, with review articles (Dann et al., 2019; Dolnicar, 2019; Guttentag, 2019; Hati et al., 2021; Ozdemir & Turker, 2019; Prayag & Ozanne, 2018; Sainaghi, 2020) that substantiate critical findings (Benítez-Aurioles, 2020).

As reference points, we tracked articles through Web of Science, Scopus and Google Scholar published in 2020 and 2021 containing the keywords "COVID" and "Airbnb", removed speculative and marginally related contributions and selected 15 papers with quantitative analyses and arguments on the pandemic's impact on the P2P accommodation market: Benítez-Aurioles (2021a; 2021b); Boros and Kovalcsik (2021); Chen et al. (2020); Dolnicar and Zare (2020); Gossen and Reck (2021); Gyódi

(2021); Jang et al. (2021); Kadi et al. (2020); Llaneza and Raya (2021); Liang et al. (2021); Martínez (2021); Trojanek et al. (2021); Yiu and Cheung (2021); and Zhu and Liu (2021).

To verify the fall in occupancy of the pandemic, we look at stays. Figure 1 shows the impact on demand and supply. Reviews, as a proxy for occupancy, fall in all cities since Q1-2020. Because guests have 14 days after leaving to review, March might show more activity; but there is a marked decline afterwards. The number of listings also supports fast supply adjustments to demand changes. Pre-pandemic, there was only a fall in supply after the summer season. This affirms supply-side adaptability to market conditions, suggesting a demand drop led to the withdrawal of accommodations with reduced expected occupancy.

Additionally, Eurostat data offers a valuable point of comparison. Table 1 displays overnight stays in EU countries from 2019 to 2020, revealing a substantial decline in tourist demand due to the pandemic. Overall, it fell by 46.7% in the European Union with inter-country variety (from 20.6% in Germany to 72.1% in Malta). Liang et al. (2021), in 12 major cities worldwide across Europe, America, Asia, and Oceania, confirm a significant decrease in Airbnb reservations during the pandemic, particularly among foreign tourists, supporting that the pandemic led to a notable fall in occupancy rates.

As for prices, Fig. 2 shows a drop in the P2P tourist accommodation market assignable to a decline in both supply and demand during the summer of 2020. However, (1) these may reflect actual exchange prices, and (2) the weighted

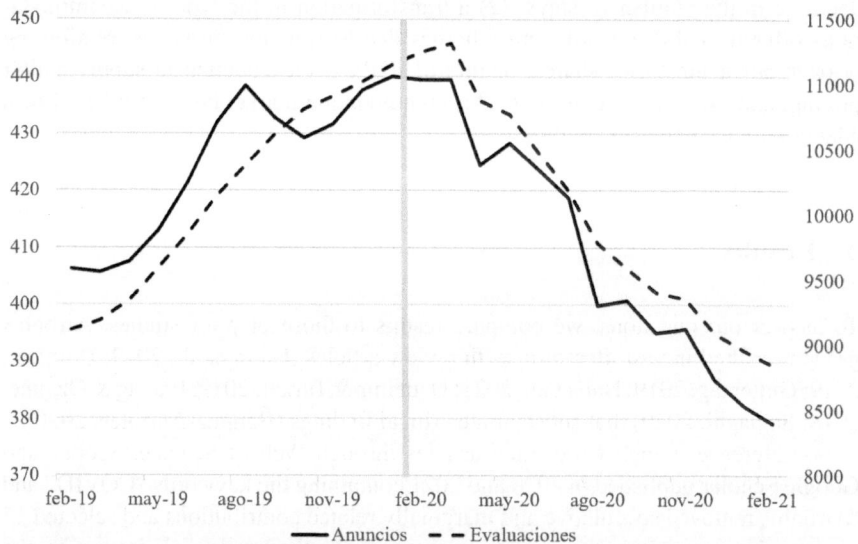

Fig. 1 Evolution of the total number of listings (rigth) and reviews (left) on Airbnb in the set of 15 selected cities (*), in thousands. February 2019–February 2021. (*) Amsterdam, Austin, Barcelona, Bordeaux, Dublin, Florence, Los Angeles, London, Lyon, Madrid, New York, Paris, Sydney, Toronto, and Vienna. *Source* Compiled from InsideAirbnb (2022)

Table 1 Overnight stays (thousands) in tourist accommodation based on data from digital platforms. Entire homes (E), shared rooms (S), percentage of E over the total (% E), percentage increase of the total between 2019 and 2020 (% Δ total)

Country	2019				2020				% Δ total
	Total	E	S	E/S	Total	E	S	E/S	
AT	15,572	14,919	653	95,8	9143	8878	265	97,1	−41,3
BE	6987	6232	756	89,2	4467	4164	303	93,2	−36,1
BG	3047	2985	62	98,0	1629	1597	32	98,0	−46,5
CY	4241	4170	71	98,3	1352	1329	23	98,3	−68,1
CZ	9401	8884	517	94,5	3639	3477	162	95,5	−61,3
DE	37,236	33,535	3701	90,1	29,583	27,902	1681	94,3	−20,6
DK	4681	4091	590	87,4	2954	2699	255	91,4	−36,9
EE	1523	1484	39	97,4	806	785	21	97,4	−47,1
EL	24,302	23,934	368	98,5	8936	8813	123	98,6	−63,2
FI	2916	2754	162	94,4	1999	1920	79	96,0	−31,4
HU	9173	8918	255	97,2	3186	3112	74	97,7	−65,3
IE	6912	5876	1036	85,0	2920	2697	223	92,4	−57,8
ES	105,602	99,511	6091	94,2	44,207	42,506	1701	96,2	−58,1
FR	99,453	94,259	5194	94,8	74,606	71,763	2843	96,2	−25,0
HR	25,630	25,151	479	98,1	10,500	10,360	140	98,7	−59,0
IT	76,044	72,383	3661	95,2	30,284	29,269	1015	96,6	−60,2
LT	1578	1527	51	96,8	992	965	27	97,3	−37,1
LU	281	213	68	75,8	187	153	34	81,8	−33,5
LV	1338	1281	57	95,7	748	726	22	97,1	−44,1
MT	3212	2850	362	88,7	897	815	82	90,9	−72,1
NL	9396	7936	1460	84,5	5901	5381	520	91,2	−37,2
PL	19,685	19,057	628	96,8	12,969	12,618	350	97,3	−34,1
PT	31,064	29,562	1501	95,2	12,577	12,134	443	96,5	−59,5
RO	4192	4044	148	96,5	2312	2252	60	97,4	−44,8
SE	3650	3229	422	88,5	2594	2426	168	93,5	−28,9
SI	2584	2478	106	95,9	877	848	29	96,7	−66,1
SK	2238	2134	105	95,4	1435	1384	50	96,4	−35,9
EU-27	511,939	483,398	28,541	94,4	271,698	260,974	10,724	96,1	−46,9

AT: Austria; BE: Belgium; BG: Bulgarian; CY: Cyprus; CZ: Czech R.; DE: Germany; DK: Denmark: EE: Estonia; HE: Greece; IF; Finland; HU: Hungary; IE: Ireland; ES: Spain; FR: France; HR: Croatia; IT: Italy; LT: Lithuania; LU: Luxembourg; LV: Latvia; MT: Malt; NL: Netherlands; PL: Poland; PT: Portugal; RO: Romania; SE: Sweden; SI: Slovenia; SK: Slovakia

Source Eurostat (2022)

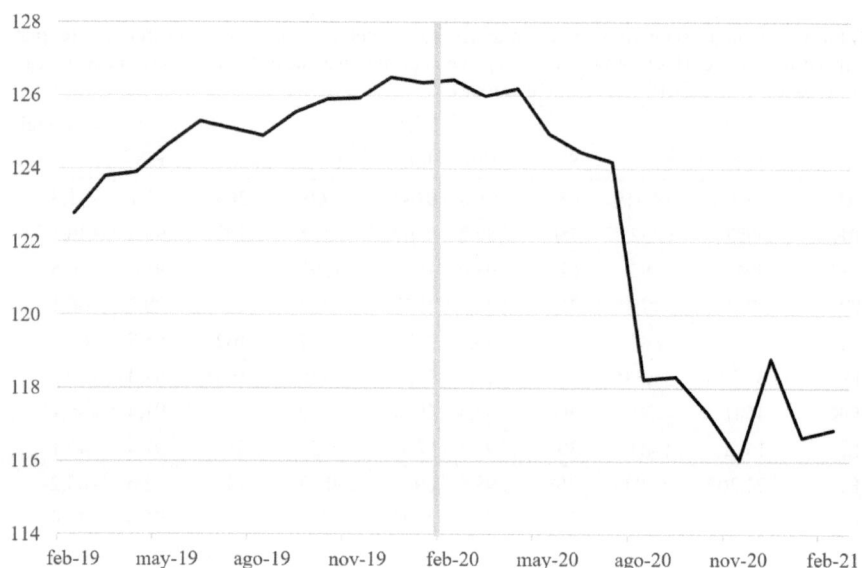

Fig. 2 Evolution of the average price for accommodation, weighted by number of ads, in the set of 15 selected cities (*), in dollars. February 2019–February 2021. (*) Amsterdam, Austin, Barcelona, Bordeaux, Dublin, Florence, Los Angeles, London, Lyon, Madrid, New York, Paris, Sydney, Toronto, and Vienna. *Source* Compiled from InsideAirbnb (2022)

average says nothing about the characteristics of the remaining post-pandemic accommodations. In sum, initial descriptive analysis suggests a reduction in both sides of the transaction, which result in a fall in volume but have an uncertain theoretical impact on price (although our data leans more to a downward movement).

To address whether the pandemic caused a drop in prices or if the supply decrease outweighed the demand decline, quantitative estimates like Benítez-Aurioles (2021b) identified statistically significant price decreases during the pandemic in 22 cities; Chen et al. (2020) reported host income losses in Sidney of nearly 90% comparing January to August 2020. Jang et al. (2021) revealed spatially diverse revenue losses in Florida destinations. These suggest that the demand drop was more substantial than that of supply.

For the question of whether the percentage of entire homes increased, we observed that there was a growing prevalence of entire home accommodations in the P2P market before the pandemic (Benítez-Aurioles, 2021a; Ke, 2017), but this amplified the trend. In most European Union countries except Malta and Estonia, overnight stays in entire homes increased from 2019 to 2020, often exceeding 95% of the total, which suggests that private and shared room rentals may lose significance within the P2P market for tourist accommodation due to health concerns related to interactions with hosts.

Assessing the adaptability and resilience of the P2P accommodation market, we remember it has lower entry and exit barriers due to small fixed costs. Temporary closures due to low tourist demand are common in the hotel industry, and seasonality in tourist demand within the P2P market is evidenced before the pandemic (Benítez-Aurioles, 2021b). Llaneza and Raya (2021), for Barcelona, identify (1) professionals adjusting prices and minimum stays and (2) non-professional hosts who do not react during the pandemic. Li et al. (2019) already showed this ability of professional hosts to stabilize as a strategic response to maximize profit. Farmaki et al.'s (2020) semi-structured interviews with P2P accommodation hosts in a series of Mediterranean countries found there were pessimistic hosts considering leaving the platforms and optimistic ones who think the pandemic could enhance the P2P sector. All of these findings support that hosts adapt according to the market incentives of each changing circumstance.

4 Conclusions

The COVID-19 pandemic has given us a chance to confirm if the trends in the P2P tourist accommodation market pre-crisis are persevering—particularly those from its rapid expansion. Given the reduced pandemic era demand, we have drawn conclusions answering our hypotheses about the changes in this industry. First, the data supports the hypothesis of a significant decrease in the number of stays in the P2P market. As revealed in our analysis, there has been a pronounced and sustained reduction in guest activity, reflected in a decline in the number of reviews. Second, prior trends indicating a shift towards entire homes in the P2P market have been reinforced by the pandemic. The substantial increase in the percentage of overnight stays in entire homes across European Union countries underscores this, primarily attributed to health concerns and the minimization of social contact with hosts. Third, the simultaneous shocks to supply and demand during the pandemic have led to a decrease in prices and income for hosts. However, professional hosts, who manage multiple accommodations, have demonstrated their adaptability by employing revenue management strategies, including lower prices and extended stay options, effectively transforming short-term rentals into a medium-term market. This strategic response, aimed at stabilizing demand, suggests that the P2P market can effectively adapt to changing circumstances. Lastly, and in the same line, we can say that despite the challenges posed by the pandemic, the P2P accommodation market has displayed resilience, evidenced by the adaptability of hosts, the market's continued operation, and the confirmation of previous observations during a period of significant demand contraction.

In terms of implications, our study distinguishes itself by analyzing multiple destinations rather than focusing on a single one. This information can be harnessed by policymakers to bolster risk management strategies, including the development of support mechanisms for P2P hosts in times of tourism crises. Moreover, aligning these insights with more robust regulations for the P2P accommodation sector can yield substantial benefits. Enhanced regulatory frameworks empower governments not only to aid but also to implement more effective taxation and oversight measures, curbing excessive activity. As for the sector itself, the growing demand for "isolated" stays has reinforced the trend toward an emphasis on entire-home accommodations. Thus, hosts who remain in the market should position their offerings as viable competitors to traditional hotels.

Future research has the opportunity to expand on these findings by confirming how effective host strategies are in recovering from the crisis's impacts. We could delve into host responses to pandemics in various geographical regions, incorporating guest perspectives and social aspects. Another avenue for research could involve comparing these findings with those from the traditional hospitality industry. This comparative analysis could help us draw implications for future responses to health emergencies. Furthermore, exploring the changing regulatory environment and its impact on the P2P market could offer valuable insights into the industry's direction in the aftermath of the pandemic.

References

AIRBNB. (2020). *Letter to the hosts. April 1, 2020.* https://news.airbnb.com/ea/letter-to-the-hosts/.

AIRBNB. (2022). *Accommodation evaluations.* https://www.airbnb.es/help/article/13/evaluacio nes-de-alojamientos?_set_bev_on_new_domain=1621762763_NjUyZGI0ZWY2OWE5.

Benítez-aurioles, B. (2020). *Peer-to-peer market for tourist accommodation: Characterization and implications.* Doctoral dissertation, University of Malaga. https://hdl.handle.net/10630/20842

Benítez-aurioles, B. (2021a). Recent trends in the peer-to-peer market for tourist accommodation. *e-Review of Tourism Research (eRTR), 18*(4), 478–494. https://journals.tdl.org/ertr/index.php/ertr/article/view/427.

Benítez-aurioles, B. (2021b). How the peer-to-peer market for tourist accommodation has responded to COVID-19. *International Journal of Tourism Cities.* https://doi.org/10.1108/IJTC-07-2021-0140.

Boros, L., & Kovalcsik, T. (2021). A COVID-19-járvány hatása a budapesti Airbnb- piacra. *Területi Statisztika, 61*(3), 380–402. https://doi.org/10.15196/TS610306..

Bugalski, Ł. (2020). The undisrupted growth of the Airbnb phenomenon between 2014–2020. The touristification of European Cities before the COVID-19 outbreak. *Sustainability, 12* (23). https://doi.org/10.3390/su12239841.

Chen, G., Cheng, M., Edwards, D., & Xu, L. (2020). COVID-19 pandemic exposes the vulnerability of the sharing economy: a novel accounting framework. *Journal of Sustainable Tourism,* 1–18. https://doi.org/10.1080/09669582.2020.1868484.

Dann, D., Teubner, T., & Weinhardt, C. (2019). Poster child and guinea pig–insights from a structured literature review on Airbnb. *International Journal of Contemporary Hospitality Management, 31*(1), 427–473. https://doi.org/10.1108/IJCHM-03-2018-0186.

Dolnicar, S. (2019). A review of research into paid online peer-to-peer accommodation: Launching the Annals of Tourism Research curated collection on peer-to-peer accommodation. *Annals of Tourism Research, 75,* 248–264. https://doi.org/10.1016/j.annals.2019.02.003.

Dolnicar, S., & Zare, S. (2020). COVID19 and Airbnb–Disrupting the disruptor. *Annals of Tourism Research, 83.* https://doi.org/10.1016/j.annals.2020.102961.

Eurostat. (2022). *Collaborative economy platforms.* https://ec.europa.eu/eurostat/web/experimen tal-statistics/collaborative-economy-platforms.

Farmaki, A., Miguel, C., Drotarova, M. H., Aleksić, A. Č, Časni, A. Č, & Efthymiadou, F. (2020). Impacts of Covid-19 on peer-to-peer accommodation platforms: Host perceptions and responses. *International Journal of Hospitality Management, 91,* 102663.

Gossen, J., & Reck, F. (2021). The end of the sharing economy? Impact of COVID-19 on airbnb in Germany. *Economic Research Guardian, 11*(2), 255–269. https://www.ecrg.ro/files/p2021. 11(2)2021ySI1y7.pdf.

Guttentag, D. (2019). Progress on Airbnb: a literature review". *Journal of Hospitality and Tourism Technology.* https://doi.org/10.1108/JHTT-08-2018-0075.

Gyódi, K. (2021).Airbnb and hotels during COVID-19: different strategies to survive. *International Journal of Culture, Tourism and Hospitality Research.* https://doi.org/10.1108/IJCTHR-09-2020-0221.

Hartmans, A. (2017). Airbnb now has more listings worldwide than the top five hotel brands combined. *Business Insider.* https://www.businessinsider.com/airbnb-total-worldwide-listings-2017-8?IR=T.

Hati, S. R. H., Balqiah, T. E., Hananto, A., & Yuliati, E. (2021). A decade of systematic literature review on Airbnb: the sharing economy from a multiple stakeholder perspective. *Heliyon, 7*(10). https://doi.org/10.1016/j.heliyon.2021.e08222..

Hotelling, H. (1929). Stability in competition. *The Economic Journal, 39*(153), 41–57.

Insideairbnb. (2022). *Get the data.* http://insideairbnb.com/get-the-data.

Jang, S., Kim, J., Kim, J., & Kim, S. S. (2021). Spatial and experimental analysis of peer-to-peer accommodation consumption during COVID-19. *Journal of Destination Marketing & Management, 20.* https://doi.org/10.1016/j.jdmm.2021.100563.

Kadi, J., Schneider, A., & Seidl, R. (2020). Short-term rentals, housing markets and COVID-19: Theoretical considerations and empirical evidence from four Austrian cities. *Critical Housing Analysis, 7*(2), 47–57. https://doi.org/10.13060/23362839.2020.7.2.514.

Ke, Q. (2017). Sharing means renting?: An entire-marketplace analysis of Airbnb. In *Proceedings of the 2017 ACM on web science conference* (pp. 131–139). MCA. https://doi.org/10.1145/309 1478.3091504.

Li, J., Moreno, A., & Zhang, D. J. (2019). Agent pricing in the sharing economy: evidence from Airbnb". In M. Hu (Ed.) *Sharing economy* (pp. 485–503). Springer. https://doi.org/10.1007/ 978-3-030-01863-4_20..

Llaneza, C., & Raya, J. M. (2021). The effect of COVID-19 on the peer-to-peer rental market. *Tourism Economics.* https://doi.org/10.1177/13548166211044229.

Liang, S., Leng, H., Yuan, Q., & Yuan, C. (2021). Impact of the COVID-19 pandemic: Insights from vacation rentals in twelve mega cities. *Sustainable Cities and Society, 74.* https://doi.org/ 10.1016/j.scs.2021.103121.

Martínez, A. (2021). COVID-19, tourist rental and cancellation policies, emergency in times of pandemic of the hidden nature of digital platforms?. *IDP. Revista d'Internet, Law and Policy, 32.* https://doi.org/10.7238/idp.v0i32.374912..

Ozdemir, G., & Turker, D. (2019). Institutionalization of the sharing in the context of Airbnb: A systematic literature review and content analysis. *Anatolia, 30*(4), 601–613. https://doi.org/10. 1080/13032917.2019.1669686.

Prayag, G., & Ozanne, L. K. (2018). A systematic review of peer-to-peer (P2P) accommodation sharing research from 2010 to 2016: progress and prospects from the multi-level perspective. *Journal of Hospitality Marketing & Management, 27*(6), 649-678. https://doi.org/10.1080/193 68623.2018.1429977.

Sainaghi, R. (2020). The current state of academic research into peer-to-peer accommodation platforms. *International Journal of Hospitality Management, 89.* https://doi.org/10.1016/j.ijhm. 2020.102555.

Trojanek, R., Gluszak, M., Hebdzynski, M., & tanas, J. (2021). The COVID-19 pandemic, Airbnb and housing market dynamics in Warsaw. *Critical Housing Analysis, 8*(1), 72–84. https://doi. org/10.13060/23362839.2021.8.1.524..

Varian, H. (1983). The nonparametric approach to demand analysis. *Econometrica, 50*, 945–973.

WHO. (2022). *COVID-19: timeline of WHO action.* https://www.who.int/es/news/item/27-04-2020-who-timeline---covid-19.

Yiu, C. Y., & Cheung, K. S. (2021). Urban zoning for sustainable tourism: A continuum of accommodation to enhance city resilience. *Sustainability, 13* (13). https://doi.org/10.3390/su1313 7317.

Zhu, X., & Liu, K. (2021). A systematic review and future directions of the sharing economy: business models, operational insights and environment-based utilities. *Journal of Cleaner Production, 290.* https://doi.org/10.1016/j.jclepro.2020.125209.

Connections Between a Tourist Destination, the Digital Ecosystem, and ICT Actors

Aurkene Alzua-Sorzabal⊙, **Volha Herasimovich**⊙,
Basagaitz Guereño-Omil⊙, **and Daniela Thiel-Ellul**⊙

Abstract The tourism sector and tourist destinations are undergoing a digital transition in order to improve their resilience and competitiveness. The way in which tourist destinations address this digital transition differs, as some incorporate more technology in their ecosystem than others, giving rise to the emergence of different types of digital tourism networks. This study seeks to determine the different ways in which a tourist destination connects with a digital ecosystem, specifically focusing on the connections with ICT actors. It is based on the theoretical framework of tourism as an ecosystem. Using web crawling, network data have been compiled on 670 tourism actors and more than 36,000 websites to which they are connected through hyperlinks. The most frequently linked entities of the discovered digital ecosystem have been identified and classified (n = 447), distinguishing between 13 types of ICT actors. The results show how the online destination network has been incorporated into the digital ecosystem. The study reveals that the configuration of the digital ecosystem surrounding a tourist destination is characterised by the different levels of importance for the network of destination actors in which the ICT actors play a central role.

Keywords Tourist destination · Digital ecosystem · ICT actors · Hyperlinks · Online network

1 Introduction

The tourism sector is currently immersed in a digital transition process in an attempt to improve its resilience and strategic autonomy (Koens et al., 2021). Digital technologies have a profound impact on the tourism industry and the digital environment

A. Alzua-Sorzabal (✉) · V. Herasimovich · D. Thiel-Ellul
Nebrija University, Sta. Cruz de Marcenado 27, 28015 Madrid, Spain
e-mail: malzua@nebrija.es

A. Alzua-Sorzabal · B. Guereño-Omil
University of Deusto, Camino de Mundaiz, 50, 20012 San Sebastián, Spain

© The Author(s) 2024   215
A. J. Guevara Plaza et al. (eds.), *Tourism and ICTs: Advances in Data Science, Artificial Intelligence and Sustainability*, Springer Proceedings in Business and Economics,
https://doi.org/10.1007/978-3-031-52607-7_20

is gaining increasing importance for improving the competitiveness of destinations and facilitating its transition towards smart solutions. The way in which tourist destinations approach the digital transition differs (Gretzel, 2022), as some incorporate more technology in their ecosystem than others: technologies such as artificial intelligence, the Internet of Things, augmented reality, and virtual reality. The result is the emergence of different structural configurations of digital tourism networks.

Understanding these configurations is vitally important for managing the digital transition in tourism, as the ICTs have the potential to modify value chains, profoundly influence the operations and strategies of tourism companies and change the power dynamics between actors (Baggio & Del Chiappa, 2013; Januszewska et al., 2015). The interaction between the ICT actors and tourism actors is important to integrate technology and facilitate technological innovations in tourism (Buhalis, 2003).

This study seeks to determine the different ways in which a tourist destination connects with a digital ecosystem, specifically focusing on the connections with the technological actors. The research adopts an unusual perspective as it uses Hyperlink Network Analysis (HNA). HNA constitutes "an important basis for the more complete empirical analysis of tourism digital ecosystems" (Baggio, 2022: 1551). The theoretical framework of this study is based on the concept of tourism as an ecosystem, drawing upon the notions of the digital ecosystem, the digital business ecosystem, and the smart tourism ecosystem (Baggio, 2022; Baggio & Del Chiappa, 2013; Gretzel et al., 2015; Nachira et al., 2007).

2 Related Literature

2.1 A Tourist Destination as a Business Ecosystem

A tourist destination is a complex system made up of interdependent social and economic actors that interact with one another and jointly produce experiences for tourism (Baggio, 2008). Their competitiveness is conditioned by their environment and geographical, economic, cultural, political, and technological characteristics (Gómez-Vega & Picazo-Tadeo, 2019; Gretzel et al., 2015). Therefore, in order to fully understand and manage the complexity of the destination it is necessary to adopt a holistic approach that takes into account the economic, technological, environmental, social and cultural dimensions.

A tourist destination can also be understood as a business ecosystem whose principal components are organisations, including suppliers, clients, competitors and another series of actors that interact and evolve jointly to create and contribute value (Baggio, 2022). The actors are integrated into the environment, which can significantly influence the power relations within the ecosystem (Gretzel et al., 2015).

Given the growing incorporation of ICTs in the operations of tourism organisations (Buhalis, 2020), it is important to determine the role of the digital environment and its actors in relation to the tourism ecosystem. This has led to conceptualisations such as the "tourism digital (business) ecosystem" (Baggio, 2022; Baggio & Del Chiappa, 2013) and the "smart tourism ecosystem" (Gretzel et al., 2015).

A digital business ecosystem (DBE) is a socio-economic and technical system composed of actors from the real world (public and private), digital objects, and technical infrastructures (Baggio 2022; Nachira et al., 2007). The emergence of digital ecosystems has been facilitated by the convergence of three networks: ICT networks, social networks, and knowledge networks (Nachira et al., 2007). As a result, a tourism organisation is represented in a DBE by a physical component and a virtual component (their technological representations such as websites), that co-evolve and intertwine to form a single entity (Baggio, 2022).

The websites of destination actors, interconnected through hyperlinks, form an online destination network (ODN). It is important to note that hyperlinks connecting websites also function as a form of interorganisational communication, specifically representational communication (Shumate et al., 2017), which is usually overlooked due to the perception that it is less efficient than direct face-to-face or technologically mediated direct communication. Representational communication is based on an organisation positioning itself with others and these connections are communicated to third parties, including the public. It may be considered as a type of "name dropping", which can reveal important inter-organisational relations (Shumate et al., 2017: 16).

The ODN is important as the websites seem to be the principal instruments for doing business in the tourism sector (Law et al., 2004; Wang & Fesenmaier, 2006). Similarly, hyperlinks are also used as service tools for providing value added to visitors, facilitating access to useful resources (Zach et al., 2019). Furthermore, the websites and the hyperlink network that connect them constitute an important instrument for giving visibility to a destination (Raisi et al., 2018; Ying et al., 2016).

As an ODN is a network of websites and hyperlinks, it forms part of a wider digital ecosystem. Therefore, the connections of the ODN with other online entities provide an initial approach to the different configurations by which a tourist destination is connected to the digital ecosystem.

2.2 ICT Actors: Supply of ICT Products to Tourism

Distinguishing the different types of ICTs to which the actors of the destination are connected can provide a deeper understanding of the place that a destination occupies in the digital ecosystem. However, this analysis is complicated, due to the difficulties in defining the ICTs as they embody a wide variety of technologies with different purposes. Furthermore, conducting an inventory of all of the ICTs is a real challenge as the websites incorporate different technologies in different ways.

In a broad sense, ICT refers to "both different types of communications networks and the technologies used in them" (OECD, 2023). It encompasses "the use of all possible means and methods offered by information technologies in the communication process (transfer of information)" (Januszewska et al., 2015: 66). The ICT sector is comprised of both "manufacturing and services industries whose products capture, transmit or display data and information electronically" (UN, 2005: 39).

Within the context of tourism, ICT products are defined as "the entire range of electronic tools that facilitate the operational and strategic management of organizations by enabling them to manage their information, functions and processes as well as to communicate interactively with their stakeholders, enabling them to achieve their mission and objects" (Buhalis, 2003: 7). Taking into account the utility significance that is attributed to ICTs in tourism, it is important to distinguish the ICT actors focused on the provision of ICT technology and, in particular, the technology that is directly designed for tourism as specific layers of the digital ecosystem.

The success of the digital transition, particularly for destinations advancing towards smartness, does not depend solely on the availability and improvement of technology (the "hard" aspect of the transition) but also on the actors of the ecosystem who represent and use this technology and collaborate, co-creating value ("soft" competences such as the attitude towards innovation) (Boes et al., 2016). Therefore, the human element is essential, which suggests that those involved in the digital transition should be considered as being as important as the technology itself.

Different tourism actors can be expected to have different connections with ICT actors, due to the interconnection between the "real" and "virtual" and the social and economic factors that underlie the structure of the network (Gonzalez-Bailon, 2009). Therefore, it is necessary to (a) explore which ICT actors are connected to the online destination network; and (b) understand whether different actors of the online destination network are connected to ICT actors in different ways.

3   Methodology

3.1   Operationalisation of Concepts

In order to research the digital ecosystem, we have analysed the different web entities, such as websites and the hyperlinks that connect them. In this study, the ICT actors have been defined as websites that principally present ICT products and/or actors that produce ICT products (companies). The ICT products refer to the tools and services used for the electronic/digital transmission of data/information at any time of the communication process (sending, transmission, data reception).

3.2   Data Collection

The data of the online destination network (ODN) have been gathered in the province of Gipuzkoa in Spain, whose largest city, Donostia-San Sebastián, has recently been accredited as a Smart Destination by SEGITTUR (a state-owned company for the management of tourism innovation and technologies in Spain) (DTI, 2023). The research employs an experimental design and utilises a convenience sample, drawing initial data from readily accessible directories provided by the Provincial Government of Gipuzkoa.

In 2021, the competent public administration facilitated an initial list of tourism actors that included 1,199 organisations from the directory of businesses and tourism activities of the Basque Country (Euskadi.eus, 2021). The authors updated the database twice: in January 2022 and April 2023. Entities that were not active were eliminated and new agents were added with their websites. The data represented six types of tourism agents: accommodations (57%), travel agencies and other reservation services (10%), destination management organisations (2.8%), natural and cultural resources (7.6%), sports and recreational activities (9.3%), and tourism-related public bodies (13.3%).

After compiling the directory, the web crawler Hyphe (Jacomy et al., 2016) was used to collect hyperlink data from the websites of tourism organisations (N = 690) in April 2023. The web crawler could not access 20 websites (2.9%), which were excluded from the final sample (N = 670). During the crawling, more than 36,000 websites hyperlinked by the ODN were discovered, together with more than 47,000 connections. Given that some actors were represented online with two or more different web domains, the sample was cleaned to guarantee that the actors were represented only once in the group of websites that obtained five or more links (for example, Euskadi.net and Euskadi.eus were merged into one web entity).

3.3 Elaboration of the Typology of ICT Actors

Due to the limited research resources, only a sample of the most popular discovered web entities was used to elaborate a typology of the ICT actors. The sample included entities with five or more links from the tourism actors of the ODN (N = 447). The elaboration of the typology was based on the analysis of information from the websites, the descriptions of the websites by the artificial intelligence of the search engine Bing, and Wikipedia entries. Following the descriptive analysis, a comprehensive coding scheme was developed to identify 13 distinct categories of ICT actors. This scheme was subsequently employed by two independent coders to categorize the websites.

3.4 Data Analysis

The data were analysed using quantitative metrics of Social Network Analysis and a qualitative analysis of the visual representation of the network with the help of Gephi 0.10.1 (Bastian et al., 2009).

4 Results

4.1 The Online Destination Network Incorporated into the Digital Ecosystem

The online destination network (ODN, N = 670) was integrated into the broader web—multiple websites connected through hyperlinks, constituting a discovered digital ecosystem (N = 36,813) (Fig. 1). The ODN connections with the discovered digital ecosystem were highly uneven, forming a power law L-curve distribution. Two types of entities were identified around the ODN: the entities linked by at least two tourism actors (n = 2374, 6%) and the majority of entities which were connected with only one tourism actor (n = 34,439, 94%) (Fig. 1). Thus, the ODN was integrated into a shared digital area and a non-shared digital area, characterised by clusters around specific tourism actors. The areas indicate commonalities and differences in the choices and interests of the tourism actors.

The most popular entities of the discovered digital ecosystem (with five or more links from the ODN) made up approximately one-fifth of the shared area (n = 447, 19%) and represented the strongest common point of the ODN. Although the ICT actors as a group constituted the minority of the "popular" discovered ecosystem (22.6%), some of them were the most important nodes of the network, appearing as the network's centre of attraction.

ODN (green, N = 670, 2%). **Discovered digital ecosystem** (all colours except green, N = 36,813, 98%). Most popular discovered entities, linked by five or more tourism actors (red, yellow, and black, n = 447): **ICT actors** (red, n = 101, 22,6%), **non-ICT actors** (yellow, n = 344, 77,0%), **unidentified actors** (black, n = 2, 0.4%). Less popular discovered entities: blue (2–4 links), grey (1 link). The **shared area** of

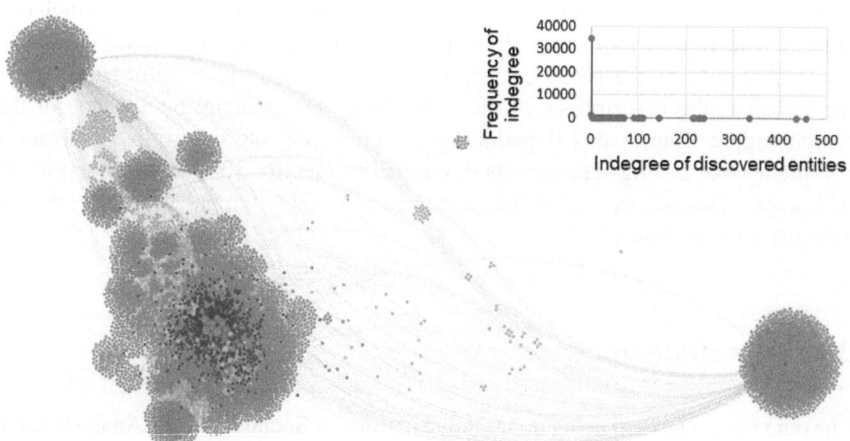

Fig. 1 The online destination network (ODN) within the digital ecosystem

the discovered ecosystem: red, yellow, blue, and black (n = 2374, 6%). The **non-shared area**: grey (n = 34,439, 94%). The colour of the links shows which type of entity they are connected to. Size: the importance, or the number of links that point at the actor (indegree).

4.2 Varying Connections of Tourism Actors to ICT Actors

The analysis distinguished 13 types of ICT actors (Table 1). Of these, three types represented tourism-related ICT actors: travel platforms, leisure platforms, and tourism management software (34.7%). Social media were the most popular actors, accounting for about 39% of all links, yet constituting only 11.9% of total actors. These were followed by software development and electronics (12.2% of the links for 5% of the actors) and multifunctional web portals (12.1% of links for 2% of actors). The tourism-related ICT actors accounted for only 13% of all links, three times less than social media, while they constituted approximately a third of all of the actors (34.7%).

There seems to be a stable predominance of certain ICT actors in the digital ecosystem, as seven of the ten principal ICT actors were the same as those in a similar research project covering the years 2013–2018 (cf. Zach et al., 2019) (Table 2).

The web entities that were subject to the grouping procedures described in the methodology section: 1, 4, 7, 8, 10.

Table 1 Types of ICT actors in the digital ecosystem of the online destination network

Types of ICT actors	No. of actors	%	No. of links[a]	%
Social media	12	11.9	1497	39.2
Software development and electronics	5	5.0	466	12.2
Multifunctional web portals	2	2.0	463	12.1
Web browsing	3	3.0	325	8.5
Travel platforms*	11	10.9	268	7.0
Web development	23	22.8	266	7.0
Videoconferencing and instant messaging	4	4.0	128	3.3
Leisure platform*	11	10.9	119	3.1
Tourism management software*	13	12.9	109	2.9
Content technology	7	6.9	98	2.6
Mapping and location technology	4	4.0	37	1.0
Marketing tools	4	4.0	34	0.9
ICT providers	2	2.0	13	0.3
Total	101	100	3823	100

* Tourism-related ICT actors
[a] Number of hyperlinks placed by the ODN tourism actors to the ICT actors

Table 2 Top 10 ICT actors related to the online destination network in 2023

Ranking	ICT actors
1	Google.com[a]
2	Facebook.com[a]
3	Instagram.com[a]
4	Twitter.com[a]
5	Youtube.com[a]
6	Apple.com[a]
7	Microsoft.com
8	Mozilla.org
9	Tripadvisor.com[a]
10	Whatsapp.com

[a] Actors coinciding with the study by Zach et al. (2019)

The actors closely related to the public domain (tourism-related public bodies, destination management organisations, natural and cultural resources) tended to have a higher proportion of links (>50%) to actors not related to the ICTs than to those related to the ICTs. On the contrary, businesses of accommodations, sports and recreational activities, and travel agencies and other reservation services had a greater proportion of links to ICT actors ($\geq 60\%$) (Fig. 2a).

(a) Connections to ICT actors vs all the other actors

(b) Connections to tourism-related ICT actors vs non-tourism ICT actors

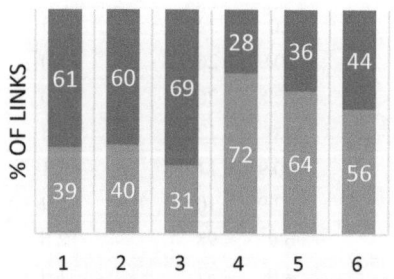
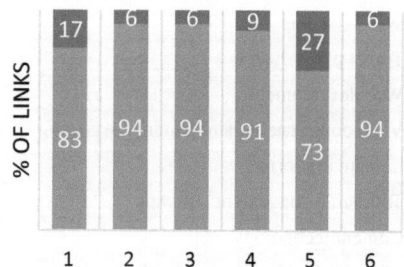

Fig. 2 Connections of the tourism agents with the ICT actors (**a**) and ICT actors specialised in tourism (**b**). 1—accommodations; 2—travel agencies and other reservation services; 3—sports and recreational activities; 4—tourism-related public bodies; 5—destination management organisations; 6—natural and cultural resources. The percentages represent the proportion of total links to the most popular discovered entities of the digital ecosystem (n = 445), except for those entities that could not be classified (n = 2)

Furthermore, tourism actors displayed differences in the way in which they referred to the different types of ICT actors: tourism-related and non-tourism ICT actors (Fig. 2b). While the majority of the sectors did not exceed the 10% barrier in terms of links to tourism-related ICT actors, two sectors stood out in their relations with tourism-related ICT agents: accommodation (17%) and the DMOs (27%), which were the most active users of the tourism-related technologies.

Tourism actors showed similar preferences when establishing links with social media, which were those most frequently used links compared to other types of ICT actors. Social media accounted for at least a third of the links to ICT actors in each tourism sector (from 33 to 53%). The higher percentages of links to social media was observed in the sectors of natural and cultural resources (53%), sports and recreational activities (46%), and travel agencies and other reservation services (46%). The second and third most popular ICT actors within tourism sectors were mainly the "multifunctional web portals" and "software development and electronics" actors, each receiving less than half the attention that social media received. Within this context of shared preferences, the DMOs stood out as they had a greater tendency to link with "travel platforms", which constituted 15% of all of their links.

5   Discussion

This study contributes to a better understanding of the digital business ecosystem of tourism, shedding light on the different configurations between tourism actors and the broader digital ecosystem, including the ICT actors. The different configurations analysed indicate different processes through which the various stakeholders become embedded in the digital ecosystem.

The results of this study reveal a highly disproportionate distribution in the degree of connectivity, with a few web entities being strongly connected to the destination and the majority being weakly connected, which is similar to the global structure of the Web, with few highly connected hubs and the lowly connected majority (Barabási et al., 2000). The existence of "shared areas", commonly linked by the destination actors, indicates possible common interests between tourism actors.

The presence of ICT actors in the nucleus of the shared area underlines the crucial role of ICTs in tourist destinations. The very small change observed in the nucleus of the ICTs compared to the most popular websites in a similar previous study (Zach et al., 2019) suggests a stable dominance of certain ICT agents in the tourism sector.

This coherence in choices is also evident in the prominent position of social media platforms within the overall digital ecosystem and within particular tourism sectors. The results confirm the solid incorporation of Web 2.0 into the tourism digital business ecosystem and ratify the evolution of social media as crucial platforms in the tourism sector (Zeng & Gerritsen, 2014).

The variances in how tourism sectors were linked to ICT and non-ICT actors, particularly between tourism sectors related to the public domain and business-focused stakeholders, suggest the role of underlying social and economic determinants. This is consistent with prior research highlighting the significance of these factors on the Web's structure (Gonzalez-Bailon, 2009). Likewise, socio-economic factors may be the reason why accommodations and DMOs had more incentives to connect to tourism-related ICTs than other tourism actors. These findings highlight the duality of tourism actors in the digital business ecosystem, where they are represented by both real-world actors and digital objects intertwined into a single entity.

One important direction for future research is the comparison of different configurations of Smart Destinations and destinations with a less developed incorporation of technology in different economic, cultural, and political environments.

Acknowledgements This research was supported by a Grant PID2021-127893OB-I00 funded by MCIN/AEI/10.13039/501100011033 and European Union Next Generation EU/PRTR.

References

Baggio, R. (2008). Symptoms of complexity in a tourism system. *Tourism Analysis, 13*(1), 1–20. https://doi.org/10.3727/108354208784548797

Baggio, R. (2022). Digital ecosystems, complexity, and tourism networks. In Z. Xiang, M. Fuchs, U. Gretzel, & W. Höpken (Eds.), *Handbook of e-Tourism* (pp. 1545–1564). Springer, Cham. https://doi.org/10.1007/978-3-030-05324-6_91-1

Baggio, R., & Del Chiappa, G. (2013). Tourism destinations as digital business ecosystems. In L. Cantoni, Z. Xiang (Eds.), *Information and communication technologies in tourism 2013. Proceedings of the International Conference in Innsbruck, Austria* (pp. 183–194). Springer, Heidelberg. https://doi.org/10.1007/978-3-642-36309-2_16

Barabási, A. L., Albert, R., & Jeong, H. (2000). Scale-free characteristics of random networks: The topology of the world-wide web. *Physica A: Statistical Mechanics and Its Applications, 281*(1), 69–77. https://doi.org/10.1016/S0378-4371(00)00018-2

Bastian, M., Heymann, S., & Jacomy, M. (2009). Gephi: An open source software for exploring and manipulating networks. In W. W. Cohen & N. Nicolov (Eds.), *Proceedings of the Third International AAAI Conference on Weblogs and Social Media*, San Jose, USA (Vol. 3, issue no. 1, pp. 361–362). https://doi.org/10.1609/icwsm.v3i1.13937

Boes, K., Buhalis, D., & Inversini, A. (2016). Smart tourism destinations: Ecosystems for tourism destination competitiveness. *International Journal of Tourism Cities, 2*(2), 108–124. https://doi.org/10.1108/IJTC-12-2015-0032

Buhalis, D. (2003). *eTourism: Information technology for strategic tourism management*. Harlow, Prentice Hall-Financial Times.

Buhalis, D. (2020). Technology in tourism-from information communication technologies to eTourism and smart tourism towards ambient intelligence tourism: A perspective article. *Tourism Review, 75*(1), 267–272. https://doi.org/10.1108/TR-06-2019-0258

DTI. (2023). *Donostia/San Sebastián obtiene el distintivo Destino Turístico Inteligente*. https://www.destinosinteligentes.es/donostia-san-sebastian-obtiene-el-distintivo-destino-turistico-int eligente/. Accessed 15 Jan 2023.

Euskadi.eus. (2021). *Registro de empresas y actividades turísticas de Euskadi.* https://www.eus kadi.eus/registro/registro-de-empresas-y-actividades-turisticas-de-euskadi/web01-tramite/es/. Accessed 10 April 2023.

Gómez-Vega, M., & Picazo-Tadeo, A. J. (2019). Ranking world tourist destinations with a composite indicator of competitiveness: To weigh or not to weigh? *Tourism Management, 72,* 281–291. https://doi.org/10.1016/j.tourman.2018.11.006

Gonzalez-Bailon, S. (2009). Opening the black box of link formation: Social factors underlying the structure of the web. *Social Networks, 31*(4), 271–280. https://doi.org/10.1016/j.socnet.2009. 07.003

Gretzel, U. (2022). The Smart DMO: A new step in the digital transformation of destination management organizations. *European Journal of Tourism Research 30.* https://doi.org/10.54055/ejtr. v30i.2589

Gretzel, U., Werthner, H., Koo, C., & Lamsfus, C. (2015). Conceptual foundations for understanding smart tourism ecosystems. *Computers in Human Behavior, 50,* 558–563. https://doi.org/10.1016/ j.chb.2015.03.043

Jacomy, M., Girard, P., Ooghe-Tabanou, B.,& Venturini, T. (2016). Hyphe, a curation-oriented approach to web crawling for the social sciences. In K. P. Gummadi, M. Strohmaier (Eds.), *Proceedings of the Tenth International AAAI Conference on Web and Social Media,* Cologne, Germany (Vol. 10, issue no. 1, pp. 595–598). https://ojs.aaai.org/index.php/ICWSM/article/ view/14777

Januszewska, M., Jaremen, D., & Nawrocka, E. (2015). The effects of the use of ICT by tourism enterprises. *Service Management 16,* 65–73. https://doi.org/10.18276/smt.2015.16-07

Koens, K., Font, W., & Neuhofer, B. (2021). *Compilation stakeholder survey results: Intermediary deliverable.* https://ec.europa.eu/docsroom/documents/48355/attachments/1/translations/ en/renditions/native. Accessed 10 April 2023.

Law, R., Leung, K., & Wong, R. J. (2004). The impact of the Internet on travel agencies. *International Journal of Contemporary Hospitality Management, 16*(2), 100–107. https://doi.org/10.1108/095 96110410519982

Nachira, F., Dini, P., & Nicolai, A. (2007). A network of digital business ecosystems for Europe: Roots, processes and perspectives. In European Commission, Directorate-General for the Information Society and Media, F. Nachira, A. Nicolai, P. Dini, M. Le Louarn, L. Rivera Leon (Eds.) *Digital business ecosystems* (pp. 1–20). Publications Office. https://op.europa.eu/en/publication-detail/-/publication/53e45e55-4bd2-42a4-ad25-27b339b051e0. Accessed 10 April 2023.

OECD. (2023). *Information and communication technology (ICT).* https://www.oecd-ilibrary.org/ science-and-technology/information-and-communication-technology-ict/indicator-group/eng lish_04df17c2-en. Accessed 26 May 2023.

Raisi, H., Baggio, R., Barratt-Pugh, L., & Willson, G. (2018). Hyperlink network analysis of a tourism destination. *Journal of Travel Research, 57*(5), 671–686. https://doi.org/10.1177/004 7287517708256

Shumate, M., Atouba, Y., Cooper, K. R., & Pilny, A. (2017). Interorganizational communication. In C. Scott, L. Lewis (Eds.) *The international encyclopedia of organizational communication* (pp. 1–24). Wiley-Blackwell. https://doi.org/10.1002/9781118955567.WBIEOC117.

UN. (2005). Core ICT indicators: partnerships on measuring ICT for development. https://www. itu.int/ITU-D/ict/partnership/material/CoreICTIndicators.pdf. Accessed 26 May 2023.

Wang, Y., & Fesenmaier, D. R. (2006). Identifying the success factors of web-based marketing strategy: An investigation of convention and visitors bureaus in the United States. *Journal of Travel Research, 44*(3), 239–249. https://doi.org/10.1177/0047287505279007

Ying, T., Norman, W. C., & Zhou, Y. (2016). Online networking in the tourism industry: A webometrics and hyperlink network analysis. *Journal of Travel Research, 55*(1), 16–33. https://doi.org/10.1177/0047287514532371

Zach, F. J., Xiang, Z., & Baggio, R. (2019). Analysing linkage between ICT and US state tourism websites. *Review Tourism Research, 17*(3), 306–316.

Zeng, B., & Gerritsen, R. (2014). What do we know about social media in tourism? A review. *Tourism Management Perspectives, 10*, 27–36. https://doi.org/10.1016/j.tmp.2014.01.001

Framework for a Tourism Intelligence System Based on Knowledge Governance: A Conceptual Model

Luana Emmendoerfer⊙, **Alexandre Augusto Biz**⊙,
and **Patrícia de Sá Ferreira**⊙

Abstract The objective of this article is to present a framework of Tourism Intelligence System (TIS) with support in Knowledge Governance (GovC) to support decision making in tourist destinations. The form of cooperation and use of knowledge should be structured through mechanisms that allow availability and reliability. The methodological framework is structured in Design Science Research (DSR) of technological and applied nature, with data collection method using a qualitative approach, classified as exploratory and descriptive, from the validation of semi-structured interviews with experts in the tourism sector and technology. This architecture was composed of three layers: knowledge application, knowledge generation and application, and knowledge generation. It focuses on the extraction of data generated by the tourist trip in the pre-trip, during trip, and post-trip phases, using Knowledge Management (KM) processes such as knowledge identification, acquisition, and use. The GovC aspect considered the mechanisms aimed at the sustainability and evolution of the TIS, as well as the hybrid structure through network and market formation, by means of knowledge centers with actors involved in the segments of the tourism production chain.

Keywords Tourism Intelligence System · Knowledge Governance · Competitive Intelligence · Tourism

1 Introduction

Each process of formatting a tourism product and visiting a destination generates a quantity of data that should be collected and used by decision makers with the aim of efficiently allocating public resources to increase tourist services and satisfaction, thus making their territory more attractive and competitive. (Soualah-Alila et al., 2016).

L. Emmendoerfer · A. A. Biz (✉) · P. de Sá Ferreira
Universidade Federal de Santa Catarina, Florianópolis, Brazil
e-mail: alexandre.biz@ufsc.br

A. J. Guevara Plaza et al. (eds.), *Tourism and ICTs: Advances in Data Science, Artificial Intelligence and Sustainability*, Springer Proceedings in Business and Economics,
https://doi.org/10.1007/978-3-031-52607-7_21

227

Studies and research on tourism governance introduced since the 1990s point to the limitations of public–private partnerships, alliances and business networks, usually focused on the economic and political side, aimed at increasing the competitiveness of the destination. (Erkuş-Öztürk, 2011; Wang & Li, 2013; Butler, 2020).

In turn, the implementation of tourism governance is related to processes and structures such as power sharing in a multilevel, diverse, and decentralized integration, through cooperation networks that allow flexibility in experimentation and knowledge creation in a differentiated way (Trentin, 2017).

With this in mind, the Tourism Intelligence System (TIS) can be a facilitator in sharing information across the destination network, be it experiences, products, services and reviews. This shows that people are increasingly dependent on data to make decisions.

Tourism governance, coupled with knowledge governance, can provide an approach to decision-making and regulation of tourism, bringing more efficiency in the development of policies and programs for the sector. Therefore, this article aims to present a framework for a Tourism Intelligence System with support in Knowledge Governance to support decision-making in tourist destinations.

2 From Tourism Governance to Knowledge Governance

Hall (2011) identified six characteristics related to governance models that bring aspects very adherent to the tourism sector, such as flexibility and revision, diversity and decentralization, and multilevel integration.

These aspects largely align with the principles of the Organization for Economic Cooperation and Development—OECD (2012) and highlight important points to consider in tourism governance, including experimentation and knowledge sharing and multi-level integration.

And the other hand, the complexity governance can be observed by Grande (2012, apud Ysa et al. 2014) describe five key elements which can be identified in governance concepts: (1) new non-hierarchical structure and mechanisms; (2) governing and the criticism of hierarchy as steering principle; (3) emergence of new actors, either private or non-profit; (4) increasing complexity of political actions, and (5) increasing cooperation and collaboration among stakeholders, and this impacts both the governance of tourism and knowledge.

About tourism governance, Bono iGispert and Clavé (2020) define it from the perspective of the actors of the system of a tourist destination, the following aspects: (i) participation, as a form of cooperation and possibility of acting together; (ii) coherence, understood as strategic planning and management; (iii) responsibility, related to the fulfillment of the functions and criteria of sustainable development; (iv) effectiveness, understood as efficiency in obtaining results; (v) know-how and quality, understood as knowledge and training; (vi) openness, related to active communication and transparency, and (vii) simplicity, understood as the ability to provide a response.

Therefore, the definition of the tourism governance model requires a conceptual framework of the platform that combines decision-making structures, collaboration facilitators and operational procedures in order to govern the platform by Tourism Information System—TIS, that is, governance relates to all activities and interactions of governance and trust (Crescencio, 2022).

So, it's necessary use the TIS to management everything and aim at the process of knowledge management. It can be considered in a general way in five: people (Government, Customer, Citizen, Stakeholders), hardware (planning, architecture), software, data (presentation method) and networks (telecommunications), that is, they are human resources and information and communication technology that need to interact to reach the desired goal within an organizational environment (O'Brien, 2020; Gregersen, 2018), and generating extensive knowledge that will require specific governance.

Knowledge governance comprising of both knowledge management governance and information technology governance whereas knowledge governance is a system that governs important knowledge operational sectors inside the company or groups, tourism governance focuses in the perspective of the actors of the system of a tourist destination (Otowicz et al. 2022).

To De Sá Freire et al. (2017) the KGM list (i) the formation of internal and external partnerships aimed at a culture of transparency; (ii) the formation of intra-organizational and inter-organizational networks through effective communication aimed at reducing cognitive distances and promoting new relationships; (iii) human resources management practices that allow the construction of psychological bonds of trust and sharing for rapprochement and understanding among parties, generating higher levels of empathy; (iv) formal incentives for KM; (v) shared property rights; (vi) promotion of organizational absorptive capacity; (vii) performance measurement and monitoring to control the costs and transaction risks of knowledge production and transfer; (viii) decentralized management coordinated by communities and project teams; (ix) promotion of inclusion for participation and collaboration; and (x) authority and leadership systems whose hierarchy is based on consensus with the social construction of meaning for decision-making.

Finally, the governance mechanisms linked to inter-organizational knowledge make the network organization smarter as a strategic business action used in the context of TIS.

3 Methodology

This article has a methodological framework in Design Science Research (DSR). According to Peffers et al. (2007), the construction of the methodological approach proposed for a DSR is the junction of several consensual elements from authors who essentially agree on the need for them in the process.

The result is understood in six stages, namely: (i) definition of the problem, (ii) definition of the artifact for its solution, (iii) design of the device, (iv) demonstration of the device solving the problem, (v) evaluation of the device, and (vi) communication of the results (knowledge).

Based on Botelho et al. (2011), for the construction of the device it was observed the state of the art of contributions to the development of theories on the concepts addressed in this research: "tourism intelligence system", "tourism governance", and "knowledge governance". The searches were carried out in academic articles found in prestigious databases recognized by the academic community, such as Web of Science, Scopus, and Scielo, as well as the Capes[1] Theses and Dissertations Bank.

In the databases, 327 publications were identified, in addition to 7 documents from the literature produced by the public and private sectors of tourism.

The third activity, called "Design and Development", concerns the artifact itself, the creation of the model, method, instances and the designed object, and what it contributes to the research. This step includes determining the desired functionality of the artifact and its architecture.

This step was outlined as a preliminary conceptual framework of a TIS based on GovC, with the idea of relating the concepts obtained from the bibliographic and documentary theoretical survey, in order to identify the elements, processes, mechanisms, and structures necessary for a TIS having as a basis the precepts of Knowledge Governance.

4   Results

Based on the researched theoretical bases, a preliminary conceptual model for a Tourism Intelligence System based on GovC can be reached. Its structure is divided into three layers: Knowledge Generation Layer, Knowledge Generation and Application Layer, and Knowledge Application Layer.

4.1   Knowledge Generation Layer

The analysis of this Knowledge Generation Layer starts with the Customer Journey, in which it is possible to identify the stages of the travel cycle that occur in three moments: i. prospective phase (pre-visit)—searching and planning, reducing decision risk, increasing interest in, building an understanding, during (on-site, the visit)—enhancing convenience and speed, experience, flexibility, engagement and enjoyment, making short-term decisions, iii. after the trip (reflective phase)—recollecting memories, sharing experiences, evaluating (making recommendations and suggestions) (Shen et al., 2020).

---

[1] Brazilian National Coordination for the Improvement of Higher Education Personnel.

The stage of knowledge acquisition includes the trail of data left by the tourist during the planning, realization and post-trip phases, whether through evaluations or reports of experiences, or even organically throughout the entire journey experienced by the tourist. In this process of acquisition and use of data is where the mechanisms of knowledge governance could already work (Bocquet & Mothe, 2010; Moresi et al., 2020; Pinho et al., 2019; Wang et al., 2009; Gold, Malhotra, & Segars, 2001; Heisig, 2009; Chen & Mohamed, 2008).

Therefore, through the identification of the knowledge management processes used and the governance structures identified, it can be seen how the governance structures are constructed from the Knowledge Generation and Application Layer. Important the variables, such as economic, social, environmental indicators and other are considered in Data Input.

4.2 Knowledge Generation and Application Layer

The format that is envisaged for the TIS is the hybrid one (Clifton et al., 2010; Butler, 2020), as it comprises both network and market structures (Foss et al., 2010; Wang & Li, 2013; Amore & Hall, 2016), through horizontal relationships and mechanisms already presented and intended for this purpose.

The first ones play a market-oriented role with horizontal relationships and strategic and competitive permanence of the destination, which requires good dialogue and communication between stakeholders (Erkuş-Öztürk, 2011).

These centers would be organized into multidisciplinary working groups, considered as learning communities in the form of thematic cells (Hoetker & Mellewigt, 2009; Gerritsen et al., 2013).

Their organization would be by thematic chambers of interest of the various segments, regarding issues relevant to all, such as training, infrastructure, economy, investments, and others that are identified as necessary to be monitored. Thus, in the face of this organization, the application of knowledge is directed to the structure from the moment the governance mechanisms already presented are involved.

4.3 Knowledge Application Layer

The third layer, Knowledge Application, is where knowledge governance would actually take place. In this layer, all the knowledge generated through the TIS is delivered to the Destination Management Organizations (DMOs) as a subsidy for decision-making and competitiveness of the tourist destination.

This environment involves several spheres, so bringing to it the notion of private/public governance would also be a premise that, if it is managed like an organization, that could have a positive effect, through routines, rules, and administrative relationships among stakeholders.

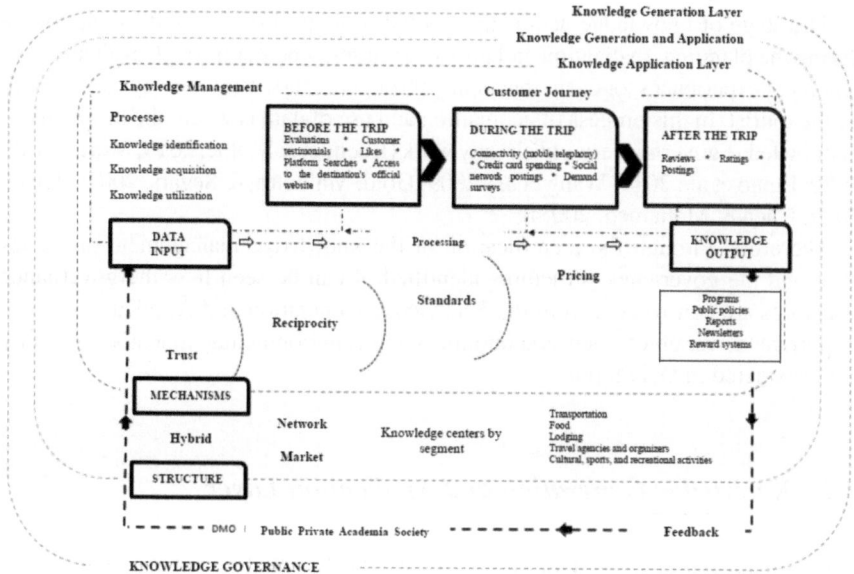

Fig. 1 Preliminary conceptual framework of a Tourism Intelligence System based on

As a preliminary conceptual framework of TIS based on GovC is represented in the Fig. 1.

The layered structure is supported by Fuchs et al. (2013), Garbani-Nerini et al. (2022), and Gretzel et al. (2015), who confirm the need to separate and identify these layers within an information system structure aimed at intelligence and destinations that want to work on knowledge. The proposed framework covered knowledge management processes to generate knowledge from the tourist's journey. The governance mechanisms present themselves as a differentiated support to the TIS, aiming at its sustainability and competitiveness by part of destiny. The TIS structure indicates the various relationships and application formats for use of knowledge by the tourist trade.

5   Final Considerations

The TIS is the conceptual artifact to be obtained as a result of the implementation of Knowledge Governance. In turn, the KG will guide it through its structures and mechanisms necessary for the understanding of the tourist journey and the sustainability of the system, making the TIS a tool to support decision-making.

On the other hand, Tourism Governance brings its contribution in the management arrangement existing in the sector and in the understanding of the knowledge that can be generated for the elaboration of programs and public policies for tourism.

Therefore, the three constructs studied in this article were Tourism Intelligence System, Tourism Governance, and Knowledge Governance, and are aligned in an interdisciplinary way, since they come from different areas of knowledge: Technology, Tourism, and Knowledge Management. The search for publications on the subject showed the incipient relationship among these three constructs in the literature, verified in the methodology.

The proposed artifact can be considered not only a structure, but a possible "knowledge product", being the preliminary result of steps 1 to 4 proposed in the methodology. From June to October 2023, it will undergo a structural verification by experts in the tourism sector and information technology of the destinations of the Latin American Smart Tourist Destinations Network (steps 5 and 6).

Acknowledgements Coordenação de Aperfeiçoamento de Pessoal de Nível Superior—CAPES/PROEX 489/2019.

References

Amore, A., & Hall, C. M. (2016). From governance to meta-governance in tourism? Re-incorporating politics, interests and values in the analysis of tourism governance. *Tourism Recreation Research, 41*(2), 109–122. https://doi.org/10.1080/02508281.2016.1151162

Bocquet, R., & Mothe, C. (2010). Knowledge governance within clusters: The case of small firms. *Knowledge Management Research & Practice, 8*(3), 229–239. https://doi.org/10.1057/kmrp.2010.14.

Botelho, L. L. R. De Almeida Cunha, C. C., & Macedo, M. (2011). O método da revisão integrativa nos estudos organizacionais. *Gestão e sociedade, 5*(11), 121–136. http://www.spell.org.br/documentos/ver/10515/o-metodo-da-revisao-integrativa-nos-estudos-organizacionais/i/pt-br.

Butler, R. W. (2020). Tourism carrying capacity research: A perspective article. *Tourism Review, 75*(1), 207–211. https://doi.org/10.1108/TR-05-2019-0194.

Chen, L., & Mohamed, S. (2008). Impact of the internal business environment on knowledge management within construction organizations. *Construction Innovation, 8*(1), 61–81. https://doi.org/10.1108/14714170810846521.

Clifton, N., et al. (2010). Network structure, knowledge governance, and firm performance: Evidence from innovation networks and SMEs in the UK. *Growth and Change, 41*(3), 337–373. https://doi.org/10.1111/j.1468-2257.2010.00529.x.

Crescencio, M. (2022). *Modelo de uma rede colaborativa suportada por plataforma digital no domínio do turismo em patrimônio mundial cultural e natural.* Tese (Programa de Pós-Graduação em Engenharia e Gestão do Conhecimento). UFSC: Florianópolis.

De Sá Freire, P., et al. (2017). Governança do Conhecimento (GovC): O estado da arte sobre o termo. *Biblios, 69*, 21–40. https://doi.org/10.5195/BIBLIOS.2017.469.

Erkuş-Öztürk, H. (2011). Modes of tourism governance: A comparison of Amsterdam and Antalya. *Anatolia, 22*(3), 307–325. https://doi.org/10.1080/13032917.2011.614354.

Foss, N. J. (2007). The emerging knowledge governance approach: Challenges and characteristics. *Organization, 14*(1), 29–52. https://doi.org/10.1177/1350508407071.

Foss, N. J., Mahoney, J. T., & De Pablos, P. O. (2010). Knowledge governance: Contributions and unresolved issues. *International Journal of Strategic Change Management, 2*(4), 263–268. https://doi.org/10.1504/IJSCM.2010.035846.

Fuchs, M.,Abadzhiev, A., Svensson, B., Höpken, W. & Lexhagen, M. (2013). A knowledge destination framework for tourism sustainability. TOURISM - An interdisciplinary journal. 61. 121–148. (2013). A knowledge destination framework for tourism sustainability: A business intelligence application from Sweden. *Tourism: An International Interdisciplinary Journal*, *61*(2), 121–148. https://hrcak.srce.hr/file/157542.

Garbani-Nerini, E. (2022). From smart destinations to personalized communication. Travel and Tourism Reserach Association: Advancing Tourism Research Globally. *TTRA International Conference*, Victoria, British Columbia, June 14–16.

Gerritsen, A. L., Stuiver, M., & Termeer, C. J. (2013). Knowledge governance: An exploration of principles, impact, and barriers. *Science and Public Policy, 40*(5), 604–615. https://doi.org/10.1093/scipol/sct012.

Gold, A. H., Malhotra, A., & Segars, A. H. (2001). Knowledge management: An organizational capabilities perspective. *Journal Management Information Systems, 18*(1), 185–214. https://doi.org/10.1080/07421222.2001.11045669.

Gregersen, E. (2018). *5 components of information systems.* Encyclopedia Britannica, 19 Mar. 2018, Disponível em: https://www.britannica.com/list/5-components-of-information-systems.

Gretzel, U., Koo, C., Sigala, M. & Xiang, Z. (2015). Special issue on smart tourism: Convergence of information technologies, experiences, and theories. *Electronic Markets, 25*(3), 175–177. https://doi.org/10.1007/s12525-015-0194-x.

Hall, C. M. (2011). Policy learning and policy failure in sustainable tourism governance: From first- and second-order to third-order change? *Journal of Sustainable Tourism, 19*(4), 649–671. https://doi.org/10.1080/09669582.2011.555555.

Heisig, P. (2009). Harmonisation of knowledge management—comparing 160 KM Frameworks around the globe. *Journal of Knowlegde Management, 13*(4), 4–31. https://doi.org/10.1108/13673270910971798.

Hoetker, G., & Mellewigt, T. (2009). Choice and performance of governance mechanisms: Matching alliance governance to asset type. *Strategic Management Journal, 30*(10), 1025–1044. https://doi.org/10.1002/smj.775.

Bono i Gispert, O. & Clavé, S. A. (2020). Dimensions and models of tourism governance in a tourism system: The experience of Catalonia. *Journal of Destination Marketing & Management, 17.* https://doi.org/10.1016/j.jdmm.2020.100465.

Moresi, E., Pinho, I., Pinho, C. & Costa, A. (2020). Mapping knowledge governance. In: *ECRM 2020 20th european conference on research methodology for business and management studies: ECRM 2020. Academic Conferences and publishing limited.* https://www.academic-conferences.org/conferences/ecrm/.

OECD. (2012). Tourism governance in OECD countries, in OECD tourism trends and policies 2012. *OECD Publishing, Paris.* https://doi.org/10.1787/tour-2012-3-en.

Otowicz, M. H., Lacerda, L. L. L., Emmendoerfer, L., & Biz, A. A. (2022). Tourism, knowledge management and its processes: An integrative literature review. *Revista Brasileira de Pesquisa em Turismo, São Paulo, 16*, e-2368. https://doi.org/10.7784/rbtur.v16.2368

O'BRIEN, J. A. (2020). *Sistema de Informação e as decisões gerenciais na era digital.* São Paulo: Saraiva.

Peffers, K., Tuuananen, T., Rothenberger, M. A. & Chatterjee, S. (2007). A design science research methodology for information systems research. *Journal of management information systems, 24*(3), 45–77. https://doi.org/10.2753/MIS0742-1222240302.

Pinho, I., Pinho, C. & Costa, A. P. (2019). Knowledge governance: building a conceptual framework. *Fronteiras: Journal of Social, Technological and Environmental Science, 8*(1), 72–92. https://doi.org/10.21664/2238-8869.2019v8i1.p72-92.

Shen, S., Sotiriadis, M., & Zhang, Y. (2020). The influence of smart technologies on customer journey in tourist attractions within the smart tourism management framework. *Sustainability, 12*(10), 4157. https://doi.org/10.3390/su12104157.

Soualah-Alila, F., et al. (2016). DataTourism: Designing an architecture to process tourism data. *Information and communication technologies in tourism 2016* (pp. 751–763). Springer.

Trentin, F. (2017). *Turismo e governança: Abordagem teórica.* Universidade de Caxias do Sul.

Wang, H. C., He, J. & Mahoney, J. T. (2009). Firm-specific knowledge resources and competitive advantage: the roles of economic-and relationship-based employee governance mechanisms. *Strategic Management Journal, 30*(12), 1265–1285. https://www.jstor.org/stable/27735491.

Wang, J., & Li, T. (2013). Review on tourist destination governance in foreign countries. *Tourism Tribune, 28*(6), 15–25. https://www.cabidigitallibrary.org/doi/full/10.5555/20133409438.

Ysa, T., Colom, J., Albareda, A., Ramon , A., Carrión, M. & Segura, L. (2014). *Governance of addictions.* European public policies. Oxford: Oxford University Press. ISBN: 9780198703303.

Funding Policies, Tourism Entrepreneurship and Innovation in the Territory: Emprendetur (Spain)

Cristina Figueroa-Domecq⊙, Laura Fuentes-Moraleda⊙,
María Rosario González-Rodríguez⊙, and María Dolores Flecha-Barrio⊙

Abstract Innovation is a vehicle for modernization and competitiveness in tourism and, even so, the report on Tourism Innovation and Smart Specialization of SEGITTUR and COTEC (2021) confirms that the tourism sector does not innovate enough. This article evaluates the call for funding for tourism entrepreneurship Emprendetur, developed by SEGITTUR (2012–2016). Through an exploratory analysis, the objective is to examine the geographical distribution of tourism entrepreneurship and innovation, as well as the type of innovation developed in each territory and the success in obtaining funding for these innovations. The main conclusion of the study is that there is a geographical inequality in the distribution of entrepreneurship and innovation in tourism in Spain. There is a concentration of applications from entrepreneurs in urban areas such as Madrid and Catalonia, as well as greater success of these applications, due to a greater emphasis on entrepreneurship and innovation focused on Information and Communication Technologies (ICTs). These results show how the design of policies to support innovation in tourism must consider regional disparities, to close the gaps generated and promote sustainable and egalitarian development.

Keywords Territory · Innovation · Entrepreneurship · Tourist destinations

1 Introduction

Tourism destinations (TD) are facing paradigmatic changes in the socio-demographic environment, digitalization and sustainability. Innovation is a fundamental vehicle for modernization and competitiveness in this environment (Divisekera & Nguyen, 2018; Hall & Williams, 2008), and despite its importance, the tourism industry does

C. Figueroa-Domecq (✉) · L. Fuentes-Moraleda · M. D. Flecha-Barrio
Universidad Rey Juan Carlos, Madrid, Spain
e-mail: cristina.figueroa@urjc.es

M. R. González-Rodríguez
Universidad de Sevilla, Seville, Spain

A. J. Guevara Plaza et al. (eds.), *Tourism and ICTs: Advances in Data Science, Artificial Intelligence and Sustainability*, Springer Proceedings in Business and Economics, https://doi.org/10.1007/978-3-031-52607-7_22

not innovate, according to the Report on Tourism Innovation and Smart Specialization (SEGITTUR & COTEC, 2021). This report highlights difficulties in access to finance, limits to business cooperation and a lack of qualified personnel.

Policies to support entrepreneurship and innovation are designed to remove many of the obstacles people face, especially in terms of access to capital and knowledge (Müller et al., 2017). However, by focusing on the universalized individual, through the "atomization" of society, the impact of these policies is limited (Ahl & Marlow, 2021). These traditional approaches to the concept of entrepreneurship and innovative capacity limit the ability to understand the different journeys of entrepreneurship and innovation and, indirectly, apply measures that replicate the limitations presented by the market (Werner et al., 2017). This essentialist conceptualization limits the impact of public policies, since, without intending to, it limits the participation of people located in certain territorial areas, women (Ely et al., 2011; Kimbu et al., 2021; Zhang et al., 2020), and other vulnerable groups (Figueroa-Domecq et al. 2022).

Theories such as Endogenous Development highlight the impact of the territory, especially on the innovation of SMEs (Jardón, 2011). Cooke and Morgan (1998) identify three major groups of actors in the relationship between innovation and SMEs: Companies, Research, Development and Innovation (R + D + i) Institutions and Political Institutions' strategies and actions. Nevertheless, this approach to innovation does not capture the impact that entrepreneurial activity itself has on other entrepreneurs, through a "spillover" effect of the innovation diffusion (Acs et al., 2009). The "Spillover Theory" incorporates a crucial element in the process of economic growth: the transmission of the indirect effects of knowledge through entrepreneurship (Audretsch, 1995). Moreover, the increase in technological innovations has increased the competitiveness of territories, while deepening the social gap between those who can afford technology and those who cannot and that consequently experience spillover effects or not (Ferreira et al., 2017; Ratten et al., 2019).

This territorial approach is used to analyse the Emprendetur funding call, developed by SEGITTUR, to support innovation in companies in the tourism sector between 2012 and 2016. Therefore, through an exploratory analysis of the Emprendetur call, the objective of this article is to analyse from a territorial point of view the distribution and typology of tourism entrepreneurship and innovation throughout the Spanish geography. Based on this general objective, the following research questions are raised:

Research Question (RQ) 1. Which territories (Autonomous Communities, provinces or municipalities) are the ones that concentrate most of the applications for innovation funding for their business activities?

RQ2. Which territories have the highest success rate in obtaining funding from Emprendetur?

RQ3. What type of innovative entrepreneurship are presented in each territory to the call for Emprendetur?

The article begins with the presentation of the theoretical framework used, to continue with the methodology and the presentation of results and conclusions.

2 Theoretical Framework and Literature Review

2.1 The Characteristics of Innovation in Tourism

Innovations and entrepreneurship play a key role in the development of increasingly fragmented and plural societies. They are seen as drivers of economic development, offering opportunities for improved competitiveness, especially in the tourism industry.

Innovation has different definitions that approach it from different points of view: innovation is the creation of something new; it is dissemination and learning; is changes in processes. Innovation can be defined as a business event and as a context-level process that sees innovation as an act that captures institutional frameworks in a geographical region (Ahmed & Shepherd, 2010). The main pilar of innovation is entrepreneurship. The entrepreneur has been widely described by Schumpeter and Nichol (1934) as a visionary who is able to visualize the new world and who creates new products and processes through the creative destruction of old institutions, processes and products.

The report on Tourism Innovation and Smart Specialization, carried out by SEGITTUR and COTEC (2021) shows how there is a low level of innovation spending by tourism companies, despite the importance that the sector itself gives to such innovation. There is a lower innovative intensity, with a scarce realization of internal R + D activities, compared to other sectors and presents a decreasing trend over the years. The largest expenditure on innovative activities is in capital and equipment expenditure, with a great shortage of own funds or public subsidies. This fact denotes a certain disconnection between tourism companies and the main existing public funding programs. Among the main constraints to tourism innovation are, firstly, access to funding (both external and from the company or business group itself); difficulties in finding cooperative partners with whom to develop innovations; the fact that the market is dominated by established companies; and finally, the lack of qualified personnel.

2.2 Innovation and Territory

Innovating and entrepreneurship are important, but impossible to do alone. The promotion of innovation within a TD involves all the actors of that destination and the interactions created and must be carried out in an inclusive way. Organizations need to cooperate with partners to bring innovative resources and capacity and generate networks (Favre-Bonte et al., 2019; Grillitsch & Trippl, 2014; Van Egeraat & Kogler, 2013).

As in the case of innovation, entrepreneurship develops within an ecosystem, which is co-created by entrepreneurs, at the same it influences people's intention to become entrepreneurs. In fact, Lowrey (2003) and Lundström and Stevenson (2005) define the entrepreneur as an individual with a perpetual desire for achievement, and entrepreneurship as an economic system consisting of entrepreneurs, an economic, social and institutional environment. To understand and promote innovative and technological entrepreneurship, it is necessary to understand and involve the entire system, the entire TD, and all its members, women and men.

Research in the field of innovation and technology has resulted in a diverse set of theoretical models that explain the intention of individuals to use technology and innovate. These studies have their origins in information systems, psychology and sociology (Dwivedi et al. 2019; Venkatesh & Davis, 2000; Venkatesh et al., 2003). This article follows the Spillover Theory developed by Acs et al. (2009) that states that entrepreneurial activity does not simply involve the identification, evaluation and selection of opportunities, but also the exploitation of intra-temporal indirect knowledge effects that established companies have not appropriated and that spill over into the environment. The theory focuses on individual agents with new knowledge endowments that allow them to identify these "spills" and use them. This theory is especially important in the case of territory and tourism, as stated by Gretzel and Koo (2021).

The combination of technology and urbanization, present in cities, promotes radical and incremental innovations, which generates an explosion of data generation of both residents and visitors, in direct relation to the development of smart cities (Andrisano et al., 2018; Silva et al., 2018). In fact, cities are clearly the context in which the concept of Smart Destinations can be developed, and the promotion of innovation and technology considering the concentration of know-how, infrastructure, services and the high density of business and tourists (Trinchini et al., 2019). And to be smart, the territory must support the intelligence of the people who settle in that territory, in addition to "smart" people encouraging the development of smart destinations. This is what Giddens identifies through his Structuration Theory (Giddens, 1984).

Based on the structuring theory of Giddens (1984), Sarason et al. (2006) emphasize that entrepreneurship does not simply respond to existing opportunities but plays a creative role in making them a reality and, therefore, can bring about changes in institutions and structures: the entrepreneur and the opportunity cannot exist independently. In addition, they argue that the different types of structure-agent interactions conceptualized by Giddens can be applied to entrepreneurs' understanding of resource discovery, evaluation, and exploitation (Shane & Venkataraman, 2000). In short, the territory and the people who relate and reside in it can attract more entrepreneurship and innovation.

In the case of leisure and tourism, Gretzel (2020) highlights that smartification leads to the connectivity of urban space, leading to cities "characterized by the hyper-connectivity of infrastructure and devices, the hypermobility of humans and data, and the hyper-personalization of tourism value propositions" (p. 394), In essence, Smartification encourages tourism to spread to all areas of the city and blurs the lines between tourists and residents. Spillover theory in leisure provides support for this trend.

Connectivity is higher in urban spaces (Magasic & Gretzel, 2020), and the need for mobile devices arises from the spatial and social complexities of cities that require "on the move" decision-making (Gretzel, 2020; Gretzel, & Koo, 2021). This approach to innovation determines the impact that the territory and its characteristics generate in innovation and entrepreneurship in tourism.

Despite the growing importance of the relationship between innovation, technology, entrepreneurship, territories and inequality, studies in this area are still very limited, when they can help the management of dynamics in territories (Ratten et al., 2019).

3 Methodology

This study analyses the financing scheme of Emprendetur that aimed to support companies in the Spanish tourism sector through the large areas or subprograms of 'Research and Development', 'Innovative Products' and 'Young Entrepreneurs' from 2012 to 2016. During this period, 996 applications were received, and 313 approved projects were approved.

A content analysis of the applications made by the participants in this call is conducted. The following is the content analysis process, detailed in Figueroa-Domecq et al. (2022):

1. Applications: Participants must submit three types of documents. First, legal documentation, which has been excluded as not relevant to this study and due to privacy concerns; secondly, a business plan, not included in this exploratory analysis; and finally, a standard application form, which includes all the relevant features of the project. Only the last document has been analysed.
2. Coding: A quantitative and qualitative content analysis allowed for topic coding. During 2021, three researchers participated in the design of the content analysis, to ensure the consistency of the coding process that adopted the following process: Two researchers participated in the coding of the 996 applications. After eliminating repeated cases and incomplete applications, a total of 932 applications were analysed. From a deductive perspective, several variables were identified as plausible and homogeneous in the coding process. The basic variables analysed were the following: name of the company, whether it has obtained funding (Binary: Yes/No), Subprogram (Nominal: 'Research and Development', 'Innovative Products' and 'Young Entrepreneurs'), Gender of the applicant (Binary: Woman/Man); Requested budget (Ordinal transformed into continuous variable); Company size (Number of employees and total budget); CNAE category; geographical location (Autonomous Community, Province and Municipality).
3. Statistical analysis: A descriptive statistical analysis was performed through SPSS. Contingency Tables have been made.

It is important to highlight the limitations of this study being based on a policy to support entrepreneurship developed between 2012 and 2016. Even so, the results are relevant in the area of policy development.

4 Results

The analysis of the results of the Emprendetur call yields relevant results in this area. There is a geographical inequality in entrepreneurship, innovation and technology, which focus, as Gretzel (2020) and Gretzel and Koo (2021) already advanced, in territories with important cities and in relevant tourist destinations at the national level.

In relation to RQ1, an analysis by Autonomous Communities shows (Fig. 1) how 33.4% of applications come from the Community of Madrid and 26.3% from Catalonia. At a great distance are Andalusia (9.1%) and the Valencian Community (6.2%). The rest of the Autonomous Communities have a minority stake. 52.04% of the applications are located in the municipalities of Madrid (246, 26.39%), Barcelona (153, 16.42%), Valencia (41, 4.4%), Palma de Mallorca (27, 2.9%) and Seville (18, 1.93%) and as a consequence the province of Madrid collects 33.37% (311) of the applications and Barcelona 23.5% (219).

The analysis of the success rates by Autonomous Communities shows (Table 1) how the regions with the highest number of applications are those with the highest success rate when it comes to finding funding (RQ2). Table 1 shows how Catalonia

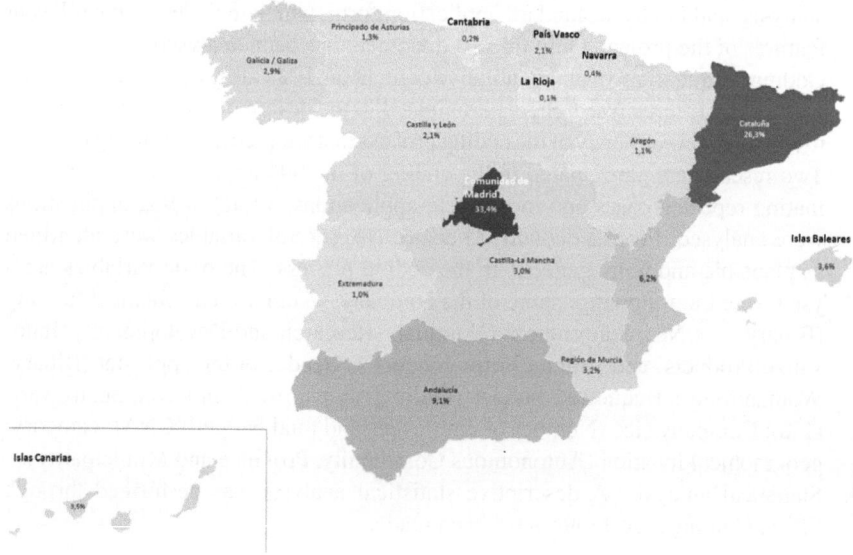

Fig. 1 Distribution of applications received by Emprendetur (% of total). *Source* Authors

is the most successful (40.4% of the proposals are approved), followed by Cantabria (40%), the Balearic Islands (38.2%) and the Community of Madrid (36.5%). Consequently, the largest negative gaps between applications and approved applications are Andalusia (−4.2%), Murcia (−3.2%) and the Canary Islands (−1.8%). And these results contrast with the Communities that receive the largest number of international tourists. According to data from 2016, the most visited Community was Catalonia (18,139,177 tourists, 24.1%), followed by the Canary Islands (17.6%), the Balearic Islands (17.3%), Andalusia (14.1%) and the Community of Madrid (7.7%). Therefore, there is no direct relationship between the number of proposals, the success and the importance of tourism in the territory, even so, there is a relationship between the number of proposals and success depending on the level of urbanization of the territory.

In a previous analysis, through a decision tree (Figueroa-Domecq et al., 2022) it was observed that the variable with the greatest classification capacity when determining the success of a proposal was the type of economic activity with which it was related (CNAE code). The most successful type of business is related to ICT, with 395 projects and an above-average success rate of 40.5%. The other two types, with below-average success rates, are "Hospitality" and the residual "Other economic activities". The type "Other economic activities" shows a success rate of 27% for 460 projects, while hospitality has a very low success rate of 5.2%, with only four of the 77 projects accepted.

In relation to RQ3, Table 2 shows how the Community of Madrid and Catalonia present the highest number of proposals related to ICTs (35.9% and 32.2%, respectively) and Professional, scientific and technical activities (43.8% and 18.3%, respectively). Then there are Autonomous Communities that only present proposals related to ICTs, such as Cantabria, hence its high level of success. The case of Andalusia stands out for a great diversity in economic areas, while they have an important participation of activity in hospitality that have not been successful when it comes to receiving funding. In hospitality, the communities with the highest % of participation, with respect to all the proposals, are Navarra (50%), Galicia (25.9%), Murcia (30%) and Ceuta (33%).

These results show that there is a direct relationship between the type of innovation in which the Autonomous Communities specialize and the level of success in obtaining funding, since ICT-related activities are the preferred in this call.

5 Conclusions

The main conclusion obtained in this work indicates the existence of a geographical inequality in entrepreneurship, innovation and technology in the tourism field. There is a concentration of applications from entrepreneurs in the regions of Madrid and Catalonia, while the autonomous communities of Andalusia and the Valencian Community have a lower level of participation. These data show a regional disparity in terms of entrepreneurship, innovation and technology in the tourism sector, where

Table 1 Projects submitted and approved by Autonomous Community (%)

	Num. applications	% applications	% approved app/ approved app in Spain	% approved app/ application in Aut.Com	Gap % applications−% approved
Andalusia	85	9.1	16.5	4.9	−4.2
Aragón	10	1.1	40.0	1.4	0.3
Balearic islands	34	3.6	38.2	4.5	0.9
Canary islands	33	3.5	15.2	1.7	−1.8
Cantabria	2	0.2	50.0	0.3	0.1
Castilla la Mancha	28	3.0	32.1	3.1	0.1
Castilla y León	20	2.1	20.0	1.4	−0.7
Catalonia	245	26.3	40.4	34.4	8.1
Autonomous community Madrid	311	33.4	33.8	36.5	3.1
Navarra	4	0.4	50.0	0.7	0.3
Autonomous community Valencia	58	6.2	27.6	5.6	−0.6
Extremadura	9	1.0	11.1	0.3	−0.7
Galicia	27	2.9	25.9	2.4	−0.5
Vasque country	20	2.1	20.0	1.4	−0.7
Asturias	12	1.3	25.0	1.0	−0.3
Murcia	30	3.2	0.0	0.0	−3.2
La Rioja	1	0.1	0.0	0.0	−0.1
Ceuta	3	0.0	33.3	0.3	0.3

Source Authors

certain geographical areas stand out for a greater activity and concentration of applications compared to others.

From the perspective of spillover theory applied to tourism entrepreneurship, it is argued that promoting entrepreneurship in tourism stimulates the creation of new companies and startups that offer innovative products and services to meet the demands of the sector. These companies can cover various areas and generate multiple spillover effects on the economy, such as the generation of direct and indirect employment, the development of supplier industries at the regional level and the

Table 2 Applications by economic activity and Autonomous Community (%)

Economic activity	Andalus (%)	Aragon (%)	Balearic islands (%)	Canary Islands (%)	Cantab (%)	C. Macha (%)	C. y León (%)	Cat (%)	Com. Madrid (%)	Navarra (%)	Valenc (%)	Extremd (%)	Galicia (%)	Vasque Country (%)	Asturias (%)	Murcia (%)	La Rioja (%)	Ceuta (%)
% application out of the total number of applications in each economic activity																		
C. Manufacture and energy	16.7	0.0	0.0	5.6	0.0	0.0	5.6	22.2	33.3	0.0	0.0	0.0	0.0	5.6	0.0	11.1	0.0	0.0
G. Wholesale and retail	10.9	1.8	3.6	9.1	0.0	1.8	0.0	27.3	32.7	0.0	5.5	0.0	1.8	1.8	0.0	3.6	0.0	0.0
I. Hospitality	11.7	0.0	2.6	5.2	0.0	2.6	2.6	3.9	33.8	2.6	10.4	0.0	9.1	1.3	1.3	11.7	0.0	1.3
J. ICTs	5.8	0.8	4.3	1.5	0.5	4.8	1.3	32.2	35.9	0.3	5.1	0.5	2.3	2.3	1.0	1.3	0.0	0.3
M. Scientific and technical activities	5.9	0.7	2.6	3.9	0.0	2.0	3.3	18.3	43.8	0.0	4.6	3.9	2.6	2.6	2.6	3.3	0.0	0.0
N. Administration and auxiliary services	15.1	2.7	5.5	4.1	0.0	1.4	2.7	28.1	23.3	0.0	7.5	0.0	3.4	1.4	2.1	2.1	0.7	0.0
R. Artistic and recreational	16.1	0.0	3.2	6.5	0.0	0.0	0.0	25.8	25.8	3.2	6.5	3.2	3.2	0.0	0.0	6.5	0.0	0.0
Others	25.8	3.2	0.0	9.7	0.0	3.2	9.7	61.3	32.3	0.0	22.6	0.0	0.0	6.5	0.0	6.5	0.0	3.2
% application on the total number of applications in each Autonomous Community																		
C. Manufacture and energy	3.5	0.0	0.0	3.0	0.0	0.0	5.0	1.6	1.9	0.0	0.0	0.0	0.0	5.0	0.0	6.7	0.0	0.0
G. Wholesale and retail	7.1	10.0	5.9	15.2	0.0	3.6	0.0	6.1	5.8	0.0	5.2	0.0	3.7	5.0	0.0	6.7	0.0	0.0
I. Hospitality	10.6	0.0	5.9	12.1	0.0	7.1	10.0	1.2	8.4	50.0	13.8	0.0	25.9	5.0	8.3	30.0	0.0	33.3

(continued)

Table 2 (continued)

Economic activity	Andalus (%)	Aragon (%)	Balearic islands (%)	Canary Islands (%)	Cantab (%)	C. Macha (%)	C. y León (%)	Cat (%)	Com. Madrid (%)	Navarra. (%)	Valenc (%)	Extremd (%)	Galicia (%)	Vasque Country (%)	Asturias (%)	Murcia (%)	La Rioja (%)	Ceuta (%)
J. ICTs	27.1	30.0	50.0	18.2	100.0	67.9	25.0	51.8	45.7	25.0	34.5	22.2	33.3	45.0	33.3	16.7	0.0	33.3
M. Scientific and technical activities	10.6	10.0	11.8	18.2	0.0	10.7	25.0	11.4	21.5	0.0	12.1	66.7	14.8	20.0	33.3	16.7	0.0	0.0
N. Administration and auxiliary services	25.9	40.0	23.5	18.2	0.0	7.1	20.0	16.7	10.9	0.0	19.0	0.0	18.5	10.0	25.0	10.0	100.0	0.0
R. Artistic and recreational	5.9	0.0	2.9	6.1	0.0	0.0	0.0	3.3	2.6	25.0	3.4	11.1	3.7	0.0	0.0	6.7	0.0	0.0
Others	9.4	10.0	0.0	9.1	0.0	3.6	15.0	7.8	3.2	0.0	12.1	0.0	0.0	10.0	0.0	6.7	0.0	33.3

Source Authors

promotion of innovation and technology, which not only benefit the tourism sector, but can also have applications in other economic sectors.

On the other hand, it is relevant to highlight that the success of tourism entrepreneurship depends on an enabling environment that encourages innovation, facilitates the creation of companies and provides support to entrepreneurs. Some of the key elements to promote tourism entrepreneurship and maximize the spillover effects on the economy include government policies, adequate infrastructure, training and access to finance.

However, considering that the call analysed, Emprendetur, has a national scope and all regions can participate on equal terms, the results raise questions about the territorial factors that can act as "drivers", causing a greater presence of entrepreneurs in some regions and not in others. The question arises as to whether entrepreneurship in tourism requires conditions or territorial factors different from those of other sectors of activity. This question becomes a relevant future research line.

References

Acs, Z. J., Braunerhjelm, P., Audretsch, D. B., & Carlsson, B. (2009). The knowledge spillover theory of entrepreneurship. *Small Business Economics, 32*, 15–30.

Ahl, H., & Marlow, S. (2021). Exploring the false promise of entrepreneurship through a postfeminist critique of the enterprise policy discourse in Sweden and the UK. *Human Relations, 74*(1), 41–68.

Ahmed, P., & Shepherd, C. D. (2010). *Innovation management: Context, strategies, systems and processes.* Pearson.

Andrisano, O., Bartolini, I., Bellavista, P., Boeri, A., Bononi, L., Borghetti, A., ... Vigo, D. (2018). The need of multidisciplinary approaches and engineering tools for the development and implementation of the smart city paradigm. *Proceedings of the IEEE, 106*(4), 738–760.

Audretsch, D. B. (1995). *Innovation and industry evolution.* MIT Press.

Bardin, L. (1986). *El análisis de contenido.* Akal.

Cassetti, V., & Paredes-Carbonell, J. J. (2019). Theory of change: A tool for participatory planning and.

Cooke, P., & Morgan, K. (1998). *The associational economy: Firms, regions and innovation.* Oxford University Press.

Davis, F. D. (1989). Perceived usefulness, perceived ease of use, and user acceptance of information technology. *MIS Quarterly, 13*, 319–339.

de Jong, A., & Figueroa-Domecq, C. (2022). Assessing the UNWTO's global report on women in tourism: Tourism's impact on gender equality. In A. Stoffelen & D. Ioannides (Eds.), *Handbook of tourism impacts: Social and environmental perspectives* (pp. 151–165). Edward Elgar Publishing.

Divisekera, S., & Nguyen, V. K. (2018). Determinants of innovation in tourism evidence from Australia. *Tourism Management, 67*, 157–167.

Dwivedi, Y. K., Rana, N. P., Jeyaraj, A., Clement, M., & Williams, M. D. (2019). Re-examining the unified theory of acceptance and use of technology (UTAUT): Towards a revised theoretical model. *Information Systems Frontiers, 21*(3), 719–734.

Ely, R. J., Ibarra, H., & Kolb, D. M. (2011). Taking gender into account: Theory and design for women's leadership development programs. *Academy of Management Learning & Education, 10*(3), 474–493.

Favre-Bonte, V., Gardet, E., & Thevenard-Puthod, C. (2019). The influence of territory on innovation network design in mountain tourism resorts. *European Planning Studies, 27*(5), 1035–1057.

Ferreira, J. J., Ratten, V., & Dana, L. P. (2017). Knowledge spillover-based strategic entrepreneurship. *International Entrepreneurship and Management Journal, 13*(1), 161–167.

Figueroa-Domecq, C., de Jong, A., Kimbu, A. N., & Williams, A. M. (2022). Financing tourism entrepreneurship: A gender perspective on the reproduction of inequalities. *Journal of Sustainable Tourism*, 1–21.

Figueroa-Domecq, C., Palomo, J., Flecha-Barrio, M. D., & Segovia-Perez, M. (2020a). Technology double gender gap in tourism business leadership. *Information Technology Tourism, 22*(1), 75–106.

Figueroa-Domecq, C., Williams, A., de Jong, A., & Alonso, A. (2020b). Technology is a woman's best friend: Entrepreneurship and Management in Tourism. *E-review of Tourism Research, 17*(5), 777–702.

Giddens, A. (1984). *The constitution of society*. Polity Press.

Gretzel, U. (2020). The growing role of social media in city tourism. In A. M. Morrison & J. A. Coca-Stefaniak (Eds.), *Routledge handbook of tourism cities* (pp. 389–399). Routledge.

Gretzel, U., & Koo, C. (2021). Smart tourism cities: A duality of place where technology supports the convergence of touristic and residential experiences. *Asia Pacific Journal of Tourism Research, 26*(4), 352–364.

Grillitsch, M., & Trippl, M. (2014). Combining knowledge from different sources, channels and geographical scales. *European Planning Studies, 22*(11), 2305–2325.

Hall, M. C., & Williams, A. (2008). *Tourism and innovation*. Routledge.

Jardón, C. M. (2011). Innovación empresarial y territorio: Una aplicación a Vigo y su área de influencia. *Eure (Santiago), 37*(112), 115–139.

Kimbu, A. N., de Jong, A., Adam, I., Ribeiro, M. A., Afenyo-Agbe, E., Adeola, O., & Figueroa-Domecq, C. (2021). Recontextualising gender in entrepreneurial leadership. *Annals of Tourism Research, 88*, 103176.

Kozinets, R. V. (2019). *Netnography: The essential guide to qualitative social media research*. Sage.

Lowrey, Y. (2003). The entrepreneur and entrepreneurship: A neoclassical approach. Office of Advocacy, US Small Business Administration Economic Research Working Paper.

Lundström, A., & Stevenson, L. (2005). *Entrepreneurship policy: Theory and practice* (Vol. 9). Springer.

Magasic, M., & Gretzel, U. (2020). Travel connectivity. *Tourist Studies, 20*(1), 3–26.

Müller, J., Castaño Collado, C., González, A., & Palmen, R. (2017). Policy towards gender equality in science and research. *Ene, 9*, 07.

Omar, F. I., Salman, A., & Rahim, S. A. (2017). The relationship between digital inclusion and support system towards the empowerment of women online entrepreneurs. *Journal of Education and Social Sciences, 7*(1), 52–57.

Organización Mundial del Turismo. (2019). Informe mundial sobre las mujeres en el turismo – Segunda edición. https://www.e-unwto.org/doi/book/10.18111/9789284422753

Ratten, V., Álvarez-García, J., & del Rio-Rama, M. D. (2019). Entrepreneurship, innovation and inequality: Exploring territorial dynamics. In *Entrepreneurship, innovation and inequality* (pp. 1–7). Routledge.

Rodriguez Sanchez, I., Williams, A. M., & García Andreu, H. (2020). Customer resistance to tourism innovations: entrepreneurs' understanding and management strategies. *Journal of Travel Research, 59*(3), 450–464.

Sarason, Y., Dean, T., & Dillard, J. (2006). Entrepreneurship as the nexus of individual and opportunity: A structuration view. *Journal of Business Venturin*, 286–305.

Schumpeter, J. A., & Nichol, A. J. (1934). Robinson's economics of imperfect competition. *Journal of Political Economy, 42*(2), 249-259.

Segittur and Cotec. (2021). Informe sobre Innovación Turística y Especialización Inteligente. https://www.segittur.es/wp-content/uploads/2021/03/Informe-Innovacion-Turistica-y-Especi alizacion-Inteligente-en-Espana.pdf

Shane, S., & Venkataraman, S. (2000). The promise of entrepreneurship as a field of research. *Academy of Management Review, 25*(1), 217–226.

Silva, B. N., Khan, M., & Han, K. (2018). Towards sustainable smart cities: A review of trends, architectures, components, and open challenges in smart cities. *Sustainable Cities and Society, 38*, 697–713.

Trinchini, L., Kolodii, N. A., Goncharova, N. A., & Baggio, R. (2019). Creativity, innovation and smartness in destination branding. *International Journal of Tourism Cities, 5*(4), 529–543.

Van Egeraat, C., & Kogler, D. F. (2013). Global and regional dynamics in knowledge flows and innovation networks. *European Planning Studies, 21*(9), 1317–1322.

Venkatesh, V., & Davis, F. D. (2000). A theoretical extension of the technology acceptance model: Four longitudinal field studies. *Management Science, 46*(2), 186–204.

Venkatesh, V., Morris, M. G., Davis, G. B., & Davis, F. D. (2003). User acceptance of information technology: Toward a unified view. *MIS Quarterly*, 425–478.

Werner, M., Strauss, K., Parker, B., Orzeck, R., Derickson, K., & Bonds, A. (2017). Feminist political economy in geography: Why now, what is different, and what for? *Geoforum, 79*, 1–4.

Zhang, C. X., Kimbu, A. N., Lin, P., & Ngoasong, M. Z. (2020). Guanxi influences on women intrapreneurship. *Tourism Management, 81*, 104137.

Framework for Enhancing the Social Impact of Tourism Research

Alba Viana-Lora⊙, Minerva Aguilar-Rivero⊙, Salvador Moral-Cuadra⊙, and Pablo Suazo⊙

Abstract This study addresses the importance of enhancing the social impact of tourism research through the implementation of a theoretical framework. The article presents the results of a review of the existing literature on the social impact of research. Key aspects for the design of a framework to enhance social impact are identified, including the identification of relevant social problems, the involvement of relevant stakeholders, a multidisciplinary approach, appropriate ethics, effective communication and impact evaluation. A series of interconnected steps are proposed to enhance the social impact of tourism research. The proposed framework seeks to address the current deficiencies in the connection between tourism research and social impact, promoting a participatory and multidisciplinary approach that generates positive change in society. Enhancing the social impact of tourism research is fundamental to maximising its effectiveness and achieving positive change in local communities.

Keywords Social impact of research · Tourism · Framework

A. Viana-Lora (✉)
Universitat Rovira i Virgili, Tarragona, Spain
e-mail: Alba.viana@urv.cat

M. Aguilar-Rivero
University of Córdoba, Córdoba, Spain

S. Moral-Cuadra
University of Granada, Granada, Spain

P. Suazo
University of Tarapacá, Tarapacá, Chile

251

A. J. Guevara Plaza et al. (eds.), *Tourism and ICTs: Advances in Data Science, Artificial Intelligence and Sustainability*, Springer Proceedings in Business and Economics, https://doi.org/10.1007/978-3-031-52607-7_23

1   Introduction

Tourism can be a powerful tool for the economic and social development of local communities. However, in practice, tourism can generate significant challenges and imbalances (Deery et al., 2012). Tourism research that seeks to enhance social impact focuses on addressing these challenges and harnessing the positive potential of tourism to generate significant change (Viana-Lora, 2023). Researchers must understand the effects of tourism on local communities so that their research can maximise benefits and minimise negative impacts (Viana-Lora et al., 2022). This calls for research into ways to strengthen local economies, promote entrepreneurship and job creation, and ensure that the profits generated by tourism are redistributed fairly and equitably (Ozanne et al., 2017). This involves investigating how tourism can respect and value local traditions, beliefs and practices, and promote respectful and meaningful interaction between visitors and host communities (Deery et al., 2012).

The potential to generate positive social impact through scientific research is undeniable. However, to maximise such impact, it is necessary to establish a theoretical framework to guide the research process and ensure the relevance and applicability of the results (Viana-Lora et al., 2023). It will be essential to ensure that tourism is a positive force for local communities, the environment and culture. For this reason, this research explores the importance of enhancing the social impact of tourism research through the design of a theoretical framework that outlines the key aspects and steps to be followed by the researcher.

2   Method

The methodology used consisted of designing a framework to enhance the social impact of tourism research. To this end, an analysis of the existing literature on the social impact of research has been carried out to enable us to extract the key theories and concepts published up to May 2023. The systematic literature review is an evidence-based technique that allows us to conduct an objective and theoretical discussion (Rother, 2007). The publications for the analysis were extracted from the Web of Science.[1] This database guarantees quality scientific content and has access to multiple databases with research in all areas of study (Mikki, 2009).

The stages carried out in this systematic literature review are depicted in Fig. 1. In this regard, the first phase consisted of searching for publications in the database through the following search algorithm:

"social impact of research" OR "social impact of the research" OR "societal impact of research" OR "societal impact of the research" OR "social benefits of research" OR "social benefits of the research" OR "social benefits of research" OR "benefits of research in society" OR "benefits of research on society"

A filter was applied to ensure that these key terms were present in the abstract, author keywords and Keywords Plus, and the publication types "Article", "Review

---

[1] https://www.webofscience.com/wos.

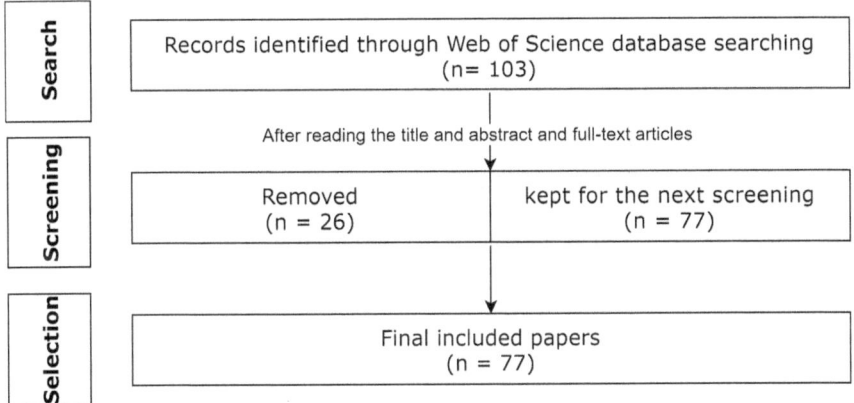

Fig. 1 Review protocol. Own elaboration

Article" and "Early Access" were selected. The search strategy yielded 103 publications. The second phase consists of filtering the publications. To do this, the information is downloaded into an Excel sheet and a first filtering is carried out by reading the keywords and the title and a second filtering by reading the full text. In this process, articles whose objective is not the social impact of the research and which are in a language other than English are discarded. This resulted in 77 publications. The third phase was based on the analysis of publications. The 77 selected articles were read, reviewed and analysed to design a framework that seeks to enhance the social impact of tourism researchers, the results of which are in the following section.

This rigorous and evidence-based methodological approach allowed us to identify and synthesize the main concepts related to the social impact of tourism research, thus laying the groundwork for the development of effective strategies aimed at maximizing this impact on society.

3 Results

3.1 Key Issues for the Framework

After analysing the publications, the key aspects to be considered by researchers in order to enhance the social impact of their research are identified.

Identifying Social Problems

The first step in enhancing the social impact of research is to identify and understand the relevant social problems that require attention (Molas-Gallart & Tang, 2011). This involves analysing and assessing society's needs and challenges in different areas, such as health, education, environment, poverty, gender equality, the pursuit of the

SDGs provides this opportunity (Dorta-González & Dorta-González, 2023; Viana Lora & Nel-lo-Andreu, 2020). The development of mobile applications and online surveys allows for the collection of data and information from affected communities and other stakeholders. This creates a closer connection between academia and society at large (De Jong et al., 2014). Research should be oriented towards addressing problems and contributing to their solution (Chen et al., 2023). Using big data analysis tools to identify whether social problems are being analyzed in related scientific publications can help researchers prioritize research areas.

Stakeholder Involvement

To achieve significant social impact, it is essential to involve relevant stakeholders from the early stages of the research (De Silva et al., 2017; Ozanne et al., 2017). This may include affected communities, non-governmental organisations, local governments, businesses, academics or residents, and other stakeholders (Senn et al., 2022). The involvement of these actors allows for a deeper understanding of social problems to develop effective strategies and evidence-based policies through co-creation and effective implementation of research findings (Soler-Gallart & Flecha, 2022; Viana-Lora & Nel-lo-Andreu, 2023). Real-time communication technologies, such as videoconferencing and webinars, can be used to facilitate interaction and dialogue between researchers and stakeholders, especially when they are unable to meet in person.

Multidisciplinary Approach

Solving complex social problems often requires a holistic perspective that integrates various disciplines and approaches (Senn et al., 2022). This collaboration between different disciplines, such as social sciences, natural sciences, engineering, technology and humanities, promotes interculturality and knowledge sharing, generating innovative perspectives and more effective solutions (Díaz Mariño et al., 2021). Fostering multidisciplinarity will allow a comprehensive approach to the social, economic, cultural and environmental aspects associated with social problems (Olmos-Peñuela et al., 2014).

Ethics and Positive Impact

An ethical approach is also essential to enhance the social impact of research (Sigurðarson, 2020). This involves ensuring respect for human rights, protection of participants' privacy and confidentiality, and responsible handling of data (Khomyakov, 2021). In addition, research should be guided by an approach based on equity, social justice and collective benefit (Huanhuan et al., 2021). The main goal should be to generate positive social impact and contribute to the well-being of society as a whole (Chams et al., 2020).

Effective Communication

Enhancing the social impact of research allows for greater democratisation of knowledge (Olmos-Peñuela et al., 2014). Science and research should not only be accessible to the academic community, but also to the general public (Viana-Lora & Nel-lo-Andreu, 2021). Using technological tools that enable data visualization to present research findings in a clear and understandable way for different audiences ensures that the information is accessible to different audiences and its findings can help inform and educate, influence public policy, and promote social change (Eschenbach, 2017; Viana-Lora & Nel-lo-Andreu, 2022). For example, the use of online platforms such as social networks, blogs and websites to disseminate research results in an open manner. This empowers people, giving them the opportunity to understand social issues, participate in the discussion and be agents of change in their own communities (Aiello et al., 2021).

Impact Assessment

A rigorous assessment of the impact of research on society will also be essential (Viana-Lora & Nel-lo-Andreu, 2021). Potential impact will be assessed in a pre-analysis (ex ante evaluation), an evaluation at an intermediate stage (in itinere evaluation), and an evaluation at the end of the research (ex post evaluation) (Holbrook & Frodeman, 2011; Viana-Lora et al., 2022). This involves measuring and analysing how the research results have contributed to addressing the identified social problems, how the proposed solutions have been implemented and what changes have been achieved (Redondo-Sama et al., 2020). Impact evaluation provides feedback to improve future research strategies and ensure greater effectiveness in generating social impact (Hill, 2016). The results of this evaluation will be stored and shared in online databases and repositories accessible to other researchers and the general public.

3.2 Steps to Follow

To enhance the social impact of tourism research, a number of interconnected steps must be followed. First, it is essential to identify and engage a variety of relevant tourism stakeholders (Ozanne et al., 2017). Each of these stakeholders brings valuable perspectives and knowledge to address societal challenges (De Silva et al., 2017). Clear and specific objectives should then be set that focus on generating knowledge for responsible and sustainable tourism, aligning them with existing societal challenges and ensuring that they are measurable (Viana-Lora et al., 2022).

Research should be based on real problems, identifying specific challenges and using appropriate approaches to analyse and solve them (Fecher & Hebing, 2021). To achieve this, collaboration and dialogue between stakeholders should be fostered, promoting a multidisciplinary approach involving experts from different fields to comprehensively address the social and environmental aspects of tourism (Díaz Mariño et al., 2021). In addition to generating theoretical knowledge, it is crucial that research produces concrete recommendations and actions that can be implemented in practice, such as policies, business practices, training programmes and awareness-raising campaigns (Viana-Lora & Nel-lo-Andreu, 2023).

To ensure the dissemination of results, it is essential to communicate them in an accessible way through reports, presentations and participation in community events, taking advantage of the media to reach a wider audience (Olmos-Peñuela

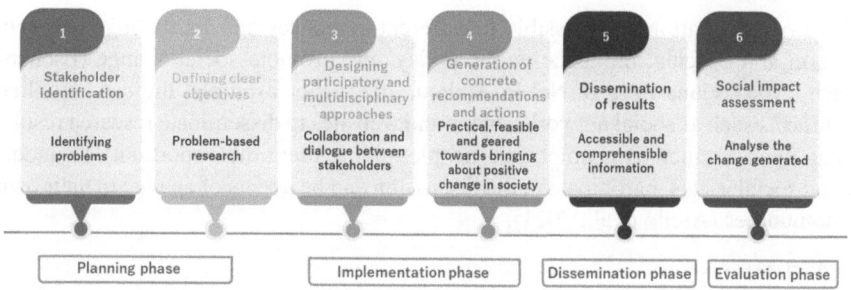

Fig. 2 Steps to follow. Own elaboration

et al., 2014). Finally, the social impact of tourism research should be evaluated periodically, measuring the change generated by the proposed recommendations and actions, and collecting comments and feedback from stakeholders involved (Viana-Lora et al., 2022). These continuous evaluations allow the framework to be improved and adapted to the changing needs of society (Fig. 2).

4 Discussion

This framework is based on a participatory and multidisciplinary approach, involving diverse stakeholders and focusing on the generation of knowledge that promotes responsible and sustainable tourism. This framework aims to address current gaps in the connection between tourism research and social impact, ensuring that research not only produces theoretical knowledge, but also concrete recommendations and actions that generate positive change in society. By following this framework, researchers can focus their efforts on addressing specific social problems, work collaboratively with relevant stakeholders, use a combination of appropriate research methods and generate concrete recommendations and actions to foster more responsible and equitable tourism.

5 Conclusions

Scientific research has the power to transform societies, address complex challenges and generate positive change. Its potential to generate knowledge and deep understanding of diverse phenomena is undeniable. However, the mere act of generating knowledge is not enough to address the complex and urgent challenges we face today. Maximizing the social impact of research has become an imperative in the scientific community and in society in general. This approach involves going beyond the generation of knowledge and focuses on the practical application of results to address social problems and improve people's quality of life. For this reason, this article proposes a theoretical framework to help researchers enhance the social impact of research and harness its full transformative potential. This approach allows us to move towards a more just and sustainable future, where scientific research is a catalyst for positive change and social progress. This involves not only solving current problems, but also anticipating and addressing the challenges we will face in the coming decades. Scientific research, when used effectively, has the power to catalyze positive change and social progress. As a society, we must recognize and support this transformative capacity of science by promoting collaboration among researchers and encouraging active engagement in the application of research for the benefit of all. Ultimately, enhancing the societal impact of research is essential to building a more resilient, equitable and sustainable world for future generations.

References

Aiello, E., Donovan, C., Duque, E., Fabrizio, S., Flecha, R., Holm, P., ... Reale, E. (2021). Effective strategies that enhance the social impact of social sciences and humanities research. *Evidence & Policy, 17*(1), 131-146.

Chams, N., Guesmi, B., & Gil, J. M. (2020). Beyond scientific contribution: Assessment of the societal impact of research and innovation to build a sustainable agri-food sector. *Journal of Environmental Management, 264*, 110455.

Chen, S., Sharma, G., & Muñoz, P. (2023). In pursuit of impact: From research questions to problem formulation in entrepreneurship research. *Entrepreneurship Theory and Practice, 47*(2), 232–264.

De Jong, S., Barker, K., Cox, D., Sveinsdottir, T., & Van den Besselaar, P. (2014). Understanding societal impact through productive interactions: ICT research as a case. *Research Evaluation, 23*(2), 89–102.

De Silva, P. U., Vance, C. K., De Silva, P. U., & Vance, K. C. (2017). Assessing the societal impact of scientific research. In *Scientific scholarly communication: The changing landscape* (pp. 117–132).

Deery, M., Jago, L., & Fredline, L. (2012). Rethinking social impacts of tourism research: A new research agenda. *Tourism Management, 33*(1), 64–73.

Díaz Mariño, B. L., Caballero-Rico, F. C., Roque Hernández, R. V., Ramírez de León, J. A., & González-Bandala, D. A. (2021). Towards the construction of productive interactions for social impact. *Sustainability, 13*(2), 485.

Dorta-González, P., & Dorta-González, M. I. (2023). The funding effect on citation and social attention: the UN Sustainable Development Goals (SDGs) as a case study. *Online Information Review*.

Eschenbach, C. A. (2017). Bridging the gap between observational oceanography and users. *Ocean Science, 13*(1), 161–173.

Fecher, B., & Hebing, M. (2021). How do researchers approach societal impact? *PLoS ONE, 16*(7), e0254006.

Hill, S. (2016). Assessing (for) impact: Future assessment of the societal impact of research. *Palgrave Communications, 2*(1), 1–7.

Holbrook, J. B., & Frodeman, R. (2011). Peer review and the ex ante assessment of societal impacts. *Research Evaluation, 20*(3), 239–246.

Huanhuan, C., Li, M., Wang, M., Roder, D., & Olver, I. (2021). Challenges for ethics committees in biomedical research governance: illustrations from China and Australia. *Journal of Medical Ethics and History of Medicine, 14*.

Khomyakov, M. (2021). Should science be evaluated? *Social Science Information, 60*(3), 308–317.

Mikki, S. (2009). Google scholar compared to web of science. A literature review. *Nordic Journal of Information Literacy in Higher Education, 1*(1).

Molas-Gallart, J., & Tang, P. (2011). Tracing 'productive interactions' to identify social impacts: An example from the social sciences. *Research Evaluation, 20*(3), 219–226.

Olmos-Peñuela, J., Castro-Martínez, E., & d'Este, P. (2014). Knowledge transfer activities in social sciences and humanities: Explaining the interactions of research groups with non-academic agents. *Research Policy, 43*(4), 696–706.

Ozanne, J. L., Davis, B., Murray, J. B., Grier, S., Benmecheddal, A., Downey, H., ... Veer, E. (2017). Assessing the societal impact of research: The relational engagement approach. *Journal of Public Policy & Marketing, 36*(1), 1–14.

Redondo-Sama, G., Díez-Palomar, J., Campdepadrós, R., & Morlà-Folch, T. (2020). Communicative methodology: Contributions to social impact assessment in psychological research. *Frontiers in Psychology*, 286.

Rother, E. T. (2007). Systematic literature review X narrative review. *Acta paulista de enfermagem, 20*, v–vi.

Senn, J., Luque-Vílchez, M., & Larrinaga, C. (2022). The role of accounting in the assessment of knowledge production from a multi-stakeholder's perspective. *Sustainability Accounting, Management and Policy Journal*, (ahead-of-print).

Sigurðarson, E. S. (2020). Capacities, capabilities, and the societal impact of the humanities. *Research Evaluation, 29*(1), 71–76.

Soler-Gallart, M., & Flecha, R. (2022). Researchers' Perceptions about methodological innovations in research oriented to social impact: Citizen evaluation of social impact. *International Journal of Qualitative Methods, 21*, 16094069211067654.

Viana-Lora, A. (2023). The societal impact of tourism research of the Research Excellence Framework 2021. *Journal of Policy Research in Tourism, Leisure and Events*, 1–16.

Viana Lora, A., & Nel-lo Andreu, M. G. (2020). Alternative metrics for assessing the social impact of tourism research. *Sustainability, 12*(10), 4299.

Viana-Lora, A., & Nel-lo-Andreu, M. G. (2021). Approaching the social impact of research through a literature review. *International Journal of Qualitative Methods, 20*, 16094069211052188.

Viana-Lora, A., & Nel-lo-Andreu, M. (2023). Pathways for the social impact of research in Barcelona's tourism policy. *International Journal of Tourism Cities, 9*(2), 481–495.

Viana-Lora, A., Nel-lo-Andreu, M. G., & Anton-Clavé, S. (2023). Advancing a framework for social impact assessment of tourism research. *Tourism and Hospitality Research, 23*(4), 494–505.

Application of Proknow-C for the Systematic Analysis of Literature on the Influence of Carbon Footprint Reduction Measures on the Choice of Accommodation Reservation

Marina Haro-Aragu📵 and Josefa García-Mestanza📵

Abstract The tourism sector is directly related to high energy consumption. In this context, measuring the ecological footprint generated by tourism is crucial to address environmental challenges. Hotels play a prominent role in this footprint due to their size and daily operations, which consume large amounts of energy and natural resources. The objective of this research is to analyze the state of the question of the influence of this carbon footprint reduction in tourist accommodation, especially hotels. The method used is based on the application of the Knowledge Development Process—Constructivist (ProKnow-C), providing a structured, rigorous procedure that minimizes the use of randomness and subjectivity in the bibliographic review process, as well as its subsequent analysis in the Bibliometrix program. As results, 7 relevant articles are obtained and aligned with the research topic, making it possible to identify the main approaches proposed by the authors of this bibliographic portfolio in relation to the problem raised. The present research can be used as a guide for the construction of knowledge in a systematic way and provides, both academics and professionals, a better overview to understand the contributions of the carbon footprint in the accommodation reservation, especially hotels. Through the bibliometric analysis, it was possible to identify relevant data from the 7 articles in the final portfolio, such as the main words and their correlation, the main authors, the production of said authors over time, etc., which can be presented as an opportunity for future researchers.

Keywords Carbon footprint · Accommodation · Sustainability · Proknow-C · Bibliometrix

M. Haro-Aragu (✉) · J. García-Mestanza
Facultad de Turismo, Universidad de Málaga, Málaga, Spain
e-mail: mharoaragu@uma.es

© The Author(s) 2024 259
A. J. Guevara Plaza et al. (eds.), *Tourism and ICTs: Advances in Data Science, Artificial Intelligence and Sustainability*, Springer Proceedings in Business and Economics, https://doi.org/10.1007/978-3-031-52607-7_24

1   Introduction

Tourism has experienced significant growth in recent decades, becoming one of the main industries worldwide (Sugathan & Roopak, 2020). However, this tourism boom has also given rise to a series of environmental concerns, especially in relation to the ecological footprint generated by this activity (Kongbuamai et al., 2020). The Ecological Footprint (HE) is a methodology widely used in the evaluation of the environmental impact of human activities due to its ability to quantitatively represent the degree to which human beings are consuming the regenerative capacity of the biosphere, and to compare said consumption with the amount of capacity still available (Goldfinger et al., 2014).

In the context of tourism, the ecological footprint has become a topic of growing interest and concern (El Archi et al., 2023; Guan et al., 2022), since the tourism sector is directly linked to significant energy consumption from fossil fuels, especially through transportation, which represents more than 75% of the total carbon emissions related to tourism activities (Zhang & Liu, 2019). In addition, for the proper development and operation of tourism infrastructure, excessive exploration of natural resources is required, which contributes to the increase in the carbon footprint and the depletion of biological capacity (Guan et al., 2022; Nathaniel et al., 2021; Razzaq et al., 2021).

In this sense, the measurement of the ecological footprint generated by tourism has become a crucial area of study to understand and address the associated environmental challenges. According to Ştefănică et al. (2021) , the ecological footprint of tourism can cover multiple dimensions, such as the emission of greenhouse gases, energy consumption, the generation of solid and liquid waste, the overexploitation of natural resources and the loss of biodiversity. These dimensions are intrinsically linked to tourism activities, from the transportation used to reach destinations to management practices and operation of tourism facilities.

Within the tourism sector, hotels play a prominent role in generating an ecological footprint due to their size, infrastructure, and daily operations. The construction and maintenance of hotels require large amounts of energy and natural resources, which contributes to their depletion and the emission of greenhouse gases. In addition, the provision of services such as water supply, waste management, and the consumption of food and cleaning products also generates a significant environmental impact.

Recent research has highlighted the importance of measuring and mitigating the ecological footprint of hotels. According to Chan (2021a, b), the precise and systematic measurement of the ecological footprint of hotels can help identify areas for improvement and establish effective strategies to reduce their environmental impact. This implies evaluating both direct emissions (for example, those generated by energy consumption in hotel facilities) and indirect emissions (for example, those associated with the provision of food and other external services).

The measurement of the ecological footprint of hotels has become a constantly evolving field of study, with the development of different methodologies and tools to assess their environmental impact. For example, the Hotel Footprinting Protocol developed by the Global Initiative for Sustainable Tourism (GSTC) provides a framework for quantifying and monitoring the ecological footprint of hotels in key aspects such as energy, water and resource consumption.

The last decade has seen significant growth in the tourism and hospitality literature on corporate social responsibility (CSR) (Font & Lynes, 2018), as the local population has also radically changed their perceptions (Goodwin, 2017). In addition, contemporary society gives more and more importance to health and well-being, physical and mental, and in general to quality of life (Edlin & Golanty, 2015). These health and well-being for all are key public values for most governments (United Nations, 2019), and are also basic needs and a human right, both crucial to achieving sustainable societies (Von Heimburg & Ness, 2021; United Nations, 2019; World Health Organization, 2016). Thorne (2021) indicates that this situation leads consumers to travel in order to meet these well-being and sustainability expectations, better known in the literature as "LOHAS" (Lifestyle of Health and Sustainability) (Pícha & Navrátil, 2019). Therefore, increasing the number of tourism companies that develop strategies for sustainable growth will also contribute positively to the commercial growth of the tourism sector (Aksöz et al., 2021).

Sustainability in the tourist accommodation sector is essential to mitigate environmental impact and contribute to community development (Ferreira et al., 2022; Font & Lynes, 2018). The implementation of Corporate Social Responsibility (CSR) initiatives has been highlighted as an effective way to achieve these objectives, while allowing sustainability, value creation and competitive advantage to be achieved (Bohdanowicz & Zientara, 2008; Cheng & Ding, 2021). In particular, the hotel industry has received attention due to its considerable financial gains and its influence on society (Wong et al., 2021).

According to Lewis (2021), CSR is of vital importance in the hotel industry, as it promotes responsible business practices that are beneficial to society. Research such as that of Wang et al. (2018) and Ferreira et al. (2022) have studied the effects of CSR practices in the context of the hotel industry, demonstrating its importance and effectiveness in addressing environmental challenges.

The environmental impact of hotels is significant, contributing approximately 60 million tons of CO_2 emissions annually and representing 1% of global carbon emissions (Lewis, 2021). It is evident that reducing the carbon footprint has become a key strategy to address this environmental problem. In addition, the recent implementation of Decree 390/2021 has promoted the energy certification of buildings, focusing on sustainability and its integration as a profitable business model in hotels.

Although marketing research in hospitality and tourism is abundant, the use of experimental design has been underutilized, mainly due to a lack of familiarity with this approach (Fong et al., 2016; Line & Runyan, 2012). However, the experimental design offers significant advantages, especially in the ability to control for external variables and examine causal relationships (Fong et al., 2016; Sparks & Browning, 2011; Sun et al., 2020).

Most of the experimental articles related to hospitality and tourism use the theory of random utility as a fundamental concept (Chou & Chen, 2014; Lee & Yoo, 2015; Sun et al., 2020), based on two components, one variable and measurable (iq), which is the function of the attributes (Xiq), and another stochastic (Eiq), which reflects, in addition to measurement and observation errors, tastes, customs, etc. of each individual. One of the experimental designs, the discrete choice model, is closely related to random utility theory, and has been adopted to examine the importance of attributes such as cities and hotels (Crouch et al., 2019; Masiero et al., 2019; Sun et al., 2020).

For example, Martin et al. (2017) examined the influence of tourists' psychological entitlement on hotel selection, finding that tourists tend to avoid hotels with great cultural distance. Kawanaka et al. (2020), studied the effect of gamification on tourist behavior and tourist satisfaction through an experimental case study. Gavilan et al. (2018) examined the impacts of online rating comments on consumer intention to book hotels through a full factorial design and revealed the interaction between ratings and online comments.

Although some companies in the hotel industry have begun to consider implementing programs that involve their stakeholders so that they can reduce their carbon footprints together, which may include saving energy and water, recycling solid waste and of food, the construction of LEED-certified buildings, and the implementation of formal environmental management systems (EMS), which can result in awards from local and international green initiatives (Chan, 2021a, b), so far only a few researchers have analyzed the influence that the implementation of these measures exerts on the consumer. In addition, in online purchase decisions, the consumer receives general information about what they are going to book, but very little about the environmental impact of their stay, or the measures taken by these hotels to contribute to it. Increasingly, different chains, such as Vincci Hotels, are incorporating carbon footprint calculators for guests into their web pages. However, no research to our knowledge has investigated the interaction between the influence that knowledge of these measures and price may have on consumer purchasing decisions.

The objective of this study is to analyze the state of the art of the influence of this carbon footprint reduction in tourist accommodation, especially hotels. This research presents the detailed application of the Knowledge Development Process—Constructivist Methodology (Proknow-C), through the creation of a relevant bibliographic portfolio through bibliometric analysis, managing to select those works highly aligned with this research topic. This constitutes an analytical study of accumulated knowledge that starts from documentary research, thanks to which we can carry out the study of accumulated knowledge within a specific area (Molina, 2005). The objective of this modality is to inventory and systematize production in an area of knowledge, an exercise that should not remain only in the inventory, but rather transcend beyond, since it allows for a deep reflection on the trends and gaps in a specific area (Vargas & Calvo, 1987). Subsequently, we will analyze the results obtained with Bibliometrix, which is an R statistical package to analyze and visualize bibliographic data from WoS and Scopus databases.

The exhaustive review of the literature carried out reveals the accumulated knowledge on these aspects and makes explicit their antecedents, causes, detection models and solutions that allow progress towards more sustainable tourism development.

2 Methodology

For the selection of the theoretical framework and construction of the necessary knowledge, the method used was based on the Proknow-C (Knowledge Development Process - Constructivist) methodology, proposed by Ensslin et al. (2010), which consists of structuring a review of the literature to build knowledge and select journals for its theoretical foundation (Vieira et al., 2019).

The objective was to carry out a systemic review in order to locate the most relevant studies based on the keywords of this research (Ravindran & Shankar, 2015), as well as a bibliometric analysis of the scientific production in this regard (Duque & Cervantes-Cervantes, 2019) by using the Bibliometrix program. The study was designed to fill in the gaps of previous reviews, examining the status, trends, and possible areas of future research, in a way that provides an overview of the research topic. For this reason, this research was carried out through a qualitative and interpretive design, which determined the procedure for selection, access and registration of the documentary sample (Vargas et al., 2015). In this way, an overview of all the research axes investigated is presented, with an interdisciplinary and comprehensive approach (Jurado et al., 2020). The design of the methodological process is organized in three phases, which are explained below.

In the first two phases, the steps followed, based on those proposed by de Carvalho et al. (2020), were the following: 1. Definition of keywords; 2. Definition of databases; 3. Search for articles in the databases with the keywords; 3. Keyword stickiness test app.; 4. Elimination of repeated articles; 5. Alignment by reading the title; 6. Alignment as scientific recognition, for example, number of citations and recent articles; 7. Alignment by reading the abstract; 8. Alignment by complete reading of articles: descriptive bibliometric and systematic analysis.

In the first phase, the lines of investigation or search are established. In our case, only one research axis is established, which is "carbon footprint reduction measures in accommodation". For our research axis, the corresponding keywords are established: carbon footprint, accommodation and hotel.

The multidisciplinary nature of tourism led to the selection of the Web of Science database, as it is the main international and multidisciplinary database that indexes only the most cited journals in their respective areas.

The search fields were used: title, abstract and keywords, and the years were restricted to the periods 1900–2021, for articles from scientific journals. The search was carried out using the following search terms, and with the boolean operators AND and OR: Carbon footprint AND (accommodation OR hotel).

Completing this first phase and to obtain the gross publication bank, an adherence test of articles with keywords was carried out, which consisted of randomly selecting several from the aforementioned bank, in order to identify the keywords of each one of them., to determine if the title, keywords or abstract are those defined in this research, so that the portfolio is as aligned as possible (dos Santos Matos & Petri, 2015).

The second phase begins with the exclusion of those that were duplicates once the first bank of gross articles of all the research axes was obtained. Since in our case we only used WOS as the database, it was not necessary to perform this step. Next, the titles were read, and from there the scientific recognition was verified by searching for the number of citations that each article had in the consulted databases. Those discarded due to their lack of scientific recognition were subjected to a re-evaluation that is detailed below. Subsequently, the abstracts of the articles were read, to select those aligned with the research topic, and the complete reading of the texts was carried out, and the bibliometric and systematic descriptive analyzes were carried out (Ensslin et al., 2010; Ravindran & Shankar, 2015; Vieira et al., 2019).

A bibliometric analysis of the results obtained was carried out using the Bibliometrix program. Various studies have highlighted the relevance and role of R and its packages in various scientific fields. For example, Li and Yan (2018) carried out a study and mapping of the use of R and its packages in Public Library of Science (PLoS) articles. Bibliometrix, for its part, is a statistical R package that allows analyzing and visualizing bibliographic data from WoS and Scopus databases. In our case, we use the WoS database. Additionally, R forms an open source environment ecosystem encompassing statistical algorithms, mathematical functionality, and visualization capabilities, making it an ideal choice for bibliometric analysis. R is compatible with Windows and Linux operating systems and has a graphical user interface (RStudio), making it easy to use for both novice and expert users.

3   Analysis and Results

With the established keywords (carbon footprint, accommodation and hotel) 161 were obtained from Web of Science. After performing the adherence test and the alignment by reading the title, 133 were discarded because they were not aligned with the objective of the research, finally resulting in 28 articles.

The alignment by scientific recognition was carried out, of which 12 were discarded for being cited less than 10 times, passing the remaining 16 to the next phase. However, those 12 discarded went through a re-evaluation, in which 6 articles were reincorporated to continue their analysis, which are added to the 16 previously mentioned, making a total of 22 articles.

Subsequently, the abstracts of the 22 articles were read, to make the selection of those that were aligned with the research topic, discarding 7. In the next phase, the accessibility of the articles was checked, discarding 8 in this process. Finally, the texts of the remaining 7 were accessed for their reading and review of the required information and the descriptive bibliometric and systematic analyzes were carried out, resulting in these being the final articles of the entire process, since on this occasion, none was discarded (Ensslin et al., 2010; Ravindran & Shankar, 2015; Vieira et al., 2019).

The analysis plan consisted of two readings: a linear one that required the consecutive review of the information obtained in the bibliographic sources, and a cross-sectional one that allowed the comparison of the sources from the applied categories to identify repetitions, gaps, confirmations, extensions, shortcomings, as well as the quality and quality of the information on the object of investigation.

The 7 articles were entered into the Bibliometrix program, obtaining the following results.

In Fig. 1, we can see, first of all, the wordcloud with the most relevant words that we find in common in the 7 articles. The results show us a combination of words closely related to our line of research. It is interesting how in all the articles there are words related to corporate social responsibility, the life cycle of products, supply chains, reducing the carbon footprint, the sustainable and economic development of cities and urban tourism and in general terms that encompass the concept of sustainability. This shows that our search has been appropriate for the topic investigated, and that the methodology has been effective in finding a bank of articles aligned with our research topic.

We can find the Treemap as well in Table 1. This is interesting, since, in addition to seeing the words that are most repeated in our texts and the interrelation between them, it also allows us to see in what percentage each one appears and, therefore, which are the most repeated in our articles, as well as the evolution and frequency of the words over time (Fig. 2).

On the other hand, Fig. 3 shows the thematic maps with their respective correlations. These interrelationships of words are linked to the concept of sustainability,

Fig. 1 Wordcloud. *Source* Bibliometrix data

Table 1 Treemap word
percentages

Word	Percentage of appearance (%)
Life-cycle	7
Emissions	5
Supply chain	4
Carbon footprint	2
Corporate social responsability	2
Inclusive leadership	2
Reduction	2
Pro-environmental behaviors	2
Ecological footprint	2
Citizenship behavior	2
Travel	4
Energy use	4
Tourist accomodation	2
Sustainability	2
Greenhouse-gas emissions	2
Transformational leadership	2

Source Self elaboration from Bibliometrix data

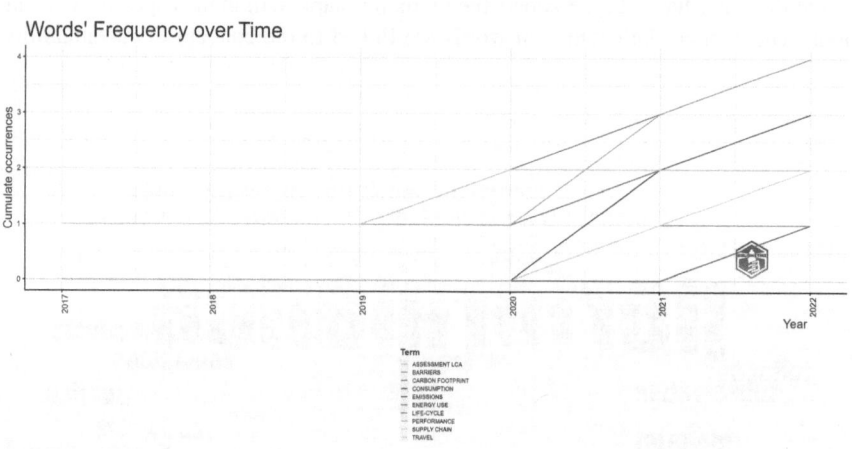

Fig. 2 Words' frequency over Time. *Source* Bibliometrix data

responsible tourism, reduction of greenhouse gas emissions and the importance of making conscious decisions to minimize the environmental impact in the tourism sector and in the supply chain of related products. All of them are grouped into sets that in turn are interrelated with each other, thanks to which we can see once again how all our articles are aligned with each other, and with our line of research.

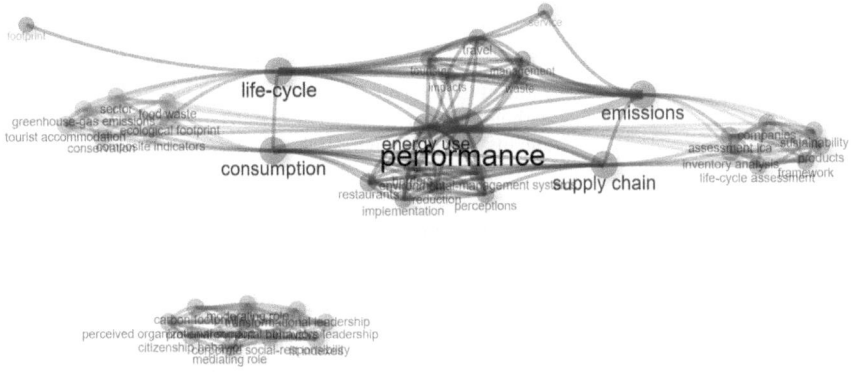

Fig. 3 Thematic map. *Source* Bibliometrix data

Continuing on, in Fig. 4, we see a very interesting data, the most relevant sources of publication. Thanks to this analysis, we can see in which magazines the authors usually publish, which are the topics that attract the most attention in each magazine, or what type of articles they usually publish.

On Table 2, we see the production of each author over time. This will allow us to analyze how they have evolved over time, who has the most scientific production, the journals in which they write the most and the years of publication.

Finally, it is also interesting to see how they show us the scientific production of each country of the articles (Table 3).

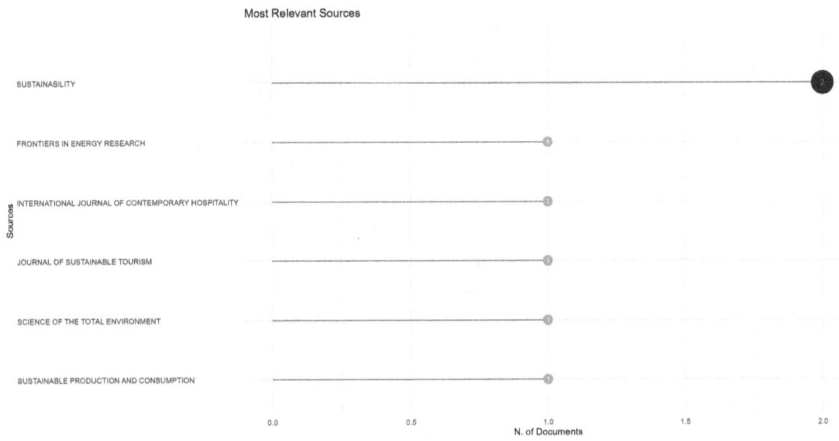

Fig. 4 Most relevant sources of publication. *Source* Bibliometrix data

Table 2 Authors production over time

Author	Year	Title	Source	TC	TCpY
Ahmad, N	2022	The role of CSR for de-carbonization of hospitality sector through employees: A leadership perspective	Sustainability	22	11,000
Comité, U	2022	The role of CSR for de-carbonization of hospitality sector through employees: A leadership perspective	Sustainability	22	11,000
Demeter, C	2022	Assessing the carbon footprint of tourism businesses using environmentally extended input–output analysis	Journal of Sustainable Tourism	5	2500
Dolnicar, S	2022	Assessing the carbon footprint of tourism businesses using environmentally extended input–output analysis	Journal of Sustainable Tourism	5	2500
Filimonau, V	2021	Strategies to improve energy and carbon efficiency of luxury hotels in Iran	Sustainable Production and Consuption	19	6333
Asadzadeh, M	2021	Strategies to improve energy and carbon efficiency of luxury hotels in Iran	Sustainable Production and Consuption	19	6333
Chan, E. S. W	2021	Why do hotels find reducing their carbon footprint difficult?	Internal Journal of Contemporary Hospitality Management	10	3333
Alberti, J	2017	Inventory analysis and carbon footprint of coastland-hotel services: A Spanish case study	Science of the Total Environment	32	4571
Chacon, L	2017	Inventory analysis and carbon footprint of coastland-hotel services: A Spanish case study	Science of the Total Environment	32	4571
Fullana-I-Palmer, P	2017	Inventory analysis and carbon footprint of coastland-hotel services: A Spanish case study	Science of the Total Environment	32	4571

Source Self elaboration from Bibliometrix data

Table 3 Countries' scientific production

Region	Frequency
China	7
Spain	4
Iran	2
Pakistan	2
Australia	1
Bahrain	1
Italy	1
Japan	1
Jordan	1
Saudi Arabia	1

Source Self elaboration from Bibliometrix data

4 Conclusions

The methodology applied in this study (ProKnow-C) has been shown to be effective in meeting the objective of selecting and analyzing a consistent bibliographic portfolio. Through the bibliometric analysis, it was possible to identify relevant data from the 7 articles in the final portfolio, such as the main words and their correlation, the main authors, the production of said authors over time, etc., which can be presented as an opportunity for future researchers. One of the results to highlight is the situation of Spain as the second country with the most scientific production on the subject, after China, which is in first place. Tourism, and in particular hotels, generate a significant ecological footprint that requires proper assessment and management. The measurement of this ecological footprint has become essential to understand and address the environmental impacts associated with tourism. As we move towards a more sustainable approach in the hospitality industry, it is essential to employ rigorous methodologies and appropriate tools to assess and reduce the ecological footprint of hotels.

Therefore, the present research can be used as a guide for the construction of knowledge in a systematic way and provides, both academics and professionals, a better overview to understand the contributions of the carbon footprint in the accommodation reservation, especially hotels, as a reference point for future research.

References

Aksöz, E. O., Aydın, B., & Esin, Y. (2021). Tourists approaches to eco-friendly hotels and determination of green hotel preferences: The case of Eskişehir. *Turizam, 25*(2), 83–95.

Bohdanowicz, P., & Zientara, P. (2008). Corporate social responsibility in hospitality: Issues and implications. A case study of Scandic. *Scandinavian Journal of Hospitality and Tourism, 8*(4), 271–293.

Chan, E. S. (2021a). Why do hotels find reducing their carbon footprint difficult? *International Journal of Contemporary Hospitality Management, 33*(5), 1646–1667.

Chan, E. S. (2021b). Influencing stakeholders to reduce carbon footprints: Hotel managers' perspective. *International Journal of Hospitality Management, 94*, 102807.

Cheng, H., & Ding, H. (2021). Dynamic game of corporate social responsibility in a supply chain with competition. *Journal of Cleaner Production, 317*, 128398.

Chou, C. J., & Chen, P. C. (2014). Preferences and willingness to pay for green hotel attributes in tourist choice behavior: The case of Taiwan. *Journal of Travel & Tourism Marketing, 31*(8), 937–957.

Crouch, G. I., Del Chiappa, G., & Perdue, R. R. (2019). International convention tourism: A choice modelling experiment of host city competition. *Tourism Management, 71*, 530–542.

De Carvalho, G. D. G., Sokulski, C. C., da Silva, W. V., de Carvalho, H. G., de Moura, R. V., de Francisco, A. C., & da Veiga, C. P. (2020). Bibliometrics and systematic reviews: A comparison between the Proknow-C and the Methodi Ordinatio. *Journal of Informetrics, 14*(3), 101043.

dos Santos Matos, L., & Petri, S. M. (2015). Balanced scorecard na gestão universitária: mapeamento sobre o tema utilizando o proknow-c. *Revista Gestão Universitária na América Latina-GUAL, 8*(2), 50–69.

Duque, P., & Cervantes-Cervantes, L. S. (2019). Responsabilidad Social Universitaria: una revisión sistemática y análisis bibliométrico. *Estudios Gerenciales, 35*(153), 451–464.

Edlin, G., & Golanty, E. (2015). *Health and wellness*. Jones & Bartlett Publishers.

El Archi, Y., Benbba, B., Nizamatdinova, Z., Issakov, Y., Vargáné, G. I., & Dávid, L. D. (2023). Systematic literature review analysing smart tourism destinations in context of sustainable development: Current applications and future directions. *Sustainability, 15*(6), 5086.

Ensslin, L., Ensslin, S. R., Lacerda, R. T., y Tasca, J. E. (2010). ProKnow-C, knowledge development processconstructivist. Processo técnico com patente de registro pendente junto ao INPI. *Brasil, 10*(4), 2015.

Ferreira, F., Ferreira, F. A., & Rodrigues, C. (2022, September). Pricing strategy for green hotel industry. In *International Conference of the International Association of Cultural and Digital Tourism* (pp. 67–80). Springer Nature Switzerland.

Ferreira, F. A., Ferreira, F., & Gomes, C. F. S. (2022). Price-setting hotel competition with corporate social responsibility. In *Proceedings of the 12th International Conference on Industrial Engineering and Operations Management (IEOM)* (pp. 325–333).

Fong, L. H. N., Law, R., Tang, C. M. F., & Yap, M. H. T. (2016). Experimental research in hospitality and tourism: A critical review. *International Journal of Contemporary Hospitality Management, 28*(2), 246–266.

Font, X., & Lynes, J. (2018). Corporate social responsibility in tourism and hospitality. *Journal of Sustainable Tourism, 26*(7), 1027–1042.

Gavilan, D., Avello, M., & Martinez-Navarro, G. (2018). The influence of online ratings and reviews on hotel booking consideration. *Tourism Management, 66*, 53–61.

Goldfinger, S., Wackernagel, M., Galli, A., Lazarus, E., & Lin, D. (2014). Footprint facts and fallacies: A response to Giampietro and Saltelli (2014) "Footprints to Nowhere". *Ecological Indicators, 46*, 622–632.

Goodwin, H. (2017). The challenge of overtourism. *Responsible Tourism Partnership, 4*, 1–19.

Guan, C., Rani, T., Yueqiang, Z., Ajaz, T., & Haseki, M. I. (2022). Impact of tourism industry, globalization, and technology innovation on ecological footprints in G-10 countries. *Economic Research-Ekonomska Istraživanja, 35*(1), 6688–6704.

Jurado-Caraballo, M. Á., Quintana-García, C., & Rodríguez-Fernández, M. (2020). Trends and opportunities in research on disability and work: An interdisciplinary perspective. *BRQ Business Research Quarterly, 25*(4), 366–388.

Kawanaka, S., Matsuda, Y., Suwa, H., Fujimoto, M., Arakawa, Y., & Yasumoto, K. (2020). Gamified participatory sensing in tourism: An experimental study of the effects on tourist behavior and satisfaction. *Smart Cities, 3*(3), 736–757.

Kongbuamai, N., Bui, Q., Yousaf, H. M. A. U., & Liu, Y. (2020). The impact of tourism and natural resources on the ecological footprint: A case study of ASEAN countries. *Environmental Science and Pollution Research, 27,* 19251–19264.

Lee, M.-K., & Yoo, S.-H. (2015). Using a Choice Experiment (CE) to value the attributes of cruise tourism. *Journal of Travel & Tourism Marketing, 32*(4), 416–427.

Lewis, A. (2021). What is greenwashing & CSR in the hospitality industry? https://www.highspeed training.co.uk/hub/greenwashing-and-csr-in-the-hospitality-industry/

Li, K., & Yan, E. (2018). Co-mention network of R packages: Scientific impact and clustering structure. *Journal of Informetrics, 12*(1), 87–100.

Line, N. D., & Runyan, R. C. (2012). Hospitality marketing research: Recent trends and future directions. *International Journal of Hospitality Management, 31*(2), 477–488.

Martin, B. A., Jin, H. S., & Trang, N. V. (2017). The entitled tourist: The influence of psychological entitlement and cultural distance on tourist judgments in a hotel context. *Journal of Travel & Tourism Marketing, 34*(1), 99–112.

Masiero, L., Yang, Y., & Qiu, R. T. (2019). Understanding hotel location preference of customers: Comparing random utility and random regret decision rules. *Tourism Management, 73,* 83–93.

Molina Montoya, N. P. (2005). ¿Qué es el estado del arte? *Ciencia y Tecnología para la salud Visual y Ocular, 3*(5), 73–75.

Nathaniel, S. P., Murshed, M., & Bassim, M. (2021). The nexus between economic growth, energy use, international trade and ecological footprints: The role of environmental regulations in N11 countries. *Energy, Ecology and Environment, 6*(6), 496.

Pícha, K., & Navrátil, J. (2019). The factors of Lifestyle of Health and Sustainability influencing pro-environmental buying behaviour. *Journal of Cleaner Production, 234,* 233–241.

Ravindran, V., & Shankar, S. (2015). Systematic reviews and meta-analysis demystified. *Indian Journal of Rheumatology, 10*(2), 89–94.

Razzaq, A., Fatima, T., & Murshed, M. (2021). Asymmetric effects of tourism development and green innovation on economic growth and carbon emissions in Top 10 GDP Countries. *Journal of Environmental Planning and Management,* 1–30.

Sparks, B. A., & Browning, V. (2011). The impact of online reviews on hotel booking intentions and perception of trust. *Tourism Management, 32*(6), 1310–1323.

Ştefănică, M., Sandu, C. B., Butnaru, G. I., & Haller, A. P. (2021). The nexus between tourism activities and environmental degradation: Romanian tourists' opinions. *Sustainability, 13*(16), 9210.

Sugathan, V., & Roopak, S. (2020). Impact assessment of the COVID-19 outbreak on international tourism. *UGC Care Group I Listed Journal, 148,* 158.

Sun, S., Law, R., & Zhang, M. (2020). An updated review of tourism-related experimental design articles. *Asia Pacific Journal of Tourism Research, 25*(7), 710–720.

Thorne, S. (2021). Are spas and wellness still considered luxurious in today's world? *Research in Hospitality Management, 11*(1), 9–14.

Vargas, G., & Calvo, G. (1987). Seis modelos alternativos de investigación documental para el desarrollo de la práctica universitaria en educación. *Educación superior y desarrollo, 5*(3), 7–37.

Vargas, M. G., Higuita, C. G., & Muñoz, D. A. J. (2015). El estado del arte: una metodología de investigación. *Revista Colombiana de Ciencias Sociales, 6*(2), 423–442.

Vieira, E. L., da Costa, S. E. G., de Lima, E. P., & Ferreira, C. C. (2019). Application of the Proknow-C methodology in the search of literature on performance indicators for energy management in manufacturing and industry 4.0. *Procedia Manufacturing, 39,* 1259–1269.

Wang, C., Nie, P.-Y., & Meng, Y. (2018). Duopoly competition with corporate social responsibility. *Australian Economic Papers, 57*, 327–345

Wong, A. K. F., Kim, S. S., Lee, S., & Elliot, S. (2021). An application of Delphi method and analytic hierarchy process in understanding hotel corporate social responsibility performance scale. In *Sustainable consumer behaviour and the environment* (pp. 133–159). Routledge.

World Health Organization. (2016). *World Health Statistics 2016 [OP]: Monitoring health for the Sustainable Development Goals (SDGs)*. World Health Organization.

Zhang, S., & Liu, X. (2019). The roles of international tourism and renewable energy in environment: New evidence from Asian countries. *Renewable Energy, 139*, 385–394.

Circular Economy in Tourism.
An Opportunity for Hotel
and Restoration Companies

Edith Georgina Surdez-Pérez⊙, **María del Carmen Sandoval-Caraveo**⊙, **and Jorge Velasco-Castellanos**⊙

Abstract The Circular Economy (CE) is an economic system focused on maintaining and increasing the economic value of goods through preservation, reduction, reuse and recycling, with the purpose of limiting and reducing environmental damage, impacting the quality of life of the beings that inhabit the planet. CE can provide the tourism sector with economic returns in the short term through the use and optimisation of resources, products and materials used to provide its services, and in the medium and long term because in tourism the conservation of nature is to a large extent what ensures the permanence of businesses. The aim of this conceptualisation work is to analyse the importance of the circular economy for the tourism sector, as well as to refer to research instruments and conclusions from various empirical studies on this topic. A qualitative and documentary type of research was carried out using scientific articles, documents generated by various organisations, among others. It is concluded that the components and benefits of CE are still not widely known by entrepreneurs in the tourism sector, mainly small businesses. Likewise, there is a shortage of research instruments to validate the CE construct for its measurement.

E. G. Surdez-Pérez · M. del C. Sandoval-Caraveo
Universidad Juarez Autonoma de Tabasco, Villahermosa, Mexico
e-mail: maria.sandoval@ujat.mx

J. Velasco-Castellanos
Instituto Tecnológico Superior de La Region Sierra, Teapa, Mexico
e-mail: jorge.vc@regionsierra.tecnm.mx

E. G. Surdez-Pérez (✉)
División Académica de Ciencias Económico Administrativas, Universidad Juárez Autónoma de Tabasco, Villahermosa, Tabasco, México
e-mail: edith.surdez@ujat.mx

M. del C. Sandoval-Caraveo
División Académica de Ingeniería y Arquitectura, Universidad Juárez Autónoma de Tabasco, Villahermosa, Tabasco, México

J. Velasco-Castellanos
División de Ingeniería en Administración, Universidad Juárez Autónoma de Tabasco, Teapa, Tabasco, México

© The Author(s) 2024
A. J. Guevara Plaza et al. (eds.), *Tourism and ICTs: Advances in Data Science, Artificial Intelligence and Sustainability*, Springer Proceedings in Business and Economics, https://doi.org/10.1007/978-3-031-52607-7_25

Keywords Circular economy · Sustainability · Tourism sector

1 Introduction

The tourism sector is of utmost importance for the economic development of countries; however, this industry, like others, has contributed to the deterioration of the environment by generating large quantities of waste. In hotels and restaurants, we can mention cooking oils, wastewater, individual soaps, paper and cardboard packaging, household appliances, mattresses, linens, utensils, plastic and glass containers, among others. The harmful results of an ecologically unplanned tourism development can irreversibly damage the resources necessary for the permanence of the project (El Insignia, 2016). According to Cárdenas (2019) the main environmental impacts of the hotel and restaurant sector are: water contamination, soil contamination by solid waste or dumping, affecting flora and fauna, atmospheric contamination and the depletion of water resources.

Another impact on the environment is linked to food waste. In this regard, the United Nations estimates that between 8 and 10% of global greenhouse gas emissions are associated with food that is not consumed (Paul, 2021). According to the study *Make the most of food: A guide to reducing food waste in the hotel, restaurant and catering sector*, between 4 and 10% of food purchased in restaurants ends up in the trash, meaning that more than 1,300 tonnes of food are thrown away annually on the planet, from the time it is prepared until it is consumed by the customer (Coderch, 2016).

On the other hand, there are some international actions of commitment to sustainability in the tourism sector among which we can mention the Global Tourism Plastics Initiative (GTPI) that brings together the tourism sector towards the development of a shared vision to address the causes and effects of plastic pollution, to lead by example in the shift towards a circular economy for plastics (World Tourism Organization [UNWTO], 2021). Another contribution is the document: *Let's make the most of food: A guide to reduce food waste in the hotel, restaurant and catering sector*, which is a useful tool published by the Environmental Office of the Autonomous University of Barcelona and the Alicia Foundation that includes concrete measures to make catering establishments more efficient by making better use of food (Universidad Autónoma de Barcelona & Fundación Alicia, 2013). It is also worth mentioning the Master Plan for Sustainable Tourism Quintana Roo 2030 (PMTS 2030), a strategic instrument characterised by a diagnosis that analyses global tourism trends and formulates a strategy for the year 2030 (Secretaría de Medio Ambiente y Recursos Naturales [SEDETUR], 2020). These efforts must continue to be added to implement, strengthen and consolidate a model of sustainable economy in the tourism sector, especially considering that worldwide travellers are opting for environmentally friendly tourism, sustainability is now an indispensable part of the competitiveness of the tourism sector (Secretaría de Medio Ambiente y Recursos Naturales [SEMARNAT], 2023),

In this context, the aim of this conceptualisation work is to analyse, based on a literature review, the importance of the circular economy for the tourism sector, as well as the research instruments and conclusions of various empirical studies on this topic. As for the methodology, the approach is qualitative and the type of documentary research, in the research procedure various sources on the subject of CE were identified, descriptors were developed to classify the information, the Mendenley reference manager was used to facilitate the organisation of documents, reading and analysis of the information.

This is because at the business level, CE practices emphasise the achievement of the twin goals of environmental and economic performance (Zhu et al., 2010).

2 Development of the Theme

2.1 Economic Sustainability

Sustainable development means "ensuring that the needs of the present are met without compromising the ability of future generations to meet their own needs" (Naciones Unidas, Asamblea General, 1987, p. 23). The concept was first used at the United Nations General Assembly by the World Commission on the Environment and disseminated in the Report of the World Commission on Environment and Development entitled *Our Common Future*. The Organización Internacional del Trabajo (OIT, 2018, p. iii) states that "achieving environmental sustainability can create jobs. The green economy will be an important driver of employment growth in the future of work".

Environmental sustainability is essential to improve the supply of jobs and in this regard, legislation is an important element in directing efforts towards decent work during and after the transition to environmental sustainability, provides support for the green economy and is helpful for emerging sectors to provide decent working conditions, and multilateral agreements between States often address labour issues, environmental rights in the workplace, employment protection, and occupational health and safety (OIT, 2018).

For his part, Tarupi (2022) points out that economic sustainability is based on productivity related to development and economic growth linked to the biosphere, labour and capital; the author adds that social sustainability, for its part, emphasises human talent with the capacity to deal with the impact suffered by ecosystems.

Sustainability thus triggers linked challenges that require a holistic programme, analysis of various disciplines and collaboration of social actors in order to achieve economic, ecological and social sustainability (Tarupi, 2022). In this sense, an important way forward is to move from a linear to a circular economy and to foster green competences in organisations.

2.2 Circular Economy

According to data from the Ellen MacArthur Foundation, 66% of the world's inhabitants will live in cities; the transition from a linear to a circular economy will take place gradually, as will the effects on waste generation. The foundation states that cities consume 75% of natural resources, account for more than 50% of global waste and produce almost 80% of greenhouse gases (MacArthur, 2017).

However, sustainability is the first reference point for understanding the CE model. In 1972, the United Nations Environment Programme was created to seek a balance between economic growth and environmental conservation. To this end, the Brundtland Report called Our Common Future was drawn up. In 2015, the Sustainable Development Summit was held in New York, at which the UN approved the 2030 Agenda with 17 goals, 169 integrated goals (Rivera & Martínez, 2021).

CE is seen as a new global socio-economic approach and paradigm for sustainable development. The European Parliament defines CE in the following terms: "The circular economy is a model of production and consumption that involves sharing, renting, reusing, repairing, renewing and recycling existing materials and products as often as possible to create added value" (Parlamento Europeo, 2022, para. 2).

The concept of CE as such was proposed in Great Britain by the environmental economists David W. Pearce and R. Kerry Turner, in 1989 with the work *Economics of Natural Resources and the Environment*, agreeing that it is an economic model focused on the optimal use of renewable and non-renewable natural resources, in one or more circular processes, as opposed to the linear model, very marked by the process produce, consume and throw away and thus move to the model or cycle that feeds back leaving the smallest possible ecological footprint (Ecofestes, 2006).

The following schools of thought contribute to the CE model: Walter Stahel's performance economics; William McDonough and Michael Braungart's Cradle to Cradle design philosophy; Janine Benyus' conceptualisation of biomimicry; Reid Lifset and Thomas Graedel's industrial ecology; the blue economy approach, as described by Gunter Pauli, among others (MacArthur, 2017).

In order to understand and frame CE, it is necessary to first identify the conceptualisation of the linear economy, which is currently the most widely used in production processes, in order to establish a comparison to understand the substantive and beneficial part of CE. Therefore, "the linear economy is the traditional model where raw materials are extracted to manufacture products, produced and then discarded, without taking into account the environmental footprint and its consequences" (Banco Santander, 2021, para. 3).

According to the Foundation, CE is based on three principles: (1) eliminating waste and pollution by design; (2) maintaining products and materials in use; and (3) regenerating natural systems.

CE is achieved through the repair, recycling, reuse, and remanufacturing of products, as in the case of automobile oil, which used to be thrown into sewers; now it is collected and has become an important input for another production process, closing cycles. On the other hand, CE also generates jobs, new markets and, according to the Economic Commission for Latin America and the Caribbean (ECLAC), it could generate almost five million jobs (Zacarías, 2018). In the challenge of consolidating CE, Scheel and Bello (2022) propose an *Extended Circular Value* model, changing the creation of value from a single delivery to cycles in a circular system through business clusters capable of generating value for all stakeholders.

However, CE relates to the Sustainable Development Goals (SDGs) that are part of the 2030 Agenda, specifically goals 12 and 13: responsible production and consumption, and climate action, as well as goals 6 (clean water and sanitation), 7 (affordable and clean energy), 8 (decent work and economic growth) and 9 (industry, innovation and infrastructure) (Pimenta et al., 2022).

Moving towards CE means reduced environmental impacts, increased competitiveness, innovation and employment, but it also means taking on challenges such as developing skills and guiding consumer behaviour (Bourguignon, 2016).

2.2.1 Circular Economy for the Tourism Sector

Tourism is considered as an economic model capable of generating wealth and quality of life for its inhabitants, especially in developing countries, and therefore with a high impact on the economy and the environment (Santacruz & Santacruz, 2020). Because of its contribution to the economy, it is important to develop the tourism sector, but within a framework of sustainability, i.e. achieving a balance between environmental conservation, economic prosperity and social welfare, to achieve this it is necessary to move from a linear economy to a CE. To achieve sustainable tourism, collaboration between actors in the sector must prevail in the planning, management and implementation of projects, as well as identifying relationships with other economic sectors that can contribute to sustainability efforts (Fusco & Nocca, 2017).

In this sense, the challenge for these companies is to maintain the value of their material resources for a longer period of time in order to reduce the generation of waste and take advantage of those that are inevitably generated either for their own benefit or for the benefit of another sector, the path is to increasingly adopt CE practices. Xu et al. (2022) argues that there is an urgent need to establish indices to assess the sustainability of the tourism industry based on CE theory.

2.2.2 Technology in a Circular Economy for Tourism

According to the graphic based on the Butterfly Diagram of the Ellen MacArthur Foundation and Doughnut Economics, CE provides purpose and drives development towards Industry 4.0 to enable the activation of circular strategies that support the two important wings: regeneration and restoration. Regeneration is capturing value at each stage of decomposition and restoration is repairing, remanufacturing, reusing and recycling. All of the above with the guiding axes of extracting (biological or technological nutrients), making and consuming or using to minimise the loss of materials and energy (Centro de Innovación y Economía Circular, 2023).

Artifact, process and organisational technologies (Villalba, et al., 2022) contribute to the transition towards a circular economy that ensures added value and sustainability. According to Schröder et al. (2020) the triumph of the transition towards CE is related to the widespread use of Industry 4.0 technologies, such as blockchain, cloud computing, big data analytics, among others. The author adds that the generation and dissemination of information on the waste stream promoted by Industry 4.0 technologies is fundamental to increase recycling rates instead of final adoptions such as landfill and incineration. All of the above with potential application to the tourism industry in terms of circular economy.

Vargas-Sánchez (2021) also mentions that:

"Artificial intelligence is also entering restaurants, more specifically their kitchens. Thus, with machine vision technology, chefs can make better decisions in order to drastically reduce both food waste and the costs of their activity" (p. 123).

2.2.3 Empirical Research on the Circular Economy

This section presents various measures to assess CE practices at the organisational level and the authors' conclusions based on the findings.

Zhu et al. (2010) presents a measure to assess CE practices, adapted from various authors, validated with expert opinion: academics, civil servants and industrial managers to verify the appropriateness of the questionnaire items and the understanding of the questionnaire, with the dimensions: Internal Business Management, Eco-design and Return on Investment. Taking this scale as a background Botezat et al. (2018) conducted a research to identify the relationship between the cooperation between the members of the eco-oriented supply chain and the practices and performance of Romanian producers with respect to the implementation of the principles of CE, they conclude that the type of cluster to which a producer belongs influences its CE practices.

Mura et al. (2020) developed a 7-point Likert-type scale to inquire about the CE practices that have been implemented in Italian SMEs, the main constraints and facilitators for the adoption of CE and sustainable business practices. They conclude that CE practices are not being widely implemented in the companies that participated in the study due to the perception that they increase costs in the organisations.

In another study, Broche-Fernández and Ramos-Gómez (2015) present a methodological instrument to quantitatively and qualitatively assess the environmental performance of small and medium-sized enterprises in the hotel sector in Cuba that includes indicators related to CE, such as: total consumption of materials, packaging, energy and water; as well as the amount of waste for disposal and recycling. Likewise for the tourism sector, Cornejo-Ortega & Chávez (2020) designed a questionnaire to measure the knowledge about CE and CE certification processes of owners and managers of restaurants and hotels, in their study they conclude that less than 50% of the participants are aware of the elements of CE and only 51.5% consider that CE certification should be unavoidable. A study on return on investment for food waste reduction involving 700 companies from 17 countries that considered restaurants and hotels, the results reported that 99% of businesses had a positive return, where the sites with the best returns tend to be restaurants between 5:1 and 10:1 (Hanson & Mitchell, 2017), a result that is important to disseminate, to eradicate the belief that environmental conservation practices only generate costs.

3 Conclusions

The CE model is starting to be aired in the tourism sector, however, it is imperative that all actors in this sector contribute to the transition towards sustainable business models, where CE is a significant alternative to achieve this.

Hotels, restaurants, and other businesses in the tourism sector should initiate or consolidate actions such as the design of green services and internal environmental management that foster commitment to environmental issues through processes throughout the value chain that promote a circular approach.

The literature review identifies that most of the research instruments to assess CE practices have content validity through expert judgement and some with reliability tests of Conbranch's Alpha, but there are few studies with construct validity tests or structural equation models that relate variables that influence CE.

References

Botezat, E. A., Dodescu, A. O., Vaduva, S. & Fotea, S. L. (2018). An exploration of circular economy practices and performance among Romanian producers. *Sustainability, 10*(3191), 1–17. https://doi.org/10.3390/su10093191

Bourguignon, D. (2016). *The loop: mew circular economic package.* Closing the loop: new circular economy package (europa.eu)

Broche-Fernandez, Y., & Ramos-Gómez, R. (2015). Procedimiento para la gestión de residuos Sólidos generados en instalaciones hoteleras cubanas. *Ingeniería Industrial, XXXV, I*(2), 240–252.

Cárdenas, H. A. (2019). *Riesgos Ambientales y Sociales en Hoteles, Restaurantes y Estaciones de Servicio. Pilotos De Innovación Financiera, negocios verdes 2019.* https://www.asobancaria.com/wp-content/uploads/2020/10/Riesgos-Ambientales-y-Sociales-sector

Centro de Innovación y Economía Circular. (2023). *Publicaciones.* https://ciecircular.com/

Coderch, I. (2016). *El coste oculto de la basura de un restaurante.* Te Lo Sirvo Verde. http://telosirvoverde.com/blog/el-coste-oculto-de-la-basura-de-un-restaurante/.

Cornejo-Ortega, J. L., & Chávez, R. L. (2020). The tourism sector in puerto vallarta: an approximation from the circular economy. *Sustainability, 12,* 1–14. https://doi.org/10.3390/su12114442

Ecofestes. (2006). *Qué es la Economía Circular ?* https://www.ecofestes.com/que-es-la-economia-circular-n-61-es

El Insignia. (2016). *Los Hoteles y su Impacto Ambiental.* https://elinsignia.com/2016/11/05/los-hoteles-impacto-ambiental/.

Fusco, L., & Nocca, F. (2017). *Del Turismo local al Circular. Aestimum, 70*, 51–74. https://doi.org/ 10.13128/Estimun-21081

Hanson, C. & Mitchell (2017). *The Business case for reducing food loss and Waste*. A report on behalf of Champions 12.3. https://champions123.org/publication/business-case-reducing-food-loss-and-waste

MacArthur, E. (2017). *Economía Circular*. https://archive.ellenmacarthurfoundation.org/es/economia-circular/concepto

Mura, M., Longo, M., & Zanni, S. (2020). Circular economy in Italian SMEs: A multi-method study. *Journal of Cleanner Production, 245*, 1–16. https://doi.org/10.1016/j.jclepro.2019.118821

Naciones Unidas, Asamblea General (1987). *Informe de la Comisión Mundial sobre el Medio Ambiente y el Desarrollo "Nuestro futuro común"*. https://www.ecominga.uqam.ca/PDF/ BIBLIOGRAPHIE/GUIDE_LECTURE_1/CMMAD-Informe-Comision-Brundtland-sobre-Medio-Ambiente-Desarrollo.pdf.

Organización Internacional del Trabajo [OIT] (2018). *Perspectivas sociales y del empleo en el mundo 2018: Sostenibilidad medioambiental con empleo*. Ginebra, Suiza. https://www.ilo.org/ global/research/global-reports/weso/greening-with-jobs/lang--es/index.htm

World Tourism Organization [UNWTO] (2021). *Tourism takes action on plastic waste and pollution*. https://www.unwto.org/news/tourism-takes-action-on-plastic-waste-and-pollution.

Parlamento Europeo (2022). *Noticias Economía circular : definición , importancia y beneficios*. https://www.europarl.europa.eu/news/es/headlines/economy/20151201STO05603/ economia-circular-definicion-importancia-y-beneficios

Paul, F. (2021). *Las impactantes cifras que deja el desperdicio de comida en el mundo (y cuáles son sus efectos)*. BBC News Mundo, 18. https://www.bbc.com/mundo/noticias-56322961.

Pimenta, D. C., Cosme, C., Cosme, C., & Costa, D. (2022). La Economía Circular como eje de desarrollo de los países latinoamericanos. *Economía y Política*. https://www.redalyc.org/art iculo.oa?id=571169753001

Rivera, P., & Martínez, R. E. (2021). Articulación de los objetivos de desarrollo sostenible con el paradigma de la economía circular. *Investigación y Desarrollo, 29*, 178–194. https://doi.org/10. 14482/indes.29.1.333.7

Santander, B. (2021). *Economía lineal y circular qué son y en qué se diferencian?* https://www.santander.com/es/stories/economia-lineal-y-circular-a-que-se-refieren-cada-uno-de-estos-terminos-y-cuales-son-sus-diferencias

Santacruz, E. E., & Santacruz, G. (2020). Consumo de agua en establecimientos hoteleros de México. *Estudios y Perspectivas En Turismo, 29*(1), 120–136. https://www.redalyc.org/articulo.oa?id= 180762690008

Scheel, C., & Bello, B. (2022). Transforming linear production chains into circular value extended systems. *Sustainability, 14*(3726), 2–17. https://doi.org/10.3390/su14073726

Schröder, P., Albaladejo, M., Alonso, P. MacEwen, M., & Tilkanen, J. (2020). *La economía circular en América Latina y el Caribe Oportunidades para fomentar la resiliencia*. https://www.cha thamhouse.org/sites/default/files/2021-01/2021-01-13-spanish-circular-economy-schroder-et-al.pdf

Secretaría de Medio Ambiente y Recursos Naturales [SEDETUR]. (2020). *Plan Maestro de Turismo Sustentable*. https://sedeturqroo.gob.mx/ARCHIVOS/PMTS/Plan-Maestro-2030.pdf

Secretaría de Medio Ambiente y Recursos Naturales [SEMARNAT] (2015). *Regulación mexicana en materia de economía circular*. http://www.sadsma.cdmx.gob.mx:9000/circular/regulacion-mexicana-en-materia-circular

Tarupi, E. A. (2022). Factores y aportes de la sostenibilidad en los planes de negocios para la gestión de emprendimientos sostenibles. *Revista Universidad y Sociedad, 14*(S5), 332–342. https://rus. ucf.edu.cu/index.php/rus/article/view/3301

Universidad Autónoma de Barcelona, & Fundación Alicia. (2013). *¡Aprovechemos la comida! Una guía para reducir el despilfarro alimentario en el sector de la hostelería, la restauración restauración y el cátering*. http://telosirvoverde.com/wp-/uploads/2016/02/guia_malbaratament_ESP. pdf